Horace Grant Underwood

**An Introduction to the Korean Spoken Language**

Horace Grant Underwood

**An Introduction to the Korean Spoken Language**

ISBN/EAN: 9783743419261

Manufactured in Europe, USA, Canada, Australia, Japa

Cover: Foto ©Paul-Georg Meister /pixelio.de

Manufactured and distributed by brebook publishing software (www.brebook.com)

Horace Grant Underwood

**An Introduction to the Korean Spoken Language**

鮮 英 文 法
션 영 문 법

---

AN INTRODUCTION

TO THE

# KOREAN SPOKEN LANGUAGE

BY

HORACE GRANT UNDERWOOD

---

IN TWO PARTS:

PART I. GRAMMATICAL NOTES
PART II. ENGLISH INTO KOREAN

---

SECOND EDITION

REVISED AND ENLARGED WITH THE ASSISTANCE OF
HORACE HORTON UNDERWOOD, A.B.

---

EUROPE AND AMERICA
THE MACMILLAN COMPANY, NEW YORK
THE FAR EAST
KELLY & WALSH, LTD., YOKOHAMA, SHANGHAI
THE KOREAN RELIGIOUS TRACT SOCIETY, SEOUL, KOREA

(ALL RIGHT RESERVED)
—
**1914**

PRINTED BY
THE FUKUIN PRINTING Co., L'td.,
YOKOHAMA, JAPAN.

# PREFACE.

It was hardly expected when this volume saw the light of day in 1889 that so many years would pass before it was supplemented by something more elaborate and better and it is only the fact that nothing else has been prepared to take its place and that the author has been so beseeched for a new edition that has led us to issue this second edition.

We have sought advice and help and suggestions for changes on every hand and regret very much that the press of work has hindered others from giving to us the assistance that would have made this book of much more value to the student of Korean.

In the present edition the author is glad to say that he has had the assistance of his son who went over the revision of the book with the enthusiasm of a new student of the language.

We regret that more changes have not been made because we feel that the imperfections of the book would have warranted a more thorough revision of the book, but a careful review of all the parts with the assistance of some of the best Korean scholars available did not result in more than what is seen in this new edition. There are one or two appendices that have been added which will contribute not a little to the study of the language  The use of the book we believe will be very much enhanced by the alphabetical indices; one, a general index in English and the other an index of grammatical forms in Korean.

Special credit should be given to Mr. Sang-Kyu Pack, Ph. B. of Brown University, U. S. A. who has assisted me throughout.

As before, so again the author would gladly welcome any criticisms or suggestions either as to form or matter with which the student of the language may kindly favor him.

Seoul, Korea, January 1914.

H. G. U.

# PREFACE.

## To First Edition.

In this introduction to the study of the Korean spoken language, a systematic grammar, in the strict sense of the word, has not been aimed at. It has been attempted simply to *introduce* the student to the study, to clear away some of the obstacles and difficulties that present themselves, and to show him the way by which he can become a proficient speaker of Korean.

Passing through Japan on my way to Korea, Dr. Imbrie's "English-Japanese Etymology" was brought to my notice; and, the plan of study there presented appealing to me as best suited to my individual needs, I decided to adopt it in the study of Korean.

In carrying out this idea, I was greatly aided by obtaining the Korean translation of Dr. Imbrie's sentences prepared by Mr. Song Soun Yong, (who had become my teacher) at the direction of Lieut. Bernardo (U.S.N.)

After correcting, arranging and adding to them, I found them of so great advantage to myself, and they proved of such valuable assistance to the many to whom I loaned them, that I determined, to carry the classification still further, to formulate rules of which the sentences should be illustrations, and to throw the whole into a form similar to Dr. Imbrie's book.

Most of this was done over three years ago, but various circumstances hindered its publication, and, in the mean time, realizing that such a work was in a measure one-sided and approached the language merely from the English standpoint, a first part, which has been called "Grammatical Notes," and which views the subject from the opposite side has been prepared.

From the very nature of the case, the second part taking English idioms and phrases and showing their Korean equivalents, assumes more of a practical than a theoretical form. On the other hand, the first part taking Korean phrases, idioms, sentences, showing their use among the Koreans, their structure, and their various forms, becomes more theoretical than practical.

This complete division of a work on a language into two parts, each of which approaches it from a different standpoint, has, it is believed, never been attempted in one book before, and yet it is felt that such a division will materially aid the student in obtaining an accurate and well *systematized* knowledge of neat distinctions, and idioms, and enable him more speedily to speak a pure and not an Anglicized Korean. It is true that at times, the one naturally overlaps the other, but is equally certain, that each has its own especial place, which the other can in no way fill, and a true conception of any language can best be obtained by viewing them separately.

The author takes pleasure in acknowledging valuable suggestions made by Prof. Homer B. Hulbert of the Royal Korean University, concerning some of the uses of the compound tenses, and also his indebtedness to Mr. A. Stewart Annand who kindly corrected much of the proof, and whose friendly assistance in many ways has greatly aided him.

Credit also is due to the pioneers in the language, the French missionaries, from whose work the author gained his first ideas of Korean grammar. To more than any one else, however, thanks are due to Mr. Song Soun Yong (宋淳容) whose sound ideas on the use of the language as it is spoken to-day, and whose intimate acquaintance with the Chinese classics, combined with his thorough knowledge of the use of the native Ernmun have been of invaluable assistance.

The author will gladly welcome any criticisms or suggestions either as to form or matter, with which students of the language may kindly favor him.

H. G. U.

Seoul Korea,
    November 1889.

# TABLE OF CONTENTS.

## PART I.

## GRAMMATICAL NOTES.

### CHAPTER I.

### Introductory remarks on the study of Korean.

1, * Difficulties surrounding the study.—2, A Korean teacher.—3, Approach the study from two sides.—4, Use of this book.—5. Korean written language.—6, Necessity for the study of Chinese.—7. Ŏnmun and Chinese rarely if ever mixed.—8, Pronounciation.—11, Arrangement of chapters.—12, Honorifics ..................... Page 1.—10.

### CHAPTER II.

### The Korean alphabet and its Sounds.

13, An alphabet.—14-22, Vowel sounds.—23-27, Diphthongs and triphthongs.—28, The consonants.—29, The part euphony plays.—30-38, Simple consonantal sounds.—39, Aspirated consonants.—41, Names of simple consonants ................................................ Page 10-23.

### CHAPTER III.

### The Noun.

42, Korean noun indeclinable.—43, Distinctions of number, subject, object not made.—44, Postpositions.—45, Methods of expressing gender.—46, Ambiguity in regard to number.—48, Reduplication of words.—51,—Compound nouns and the use of a knowledge of Chinese.—52,

\* These numbers refer to the paragraphs.

Uses of 군, 장이, 질 etc.—53, Verbal nouns.—54, Surnames.—56, Korean titles.—57, No names for women.—58, The wrong and proper use of the term 부인 .................................................................. Page 24—39.

## CHAPTER IV.

## Pronouns and Pronominal adjectives.

59, All pronouns really nouns.—60, Personal Pronouns.—62, Personal pronouns and postpositions united,—63, No third personal pronoun in Korean.—65, Reflexive pronouns.—66, All Korean interrogatives also indefinite.—67, 어느, 엇던, and 무슴 used adjectively.—69, Use of 아모.—71, Demonstrative pronouns.—72, Words derived from these.—73, The relatives 쟈 and 바 .................... Page 40—53.

## CHAPTER V.

## The Numeral.

74, Two sets of numerals. Adjective and substantive forms.—75, Sinico-Korean numerals have only an adjective form.—77, Specific classifiers.—79, Money.—81, Oriental numbers.—82, The months of the year.—83, Days of the month.—85, Hours of the day—86, Fractions.—87,—Multiples,—88, Interest on money.—89, The Korean word 번.—90, Weights and measures.—92, The peculiar use of 호 and the meaning of 조음 ..................................................... ............ Page 54—71.

## CHAPTRR VI.

## The Postposition.

93, Kinds of postpositions.—94, Simple postpositions.—95, Euphonic changes that may creep in.—109, 나 and 가 considered as postpositions.—111, Composite postpositions,—113, Verbal postpositions.

Page 72—86.

## CHAPTER VII.

## The Verb.

114, Difficulties; terminations and conjunctions not distinguished.—115, Verb impersonal and no number.—118, A few so called "personal forms.—119, Two kinds of verbs, active and neuter; active verbs.—120, Neuter verbs.—121, Three voices; active, causative and passive.—122, Method of forming the passive voice. Method of forming the causative.—123, Causative in 치.—125, But one conjugation.—127, The Basal Conjugations.—128, Each part divisible into three parts.— The stem.—129, The tense root.—132, The particle 더.—133, Simple and compound tenses.—134, The use of the simple tenses.—135, The use of the compound tense.—136, The form 더 defective and lack of discrimination between terminations, and conjunctions.—137, Different kinds of terminations.—138, Declarative terminations.—141, Interrogative terminations.—144, Propositive terminations.—145. Imperative termination.—146, The parts of the Basal Conjugations.—147, Indicative mood.—148, Volitive mood.—149, Two kinds of participles.—150 Verbal participles.—151, Different forms of past verbal participle have caused discussion.—153, Postpositions may be affixed.—155, The use of the verbal participle; As connectives.—156, Introducing cause, manner, means.—157, Used also with object of principal verb.—158, In making compounds.—159, The future verbal participle.—160, Relative participles.—161, The four most common.—162, The present, its form and use.—163, The past, its form.—164, It uses.—165. Past relative participle of neuter verbs.—166, The future relative participle.—167, Future past relative participle.—168, Progressive participle.—169, Each tense has its relative participle.—170, The Former Supine.—171, Verbal noun in ㅁ,—172, Verbal noun in 기—176, The desiderative base.—177, The negative base.—178, The principle parts.—179, The paradigm of the basal conjugation—180. Other verbs to illustrate.

Page 87,—142.

## The Verb (*Continued*).

181, The verb with conjunctions.—182, List of these conjunctions.—183, Their union with indicative tenses.—185 to 203, The use of these conjunctions considered individually.—204, The desiderative form.—205, Another desiderative form.—206, Negative particles.—207, Formation of negative verbs.—208, The negative verb 마오.—209, Certain other negative forms.—210, Auxiliary verbs.—211, A list of some of them.—212 to 219, The uses of these auxiliaries.—220, Modifications produced by nouns forming new verbs.—221, List of these words and their uses.—227, Adverbial effect produced by nouns with postposition when used with the verb.—223, Verb in indirect

discourse.—229, The imperative verb.—230, Contractions and ellipses.
—242, The principal parts of some verbs ............... Pages 142—193..

## CHAPTER VIII.

## The Adjective.

243, True adjectives.—244, Adjectives used attributively and predicatively.—245. Distinctions attainable through adjectival verbs.—246, Formation of adjectives,—247, Adjectives in 스럼 —248, Adjectives formed by reduplication of stem.—249, Nouns used as adjectives.—250, Comparison of adjectives—little used.—251, How formed.—252, Use of 보다—253, Use of 에서—254, Superlative how formed.

Page 194—199

## CHAPTER IX.

## The Adverb.

255, Primitive adverbs.—256, Derived adverbs. Those derived from verbs.—257, The future verbal participle used as an adverb.—258, Distinctions between these two classes of adverbs.—259, The Korean past verbal participle used as an adverb.—260, Adverbs derived from nouns and pronouns.—261, Comparison of adverbs,—262, Primitive adverbs used with postposition.—263, Numeral adverbs.—264, Position of adverb in sentence.—265, Korean responsives.—266, Answers to negative questions ............................ Pages 200—204.

## CHAPTER X.

## The Conjunctions.

267, Two classes of conjunctions—Co-ordinate and subordinate.—268 and 269, Uses of co-ordinate conjunctions.—270, Subordinate conjunctions etc. ................................. Pages 205—207.

## CHAPTER XI.

## Honorifics.

271, Importance of use of honorifics.—272, Persons spoken of, how honored.—273, Honorific form of verb how constructed.—274, Honorific verbs honoring the subject.—275, Honorific verbs honoring the object.—276, The two honorifics combined.—277, The use of honorific nouns, postpositions etc.—278, List of some of these nouns.—279, These honorifics not the same in all the provinces.—280, Terms for addressing servants etc.................................................... Pages 208—212.

## CHAPTER XII.

## The Structure of the sentence.

281, The general rule.—282, Position of the different parts of speech in relation to the words they govern or are governed by.—283, Position of the parts of a sentence.—284, Several verbs connected.—how used.—285, Indefiniteness of Korean sentences.—286, Use of two negatives.—287, The use of elliptical forms.—288, Constant absence of postpositions—verbal modification etc.—289, Use of conjunctions; the sentence and paragraph the same.—290, Need of practice.

Pages 213—217.

# PART II.

# ENGLISH INTO KOREAN.

Chapter I. THE VERB.
 § I. The verb "To be" .................... Page 221
 § II. The verb "To have" .................... „ 225
 § III. Auxiliaries.
  Am, Is and Are—Was, Were—Do and Did—Have, Has, and Had—Shall and Will—Should and Would—Can and Could—May and Might—Let, Make, Have and Get—Must—Ought and Should—Think and Suppose—Intend—Want—Wish and Hope—Need—Seem and Look .................... Pages 227 to 257
 § IV. The Infinitives .................... „ 258 „ 262
 § V. Passive Construction .................... „ 262 „ 266
 § VI. Conditional Sentences .................... „ 267 „ 268
Chapter II. THE NOUN .................... „ 269
Chapter III. THE ARTICLE .................... „ 270 „ 271
Chapter IV. THE PRONOUN .................... „ 272 „ 279
 § I. Personal Pronouns.
  Simple and Compound .................... „ 272 „ 275
 § II. Relative Pronouns .................... „ 275 „ 277
 § III. Interrogative Pronouns .................... „ 277 „ 279
Chapter V. PRONOMINAL ADJECTIVES.
 This, That, and Such—Either, Neither and Both—Each—Some—Any—Every—No, None and Nobody—All—Several—Few—One, Ones—Other, Another—Same—Much—Many—Most—Enough .................... Pages 280 to 319
Chapter VI. THE ADJECTIVE.
 § I. Used Attributively, and Predicatively .................... Pages 320 to 322
 § II. The Comparison of Adjectives.
  Comparative degree—Superlative degree .................... Pages 322 to 325
Chapter VII. THE ADVERB.
 § I. Adverbs of Place.
  Here—There—Where .................... Pages 326 to 331

§ II. Adverbs of Time.

Always—Whenever—Usually—Often and Frequently—Sometimes—Seldom—Never and Ever—Again—When—While—As—Then—Now—Already—Formerly—Recently, and of Late—Ago—Just Now—Still and Yet—Till and Until—By and By—Soon—Directly—Before—After and Since—Long Time—Sometime—Finally and At Last .................... Pages 331 to 359

§ III. Adverbs of Cause, Manner and Degree.

Why—Accordingly, Consequently, and Therefore—How—So—Like and As —Very—Only—Too—Even—Almost—About.

Pages 359 to 368

Chapter VIII. The Numerals........................... ,, 369 to 370

Chapter IX. The Preposition.

At—In—On—To—From, Out of and Off—By—Through—With—Without—Of—For—Across, Over, and Beyond—Among—Around—Before—Behind—Between—During—Except, Besides and But—Instead of—Over and Above—Under and Below—According to—In accordance with ........... Pages 371 to 391

Chapter X. The Conjunction.

And—Both......and—Too, Also—But—Though, Although, and Still—Either, Or, and Whether—Neither.........Nor—If, and Unless—Because—Then—That—Than............Pages 392 to 406.

# PART I.

# GRAMMATICAL NOTES.

## CHAPTER I.

INTRODUCTORY REMARKS ON THE STUDY OF KOREAN.

1.—The study of Korean is as yet in its infancy, ways and means are few, and good books written in the native character are still fewer.

Despite the fact that twenty odd years have passed since the first edition of this book was published and that new Missionaries have many facilities provided in the form of organized language classes and several very helpful books; the difficulties are still many. Obviously even in that part of the language which we get through books we must have the assistance of native teachers, and Koreans with an accurate knowledge of the rules of grammar or with any idea of the real functions of a teacher are still rare.

Under these circumstances, the difficulties which surround the student are numerous, and while in these pages the writer tries in part to systematize the language, and to aid the student, it must be remembered that no language was ever learned entirely from books, and from the very start he must accustom his ear to accurately hear, and to retain every variety of sound, and by unremitting effort train his tongue to reproduce them exactly.

The test of exactness in pronunciation is the ability to make oneself understood, not merely by one's own teacher and native associates, who will soon become accustomed to the wrong pronunciations, and mistakes of a foreigner, but by strangers and outsiders. The writer would therefore strenuously urge upon the learner the necessity of daily use among the people, of what he learns. Let him not be afraid of mistakes, by mistakes he must learn. Let him from the very first day, though he knows but one or two words, go out and begin to use them.

We have said that the test of exactness in pronunciation, is the ability to make oneself understood by strangers and outsiders. Here we must remember that another element besides that of the individual word enters in, that of the *rate* of pronunciation of the combinations of syllables and words which make up, what is in fact the unit of effective speech, the sentence. Let each word be pronounced ever so correctly if the rate of speech in the completed sentence be not at least approximately correct, the result if understood at all, will be stilted and laughable.

2.—A Korean teacher is of course indispensable, but he cannot be expected to teach in any sense of the word as we understand it. He is to give the exact pronunciation, to assist in reading the character, to explain forms of expression and idioms, if possible give distinctions between synonyms, and to correct the mistakes of the learner. From him the student is to get all he can, and upon him to practice at every opportunity. He should be a good Chinese scholar; as the Chinese enters so largely into the composition of words, and as far as possible, a man well acquainted with the native Korean character, and having no knowledge of English, so that the student shall from the start be thrown upon his own resources.

3.—It must be borne in mind, that not only are the characters and words different from those to which we have been accustomed, but also the forms of expression and the idioms. The surroundings of the Korean are entirely different and his habits of thought are necessarily as unlike ours as his surroundings; hence " Put yourself in his place" should be the motto of the student; he must early learn *to put himself in the place of the Korean.* He must learn to hear with Korean ears, to see with Korean eyes, to enter heartily into the life and surroundings of the Korean, to appreciate fully all their circumstances, and as far as possible in fact, to think Korean. Until this is done at least in part, no one can become a speaker of Korean, and as long as the student continues to think in English, and to translate word for word into Korean, he will not be speaking Korean at all, but simply an Anglicized jargon of words, almost as unintelligible to the uninitiated, as Pidgin English is to the foreigner when he first lands on Chinese soil, and in many cases he will convey a meaning directly opposite to what he intends.

4.—To accomplish this end and think in Korean, we must approach the language from two sides, the Korean and the foreign. This has been the object in this work. In the first or grammar part of the book, the effort has been made to present Korean from the Korean stand point. That is to say ; to take the Korean as it is, systematize it in part, divest it of everything foreign, show as far as possible how the Korean thinks and how he constructs his sentences. In the second part, on the other hand, we have tried to approach the language from the foreign standpoint, and taking English ideas, English thoughts and English methods of expression, to show how they would be expressed by the Korean. These have been named for convenience Parts I and II, not because the one should be studied before the other, or is of more importance, for they should be studied together, and we should try to approach the language from the two sides at once.

I would particularly emphasize this last as many, even among those who teach the language, seem to consider Part I proper for the beginner and Part II a fitting study for the second year, As a matter of fact Part II would be better for the beginner, if the two parts are to be studied separately, but really the two must be taken together if the student would secure the greatest benefit from the use of this book.

In the study of the second part, the student is urged to take each sentence and analyze it carefully, ascertain the " whys " and " wherefores," notice its structure and *memorize* it; at the same time reading carefully Part I, and comparing what it says with what he finds put in practice in Part II. Of course the chapter on The Alphabet and its Sounds, must be mastered first, but as soon as this is done let the student begin on the sentences in Part II, while he is at the same time reading carefully, and learning all there is to be learned in the chapter on the noun. He need not wait till he has studied the verb but simply glance at such words and terms as may be necessary.

5.—This work does not enter into the study of the Korean written language, which differs from the spoken, largely in verbal terminations and a few expressions never used in the colloquial. A little careful study, will soon acquaint one with these and their meanings, and while much hard work would be needed to make one a proficient and exact writer of " the book language," one may soon with comparative ease understand it.

6.—In the writing of Korean, two forms of character are used, the native Ŏnmun and the Chinese, In all official correspondence, philosophical books, and in fact in nearly all books of real value, the Chinese character was used in the past, the native Ŏnmun being relegated to a few trashy love stories and fairy tales. This difference in the written language, led to the assertion that there are two languages in Korea, and we sometimes hear foreigners talk of "speaking in the Ŏnmun." There are not two languages and this expression is wrong, for the " Ŏnmun " is simply a system of writing, and it would be as sensible to talk of "speaking in Munson's system of short hand." The idea that there are two languages in Korea is strengthened by the fact, that foreigners, who are perhaps tolerably well acquainted with words purely Korean, have, when they heard conversations carried on between officials and scholars, been unable to understand what was said. They have been on their way to the houses of the officials and passing through the streets and hearing the merchants the middle classes, and the coolies, talking among themselves, have been able to understand, while when they came into the presence of the officials, they have been unable to comprehend the meaning of statements and questions addressed directly to them. At once they have said "There are two languages" while the truth is that the officials have simply been using those Korean terms which have been derived from the Chinese. Chinese may be called the *Latin* of Korea. It is more polite and scholarly to use "*Latinized*" Korean; but among merchants, middle classes, and in common daily conversation this is not largely used : the learner does not hear it, hence the difficulty. This however being the case, it becomes necessary to make a study of these Sinico-Korean terms, for which he will find frequent and important use.

In connection with his use of these terms one thing must be borne in mind, that if a Sinico-Korean noun is used, the adjective or pronominal adjective used to qualify or limit it, should also be Sinico-Korean and *vice-versa*. All such words however undergo inflection and change as though pure Korean. This rule is more apparent, and is more necessary of observation in connection with the formation of compound words.

7.—Reference was made in the previous paragraph to the two forms of writing used. They were however for the most part, kept entirely distinct, and unlike the Japanese, the two were seldom mixed. Now and then in a letter written in the Chinese, Korean particles might be interspersed to assist the reader, or in a letter written in the "Önmun" the names of persons, places, etc., might be written in the Chinese. A few books were to be found witten in both the Chinese and the "Önmun" but for the most part, the Chinese character was written on one page with its equivalent in Ŏnmun on the other, The rule was, as we have stated, not to mix the two characters, and the almost universal practice to use either the Ŏnmun or Chinese alone.

8.—Before leaving the subject of Chinese and " Ŏnmun we would call attention to the fact that the great majority of the students of Korean utterly neglect the study of the Chinese characters on the ground that they cannot study two languages at once and prefer to study Korean." Nothing could be more ridiculous or more short sighted. The study of the Chinese character is not the study of a different language but the study of Korean derivations carried on in Korean and opening up new etymological avenues leading the student to a clearer understanding of the language which he hears, and nearer to a mastery of elegant and scholarly speech. It will bring him the respect and regard of scholarly Koreans and broaden his vocabulary with astonishing ease and speed as new words will appear as merely new groupings of old friends.

This lack of vocabulary on the part of missionaries is often remarked among Koreans and indeed it would be laughable were it not rather disgraceful to notice how completly at sea many even of the older missionaries are when a conversation takes a turn not directly religious or domestic or when any but a religious book is taken up. It may be claimed that a perfect knowledge of a foreign language is impossible, but whether we dispute this point or not, we ought simply to bring our knowledge to a point where we can join intelligently in conversations outside the ordinary domestic and religious lines and read with a fair amount of ease literature more difficult than the Bible and translated hymns.

9.—Great care must be exercised in the matter of pronunciation.* An effort has been made in the chapter on the alphabet and pronunciation, to give rules to aid in this, but do not be satisfied with these, test each rule given, for yourself, try them with your teacher, and prove the result by conversation with natives, who have not accustomed themselves to your peculiarities and mistakes.

There must be from the start systematic drill of both ear and tongue. Which of the two is most important it is not easy to state, but certainly if one does not manage to distinguish with the ear the different sounds it will be impossible to reproduce them with the tongue.

One must as far as possible daily go where he will hear the Koreans talking among themselves. He should do this from the second day of his arrival and note-book in hand mark down the sounds as he hears them. This should be his constant practise. He should never allow himself to get to the place where words and sounds pass him unnoticed. Get aquainted with some Korean who is popular, and has a large circle of friends, become a regular habitue of his Sarang at the hour when you know the Koreans will be assembling. At the start, it will seem as though the Koreans speak with unusual rapidity until your ear becomes more accustomed to the sounds.

The tongue also must be drilled. Various are the exercises that may be suggested but the best the writer knows, is to take a good long Korean sentence learn it off by heart, practice clause by clause until the whole can be repeated at least as fast as by the fastest Korean speaker. In order to secure this, time yourself with a watch and be sure you reach some standard, such for instance, as that suggested by Prof.

---

* See Appendix on phonetics.

Cummins of 5 syllables per second. After such a sentence has been thus learned, begin again with another until it becomes one's habit to speak and talk as fast as the ordinary Korean. In this drill however from the very start one must articulate clearly and correctly, or the speed will be worse than useless.

10.—As has been observed above, Koreans think along entirely different lines from the foreigner, and we would here warn the learner against a few mistakes into which, on this account, he is apt to fall. As will be stated further on, in many cases Koreans do not use the terminations, signifying number, case, etc. unless ambiguity would be caused by their absence. It is not a universal rule, but it is so common that one is almost safe in adopting it as such, and saying : " Never use such terminations unless a true interpretation of the sentence requires them."

Foreigners are apt in their efforts to speak correctly to use postpositions wherever possible, and thus to speak in what the Korean must consider a stilted manner. This almost *laconic conciseness* of speech is much more observable in the use, or rather neglect of use of the personal pronouns, and here more than anywhere else the foreigner is most apt to blunder.

11.—Native grammarians make but three parts of speech, namely ; Nouns, Verbs, and Particles : and, while it might have been well in some respects to have confined ourselves to this division, it has been deemed best for the sake of convenience, to classify and arrange these three divisions under nine heads, namely : Nouns, Pronouns, Numerals, Postpositions, Verbs, Adjectives, Adverbs, Conjunctions, and Interjections.

As all pronouns are in reality nouns, the chapter, on the former, immediately follows that on the latter. As nearly all true Korean adjectives, are really verbs, the chapter on verbs precedes that on adjectives.

12.—Finally we would urge that much care and pains be taken in the study of Korean honorifics. At first sight they appear so numerous and varied that the student is almost discouraged, but he will soon learn that with some trifling exceptions, the whole matter is governed by but a few rules. It is important that he address servants and attendants in low terms, and speak of himself in higher terms ; while in the presence of officials and men of high rank, he must always speak of himself in low terms and address them in the highest forms. While this in theory is so contrary to the Christian idea, in practise in Korea it is almost a necessity, unless one desires to be considered entirely ignorant of both language and propriety.

## CHAPTER II.

### TEE KOREAN ALPHABET AND ITS SOUND.

**13.**—Unlike most languages of the East, Korean has neither a syllabary like the Japanese, nor a system of characters representing individual ideas, like the Chinese, but a true native alphabet. The writing is always in syllables, each syllable forming we might say a separate character, but divisible into its component parts.

**14.**—The Korean alphabet contains twenty-five letters, of which eleven are vowels and fourteen consonants. They are as follows:—

VOWELS.

아 a, ㅑ ya, ㅓ ŏ, ㅕ yŏ, ㅗ ō, ㅛ yō, ㅜ u, ㅠ yu, ㅡ eu, ㅣ i, ㆍ a.

CONSONANTS.

ㄱ k, ㅁ m, ㄴ n, ㅂ p, ㄹ r or l, ㅅ s *or final* t, ㄷ t, ㅈ j, ㅇ ng, ㅋ hk, ㅍ hp, ㅌ ht, ㅊ tj *or* ch, *and* ㅎ h.

As is stated in all books on foreign languages, it is an impossibility to give the exact pronunciation of all the letters of one language in that of another, but a few words here concerning the pronunciation and use of the above alphabet, may be a help in the study of Korean.

Of the vowels, it will be seen at once that the second, fourth, sixth, and eighth are simply modifications of the first, third, fifth and seventh, and it will be noted that this modification is shown in the writing, by the reduplication of the characteristic sign of the vowel, and expressed in the speaking, by the interposition of the sound of the English consonant *y* before the vowel sound. If then we give the sounds of the first, third, fifth and seventh, we will at once have the sounds for all of the first eight vowels.

Note.—No vowel can stand alone at the commencement of a Korean syllable, but if it has no consonant of its own must be preceded by the consonant ㅇ, which is then mute.

PRONUNCIATION OF THE VOWELS.

Whereas English vowels may have a glide such is not the case as a rule with the Korean vowels even though final.

15.— 아. This vowel has two sounds.

(1) That of the Italian ä found in the English words *father, arm,* etc.

Ex. 알, äl, (*egg*) ; 안경, än-gyeng, (*spectacles*).

(2) That of the regular English short ă found in *mat, add,* etc.

막닥이, mäk-tă-gi, (*a stick*).

16.— 어. This vowel has two sounds.

(1) That of the regular English short ŏ seen in *not, odd,* etc.

Ex. 얼핏, ŏl-hpit, (*quickly*) ; 어듸, ŏ-dai, (*where*) ; 업소, ŏp-sŏ, (*to carry on the back*).

(2) That of the German ö, or the English *ur* of *urn*.

Ex. 어루신너, ö-rŏ-si-nai, (*father*) ; 어룬, ö-run, (*adult*), and 업소, öp-sŏ, (*to be lacking, to be not*).

17.— 오. Here we can use the regular long and short English *o* sounds.

---

* See Appendix on phonetics.

(1) Long ō, of old, etc. is for the most part found in open syllables.

Ex. 호랑이, hō-rang-i, *(a tiger)* ; 오, ō, *(five)*.

(2) The short ŏ of lot, etc. occurs generally in closed syllables.

Ex. 봉, pŏng, *(an envelope)* ; 공사, kŏng-sa, *minister)* ; 오늘, ŏ-nel, *((to-day)*.

**18.—우.** From this vowel we get the sound of either the long o͞o of *moon*, or the short o͝o of *wool*.

(1) Ex. 구경, koo-gyeng, *(a sight)* ; 부리, po͞o-ri, *(a beak)* ; 눈, no͞on, *(snow)*.

(2) Ex. 풀, hpo͝ol, *(herbage)* ; 눈, no͝on, *(eye)*.

**19.**—As has been said above, the compound vowels 야, 여, 요, 유, have respectively the sounds of the above four simple vowels with *y* preceding.

Then. 야 will be either yä or yă.
  여 will be either yŏ or German yö.
  요 will be either yō or yŏ.
And  유 will be yoo.

**20.—으.** Here we have the sound of the French eu, as in *feu* (fire)

Ex. 그, keu, *(that)* ; 그늘, keu-neul, *(shade)* ; 늙은이, neulk-eun-i, *(an old man)*.

**21.— 이.** This vowel has two sounds.

(1) The sound of *i* in the words *machine, pique*.

Ex. 비, pï. *(rain)* ; 시, sï, *(hour)* ; 이상하오, ï-sang-ha-o, *(to be strange)*.

(2) The sound of the regular English short *ĭ* of *ill, hit*, etc.

Ex. 기다리오, kĭ-da-rĭ-o, *(to wait)* ; 십, sip, *(ten)*.

22.— 으, This vowel has really four sounds.

(1 & 2). The same two sounds as given for 아.
Ex.

(1) 한하오, hän-ha-o, (*to hate*); 수신, sä-sin, (*ambassador*).

(2) 기드리오, ki-dä-ri-o, (*to wait*).

(3) Most commonly the sound is that of the short Italian *a seen* in staff.

Ex. 물, (*horse*); 으히, à-hai, (*boy*).

(4) The sound of *e* in cable, 오늘, ŏ-nel, (*to-day*); 고름, kò-rem, (*pus*); 기름, kï-rem, (*oil*).

Note —In spelling the Koreans distinguish between 아 and 으 by a reference to their position in writing, (calling 아 "upper *a*" and 으 "lower *a*."

23.—Before we turn to the consideration of the consonants it would be well to linger a little while over a few combinations, of vowels. In the following diphthongs and triphthongs it will be seen that 오 and 우 placed before other vowels in the syllable generally give the sound of the English *w*.

The combinations most commonly used with their pronunciations are as follows.

1st. 애, has the sound of the *ai* before *r* in *air* etc.

Ex. 개, (*a dog*); 내, (*I*); 대개, (*for*); 새, (*new*).

2nd. 이, has the same sound as the preceding:

Ex. 티신, (*instead*); 미우, (*very*).

24.—3rd. 에, has the regular long sound of the English *a* in *day*.

Ex. 네, (*you*); 셋, (*three*).

Sometimes also it has the sound of the short English *e* in *end*.

Ex. 메누리, (*a daughter-in-law*).

It has also though very rarely, the sound of *i* in *machine*.

Ex. 메토리, *(hempen sandals)*.

4th. 예, properly has the sound of the English word *yea*.

Ex. 계란, *(eggs)* ; 예비호오, *(to make ready)*.

However, after consonants where it would be hard to pronounce the *y*, the sound is the same as 에, though perhaps a little prolonged.

Ex. 뎨일, *,(the first)* ; 셰샹, *(the world)*.

25.—5th. 와, has the sound of *wä*, the *a* being the long Italian *a* which is seen in *father*, etc.

Ex. 과히, *(excessively)* ; 화초, *(flowers)* ; 실과, *(fruit,)*.

6th. 왜. Here we have No. 1 preceded by 오 which having the effect of *w* gives us the sound of *wa* in *ware*.

Ex. 왜국, *(Japan)* ; 홰, *(a torch)*.

7th. 외. The exact sounds that this diphthong may have, can only be learned by practice.

Sometimes it may have the sound of *we* in *were*, as 되오, *(to become)* ; 피롭소, *(to be troublesome)* ; sometimes that of *wa* in *way*, as 너외, *(husband and wife)* ; sometimes almost this same sound with the *w* less distinct, as 죄, *(sin)* ; and sometimes also the sound of French *eu*, as 쇠, *(metal)*.

26.—8th. 워, consists of 우 placed before 어, and may therefore have either of the two sounds which are derived respectively by placing *w* before the two sounds of the latter vowel,

Ex. 1st, 월, *(moon)*. 2nd, 원호오, *(to desire)* ; 권호오, *(to exhort)*.

At times also it may have the sound of *wo* in *won*.

Ex. 원, *(a mandarin)*; 권, *(a volume)*.

9th. 웨, may have any of the sounds of 에, preceded by *w*, but for the most part it is restricted to the sound of *wa* in *way*.

Ex. 궤, *(a box)*; 왜, *(why)*.

10th. 위. This diphthong has the force of *w* before the long continental *i* sound and may be pronounced like the English *we*.

Ex. 귀, *(ear)*; 귀ᄒᆞ오, *(to be rare)*; 뒤, *(back)*.

11th. 위. This combination of vowels is rarely found, and it has the same sound as 위 though perhaps a little more prolonged.

Ex. 취ᄒᆞ오, *(to be intoxicated)*.

27.—12th. 의. The effect of this diphthong is produced by pronouncing the two sounds of 오 and 이 together, running them into one.

Ex. 긔슈, *(a soldier)*.

Note.—There is a tendency among foreigners to pronounce this like the short *i* of hit, but this is wrong and should be carefully avoided.

Sometimes this becomes almost the same as the English *we* without movement of the lips.

Ex. 의심, *(doubt)*.

## The Consonants.

28.—Of the Korean consonants, nine are simple and five are aspirated.

The simple are ㄱ k, ㅁ m, ㄴ n, ㅂ p, ㄹ r or l, ㅅ s, ㄷ t, ㅈ j, and ㅇ ng.

The aspirated are, ㅋ, ㅍ, ㅌ, ㅊ and ㅎ.

Five of the simple consonants, ㄱ, ㅂ, ㅅ, ㄷ, and ㅈ are often doubled when they can be written as such, or the doubling is expressed by placing ㅅ before the letter. This ㅅ is then called "twin siot." These double consonants may then be written :—

ㄲ, ㅃ, ㅆ, ㄸ, ㅉ,
or ㅅㄱ, ㅅㅂ, ㅆ, ㅅㄷ, ㅅㅈ.

The effect of the doubling, is generally expressed by a harder and more incisive utterance of the double consonant, while that of the aspirating, by a decidedly rough breathing. These differences can only be learned and reproduced by careful study and constant practice.

29.—In connection with the consonants and their sounds, euphony plays an important part, sometimes completely changing the sound of the consonant itself, sometimes merely modifying, and sometimes rendering it absolutely mute. The rules of euphony cannot all be here given, but in describing the sounds of the consonants, an attempt is made to so explain them and their changes that the main difficulties may be overcome.

It may be well to notice here, that euphony plays such an important part in Korean, that it ofttimes completely changes the initial consonant of postpositions and other suffixes. In a language where the character is syllabic like the Japanese, there is not the same latitude for such changes as in a language purely alphabetic like the Korean. It is these euphonic changes in the postpositions which have led foreigners to follow and tenaciously hold to, the example of the French Missionaries, in Latinizing the noun and giving five distinct declensions with eleven cases each.

CONSONANTAL SOUNDS.

30.—We will consider first the simple consonants.

1st. ㄱ. This has commonly the sound of *k* in *king* As, 갑, kap, (*price*) ; 가오, ka-o, (*to go*).

Sometimes it may have the sound of *g* in *give*.

Ex. 잇다가, it-ta-ga, (*in a little*), and 막다이, mak-tă-gi, (*a stick*).

When before ㅁ (m), ㄴ (n), or ㄹ (r) ; this letter has the sound of *ng*.

Ex. 약물, yang-moul, (*medicinal water*).
넉넉이, nŏng-nŏk-i, (*enough*).
약력, yang-ryok, (*medicinal effect*).

31.—2nd. ㅁ. This is pronounced like the *m* of *money*.

Ex. 머므오, mŏ-meu-o, (*to tarry*).

32.—3rd. ㄴ. This for the most part has the common sound of *n* in *panel*.

Ex. 나는, na-năn, (*as for me*) or 눈, noon, (*eye*).

Sometimes when followed by the vowel *i*, it has the effect of the English *y*, or may be mute.

Ex. 니, yi, (*a tooth*) ; 니히오, ig-hi-o, (*to be cooked*).

When preceded or followed by ㄹ *l*, both consonants take the sound of *l*, in *calling*.

Ex. 별노, pyel-lo, *specially* ; 날너, nal-lai, (*swiftly*).

33.—4th. ㅇ. Before a vowel this is mute. In Korean no vowel is allowed to stand alone, or to begin a syllable, and in cases where this would occur ㅇ is used.

Ex. 아오, a-ō, (*to know*) ; 아마, a-ma, (*perhaps*).

At the end of a syllable, this has the sound of *ng* in *song*.

Ex. 양, yang, (*sheep*) ; 병, pyung, (*a bottle*).

**34.**—5th. ㅂ. This commonly has the sound of the unaspirated *p* in English.

 Ex. 밥, pap, (*rice*) ; 보오, po-o, (*to see*).

Sometimes it may have the sound of *b*.

 Ex. 아바지, abaji, (*father*) ; 불가불, poul-ga-boul, (*of necessity*).

Before ㅁ (m), *or* ㄴ (n), *or* ㄹ (r), it generally has the sound of *m*.

 Ex. 협문, hyŏm-mun, (*side gate*) ; 압니, am-ni, (*front teeth*) ; 십리, sim-ni, (*ten ri*).

**35.**—6th. ㄹ. This consonant may have the sounds of *l, n,* or *r*.

It has the sounds of *l* :—

 (*a*). At the end of a word.

 Ex. 물, mal, (*horse*) ; 불, pul, (*fire*) ; 밀, mil, (*wax*).

 (*b*). When it is followed by another consonant in the same syllable.

 Ex. 의둛소, ai-dalp-so, (*to hate*) ; 사둙, ga-dalk, (*reason*).

 (*c*). When it follows or precedes the consonant ㄴ

 Ex. 칼노, kal-lo, (*with a knife*) ; 환란, hwal-lan, (*calamity*) ; 말니오, mal-yi-o, (*to prevent*).

It is pronounced *n* :—

 (*a*). At the beginning of a word.

 Ex. 릐일, nai-il, (*to-morrow*).

 (*b*). Sometimes at the beginning of a syllable in the middle of a word.

 Ex. 공론하오, kong-non-ha-o, (*to consult together*).

It generally has the sound of *r*, when coming between two vowels, or between a vowel and ㅎ.

Ex. 아름답소, a-ram-tap-so, (*to be beautiful*) ; 일홈, ir-hom, (*a name*).

Sometimes before ㅣ, and the compound vowels, it has the sound of *y*.

Ex. 리, yi, (*profit*) ; 료량, yo-ryang, (*deliberation*).

36.—7th. ㅅ. At the beginning of a word this letter has the sound of *s*.

Ex. 삼가오, sam-kao, (*to take care*) ; 삭, sak, (*pay*).

At the end of a word it has the sound of *t*.

Ex. 갓, kat, (*hat*); 낫, nat, (*mid-day*) ; 몃, met, (*how many*).

The sound of this final ㅅ is however sometimes modified by the initial letter of the syllable which follows it.

Before another ㅅ it becomes *s*.

Ex. 갓소로, kas-sa-ro, (*with a hat*).

Before ㄱ, it has the sound of *k*.

Ex. 삭기, sak-ki, (*young*) ; 잣고, chak-ko, (*frequently*).

Before ㅁ, it becomes *n*.

Ex. 갓모, kan-mo, (*hat covering*).

When the compound vowels ㅑ, ㅕ, ㅛ, ㅠ, are preceded by ㅅ, the *y* is mute, and they have the sounds of the corresponding simple vowels.

Ex. 샹관, sang-gwan, (*importance*) ; 세샹, sō-sang, (*the world*).

37.—8th. ㄷ. This letter has generally the sound of *t*, in *told*.

Ex. 답쟝, tap-jang, (*answer*); 달소, tal-so, (*to be different*).

Sometimes it may have the sound of *d* in *dance*.

Ex. 틱답호오, tai-dap-hao, (*to answer*); 견틱오, kyun-dai-o, (*to endure*).

Before ㅣ, or any of the compound vowels, the *y* sound of the compound vowels disappears, and ㄷ has the force of *ch*.

Ex. 디경, chi-gyung, (*territory*); 됴소, cʻio-so, (*to be good*).

Note.—This rule does not hold in the province of Pyang An Do where ㄷ always retains the sound of ㄷ and the *y* sound is retained in the double consonants.

At the end of a syllable ㄷ becomes ㅅ, although retaining the sound of *t*. but in some ancient books it is still found as ㄷ.

38.—9th. ㅈ. This consonant for the most part has the sound in *ch* in *choose*.

Ex. 잡소, chap-so, (*to catch*); 쥐, chwi, (*a rat*).

Sometimes it may have the sound of *j* in *joy*.

Ex. 죽이오, ju-gi-o, (*to kill*).

As in the case of ㅅ so also in the case of this consonant, when followed by the compound vowels, the *y* sound is lost and that of the simple vowel only, remains.

ASPIRATED CONSONANTS.

39.—The aspirated consonants are.

ㅋ, ㅍ, ㅌ, ㅊ, ㅎ.

As has already been said the exact pronunciation of these aspirated consonants cannot be expressed in English. Suffice it to say that, each one has a rough explosive sound of the corresponding simple consonant.

ㅋ, is aspirated k.

Ex. 칼, hkal, (*a knife*)? 퀴, hkeui, (*height*); 코, hkŏ, (*nose*).

ㅍ, is aspirated p.

Ex. 픔, hpeum, (*rank*); 풀, hpōōl, (*grass*); 팔, hpal, (*eight*).

ㅌ, is aspirated t.

Ex. 탐심, htam-sim, (*envy*); 토하오, hto-ha-o, (*to vomit*).

ㅊ, is aspirated ch.

Ex. 차, cha, (*tea*); 착하오, chak-ha-o, (*to be honest*).

ㅎ, being ㅇ aspirated has the effect of h in house.

Ex. 합하오, hap-ha-o, (*to unite*); 혼인, hon-in, (*marriage*); 흥샹, häng-säng, (*always*).

### DOUBLED CONSONANTS.

40.—It is no easy task to properly reproduce the sound given by Koreans to the doubled consonants, much less to describe them accurately. It may be said however that as a rule the effect of the "twin siot" or doubling is to change the natural surds $k, p, s, t$, to the sonants $g, b, z$, and $d, j$. These sounds like all others must be obtained from the Koreans direct, and ear, and tongue drilled and drilled till they are distinguished and can be reproduced.

까투리 gatouri, (female pheasant); 까다 gata, (to peel)

셰앗다 bai-ät-ta, (to seize) 쌀너 ballai, (washing)
쌉쌀하다 Zapsalhata (*to be bitterish*); 쓰다 zeuta (*to be bitter*)
따 da, (*the earth*) 뛰다 dwita, (*to jump*)
짜다 Jata, (*to be salt*) 쫏다 Jotta, (to pursue)

41.—The Koreans have given names to the nine simple consonants, but the vowels and aspirated consonants have no distinctive names, and can only be expressed by the sounds they represent. The names of the nine simple consonants are,

ㄱ—기억, ki-ok.
ㅁ—미음, mi-om.
ㄴ—니은, ni-eun.
ㅂ—비읍, pi-op.
ㄹ—리을, li-eul.
ㅅ—시옷, si-ot.
ㄷ—디긋, ji-keut.
ㅈ—잣, jät.
ㅇ—이힝, i-haing.

It will be noticed that for the most part the name gives the initial and final sound of the consonant it represents.

Enough has now been said to enable the student to gain an idea of the true sounds of the Korean alphabet, and some of the various modifications that they undergo. No book can ever tell him when and where long and short sounds should be used. These he must learn by practice.

## CHAPTER III.

### THE NOUN.

42.—Heretofore it has been the custom to consider that the Korean noun is declinable, and grammarians have variously classified the noun as belonging to, from one to five declensions, each having a number of cases varying from six to ten. There have been two causes for this, first the intimate acquaintance of those who have tried to systematize the language, with Latin and Greek, and the tendency that would thus naturally arise to make the languages conform. Secondly, on coming to Korea they found different nouns with various endings to express the same idea, and losing sight of the fact that they were but euphonic changes of various postpositions, called them cases.

The Korean noun is however indeclinable. In what has heretofore been regarded as declension, the noun itself is not *declined*, undergoes no change,* remains the same

---

\* Note.—There are probably only three exceptions to this rule 것, 무엇 and 여럿 which may really be considered as one, since 여럿 and 무엇 are but contractions and were originally 여러 것 and 무슴 것. In all these words the final *t*, or *s*, is taken from the stem and prefixed to the postposition. At times also, still further contractions are made and we can have 걸 for 거 슬, 무얼 for 무 어 슬, etc.

throughout, and the particles affixed, which have been considered as representing various cases, are rather distinct words or postpositions. These postpositions undergo a variety of changes according to the final letter of the noun to which they are affixed, but in no case do they change the noun itself. They represent the English prepositions.

**43.**—The distinctions of number, subject, and object, of a sentence etc, may be designated by postpositions or may be left to the context.

For Ex. 그 사룸 의게 칙 주어라.
*lit. that man to book give.*

The *exact* meaning of this sentence can only be understood by a knowledge of the circumstances. It may mean, give a book, or books, to one man or two. The man, (사룸), may be man or woman, boy or girl. This indefiniteness of expression, which is a characteristic of most eastern languages, is more apparent in Korean than in Japanese. It would have been perfectly correct to have omitted the 의게 from the sentence given above. In the case of the subject and object of a sentence we find the same difficulty. As has been said before, the general rule is to omit the postposition unless the sentence taken with its context and circumstances would be ambiguous without them.

The use of the postposition giving definiteness to the sentence, often has the effect of the English definite article; and, where ambiguity would arise without them, they may be used to express this. In the example given above, the accusative postposition is not expressed, but if we desired to be definite we would say.

그 사룸 의게 척 을 주어라.
which would be "Give that man *the* book."

As also. 병뎡 왓소   병뎡 가 왓소
A soldier has come.   The soldier has come.

문하인 이 교군 을 불넛소.
The gateman has called *the* chair coolies.

**44.**—For a full account of the postpositions, and the various euphonic changes that they undergo, see Chapter VI. For convenience, however, we give in this place the postpositions representing some of the various case relations of the noun.

Nominative or subjective by. 이 or 가.
Genitive by ..................... 의.
Dative by........................ 의게 or 안테.
Accusative by ................. 을.
Instrumental by ·.............. 으로.
Ablative by ..................... 에, 에셔, or 브터.

These postpositions are added to the noun and give the various ideas given by the above arrangement of cases, but undergo a variety of changes according to the final letter of the noun.

**45.**—Gender where necessary may be expressed by employing particles denoting male and female, or by the use of distinct words.

Thus we have in the case of human beings :—

A man, 사나희, 남조, 남인.
A woman, 계집, 녀인, 녀편네.
A child, 으히 ; a boy, 사나희 ; a girl, 계집으히.

In the case of relations, different words are used.

아 바 지, Father ;   어마니, Mother.
할 아바지, Grandfather ;   할마니, Grandmother.

The gender of animals also is distinguished by particular names or by the prefixing of 슈 male and 암 female.

둙, a fowl ;       슈둙. a cock ;        암둙, a hen.

쇼, a bull or cow ;  슈쇼 } a bull ;    암쇼, a cow.
                    황쇼

꿩, a pheasant ;   슈꿩 } a male      암 꿩 } a female
                   쟝끼  pheasant ;   ᄭᅡ투리 pheasant.

말, a horse ;      샹마 } a stallion ;  피마 } a mare.
                   슈물                암물

The particles 암 and 슈 are not employed alone and are never applied to human beings except as terms of extreme contempt. If then we desire to speak of the gender of an animal without repeating its name, we say for the male 슈놈 or 슈것, and for the female, 암놈 or 암것.

그 거시 슈둙이냐 암둙이냐.
(*That thing male chicken is? female chicken is?*)
    " Is that a rooster or a hen? "

In this sentence 암 and 슈 are used adjectively, but in the following sentence we see the use of 암것 and 슈것.

그 톡기 슈 거시냐 암 거시냐.
(*That rabbit male thing is? female thing is?*)
    " Is that rabbit a male or a female."

Here the word rabbit, is not repeated, so 암것 and 슈것 are used.

46.—The same ambiguity that has been referred to in the matter of case, etc., also exists with reference to number. The Korean noun in fact has no number. Context or circumstances decide this also.

# THE NOUN.

병인 다숫 오놀 아춤 왓소.
*(patient five to-day morning came.)*
"Five patients came this morning."

날 드러 골으라고 물 셋슬 가져왓소.
*(me—to choose-order horse three (accu) brought.)*
"They brought three horses for me to choose from."

그 목련화 나모에 오빅 송아리 잇슬 터히오.
*(that magnolia tree on five hundred blossom must be.)*
"There must be five hundred blossoms on that magnolia tree."

Note.—*Must* is not always rendered in this way. For its various renderings see Part II Chap. I. ¿ 3 Sec, 10.

47.—At times however, either for the sake of emphasis or to avoid ambiguity, it is desirable to express a plural idea ; and this may be done by the use of the particle 들 affixed to the nouns, to which in turn may be affixed any one of the postpositions.

| | | | |
|---|---|---|---|
| 동싱, | Brother. | 동싱들, | Brothers. |
| 눈, | Eye. | 눈들, | Eyes. |
| 물, | Horse. | 물들, | Horses. |
| 꼿, | Flower. | 꼿들, | Flowers. |
| 양, | Sheep. | 양들, | Sheep. |
| 사슴, | Deer. | 사슴들, | Deer. |

This particle 들 may also be used without the noun, and is then generally affixed to an adverb in the sentence, and gives a plural idea.

As :—

어셔 들 오시오.
*quickly (plur) come.*
Please come quickly.

## THE NOUN.

잘 들 ᄒᆞ여라.
*well (plur) do.*
Do   it   well.

The particle 들 used in this way, generally pluralizes the subject of the verb; and in both the above sentences it shows that the request in the first case, and the command in the second, was addressed to more than one.

**48.**—Students in Korea soon begin to notice the constant reduplication of nouns, verbs, syllables etc. In verbs it has the effect of signifying continued action, and is found frequently in onomatopoetic words, to designate sounds and the like, and in nouns it gives the idea of universality, or variety,

As:—

집집, Every house.
식식, All colors or sorts.
곳곳, All places or everywhere.
나라나라, All countries.

**49.**—These then are the various ways of expressing case, gender, and number, which may be employed if desired, and are at times used by Koreans even when ambiguity would not exist without them. It cannot however be too carefully borne in mind that as a rule Koreans do not express these distinctions.

**50.**—In a few cases there are distinctive words which have a plural sense. They are, for the most part, compound words of Chinese origin, and to them again, if special emphasis is desired the plural ending 들 may be added.

As :—

부모 or 부모들 (rare), Parents.
식구 or 식구들, Members of a family.
형데, Brethren.

## COMPOUND NOUNS.

**51.**—There are of course a large number of compound nouns, and these by the use of Chinese may be formed at will. They may consist either of nouns alone, nouns and adjectives, nouns and verbs, or of verbs alone. A knowledge of the Chinese characters and their sounds in Korean, will enable the foreigner, not only to recognize these and understand their meaning at once, but also to form them for himself. We would then urge the student not only to learn these compounds whenever he meets them, but to analyze them, ascertain their derivation, learn the Chinese character and its Korean sound and thus be able when next he meets the same characters, though perhaps in different combinations, to recognize them at a glance. This study of words and their derivations will also be a great help in giving definiteness and precision to his style.

안경, " Spectacles " from 안 " eye " and 경 " a glass."
안질, " Ophthalmia " from 안 " eye" and 질 " disease."
쳔리경, " Telescope " from 쳔 " thousand," 리, "li," and 경 a " glass."
현미경. " Microscope " from 현, " exhibiting," 미, " smallness " and 경 a " glass."
화학, " Chemistry " from 화 " change " and 학, " study."

No attempt can here be made to give all, or even the most important of the words belonging to this class. The few that have been given above are sufficient to enable the student to understand this method of forming compound words, so that he can go forward and analyze these words for himself. A little care in this line will be a great help to him in his study of this class of words, and if from the beginning he makes a systematic study of all such words, in but a short time he will be able to understand without difficulty most, if not all the Sinico-Korean terms so much used in polite discourse.

52.—There are also a few words which are joined to verbs and sometimes to other nouns, making compound nouns having the sense, of "*the work of*" "*doer*" etc. Among these are 군, 쟝이, 질, etc.

The first two of these refer to the *maker* or *doer* of something, both have nearly the same meaning but are restricted in their use.

쟝이, the more restricted, has properly the sense of "*the worker in*," "*the maker of*" and is affixed to the name of the *thing made*, or *the work done*.

군, the more generally used, is a termination equivalent to the Latin "*ator*," or the English "*er*," and may be added to almost any word with which work of any kind is connected. Neither of these terms are respectful and are only applied to artisans, coolies, or people whose actions have, in the eyes of the Koreans, brought them to that level.

| | | | |
|---|---|---|---|
| 일군, | Workman, coolie. | 미쟝이, | A mason. |
| 교군군, | A chair-man. | 개와쟝이, | A tiler. |
| 보힝군, | A walker. | 붓쟝이, | A pencil-maker. |
| 작란군, | A player, a trifler. | 통쟝이, | A hooper. |
| 슈직군, | A guard. | 숫쟝이, | A charcoal-burner |
| 농군, | A farm-hand. | 쥬막쟝이, | A hotel-keeper. |

## THE NOUN.

소릭군, A (noiser) singer.　쇼목쟝이, A cabinet-maker.
나모군, A woodman.　　갓쟝이,　A hat-maker.
노름군, A gambler.　　오입쟝이, A dissolute-fellow.

With reference to the termination 질, it may be said that its use varies greatly with the locality.

It has properly the sense of "*the work of*," and is commonly joined to the name of the tool or instrument with which any work is done. By certain people, and in certain places however, its use has been very much enlarged and in the province of Kyeng Sang Do it may be heard affixed to almost any noun or verb.

The following examples illustrate its proper use:—

> 바누질,　Needlework.
> 다림이질, Ironing.
> 채직질,　Whipping.
> 로질,　　Rowing.
> 붓쳐질,　Fanning.

### VERBAL NOUNS.

53.—In Korea there are two regular ways of forming verbal nouns. They are formed by adding ㅁ and 기 to the verbal stem. With the verb 호오, they will then be 홈 and 호기 and we designate them verbal noun in 홈, and verbal noun in 호기. While a large number of Koreans have come to consider these as synonyms, and to use them interchangeably, they are not the same, and good scholars never consider them so. The distinction made by the French missionaries in their admirable "Grammaire Coréenne" should always be maintained.

The noun in 홈, is an abstract noun referring to the quality or attribute as *love*, *hate*, and *fear*.

# THE NOUN.

The noun in 기, retains more of the verbal idea and is rather, the act of *loving, hating, fearing*, and would be used where we would employ either the infinitive of the verb, *to love, to hate, to fear*, or the present participle.

It is about equivalent to the Latin Supine, being a verb in force and a noun in form and inflection. It can both govern and in turn is governed. In use it is generally employed as we would employ the ablative Supine.

An examination of the following sentences will make this distinction plain.

Illustrating the use of Verbal noun in 훔 :—

무셔옴이 겁쟝이 의게 당훈 거시오.
*Fear belongs to cowards.*

착훔이 덕이 되오.
*Honesty is a virtue.*

분홈이 고로옴 을 내오.
*Anger brings trouble.*

Illustrating the use of verbal nouns in 기 :—

원슈 용셔기가 어렵소.
*It is hard to forgive an enemy.*

시방은 온 셰샹을 도라 둔너기 쉽소.
*Now, it is easy to go round the whole world.*

그런 사롬 사랑기 어렵지안소.
*Loving such a man as that, is not hard.*

Illustrating the use of both verbal nouns together :—

무음에 사랑훔이 잇는 사롬 눔을 사랑기 쉽소.
*It is easy for a man who has love in his heart to love others.*

죽옴이 압회 잇신즉 죽기를 면홀수 업소.
*As death is before us, to avoid dying is impossible.*

## NAMES AND TITLES.

**54.**—A few words here about Korean given names and titles, may be a help to the student. The Korean surnames are but few and for the most part consist of but one syllable. A few, but five or six at the most, consist of two syllables. The total number of surnames in Korea, being under a hundred, can be learned with comparative ease. In writing their surnames they seldom use any but the Chinese character, and it is a necessity for almost any one who expects to have much dealing with Koreans, to learn these eighty or hundred characters. The ending 가 may be added to the surnames with the sense of *the family, tribe, household of,* as 민가 "The Min family" or "the Mins," 리가 "The Yi family" "the Yis" etc. While it is perfectly proper, and no act of disrespect to use this ending in speaking of any family or person; in their presence or in addressing them, it is not polite.

Note:—This ending 가 is also used in speaking of servants. It would not be proper in sending for your gateman to say—

박서방 불너 오너라 or "Call Mr. Pak."

but—

박가 불너 오너라. "Call Pak."

It may be well here, however, to state that the ordinary Korean way of summoning a servant, is not to use the surname at all, but the given name or the office that they fill.

To these surnames may be prefixed or affixed names of towns or places. If the name of the town precedes the surname, it signifies that the place mentioned was the original home of the branch of the family spoken of. In a country where surnames are so limited, this becomes a necessity.

When the names of the place follows the surname it may have one or other of two significations; that most common is, that the party referred to, is now, or was lately the magistrate of that place.

Among travelling pedlars however, this same method has been adopted to designate their domicile.

| | | |
|---|---|---|
| 안동 | 김가 | The "An Dong Kims," or the Kims of An Dong. |
| 쳥풍 | 김가 | The "Chyeng Pung Kims." |
| 젼쥬 | 리가 | The "Chyeng Ju Yis." |
| 연안 | 리가 | The "Yern An Yis." |

but—

| | | |
|---|---|---|
| 죠 | 쥭산 | "Cho Chuk San" means the Cho who is now, or was lately, magistrate at Chuk San. |
| 리 | 고양 | "Yi Ko Yang," the Yi who was, or is, magistrate at Ko Yang. |

Among pedlars—

| | | |
|---|---|---|
| 리 | 강계 | "Yi Kang Gay" means that Kang Gay is Mr. Yi's home. |
| 한 | 의쥬 | "Han Eui Ju," that Eui Ju, is Mr. Han's home. |

**55.**—In connection with the Korean given names there appears to the foreigner an almost unlimited amount of confusion. He hears a man with whose name he is acquainted called by a name entirely different, and is told that it is still his name, his given name. A boy whom he has known for years, marries; and coming to pay his respects, sends in a card bearing a name that he has never before seen. This too, the foreigner learns is his given name. This apparent confusion arises from the fact that each Korean has several given names, and that by which he was known as a boy, is entirely put aside on his attaining manhood.

THE NOUN.

We shall here speak of but three classes of names: the civil name, the name held during boyhood, and that given at marriage.

The civil name is properly only found among the nobility and upper classes. It is the name by which the individual is legally known from boyhood up, and continues with him throughout life. It always consists of two characters, one of which will have been settled generations before, and all the members of the same generation of any one family will have this same character and will be *called* brothers.

As:— 김틔호, 김두호, 김겸호.

Here the presence of the same character 호, as the last half of all their names shows that they are of the same generation. Their sons will be—

김영익, 김영균, 김영환.

Here the second character 영, is the same throughout. In the next generation it will again be the third character that will be the same and it will be 식.

As:— 김응식, 김뎡식, 김궁식.

And thus it alternates from the second to the third character of their names, the surname of course as in all Eastern languages coming first and the remaining character being left to the option of the parents.

In common use among friends, however, this civil name is seldom used. As a boy, he has a boyish name, given him by his parents at his birth, which remains with him until his marriage. On this occasion, his parents *again* give him another name: that by which he was known as a boy is no longer used, and his friends now call him by his 字, or name given at marriage. At times, also, friends give complimentary names and nicknames of which we need not speak here.

Here as in other things the times are making great changes. The old habits are passing away and the advantage as well as necessity of maintaining one's individuality is causing people more and more to use one name and that the civil.

56.—The titles by which Koreans are known and addressed : with the officials, follow the office held ; with those who are not officials, they are 셔방 (Mr.) 셕ᄉ (Esq.) 싱원 (Revered Sir) and many others. To these at times are added the honorific particle 님, and we have 셔방님, or 싱원님. More lately the terms 샹 and 공 have been used and we hear 감샹, 김공, etc. All these are affixed to the surname, and when used, the civil, or given name must be dropped. In addressing or speaking of old men or those whose rank gives them the right to wear the jade button, we use the word 령감 : and those whose rank gives them the right to wear the gold button, are spoken of as 대감. But when these words are used, it is as independent titles without the surname. The use of the surname with either of these words is habitual among certain classes ; but is not considered good Korean and should be avoided.

57.—One of the surprising facts which met the Westerner on his arrival in Korea, was that the girls and women of the land had no names. Parents give a pet name to little girls as well as to boys, at their birth ; but after they have reached the age of ten, this name is no longer known. From this time on, they were known as "Mr. Kim's daughter" or even "Mr. Kim's girl baby ;" and strange to say the latter term is the more honorific.

When there is more than one daughter in the family, they are distinguished by such words as: "big" (for the eldest), "second," "third," "fourth," etc.

After marriage, they are still, often known by their husband's name and title, with the word 되 or 집 (house) affixed.

As:—

김 셔 방 되   Mrs. Kim.
리 참 판 되   Mrs. Yi Champan or Lady Yi.
한 셔 방 집   Mrs. Han.

Of these two, 되 is the more honorable.

They may also be designated by the name of the place from which they came when marrying, prefixed to such words as 마 님 or 마 루 라 님, if the person is old; or to 아 기 씨 or 아 씨, if young.

As:—고 양 마 님 or 고 양 마 루 라 님, The old lady who came from Ko Yang.

공 쥬 아 씨 or 공 쥬 아 기 씨, The young lady from Kong Ju.

It should always be remembered in connection with the names for women and girls that it is not customary in Korea for any except relatives or those extremely intimate to ask concerning the female members of another's family.

Christian civilization has however been changing all this. The baptismal names are more and more being used. The individuality of the woman as distinct from her husband is being asserted. All over the land it is more and more becoming the custom for the women to have their distinct names. In fact now the new laws of the Empire require it.

58.—Before closing this subject, a remark or two on the Korean employment of the word 부인 that has come into such common and erroneous use by foreigners, should be given. This term 부인 was properly equivalent to the English title,—"Lady": and if strictly used could only be applied to the wives of high officials. Even then it was not in common use, and the official himself would not use it in speaking of his own wife; unless perhaps in addressing a foreigner, who, he feared might not understand another word. It would however have been proper in speaking *of* the wife of a high official to use this term where in English we would use "Her Ladyship." A change has been brought about of late years and it is now proper to refer to the wife of another as 부인 but never to use the term in speaking of one's own wife. In speaking of one's own wife the terms 안 히, 안 악, 안, etc., would be used; or in addressing an inferior, 아 씨, 아 기 씨, 마 님, 마 루 라 님.

# CHAPTER IV.

### PRONOUNS AND PRONOMINAL ADJECTIVES.

59.—With reference to Korean pronouns, it is doubtful whether such in the true sense of the word really exist. It is so easy, with most of the words used for pronouns to trace out their original meaning, and to show that they are really nothing but nouns which have either become restricted in use to one or other of the three persons, or else are convenient words, either by the designation of one's self or others, for rendering honor or its opposite to the person spoken to or of; that we are tempted to believe that by diligent research we should find that all the pronouns were originally nouns. We are strengthened in this idea by the fact that the native grammarians arrange their words into but three classes, including all pronouns under the head of nouns. For the sake of convenience, however, it has been deemed best to treat of these words by themselves; and in the consideration of Korean pronouns and pronominal adjectives, we will divide them into Personal, Reflexive, Interrogative, or Indefinite, Demonstrative, and Distributive.

## Personal Pronouns.

**60.—The First Person.** The word most commonly used to render the first person is 나, 내, or 내가 : many other words, however, are also used, as, 즈긔, 제가, 쇼인, 이사룸, 본인, as well as many others. 즈긔 is properly "one's self"; 제가, "this one," 쇼인 "the little man."

우리 or 우리가, is used to express the first person plural; and to this may be added the plural ending 들 which hardly makes a plural of a plural, but simply emphasizes the *we*.

우리 is not restricted in meaning, to the first person *plural*, but is a somewhat more polite way than 나, of expressing the first person singular.

For Ex :—우리 집, *lit.* "*our house,*" means, "*my house,*" "*home.*"

우리 안히, "*our wife,*" means, "*my wife.*"

It would hardly be considered proper to say 내 안히.

**61.—The Second Person.** The equivalents of a pronoun of the second person, from the very nature of the case, are extremely numerous : the most common is 너, 네 or 네가. This word however has a low or disrespectful meaning, and while it is applied for the most part, to none but inferiors it is still the nearest to a true personal pronoun of the second person. When we come to use any other word, it at once assigns a rank or grade, which 너 does not, and hence it has been used for the second person in addressing the Deity, as in the form used in the Lord's Prayer by some. A study of the true meanings of any of its equivalents, some of which are given below, will at once make plain the impossibility of using any one of them, and the necessity of either using 너 in this case, or of not translating the word *thou* at all, but of replacing it by some other word, such as 쥬 (*Lord*). Other words that may be used to represent the second person are 즈네, 공, 당신, 로형, (Elder brother), 어루신네, (Aged father).

The plural of the 2nd Person is 너희 to which, like 우리, may be affixed the plural ending 들, and with the same effect.

62.—As in the case of nouns, so also in the case of these pronouns, they may be followed by postpositions; but, like other nouns, the postposition need not be affixed unless the sense demands it.

Euphony has played more than its accustomed havoc with the postpositions when affixed to the pronouns 나, 우리, 너, 너희. Various contractions have taken place, so that it may be said that the personal pronoun and postposition have become one ; and no matter what may have been the condition of affairs originally, the contractions as they exist to-day, present us with what may be termed a declension.

For the convenience then of the student, we give these pronouns with their postpositions affixed, and the contractions they have undergone though it must be remembered that in many cases the uncontracted form is preferable.

| | | | | | |
|---|---|---|---|---|---|
| Stem. | 나 | | | | I. |
| Nom. | 내 or 내가 | | | | I. |
| Gen. | 나의 | contr. into. | | 내 | My. |
| Dat. | 나의게 | „ | „ | 내게 | To me. |
| Accus. | 나룰 | „ | „ | 날 | Me. |
| Instrum. | 나으로 | „ | „ | 날노 | By me. |

## PRONOMINAL ADJECTIVES. 43

| | | |
|---|---|---|
| Stem. | 우리 | We. |
| Nom. | 우리가 | We. |
| Gen. | 우리의 contr. into. 우리 | Our. |
| Dat. | 우리의게 ,,  ,, 우리게 | To us. |
| Accus. | 우리를 | Us. |
| Instrum. | 우리로 | By us. |

| | | |
|---|---|---|
| Stem. | 너 | Thou or you. |
| Nom. | 네 or 네가 | Thou or you. |
| Gen. | 너의 contr. into. 네 | Thy or your. |
| Dat. | 너의게 ,,  ,, 네게 | To thee, or to you. |
| Accus. | 너를 | Thee or you. |
| Instrum. | 너로 | By thee or by you. |

| | | |
|---|---|---|
| Stem, | 너희 | You. |
| Nom. | 너희 or 너희가 | You. |
| Gen. | 너희의 contr. into. 너희 | Your. |
| Dat. | 너희의게 ,,  ,, 너희게 | To you. |
| Accus. | 너희를 | You. |
| Instrum. | 너희로 | By you. |

63.—Third Person. There is in Korean, no third personal pronoun; and we are safe in saying that this language has no equivalents for *he, she, it, they*, etc.

The words and phrases that foreigners are apt to use in the place of these pronouns are in no sense their equivalents. We do not mean to say, that the phrases and sentences in which those equivalents are used are not good Korean; but we do mean to say that they are not true translations of the sentences which they are meant to represent.

For Ex :—Among the words most commonly used by foreigners, and by Korean students of English, to represent these terms, are the Korean demonstrative pronouns either with or without an additional word as 것, or 사롬, and

뎌 사 롬 왓 쇼.
has been taken as the equivalent of
*He has come.*

The sentence given above is correct enough Korean, but it does not mean ;"he has come;" and never can be properly used where we would employ those words, it means simply.

That man has come.

Again 뎌 것 가 져 오 너 라,
does not means.

" Bring *it* ; " but " Bring *that* ; "

Where in English we use the personal pronouns of the third person, it is always when immediately speaking of the person, thing, or place represented by the pronoun; and when in Korean we do this, the pronoun is *not translated.*

*He has come*
becomes then simply, 왓쇼.

Bring *it*
is simply, 가져 오너라.

In places where special emphasis is needed, or where in contrast, one party or thing is spoken of with the personal pronoun, a circumlocution such as "the person spoken of," or either a demonstrative, or reflexive pronoun may be used.

The few examples given below will help to illustrate this point :—

PRONOMINAL PDJECTIVES. 45

송셔방이 어제 와셔 돈 줄수 업다 ᄒᆞ엿소·
*Mr. Song came yesterday and said he could not let me have the money.*

내게 돈 주면 모르게 ᄒᆞ시오·
*If you give me money don't let him know about it.*

아바지는 흉보고 어마니는 ᄉᆞ랑ᄒᆞ오·
*He ridicules his father but he loves his mother.*

유모 보거든 오라고 ᄒᆞ시오 아기를 니져 ᄇᆞ려셔 발셔 브러 울엇소·
*If you see the Amah tell her to come; she has forgotten the baby, and he's been crying a long time.*

이ᄉᆞ이 김셔방을 보앗소 아니오 졔물포 가셔 아직 도라오지 아니 ᄒᆞ엿소·
*Have you seen Mr. Kim lately? No, he went to Chemulpo and has not come back yet.*

나는 이둘 안희 다 갑겟것 마는 그는 티월 안희 못 갑겟소·
*I will pay you all this month, but he won't pay till next month.*

아니오 우리 형님은 쟝ᄉᆞ요 그는 션ᄉᆡᆼ이오·
*No, my brother is the merchant: he is the teacher.*

**64.**—These then are the various ways that Koreans have of expressing the first, second, and third persons; but it must not be forgotten that their use is much more restricted by the native than by the foreigner. For the most part it is left entirely to the surrounding circumstances, or to the context, to decide what may be the subject or object in the sentence. Throughout this work, in many places where we have translated I, it might equally well have been *he* or *you*, or *vice versa*. Of course with reference to the second person, one is so often desirous of being polite or of assigning to the person spoken to his proper station, that words are much more frequently used to represent the second person, than any other.

### REFLEXIVE PRONOUNS.

65·—There are a few words in Korean that are used with or without the personal pronouns given above and have a reflexive sense. They are:—

저, 제, 제가, and 즈긔.

These words have properly the sense of *self, one's self, himself*, etc.

There are several other words that also have this same reflexive idea: 친히 (properly), 스스로 (of itself), 손슈 or 손조 (with his own hand), 즈하로 (of itself), and 절노 (by nature). These latter cannot be called reflexive pronouns, those first given, only are such. But these which are really adverbs or nouns with the postposition 로 are given here as they have the same effect.

The word 서로 (*mutually*) may be termed a reflexive pronoun, and will be rendered into English by *each other* or *one another*.

The word 피츠 may in a sense be termed a reflexive pronoun. It has the sense of "*either this or that*," "*both*," and is used largely when comparing two people or things etc. It can sometimes be translated by the English "*each other*."

| 은젼 이나 지젼 이나 쓰기는 피츠 굿소. | As far as use is concerned, the silver dollar and the paper dollar equal each other. |

아라사 황뎨와 덕국 　(As for the Emperors of Ger-
황뎨가 권은 피ㅊ 　{ many and Russia, in rank,
곳소. 　　　　　 　(the one equals the other.

This same reflexive idea is given to certain verbs derived from the Chinese, by prefixing 즈 as 즈매ᄒᆞ오, (to sell one's self); 즈침ᄒᆞ오, (to lance one's self); 즈득ᄒᆞ오, (to obtain by one's self) and many others.

(For examples please see Reflexive Pronouns. Part II.)

### INTERROGATIVE OR INDEFINITE PRONOUNS.

**66.**—All Korean interrogatives have also an indefinite sense: hence, what would be two classes in English, form but one in Korean.

They are:—

누, 누구, 누가, 뉘, 뉘가, Who, some one.
어느, Which, a certain, some.
엇던, Which, what kind of, a certain.
웬, What kind of, a certain.
무솜, What, some.
무엇, What, something.

Of these 누, in its various forms, and 무엇 having more of a pronominal than an adjectival use, may be joined to any of the various postpositions, and when this is done like the personal pronouns they undergo various contractions. For convenience, then, they are given below with the various postpositions and their contractions.

Stem. 누 or 뉘 ................ Who or some one.
Nom. 누가 or 뉘가 ............ Who or some one.
Gen. 누의 contr. into 뉘 ...... Whose or some one's.
Dat. 누의게 ,,   ,, 뉘게 ... To whom or to some one.
Acc. 누롤 or 누구롤 ......... Whom or some one.
Instr. 누로 or 눌노 ............ By whom or by some one.

Stem. 무엇.......................... What or something.
Nom. 무엇 or 무어시 ......... What or something.
Gen. 무어시..................... Of what or of something.
Dat. 무어시게.................. To what or to something.
Acc. 무어슬 contr. into 무얼.. What or something.
Instr. 무어스로 ,,   ,, 무얼노. By what or by something.

67.—어느, 엇던 and 무솜, being always used adjectively, cannot be united with the various postpositions. If it is desired to use these as pronouns it can only be done by joining them to such words as 사룸, 이, 것, etc. The distinctions between these are not always observed by Koreans.

엇던 means rather, *what kind of*, or indefinitely *a certain*.

어느, Means rather, *which* of a number.

무솜, Has the idea of *what*.

As :—  엇던 사룸 이오.
*What kind of a man is he?*

어느 사룸 이오.
*Which man is it?*

뎌 무솜 사룸 이오
*What man is that?*

The answer to the first would tell whether the man was good or bad, rich or poor ; the answer to the second simply decides which one of a number ; while the answer to the third states whether he is a farmer, labourer, or what his business is.

In using these words indefinitely an adherence to these distinctions should be aimed at, though it is not always possible.

68.—These interrogatives, may be made still more indefinite by affixing to them the Korean equivalent of the English *either* or *whether*. As 누구나, 누구던지, (A contraction of 누구이던지), 누굴넌지, (A contraction of 누구일넌지), 누구라도.

These really have rather the sense of *any one whatever, whoever*, and the other pronouns may be treated in the same way, with a like result.

69.—It has been said above that the interrogative pronouns take the place of the indefinites; but the pronoun 아모 (*any*) has an indefinite sense only, and may be used both adjectively, and pronominally. When used pronominally it may be joined with any of the various postpositions. Like the other indefinites it may be made more indefinite as in ¶ 68.

70.—Some of the numerous distributive pronouns are as follows.

더러. (*some*) signifies a part or portion of anything. 더러…더러 or 더러는…더러는 are equivalent to the English " some one " or " some others."

놈, (*other, others, another*) applies to people generally, as distinguished from oneself.

다, 모도, 모든, 온, (*all*) may be used almost interchangeably. 다 and 모도 are employed substantively, and at times we can use them with one or other of the postpositions, 모든 can only be used adjectively, and cannot therefore be united with postpositions; 온, signifies all in the sense of the whole, with reterence to extent or duration. It is used solely as an adjective, and can only be used as a pronoun by the addition of some such word as 퉁, becoming then 온퉁 (*the whole, the entirety*).

여러, 여럿, 여러히, (*several, a good number, many*).

The first form alone can be employed as an adjective ; and to the other two only, can the postpositions be affixed.

마다, 매 (*every*), 각 (*each separate*) and 식 (*a piece*) are all distributive indefinite pronouns and may at times be used interchangeably. They differ, however, in their use in some respects.

마다 and 매 are, respectively, the pure Korean and Sinico-Korean equivalents for the same idea. 마다 should then, properly, be only used in connection with pure Korean terms, and always follows the noun which it distributes. 매 On the other hand can only be used with Sinico-Korean terms, and precedes its noun.

Note.—While with most words this rule is rigidly observed, there are exceptions with these terms, and we do find 마다 at times acting as distributer for a Sinico-Korean term, and 매, for a pure Korean; but this is not elegant.

매 and 마다 have properly the sense of *every*, and refer to the separate individual parts constituting a whole, regarded *one by one*. 매 precedes while 마다 follows the word it limits.

각 on the other hand, refers rather to *each separate individual* ; and denotes *every one* composing a whole, considered separately from the rest.

식 generally means *at a time, together ;* but used with the pronoun 하나, has the sense of *one at a time* or *each*. Quite often we find this used together with 각, 마다, or 매.

It may also, at times, have the sense of *each* when standing alone.

## PRONOMINAL ADJECTIVES.   51

셋식 주어라 ............ { Give three each, or Give three of each.

민명 열량 밧앗소 ...... { Every man received ten nyang.

사룸 마다 먹을 거슬 넉넉히 주어라. { Give every man enough to eat.

몰 마다 사룸 흐나식 홋소. { Each horse had a rider.

각 나라 풍속이 다르오. { Each country has its own customs.

For further examples see Part II. the chapter on Pronominal adjectives.

### DEMONSTRATIVES.

**71.**—In Korean there are three commonly known, and constantly used, demonstrative pronominal adjectives: 이, 뎌 and 그. While at times they are employed substantively, they are for the most part used as adjectives: and when the pronominal form is needed, it is more common to affix such a word as 것 or 사룸 etc., than to use the demonstrative alone. It is admissible, however, to employ any one of them substantively, and then there may be affixed, any of the various postpositions. This use is not at all common, and when referring to persons, is extremely disrespectful and contemptuous. In uniting with the various postpositions there are no contractions.

Used as adjectives, of course they cannot be joined to the postpositions, and they precede the noun they limit.

이 is equivalent to *this*.

뎌 is equivalent to *that*, and is used of things near at hand or in sight.

그 also is equivalent to *that*; but refers to things remote and not in sight.

**72.**—From these three demonstratives are formed various adverbs, verbs and adjectives, that are much used by Koreans and all of which retain these distinctions. We have from 이 ; 이러 (*thus*), often corrupted into 요러 which becomes a verb 이러하오 (*to do thus*) or 이럿소 (*to be so*). From this verb we get 이러한 or 이런 an adjective meaning *such*, in the sense of *such as this*: and the adverb 이러케 (*thus in this way*). From 이 we also get 이리 (*here*), and 이리로 (*by this way* or *hither*.)

In like manner we get adverbs, verbs and adjectives from all of these demonstratives, and the following table of some of them may be of use.

| | | | |
|---|---|---|---|
| 이, This (Subst. and Adj). | 뎌...(near)... | 그, (far) | That (Subst. and Adj). |
| 이것, This (Subst). | 뎌것......... | 그것, That (Subst). | |
| 이러하오 } To do it in this way. <br> 이럿소 } To be so. | 뎌러하오 } <br> 뎌럿소 } | 그러하오 } <br> 그럿소 } | To do it in that way. <br> To be that way, thus. |
| 이러한 } This kind of. <br> 이런 } Such as this. | 뎌러한 } <br> 뎌런 } ... | 그러한 } <br> 그런 } | That kind of. <br> Such as that. |
| 이러 } In this way, <br> 이러케 } thus. | 뎌러 } <br> 뎌러케 } ... | 그러 } <br> 그러케 } | In that way, thus. |
| 이리. Here. | 뎌리......... | 그리, There. | |
| 이리로 { By this way, hither. | 뎌리로...... | 그리로 { By that way, thither. | |

Note.—From these three words again, have been derived three exclamatory demonstrative pronouns expressing disgust. They are, 요, 조, and 구. They are much used, but only as exclamations of disgust, and cannot be called elegant Korean. Ex. 요놈, This fellow.

**73.**—In Part II. it is stated that there are no relative pronouns in Korean, There are, however, two words that have, by some, been classified as demonstrative pronouns, and that in a sense hold this place. They are the words 자 and 바. They are only used with relative participles, and may be said to express *that which*, *he who*, etc. The "which" or "who" being then considered the subject of the verb contained in the preceding participle. It must be remembered, however, that the employment of these words is largely restricted to books.

# CHAPTER V.

## NUMERALS.

**74.**—From the very nature of the case, the conditions of the Korean language present us with two sets of numerals. The one pure Korean, the other Sinico-Korean.

The pure Korean numbers carry us only as far as ninety-nine, and above this we are forced to rely entirely upon those derived from Chinese.

The pure Korean numbers may serve either as substantives or adjectives, and a few of them have two forms, which may be termed, respectively "*substantive form*," and "*adjective form.*" With the number 흐나 the substantive form can never be used adjectively, in all the others it may; but the special adjective form can never take the place of the substantive. To the substantive forms may be affixed the various postpositions, but this of course cannot be done with the adjective forms. Commonly the adjective forms are only used as high as six. Of course the rule given before, concerning the use of Sinico-Korean and pure Korean terms, holds here also: and properly the pure Korean numerals can only be used qualifying pure Korean nouns.

NUMERALS.  55

When the substantive form is used substantively it does not qualify the noun as an adjective; but stands in apposition to, and follows it. This being the case, when this is done, we may often find a Sinico-Korean word standing in apposition to a pure Korean numeral substantive.

The adjective and substantive forms from one to six are given below.

| ADJECTIVES. | SUBSTANTIVES. | |
|---|---|---|
| 흔 | 하나 | One. |
| 두 | 둘 | Two. |
| 세 | 셋 | Three. |
| 네 | 넷 | Four. |
| 닷 | 다섯 | Five. |
| 엿 | 여섯 | Six. |

**75.**—The numerals derived from the Chinese have but one form, and that adjectival. Until we get above ninety-nine they may only be properly used with Sinico-Korean words, and must always precede the words which they qualify. When a substantive form is desired, it can only be rendered by the use of some other Sinico-Korean word, or one of the numerous " Specific Classifiers " some of which will be given further on, which word will then stand in apposition to the noun. As in the case of the pure Korean numeral, so also here, when this is done we may have a Sinico-Korean numeral, qualifying a Sinico-Korean noun, which latter stands in apposition to a pure Korean noun. In paging, figuring and numbering, the Chinese characters themselves are used, and one seldom meets with the Korean numerals spelled out in the Ön-mun. Even in Önmun books, the paging will be in

Chinese characters, and quite often in letters written in the native character, where numbers are mentioned, the Chinese characters may be used.

76.—We give below a list of the Korean cardinal numbers, giving first the Chinese character, then the pure Korean, and lastly the Sinico-Korean.

|   | KOREAN. | SINICO-KOREAN. |   |
|---|---|---|---|
| 一 | 호나 | 일 | One. |
| 二 | 둘 | 이 | Two. |
| 三 | 셋 | 삼 | Three. |
| 四 | 넷 | 亽 | Four. |
| 五 | 다숫 | 오 | Five. |
| 六 | 여숫 | 룩 | Six. |
| 七 | 닐곱 | 칠 | Seven. |
| 八 | 여쯞 | 팔 | Eight. |
| 九 | 아홉 | 구 | Nine. |
| 十 | 열 | 십 | Ten. |
| 十一 | 열호나 | 십일 | Eleven. |
| 十二 | 열둘 | 십이 | Twelve. |
|   |   |   | Etc. |
| 二十 | 스물 | 이십 | Twenty. |
| 二十一 | 스물호나 | 이십일 | Twenty-one. |
| 二十二 | 스물둘 | 이십이 | Twenty-two. |
| 三十 | 설흔 | 삼십 | Thirty. |
| 四十 | 마흔 | 亽십 | Forty. |
| 五十 | 쉰 | 오십 | Fifty. |
| 六十 | 예순 | 룩십 | Sixty. |
| 七十 | 닐흔 | 칠십 | Seventy. |
| 八十 | 여든 | 팔십 | Eighty. |
| 九十 | 아흔 | 구십 | Ninety. |

| | | |
|---|---|---|
| 百 | ............빅 or 일빅 | ......One hundred. |
| 二百 | ............이 빅 | ...............Two hundred. |
| 三百 | ............삼 빅 | ...............Three hundred. |
| 四百 | ............ᄉ 빅 | ...............Four hundred. |
| 五百 | ............오 빅 | ...............Five hundred. |
| 千 | ............천 or 일천 | ......One thousand. |
| 二千 | ............이 천 | ...............Two thousand. |
| 萬 | ............만 or 일만 | ......Ten thousand. |
| 二萬 | ............이 만............... | Twenty thousand. |
| 十萬 | ............십 만 or 億 억... | One hundred thousand. |
| 百萬 | ............빅 만 or 兆 죠 | ...One million. |
| 千萬 | ............천 만 or 京 경 | ...Ten million. |

### Specific Classifiers.

**77.**—As has been said above, the Korean numeral has both an adjective and a substantive form. Its adjective form may be used in direct connection with the word which it limits, when it precedes it; but the Korean much prefers to place the numeral with some other word, which stands in apposition to the noun limited, after the noun. As in English, we speak of so many "head of cattle" so many "sheets of paper," so also in Korea is this form used. It is, however, carried much further here; and we find a large class of words that are used for this purpose. They have been variously termed "numerals," "auxiliary numerals," "classifying numerals," and "classifiers;" but it seems to us that the term "specific classifiers," answers more nearly the demands of the case. The following list of those most commonly in use, will greatly aid the student; and we would urge that he take pains to make himself intimately acquainted with all, and with their use, as a mistake in this line is extremely ridiculous in the eyes of the Koreans.

개, 箇, Numeral for almost all small things, or of things of which a number may be used.

뭇, Piece, roll, bolt. Used for all piece goods.

길, Set as of books.

권, Volume, numeral for books. *Also* a measure of paper consisting of twenty sheets.

켜리, Pair, numeral of all things that are made in pairs.

마리, Numeral for all animals.

명. Numeral for men.

낫, (*A grain*). Used for almost all extremely small things.

립, Numeral for hats, mats, etc.

벌, Suit, suite, a complete set, an outfit. Numeral for sets.

부, The same as 켜리, used for things made in pairs and also for books.

병, The same as 자로. Numeral of things that one grasps in using.

필, Numeral for horses and oxen. Also used for 뭇 *q.v.*

편, Slice. Used of dried beef and fish, etc. Also, Page, chapter, book.

쌍, Brace, couple, pair. Of animals and things that go in couples but whose usefulness is not impaired when used singly.

셤 or 셕, Bag, sack. Used of grains, etc.

## NUMERALS.

떼, Numeral for flocks, broods, crowds, etc. A company, a crowd, a flock.

덩이, Measure of paper. 100 권. Numeral of all large round things, as,—pumelos, loaves of bread.

동, Bundle. Numeral of things bound together.

자로 The same as 병. Numeral for all things that are grasped in using.

싹, Numeral for one of pairs.

쟝, Sheet, leaf. Numeral for such, and for letters and notes. Used also for chapters of a book.

좌, Numeral for houses, tables, chairs or anything that sets firmly on a broad base.

쏙, Piece, numeral for parts of anything.

쳑, Numeral for boats, and ships.

**78.**—The following are a few examples of the use of the above words.

| | | |
|---|---|---|
| 개. | 비 흔 개 사 오너라.. | Buy a pear. |
| 켜리. | 집신 흔 켜리 사면 됴켓소. | You had better buy a pair of straw shoes. |
| 마리. | 개 두 마리가 서로 싸호오. | Two dogs are fighting together. |
| 명. | 일본 군스가 멋 명 이오. | How many Japanese soldiers are there? |
| 낫. | 곡식을 흔 낫 도 흘니지 마라. | Do not drop a single grain of corn. |
| 쌍. | 뎌 집에 비둙이 두 쌍 이 잇소. | There are two pair of pigeons on that house. |
| 동. | 나모 흔 동에 갑시 얼마오. | What is the price of a bundle of wood? |
| 자로. | 붓시 흔 자로 도 쓸 것 업소. | There is not a single pen that can be used. |

쟝. 오늘은 칙 몃 쟝 쎳 How many double pages of
느냐. the book have you written
to-day.

쏙. 춤외 호 쏙 먹어라. Eat a piece of muskmelon.

## KOREAN MONEY.

**79.**—When foreigners first came to Korea the Koreans had only, what is known in the East as "cash" as a circulating medium. Around the capital the "five cash piece" and in the interior the old one cash piece were in use. The unit of currency, however was not the cash. Foreigners coming from China had taken this as the unit, and had thus made for themselves and others much confusion. The native unit was the 량 (nyang) or one hundred cash, this was divided into ten 푼 (poŏn) or 닙 (nip). This last stood simply for "one piece" (of money) and 호 might as a consequence, referring to the old cash, mean either simply "one cash" or referring to the new cash mean one five cash piece. On account of this difficulty, it was quite customary, when speaking of prices of small things which cost only a few cash, when the word 푼 was used, if the "five cash piece" was meant to precede the price by the words 당오.

당오 호푼, meant five cash.

당오 두푼, meant ten cash.

In the reading of old books this must be kept in mind as well as the fact that before the introduction of money, barter was commonly assisted by the use of gold and silver according to weight in 량 and 돈.

## NUMERALS.

**80.**—After the advent of foreigners, the yen and Mexian dollar came into constant use.

Now of course the monetary system of the whole Empire applies equally here. The old Korean terms are still sometimes used and confusion has arisen from a lack of uniformity. In certain sections the 량 is used to designate twenty sen, in Seoul it most commonly means two sen and in most of Korea ten sen. More and more however the terms 원 for yen and 젼 for sen are coming into vogue all over the country.

### ORDINAL NUMBERS.

**81.**—Just as there are two sets of cardinal, so there are two sets of ordinal numbers. They are formed from the pure Korean by affixing 재 to the substantive form. In the case of the first, generally the term 첫 replaces 하나. They are formed from the Sinico-Korean by prefixing the term 뎨. From one to one hundred then they are as follows:—

| KOREAN. | SINICO-KOREAN. | |
|---|---|---|
| 첫재 | 뎨일 | First. |
| 둘재 | 뎨이 | Second. |
| 셋재 | 뎨삼 | Third. |
| 넷재 | 뎨사 | Fourth. |
| 다숫재 | 뎨오 | Fifth. |
| 여숫재 | 뎨륙 | Sixth. |
| 닐곱재 | 뎨칠 | Seventh. |
| 여덟재 | 뎨팔 | Eighth. |
| 아홉재 | 뎨구 | Ninth. |
| 열재 | 뎨십 | Tenth. |
| 열훈재 | 뎨십일 | Eleventh. |

NUMERALS.

| KOREAN. | SINICO-KOREAN. | |
|---|---|---|
| 열둘재 | 뎨십이 | Twelfth. |
| 스물재 | 뎨이십 | Twentieth. |
| 스물훈재 | 뎨이십일 | Twenty-first. |
| 스물둘재 | 뎨이십이 | Twenty second. |
| 설흔재 | 뎨삼십 | Thirtieth. |
| 마흔재 | 뎨ᄉ십 | Fortieth. |
| 쉰재 | 뎨오십 | Fiftieth. |
| 예슌재 | 뎨륙십 | Sixtieth. |
| 닐흔재 | 뎨칠십 | Seventieth. |
| 여든재 | 뎨팔십 | Eightieth. |
| 아흔재 | 뎨구십 | Ninetieth. |
| 빅재 | 뎨빅 | One hundredth. |

TIMES AND SEASONS.

82.—The Koreans do not make a distinction between the terms month and moon, as since their calendar month is a lunar month, they are co-ordinate. They designate them, then, as the "first moon," "second moon," etc, using Sinico-Korean terms: and every third year adding a thirteenth month, which they call 윤돌, or 윤월, which is variously interspersed, their calendar corresponding with the Chinese. The names of the months are:

정월.........................The first moon.
이월.........................The second moon.
삼월.........................The third moon.
ᄉ월.........................The fourth moon.
오월.........................The fifth moon.
륙월.........................The sixth moon.
칠월.........................The seventh moon.

팔월.........................The eighth moon.
구월.........................The ninth moon.
십월.........................The tenth moon.
십일월 or 동지둘 .........The eleventh moon.
십이월 or 섯둘 ............The twelfth moon.
윤월 or 윤둘 ............... { The extra month in the Korean leap-year.

Note.—As will be seen, pure Korean terms may be used for the eleventh, twelfth, or leap months.

The western calendar has however now been the legal calendar for some years and little by little it will displace the old.

83.—Their months vary in length from twenty-nine to thirty days, and are designated respectively from their size 적은 둘 or 쇼월 (*little moon*) and 큰둘 or 대월 (*big moon*).

In naming their days, either series of numerals may be used, but of course with the corresponding term for day. The pure Korean terms have undergone certain contractions and modifications, as can be seen from the table below. In speaking of the day of the month from the first to the tenth, the term 초, is prefixed and we speak of the "first first" the "first second" the "first third," etc. This arises from the fact that when they speak of those above ten or twenty, it is not necessary to prefix the ten or the twenty. Koreans suppose that most people will know whether they are in the first, second or third ten days. If then it is the seventh, seventeenth or twenty-seventh, and they are asked what day of the month it is, it is perfectly proper, and in fact customary for them simply to reply "The seventh." If, even then, it is not certain what day of the month it is, the inquirer would again ask "Which seventh?" and the reply would be, "The first seventh," "the seventeenth," "or the twenty seventh" as the case might be. This practice is not universal, but quite common and follows out the Korean custom of using as few words as possible. We have then the following as the days of the month.

| KOREAN | SINICO-KOREAN. | |
|---|---|---|
| 초ᄒᆞ로 | 초일일 | The first. |
| 초이틀 or 잇흘, | 초이일 | „ second. |
| 초사흘 | 초삼일 | „ third. |
| 초나흘 | 초ᄉᆞ일 | „ fourth. |
| 초닷시 | 초오일 | „ fifth. |
| 초엿시 | 초륙일 | „ sixth. |
| 초닐헤 | 초칠일 | „ seventh. |
| 초여드리 | 초팔일 | „ eighth. |
| 초아호리 | 초구일 | „ ninth. |
| 초열흘 | 초십일 | „ tenth. |
| 열ᄒᆞ로 | 십일일 | „ eleventh. |
| 보롬 | 십오일 | „ fifteenth. |
| 스무날 | 이십일 | „ twentieth. |
| 스무ᄒᆞ로 | 이십일일 | „ twenty-first. |
| 스무이틀 | 이십이일 | „ twenty-second. |
| 금음 | 삼십일 | „ last day of the month. |

84.—If we drop off the 초, which precedes the first ten of the above days of the month; the names of the days may also be used to express duration of time: and ᄒᆞ로, or 일일, may mean either *one day* or *the first day*;

열흘, or 십일, may mean *ten days* or *the tenth day*; 보름, or 십오일, *fifteen days* or *the fifteenth day*.

Often when used this way, they will affix such words as 간, 동안, meaning *space, duration.* 금음, meaning *the last day* of the month, cannot of course be used in this way.

85.—Until recently Koreans divided their day into twelve, instead of twenty four hours; and, in speaking of the hour, they did not as we do, refer to the end of the hour, but to the whole time covered by it. Thus 오시, which is the Korean hour which comes in the middle of the day, and corresponds to our time from eleven A.M. to one P.M., means neither, eleven, twelve, nor one o'clock, but the whole time from eleven to one. To say then, that you will meet a person at 오시, or noon, is extremely indefinite. If one desires to be more definite the terms 초 "the beginning," 중 "the middle," and 말 or 끗 "the end" may be used: 오시초, will then be *a little past eleven*, 오시중, *about twelve*, and 오시끗, *a little before one.*

The times of the night were known throughout the country, by the five watches; the beginning of which were signalized at each magistracy, either by drum beating or horn blowing. In the farming sections, where sundials and anything resembling a time-piece is unknown, such primitive terms as "sunrise" and "sunset," "when the sun is high in the east" or "low in the west," the "first" and "second cock-crowing," are used to mark the time.

The introduction of foreign time-pieces, however, has changed all this; and the foreign hours are marked by the use of the adjectival numerals, either pure or Sinico-

Korean, with the word 시 (*time, or hour*). It should be noted that while the Sinico-Korean numerals may be used ; the pure Korean are more commonly heard. The minutes are represented by the word 분 together with generally the Sinico-Korean numerals ; but either may be used. In speaking of the time then, the hour preceded by its numeral comes first, and then the minute preceded by its numeral.

As :—

열시 or 십시............... Ten o'clock.
열두시 or 십이시......... Twelve o'clock.
다솟시 오분............... Five minutes past five.
여솟시 십오분............ A quarter past six.
닐곱시반................... Half past seven.

or 닐곱시 스십오분 } ...... A quarter to eight.
여듧시 십오분전 }

The difference between "A.M." and "P.M." can only be marked by such words as, "before noon" and "afternoon," "morning" and "evening."

## FRACTIONS AND MULTIPLES.

86.—Fractional numbers are not used by Korean to the same extent as by foreigners. We find such words as 반 and 절반 to express *half*, and 반반 or "half, half," to express *a quarter*. Other fractions may be expressed by the use of 분 "a part," which being Sinico-Korean generally requires corresponding numerals.

삼분 지일 { " three part-of, one " or " of three parts, one " } =One third.
슷분 지일, " Four part-of, one "   =One fourth.
오분 지삼, " Five part-of, three " =Three fifths.
십분 지륙, " Ten part-of, six "    =Six tenths.

These same quantities may be expressed by the use of Pure-Korean numerals; but if such is done, the postposition must be used, and the result is clumsy and awkward. We would then have :—

세분 에 두분 "Three part-in two part" = two thirds.
다섯분 에 네분 "Five part-in four part" = four fifths.
두분 에 혼분 "Two part-in one part" = one half.

87.—Various words such as, 갑, 동갑, 갑절, 곱, 곱절, 비, etc., hold the place of multiples in Korean, and are affixed to the various numerals. 비, being Sinico-Korean, must be used with the corresponding numerals; the others, for the most part, being restricted to pure Korean numerals; 동갑, 갑절 and 곱절, may be used independently, without any numeral, and have then the sense of *double*.

The following examples will illustrate the use of these words :—

| | |
|---|---|
| 이 보다 삼비 가져 오너라. | Bring three times as much as this. |
| 갑시 갑절 되엿소. | The price is twice as much. |
| 이 거시 그것 보다 크기 동갑 이오. | This is twice as large as that. |
| 어제 가져온 거슨 오늘 열곱 이오. | What you brought yesterday was ten times what you have to-day. |

88.—Interest on money is, for the most part, reckoned per month; and the rate is expressed by so many cash per nyang, though the word *nyang* is universally left to be understood. The word 변 (*interest*) is affixed to the amount and, 혼푼변, means *one cash interest* or "one cash per hundred" and equals *one per cent*. Interest at less than one per cent is seldom spoken of in Korea, and when it is, the term 리 (equivalent to one tenth of a 푼 or cash) is used. We have then the following :—

훈리변 or 일리변 ............ $\frac{1}{10}$%.
오리변 ........................ $\frac{5}{10}$% or $\frac{1}{2}$%.
훈푼변 or 일푼변 ............ 1%.
훈돈변 or 대돈변 ............ 10%.

Discount on bills or prices is expressed by the use of 할리 (割利) prefixed of the numerals and means "*tenth discount*" and we have the following :—

일할리 equals $\frac{1}{10}$ or 10% discount.
이하리 „ $\frac{2}{10}$ s or 20% „
ᄉ할리 „ $\frac{4}{10}$ s or 40% „
오할리 „ $\frac{5}{10}$ s or 50% „
팔할리 „ $\frac{8}{10}$ s or 80% „

89.—The Korean word 번, which has by some been termed a multiple, has the sense of the English word *time* or *times*; and is affixed to numerals of either kind. Then 세번 or 삼번 means three times; 네번 or ᄉ번, four times, etc. To these may be added the particle 재, which gives an ordinal sense; and 세번재 becomes "the third time;" 네번재, "the fourth time;" 다솟번재, the fifth time. While this 재 may at times be affixed to 번, when accompanied by Sinico-Korean numerals, it is not common and is considered ine'egant.

## WEIGHTS AND MEASURES.

90.—To the student of Korean, a knowledge of all the weights and measures used in Korea is unnecessary;

but a few words concerning those most commonly used may be of service. The one main difficulty everywhere was, that there was no one authorized and regularly acknowledged standard.

In measures of small length, carpentering, etc., the 자 or what we might call *foot*, is the unit; but the 목척 or carpenter's 자, varies considerably from that used to measure cotton goods; and this again from that used in measuring silks, satins, etc. Whatever the 자 used, one tenth will be one 치 or *inch*, which is again divided into ten 푼; the 치 and 푼 varying of course with the 자. The 목척 exactly equals the English foot of twelve inches. The 자 used in measuring cloth goods, varies from eighteen to twenty-two inches, but the usual length is about twenty inches. In measuring cord, wire and the like, the 발 (*fathom* or *brace*), the distance from hand to hand with arms outstretched; in measuring depths, the 길 (*man's height*); and in measuring small lengths quite frequently, the 썜 (*span*), the distance from thumb to middle finger, are used.

The measure of distance, or 리, has been said to be about one third of a mile, but the 리 itself varies so much in different localities, that no definite comparison can be made. It is short among the mountains and long on the plains; and it has been aptly remarked that the Korean 리 is hardly a measure of distance, but should rather be called a measure of the time taken to travel the distance; as, in ordinary Korean travelling with coolies and pack ponies, it averages an hour for every ten 리 whether they be long or short.

91.—The Korean weights were the same as the Chinese, and the 근 or catty, was about one and one third English pounds. It is divided into sixteen 량 (nyang), or ounces, which are again divided into ten 돈, the 돈 into ten 푼, the 푼 into ten 리.

In the measuring of grain still greater confusion existed. The system used in the country districts differed entirely from that used in Seoul. The measures used in the country were as follows:—

    Ten           슈 =one 홉 or about one handful.
    Ten           홉 =one 되.
    Ten           되 =one 말.
    Twenty 말 =one 셤 or 셕 or one bag.

Note.—The 슈 is only used in computing government taxes.

The measures used in Seoul differed largely from these.

It took three of the above 되 and a little more, to make one 화인되.

Ten 화인되, (commonly spoken of as ten 되) =one 말.
Four 말 =one 셤 or bag.

This latter 말, contained about one and a half pecks.

All this has however been now changed: standard weights and measures have been introduced throughout the whole land and correspond to those in use in Japan proper.

Land was measured either by the amount of grain taken to sow it, (and from the above we get the measures 셤 직이, 마직이, 되직이): or, as in some parts of the United States, by the number of days it will take to plough it.

92.—In closing this chapter on numerals, we would notice a peculiar use of the adjectival numeral 호. It is often placed before other numerals, or nouns signifying quantity, distance, amount, etc., to give an indefinite sense; and may then be translated by the English word "*about.*" 즈음, placed after the numeral, has also this same effect and may often be used in conjunction with 흔, following the numeral or quantity which 흔 precedes.

Ex. :—

그 집이 흔 륙십 간되 오.   That house contains about sixty kan.

나히 흔 오십 즈음 된 듯   His age is probably some-
흔오.                      where about fifty.

Note.—In the Chapter on nouns, as well as elsewhere, attention was called to the fact, that the plural ending 들, like the postpositions, was only to be used when its absence would cause ambiguity. We would here remind the student, that when numerals are used, (according to the rule then given) unless special emphasis is desired, 들 should not be used. Let him then, when talking Korean, not speak of five houses but *five house*, etc.

## CHAPTER VI.

### THE POSTPOSITION.

93.—There is a large class of words, which are affixed to nouns, and show their relation to some other word or words in the sentence. Some of these have arbitrarily been taken and made to stand as case inflections or parts of the noun. For such an arbitrary selection, there can be no authority. If some are case inflections all should be taken as such. Such a method would, however, complicate matters greatly, and it is far more simple to consider all these, as separate words or postpositions. Most of them were originally nouns or parts of nouns; this, however, is not the place to enter upon a study of derivations and the original meanings of words, since we are neither making a language nor trying to force one that exists at present to conform to ancient and now obsolete rules, but taking a language as we find it to-day, and trying to systematize it and show how it is used. In this connection, it may be well to note that certain compound postpositions, and other words, have in the course of time undergone changes; and the form of the original simple postposition, from which these compounds were made, has been lost. Some have desired to change this and go back to the original and correct form. This, however, is not the part of a gram-

THE POSTPOSITION. 73

marian, who must take facts as he finds them, and show perhaps the order of the change, but can go no further.

We find three classes of postpositions which we will call Simple, Composite, and Verbal: Composite being made up of a noun and a simple postposition.

SIMPLE POSTPOSITIONS.

94.—The simple postpositions are :—

| | |
|---|---|
| 이, 가, 씌셔 | Signs of the Nominative. |
| 이 | The man who. |
| 의 | Of; sign of Genitive case. |
| 의게, 안테, 드려, 씌 | To, from, at, unto; Signs of the Dative case. |
| 에 | In, into, to, at; called by some the sign of Locative case. |
| 을 | Sign of Accusative case. |
| 로 or 으로 | By, with, by means of, for; Sign of Instrumental case. |
| 아 | Sign of Vocative case. |
| 에셔, 브터 | From, at, since; Sign of Ablative case. |
| 은 | As for, as far as, regarding; Sign of Oppositive case. |
| 성지* | To, up to, as far as. |
| 야 | Only, but, merely. |

95.—Before we speak of all the various postpositions and their uses, it may be well to mention a few of the rules governing the euphonic changes that these particles undergo, in uniting with the nouns.

---

\* The Korean word 성지 is more than the English equivalent here given and means *up to and including* being always used thus inclusively f the word it modifies.

Nouns ending with ㅂ or ㅅ generally interpose an ' ㅅ before the postposition : A few nouns in ㅅ may interpose ㅊ, but when this is done, it will be generally found that there are two forms, and that either the form in ㅅ or ㅊ can equally well be used.

Note.—We are pretty safe in saying that this difference between 시 and 치, arises from what was originally a difference in the final letter of the word. No word can end in ㄷ; no word ending in ㅅ is pronounced as though it were an s; consequently the distinction between words ending in ㅅ and ㄷ, was lost. It re-appears, when a postposition, beginning with a vowel is affixed. For example 갓 (*hat*) pronounced now kat, was evidently originally pronounced with the sound of s. 밭 (*field*) on the other hand evidently ended originally in ㄷ, which being unable to stand at the end of a word became ㅅ. When the postposition is added, however, the old difference of sound re-appears, and we have 갓시 for hat with the nominative ending; and 밭 치 for field.

The Korean does not like to have the vowel ㅡ (eu) in a syllable preceded by ㅅ, ㅊ, or ㄹ; consequently in all such places, this letter is replaced by ㆍ ("*lower a*"). In a few cases of nouns ending in vowels, and some, ending in ㅂ, the letter ㅎ is interposed and becomes the initial letter of the postposition. In many cases of nouns ending in vowels, contractions occur; but for the most part, these are not allowable in writing.

96.—이, 가, 쎄셔. These three postpositions are all signs of the Nominative case, but (like all postpositions, as has been said before) are only used when the sense requires it.

이 may be joined to any noun; and, according to the rules given above, may become 시, 치, or 히. When preceded by a vowel the initial ㅇ may be dropped, and, without any initial consonant, it may be placed below its noun.

가 can only be used with nouns ending in vowels. With such, the postposition 가 is more commonly used than 이, though the latter may always be used.

씌셔 is an honorific, and is commonly used, for the Nominative case. At times, it is used to represent other cases; but such a practice is wrong and should be avoided.

| | |
|---|---|
| 어제 보낸 사롬이 다 왓소. | All the men you sent yesterday have come. |
| 갓시 대단이 비싸오. | The hats are terribly dear. |
| 죠션에 호랑이가 만소. | Tigers are plentiful in Korea. |
| 님금 씌셔 오놀 거동ᄒ오. | The King goes out today. |

**97.**—The postposition 이 has also another use: it is added to Relative Participles in the sense of—*the man who, he who*. Used in this sense, it is probably derived from 인, the ㄴ having been elided; and when so used, it can be followed by any one of the other postpositions.

| | |
|---|---|
| 어제 온이. | He who came yesterday. |

**98.**—의. This postposition means *of*, and denotes the Possessive case. According to the rules given above this may become 회, or 시, or, when preceded by a vowel, a contraction may occur. While, for the most part, any such contractions would not be allowable in writing, in certain words, prominent among which are the personal and interrogative pronouns, they are both allowable and common.

| | |
|---|---|
| 내 칙 왓소. | My books have come. |
| 오놀은 님금의 탄일이오. | Today is the King's birthday. |
| 그 옷시 빗츨 슬희여 ᄒ오. | I don't like the color of these clothes. |

## THE POSTPOSITION.

99.—의게, 안테, 드려, 셔. These four all mean—*to, from, at, unto*, etc., and denote the Dative case. 의게 may become 희게, 시게, and at times, simply 게. This last, although quite common in speaking is, with a few exceptions, not allowable in writing. 의게 can be replaced by 안테 or 드려, which have exactly the same effect, or 셔, which is honorific. While these words originally meant *to, unto, at,* they are also used with verbs of receiving, in the sense of *at the hand of,* or *from.*

| | |
|---|---|
| 이 칙 리셔방 의게 주어라. | Give this book to Mr Yi. |
| 박셔방 안테 내가 은젼 십원 밧앗소. | I received ten dollars from Mr. Pak. |
| 글닑고 시분이 의게 칙이 긴 호오. | Books are valuable to one who wants to read. |
| 민판셔 의게 하인이 대단이 만소. | There are a great many servants at Min Pansa's. |

With Passives and Intransitives, 의게 and 안테 often correspond to the English word *by*.

| | |
|---|---|
| 포교 안테 잡혓소. | They were arrested by the police. |
| 도젹놈 의게 죽엇소. | He was killed by robbers. |
| (Here the Koreans use the intransitive, *he died*). | |
| 그 사롬 안테 속엿소. | I was cheated by that man. |

100.—을 is the sign of the Accusative case. It may become according to the rules given above 흘 or 슬, etc. After nouns ending in a vowel, it commonly becomes 를. In many places where we would suppose it necessary, it is omitted: and its presence in a sentence where it is not really needed, has the effect of the definite article.

| | |
|---|---|
| 그 사롬 이 제 개를 죽엿소. | That man killed his dog. |

| | |
|---|---|
| 의원이 약을 주엇소. | The doctor gave *the* medicine. |

Sometimes this postposition may also be translated by the English, *for, about, of, to*.

| | |
|---|---|
| 그 사람을 다슷 시룰 기드럿소. | I (or he) waited five hours for him. |
| 칙은 그 사람을 주어라. | As for the book, give it to that man. |
| 로형이 어제말 ᄒᆞ던 거슬 말 ᄒᆞ엿소. | We were talking about what you told us yesterday. |
| 곡 시방공을 말 ᄒᆞ엿소. | We were speaking of you just now. |

**101.**—에 The original sense of 에 is *in, into, to, at*, and it may consequently many times be used for 의게. It may be changed for euphony into 혜 or 시.

The distinction between 에 and 의게, is, while not always rigidly adhered to, that 의게 cannot be used of any but animate objects. Thus you would not say 칙 의게 두어라; but 칙에 두어라 (*Put it in the book*); you would not say 집 의게 가거라 but 집에 가거라; (*Go home*). *Properly,* 에 should only be used with inanimate objects.

| | |
|---|---|
| 내 가락지 강에 빠젓소. | My ring fell into the river. |
| 공의 동너에 미국 사룸 사는이가 잇슙ᄂᆞ니 잇가. | Do any Americans live in your neighbourhood? |
| 칙에 잇소. | It is in the book. |
| 그 거시 집에 만소. | There is plenty of that at home. |
| 케에 너허라. | Put them into the box. |
| 이 오리롤 쥬방에 보내여라. | Send this duck to the kitchen. |

With intransitive and passive verbs, at times 에 corresponds to the English words *by* or *with*.

칼에 죽엿쇼.  He was killed with a knife.
불에 탓쇼.  It was burnt by fire.

Note—The distinction made in the use, on the one hand of 에, 의게 or 한테; and on the other hand of 로; with the Passive or Intransitive verb is not always adhered to.

Where the instrument is considered as the instrument in the hands of some one else, 로 may be used; but when it is considered as the agent accomplishing the result 에 or 의게 must be used.

On this account we cannot say—포교로 잡혓쇼; but as seen above we may say—포교의게 잡혓쇼 (he was arrested by the police).

Of course the distinction between 에 and 의게 mentioned above is maintained here also.

102.—로. This postposition has the sense of—*by, with, by means of, for*. It generally denotes that by which anything is accomplished—*the instrument used*.

When joined to a syllable ending with a consonant, it becomes 으로. This, again, according to the rules given above, may become 호로, 소로, or 초로. When preceded by the consonant ㄹ, there is no need for the interposition of the vowel: 로 becomes 노, and the ㄹ and ㄴ coming together have the sound of *double l*.

칼노 버혀라.  Cut it with a knife.
노끈으로 미여라.  Fasten it with a string.
이것 죠션 말노 무어시  What is this called in
라고 호오.  Korean?
산꼴 길노 왓쇼.  We came by the mountain road.
공을 송셔방으로 알앗쇼. I took you for Mr. Song.

This postposition has also the sense of *to*, and *from*. From its meaning as the instrument, it comes to mean the place *from* which one begins, or *at which* one ends a journey.

평양 으로 와셔 꽁쥬로　I came from Pyeng Yang
가 오.　　　　　　　and am going to Kong
　　　　　　　　　　Ju.

Note.—From this use of this postposition ambiguity may arise, and 숑도로갓소 may mean either that he ends his journey at Song Do, and has gone there; or that on his way to some other place, he has gone *via* Song Do.

103.— 아 This postposition was probably originally derived from 와 but has now lost its original meaning, and is used as an exclamatory particle, representing what may be termed the "Vocative Case." From the very nature of the case, it is not as commonly used as many of the other postpositions. It may at times become 야, and generally does so when following a vowel, and of course like the other postpositions becomes 사 or 하, and at times, though very rarely 어.

104.— 에셔. This postposition is properly a contraction of 에 and the verbal participle 잇셔 from 잇소 (*to be*); and has the sense of—*being at*, or, *having been at*. From this, then, we get, in English, the sense of —*from, since, at*; referring to the time or place *at which*, or *from which* anything takes place. Euphonically it may change to 헤셔 or 시셔, and quite often is contracted to simple 셔. It has generally been regarded as the sign of the Ablative case.

미국 셔 계 왓소.　　　　A box came from America.
외아문 에셔 맛낫소.　　I met him at the Foreign
　　　　　　　　　　　　Office.
여긔셔 숑도가 몃 리오.　How far is it from here to
　　　　　　　　　　　　Song Do.

**105.**—은 This postposition has generally been classified as the sign of the Oppositive case, because of its constant use in contrasts. It has the effect of emphasizing the word to which it is joined, and may be translated into English by the words—*as far, as far as, with regard to*. In many places where in English, the contrast of the words, or the emphasis desired to be given, is sufficiently plain without these words, in Korean this postposition will be used. For instance, with the indefinite pronominal adjective 더러 (some), in English we consider the repetition of the word sufficient emphasis, and, while this is allowable in Korean, the two words, each with the postposition would be preferable.

Following a vowel, this becomes 는, and according to the rules given at the beginning of this chapter, it may also become 흔, or 슨, or 츤.

| | |
|---|---|
| 내가 시방은 아조 낫소. | Now I am quite well. (I have been sick). |
| 이 릉금은 미우 낫소. | These apples are much nicer. |
| 공의 편지 는 쓰겟소. | With regard to your letter, it will do. |
| 꼿촌 릭월에 쓰겟소. | As far as the flowers are concerned, next month will do. |

This same postposition may be added also to verbal participles, when it has a conditional effect; and may be used either of the present or future. Sometimes its effect is simply temporal.

눈이 붉아셔는 칙 잘 보앗소.
(Lit. Eyes having been clear as far as, books well I read).

When my eyesight was good, I could read books easily.

물에 빠자셔는 죽겟소.
(Lit. Water in, having fallen, as for will die).

If you were to fall into the water, you would drown.

이것아니먹어셔는죽겟소.
(Lit. This thing not having eaten, as for, will die).

If you don't take this, you will die.

This postposition also may be, and is quite frequently, added to other postpositions. It emphasizes thereby, not the postposition, but the word to which that postposition is joined.

**106.—브터.** The postposition 브터 has the sense of *from, since*, and refers to either time or place. In many cases, it takes the place of 에셔. It may be written 브럼.

Note.—This word will often be found written with a ㅜ instead of ㅡ but the best authorities write 브터, and 부터 is seldom met with to-day.

오눌 브터 일잘 ᄒ여라.

From to-day on, do your work well.

그저씌 브터 조곰도 아니 먹엇소.

I have not eaten a morsel since the day before yesterday.

당신이 갈 때 브터 추추 덧쳐 갓소.

He has been getting worse from the time you left.

황쥬 브터 즁화 ᄭᆞ지 말쌍 진흙 뿐이오.

From Hwangju to Chungwha there was nothing but mud.

**107.—ᄭᆞ지** is the opposite of 브터 and means, *up to, as far as, to*. It is *inclusive*.

The English words *to, up to, till* etc are not the exact equivalents for 싸지, for it must always be remembered that the Korean word means *up to and including.* Thus 십삼 쟝싸지보라 means read up to and including the thirteenth chapter.

| | |
|---|---|
| 내가 십 환 싸지 보아도 아니 밧앗소. | I offered, up to ten *yen* but he would not take it. |
| 오리골 싸지 가셔 맛낫소 | We went as far as Oricole, and met them there. |
| 물이 물 가슴 싸지 왓소. | The water came up to the horse's chest. |
| 요한복음십칠쟝싸지보라. | Read to the eighteenth chapter of John's Gospel. |
| 칠월싸지잇스라고호엿소. | He asked me to stay till the end of the seventh month. |

In a few cases, but rarely, this word is found written 싸종 but it is not elegant and should not be imitated.

108.—야. This postposition has heretofore been overlooked as such. It may be joined to nouns, adverbs and is largely found added to verbal participles. It is exclusive in its use and has the sense of.—*only, merely.*

With a verbal participle, and followed by the future of 호오 and 쓰오 it has the effect of the English word *must.* Followed by the future of any other verb it has the effect of stating what *must* be done in order to accomplish the act, or bring about the state expressed in the principal verb.

| | |
|---|---|
| 대포가 잇시니 활이야 쏠티 잇느냐. | As there are cannon, is there any use in mere bows? |

| | |
|---|---|
| 그 사롬이 발셔 죽엇 시니 약 가져와야 쓸디 업소. | Since that man has been dead for some time, the mere bringing of medicine is useless. |
| 그런 거슨 대궐 에야 엇 겟소. | Such as that can only be found in the Palace. |
| 비 라야 바다를 건너 겟소. | One must have a boat to cross the sea. |
| 사롬이 먹어야 살겟소. | Man must eat to live. |
| 일 ᄒ여야 삭을 밧게소. | You must work, to receive wages. |
| 됴희가 잇셔야 글시를 쓰 겟소. | I must have paper to write on. |
| 목슈가 와야 일을 훈가 지로 ᄒ겟소. | The carpenter must come, if we are to work together. |
| 릭월에 내가 함흥 가야 쓰겟소. | I must go to Ham Heung next month. |

**109.—나.** This word is properly a conjunction, but in many cases it takes the place of a postposition. It may be written 이나 and corresponds to the English "*or*," "*either*." Repeated it is "*either...or*." Used alone as a postposition joined to a noun, it has the sense of, *at least*. Joined to verbs it has a concessive force. In this place, however, we have but to deal with it as a postposition meaning, *at least, even*.

| | |
|---|---|
| 나 나 가겟소. | I at least will go. |
| 이 거시나 쓰겟소. | Even this will do. |

**가.** This word, also, can hardly be called a postposition as it is not added to nouns. It is joined to almost any verbal form, and asks a question. It is not used so much in asking questions of another, as in soliloquies where one is in doubt or in hesitation.

| | |
|---|---|
| 내가 갈가. | Shall I go ? |
| 가져 가리잇가. | Shall I take it away ? |
| 오놀 비 올가. | Will it rain to-day ? |
| 됴흔가. | Is it good ? |
| 약 먹으면 병 나흘가. | If I take the medicine shall I get better ? |
| 먹을가 말가. | Shall I eat it or not ? |

100.—In many cases one or more postpositions may be combined, just as in English we use one or more prepositions.

In these cases, for the most part, the effect of all the postpositions is manifest.

The following sentences will illustrate this :—

| | |
|---|---|
| 그 사룸의 지조 로논 못 호겟쇼. | I can't do it with such skill as that man shows. |
| 이 칙 에셔논 못 본 말 이오. | That's something I have not seen in this book. |
| 님금 씌셔 논 미우 착 호오. | As far as the king is concerned, he is a good man. |
| 일본 으로셔 왓소. | He came from Japan. |
| 리셔방 의게로 보내여라. | Send it to Mr. Yi. |
| 님금 씌로 가기가 조심 스럽소. | It is well worth taking great care, in paying a visit to the king. |

Composite Postpositions.

111.—The composite postpositions are nouns to which are affixed simple postpositions, and which are now in turn affixed to other nouns in a sentence and hold the same place as simple postpositions. A few of them are

THE POSTPOSITION.

given below. It will be noticed that in some cases the simple postposition has slightly changed its form.

| | | | |
|---|---|---|---|
| 안희, | Inside of, inside. | 아래에, or 아래, | Lower part of, below. |
| 밧긔, | Outside of, outside. | 이편에, | This side of, on this side, |
| 우희, | On the top of, above. | 뎌편에, | That side of, on that side. |
| 밋희, | Below, underneath. | 딕신에, 딕신으로, | Instead of, in place of. |
| 겻희, 엽희, | At the side of, beside. | 속에, | Inside of, inside. |
| 뒤희, | Behind. | 것희, | Outside of, outside. |
| 압희, | Front of, in front. | 후에, | After. |
| 씨문에, | On account of. | 전에, | Before. |
| 사록으로, 연고로, | Because of. | 끗희, | At the end of. |
| | | 가희, | At the side of. |

112.—In the use of these composite postpositions, originally the simple postposition 의 was placed after the noun before the composite postposition; but this is no longer done except in a few very rare instances, the composite postposition directly governing the noun.

| | | | |
|---|---|---|---|
| 집 압희, | In front of the house. | 그 사롬, 씨문에, | "On account of that man." |
| 궤 속에, | Inside the box. | 뜻 밧긔, | Outside of thought, unexpectedly. |
| 상 우희, | On the table. | 너딕신에, | Instead of you. |
| 궤 밋희, | Beneath the box. | 길이편에, | "On this side of the road." |

## Verbal Postpositions.

**113.**—There are a number of verbal participles that are now used as postpositions. They can follow a noun, or at times are preceded by a simple postposition. When met with, they can generally be recognized in a moment, but a few are given below as examples.

위ᄒᆞ야, "In behalf of," "For the sake of."
인ᄒᆞ야, "Because of," "On account of."
넘어, "Having gone over," beyond.
건너, "Having crossed," across.

# CHAPTER VII.

## THE VERB.

**114.**—It has been said, and that rightly, that the verb presents the greatest difficulty which the student has to meet in the study of Korean. This difficulty arises not so much from the great variety of forms to express time and mood, through which the verb may be carried: as from the number of nouns, adverbs, conjunctions etc., which may be joined to it, slightly changing its meaning, or from the way in which any verb can play into almost any other. No fully adequate classification of these various words and forms has as yet been made. They have been joined to the verb, and most of them classed under the general head of terminations. Admitting, as all those in the verb form do, of being put in turn through a complete conjugation, the whole subject has presented to the student, an almost impassable barrier. If, however, we can take these various forms, separate them into their elements, and show rules by which they are joined, matters will be greatly simplified.

An attempt to do this has been made in the following pages, and while the writer realizes how inadequately this has been done, he trusts that the classification aimed at and begun, will enable the student not only to carry it to its completion, but to gain a firm grasp of the verb in all its forms.

115.—One thing to be remembered in connection with the Korean verb is its absolute impersonality, and its entire lack of number. This was hinted at, while speaking of the Korean personal pronoun. The same form is used for first, second, or third person, singular or plural, and, as has been said before, these distinctions are left to the context.

116.—There are a few forms, which from the very nature of the case, can only belong to one or other of the persons. In such cases, however, the person is expressed rather in the *sense* of the verb than in its form. For example, in the expression for direct command, one does not "command" oneself, nor can the "command" be said to be in the third person, it can only be in the second.

As :— 어셔 가거라.
(*Go quickly*).

Here of course this can only be in the second person ; and as in English, it may be addressed to one or more. If one is desirous of showing that the direction is addressed to more than one, it may be done by the insertion of the plural particle 들, immediately after the adverb, and we have.

어셔 들 가거라.
(*Go '(plur)' quickly*).

This last shows that the command is addressed to more than one.

## THE VERB.

**117.**—Again in what we have termed *Volitive mood, first person*, the first person exists in the very meaning of the word. It is a proposition, that the speaker, together with the person or persons addressed, shall act. We can then but call it, "first person plural," making it equivalent to the English "Let us."

As 남산 올나 갑시다.
(*Let us go up Nam San*).

**118.**—There are also a few forms which have been said to designate the first person, but these too, as was remarked above, get their *first person* rather from their sense, and may be termed forms of *assent*, or *compliance*.

Thus we have the termination 마, which is affixed to the stem of the verb giving it this sense.

Note.—Sometimes euphony requires that 으 shall be inserted between the stem and this ending.

Then, in reply to a request, in assenting, we have :—

그러면 가마.
(*Then I will go*).
or 믄들마
(*I will make it*).

We have also a first personal termination 노라, which may replace the termination of any one of the simple tenses, and can then only refer to the person speaking. This is commonly a book form.

| 그것호노라, | I am doing that. |
| „ „ 호겟노라, | I will do that. |
| „ „ 호엿노라, | I did that. |

With these exceptions, which in reality can scarcely be called such, we repeat; "There is no such thing as person or number in Korean verbs."

### DIFFERENT KINDS OF VERBS.

**119.**—We divide Korean verbs into two classes, *Active* and *Neuter*, giving to these terms not the sense in which they are used by most grammarians, but that given in the "Grammaire Coreenne." All verbs that express *action*, whether the subject acts or is acted upon, whether the action does or does not terminate on some object, we call *active* verbs.

From the standpoint then of foreign grammarians, the Korean active verb may be either, active or passive, transitive or intransitive.

**120.**—Neuter verbs are those which predicate a quality of the subject, and have been termed by many, "Adjectival verbs." As will be seen further on, there are but few true adjectives in Korean, and even these few were originally nouns. For the most part when a quality is predicated of a noun, a verb is used; and if the adjectival form is desired, the relative participle must be employed.

**121.**—It may be said that Korean verbs, have three distinct voices, *Active*, *Causative* and *Passive*. From the very nature of the case, many verbs do not admit of all three voices, and in some we find but an Active and a Causative, in some simply an Active and a Passive, but in some again, all three. A large number of Korean active verbs have a passive sense as 속 소 (to be cheated) and these when put in the causative voice give us naturally the equivalent of the English transitive verb. Such verbs admit of no passive voice, and although according to rule, it might be formed, from the nature of the case it is useless. Some neuter verbs on the other hand, forming a causative give us the effect of the English transitive verb. A passive of these causatives may be formed, but the Korean prefers to return to his neuter form. For example the neuter verb

     마르오, To be dry.
becomes  말니오, To make to be dry, or to dry.

The passive of this can be formed and we would then have

     말니이오, To be dried.

This last is perfectly correct according to rule, but it is not what the Korean would use. He would prefer to return to the neuter verb and say simply, "It is dry."

122.—The method of forming the passive and causative voices being so similar, among Koreans themselves there is much confusion in this matter. The causative voice may be formed by the addition of 이, 오, or 우 to the verbal stem. Causative forms usually are made from neuter or intransitive verbs, or even from those transitive verbs which are used at times intransitively. The addition to the stem of the verb is of course much modified by the final letter of the stem. After vowels we commonly find the form in 오 or 우, though the form in 이 is also quite frequent. After ㅁ or ㅅ; ㄱ is often inserted, giving us 기 instead of 이; after ㅂ, or a form in which there is a latent aspirate; 히 will be used. But these changes, as will be seen at a glance, are all euphonic, and to these rules there are many exceptions. A few of these causative forms are given below.

녹소, To melt (v.i.) ......... 녹이오, To make to melt, to melt (v.t.).
죽소, To die ............... 죽이오, To kill.
우오, (r. 울) To cry........... 울니오, To make to cry.
지오, To carry ............. 지우오, To load.
먹소, To eat .............. 먹이오, To feed.
붉소, To be bright ........ 붉히오, To make bright, to lighten.
식소, To be cold .......... 식히오, To cool.
놉소, To be high .......... 놉히오, To elevate.
너르오, To be broad ........ 널니오, To broaden.
보오, To look ............. 뵈오, To show.
세오, To awake............ 세우오, To waken.
더웁소, To be hot.... 데오, or 데우오, To heat.

123.—All verbs do not admit of such a causative from, but a causative sense can always be given by the use of the future verbal participle with 호오, which, however, often has the sense of *to force, to make, to oblige, to compel*, and is the stronger of the two.

가게호오, To make him go.
오게호오, To make him come.
곱게호오, To make to be beautiful.

124.—The passive voice is formed by affixing 이 to the stem, and, as has been noted above, it may be affixed to the stem of either an active or causative verb. From the nature of the case the passive voice can only be formed from verbs having a transitive sense. For the most part, however, the Koreans prefer not to use these forms, and as is noted in Part II on-passive constructions, the English passive is generally rendered into Korean by a change of form. As was seen in ¶ 121, where there is an intransitive verb expressing the idea of the passive, it is preferred. The Korean verb "*to kill*" being the causative voice of their verb "*to die*," in place of saying "he was killed," which would be a passive of their causative voice, they would simply say, "he died;" and in expressing the agent "he died by" or "he died at the hands of." A few passive forms are in constant and frequent use. Which these are, the student must learn from practice; but he will be always safe and much more in accordance with Korean usage, if he changes the form and employs an active construction. The following are sufficient to illustrate.

닷소,     To shut ................ 닷치오, To be shut.
여오 (*r.* 열) To open ............ 열니오, To be opened.
잡소,     To seize ................ 잡히오, To be seized.
막소,     To stop ................ 막히오, To be stopped.

### The Conjugation.

**125.**—It has been said, and rightly, that the Korean verb has but one conjugation, and in the formation of the various moods and tenses, there are certain regular and well defined governing laws; and these laws may in a sense be said to be the same throughout all the moods and tenses. What these laws are and how they are used, will be developed in the following paragraphs.

**126.**—Throughout what have been termed the various voices and forms of the verb, as, *active* and passive, dubitative, desiderative etc., we find these same rules holding good, and a thorough acquaintance with what we have termed the "Basal Conjugation" and its various euphonic and other changes, will enable us to comprehend almost at a glance any other part. We shall enter, then, into a careful consideration of this conjugation.

## THE BASAL CONJUGATION.*

**127.**—This conjugation is the basis of all other forms. All other voices or forms of what have been termed various conjugations, no matter what they may be, are not only derived from some one or other part of the Basal Conjugation ; but, after they have been so derived, they may in turn, be carried through all its various forms.

Each part of the Basal Conjugation, except the participles, supine, and bases, may be divided into three parts. The *Stem*, the *Tense root* and the *Termination*.

Note.—The student should not confound this division with the division made with similar terms in the "Grammaire Coréenne." Their "sign of the time" did not include all that the "tense root" here does and in fact the "tense root" here given includes their "sign of the time" and part of their "termination." The "termination," as used here, differs entirely from theirs.

**128.**—**The stem** of the verb expresses simply what the action or state may be, and therefore generally remains the same throughout. It may be the stem of a simple verb, when it may also be called the *root ;* it may be causative or passive, when it will have the causative or passive ending affixed. If the verb is in one of the more complicated forms, such as desiderative, intentional, etc., the verbal stem may include more than one word. It was just noted that the stem generally, remains the same. This was so put, because there is a class of verbs (and that

---

\* For the complete paradigm see p. 179 and 180.

not a small one) in which, in the present tense the stem undergoes a slight change, which holds also in the relative participles.

> In 가오 (*to go*) the stem is 가.
> „ 먹소 (*to eat*) „   „   „ 먹.
> „ 여오 (*to be open*) the stem is 열.
> „ 열니오 (*to be opened*) the stem is 열니.

And in 가져오라고호오 (*to order to bring*), it is 가져오라고호. In this last example, we have first 가져 the past verbal participle of the verb 가지오 (*to take*); 오 the stem of the verb 오오 (*to come*); 라 the contraction of the imperative ending, showing that it was an order; 고 the conjunction uniting it to 호오 and used commonly in indirect discourse; and 호오, with the sense here of *to say*. Dropping then the termination 오 we have the stem of the verb, *to order to bring*, and this may in turn be carried through the whole Basal Conjugation.

**129.**—**The Tense Root,** shows the time of the action, whether past, present, future, perfect or imperfect or even continued action. For the most part, when no tense root is expressed, the present is understood, but with Korean active verbs, we find 는 contracted into ㄴ after a stem ending in a vowel, acting as a present tense root. In the indicative, however, except in the form used to inferiors, no present tense root is used.

**130.**—To express past time, we have the tense root 엿 or 엇, and quite frequently 앗. Whether the compound or simple vowel should be used is entirely a matter of euphony, and it seems as though the distinction between 아 and 어 depended also on the same cause. It has been suggested that, on account of this difference in the past tense, we classify the Korean verb as having two conjugations, the one forming its past in 아, the other in 어. This may be advisable, but when the difference exists simply in the tensal root of the past, and in the past verbal participles, and as it can be accounted for on the score of euphony, it hardly seems necessary. The past tense in this matter follows the lead of the verbal participle, and it will be noticed, that nearly all verbs the ultima of whose stem has the sound of 아 or 오, take their past tense root in 앗 while nearly all others take it in 엇. It will also be seen that euphony goes still further, and where the ultima of the stem requires it, we shall find a consonant prefixed to the tense root. Stems ending in ㄹ, generally prefix ㄴ, those ending in ㅂ or containing a latent aspirate, prefix ㅎ, and at times we find a final vowel uniting with the tense root.

131.—The future tense root 겟 is the simplest of all, and except in the case of verbs whose stems contain a latent aspirate, when it becomes 켓, it is always the same.

There is also another future tense root 리 though this is somewhat defective in its use with the various terminations.

Note.—The true distinction between 겟 and 리 though not always adhered to, is that 리 signifies *purpose, intent;* while 겟 is simple future.

These signify simple future time and are used where we would use the future. The future is at times, though rarely employed to render the English present and such phrases as, 알겟소 and 모르겟소 need have in truth, no future significance; but should be rendered into English by the present, *I know,* and *I do not know.* This use of the *future* for the *present,* is comparatively rare, but on the other hand the expression of a vivid future, by the simple present is quite common.

The *past tense root* may be repeated giving us through euphony 엿썼 and the effect, "*have have done*" or *have already done* or a *Complete* or *Perfect Past*.

The future tense root is at times used together with the past tense root, 엿겟 giving us, as we might expect, a future past. When used in this way, the future follows the past tense root, which will be seen, is the reverse of the English method. The Korean says "I have will go," where we say "I will have gone."

**132.**—The particle 더 shows that the action signified by the verbal stem, was continuing or progressing, at the time shown by the tense root, and may be used alone, or with either the past or future tense root, or with both. When used alone, it signifies that the action was continuing or progressing, and can be used with either present or past time.

김셔방 오놀 그 일 ᄒ더라.    Mr. Kim is doing that to-day,

김셔방 어제 그 일 ᄒ더라    Mr. Kim was doing that yesterday.

When used with either the future, perfect, or future-perfect tense root, this same progressive idea holds, and has the effect of taking the speaker and placing him in the time of the principal tense root. That is to say, if used with the past root, it causes the speaker to view the action not from the present as something done, but from the past, as something done in the past, giving us then, almost the exact equivalent, of the English pluperfect. With the future tense root, on the other hand, the speaker is caused not to look at the action from the present, as something *to be done* in *the future*, but is projected forward into the future, and made to view the action as progressing then.

**133.**—We thus get, by the use of these various tense roots with the verbal stem, two classes of tenses which we have called "Simple" and "Compound," The simple, are formed by the use of either no tense root, or the future, or past, or both; giving us then as—

### Simple Tenses.

Present.
Past.
Perfect Past.
Future Past.

The compound tenses, we have so named because they contain the two ideas of present, past, or future, together with that of progression. We have then, as—

### Compound Tenses

The Progressive (*present or past*).
„ 1st Pluperfect.
„ 2nd Pluperfect.
„ Continued Future.
„ Probable Future Past.

**134.**—A few words on the use of these tenses :—

The **Present** represents action simply as in present time, whether continuing or not.

(A)

It is used to *express general truth;*

쟝마가히 마다 여름에지오   The rainy season comes every summer

이슬이 밤에 누리오   Dew falls at night,

## THE VERB.

(B)

or as *a vivid future;*

우리가릭일셔울가오    We go to Seoul to-morrow.
목슈가그집을모레필역하나   Will the carpenter finish that house by the day after to-morrow?

(C)

or in *historic narration* as a preterit.

헤롯왕째에예수씌셔유대    Now when Jesus was born
벳을네헴에나시니박수      in Bethlehem of Judea in
들이동방으로브러예루      the days of Herod the
살넴에니르러말하되          king, behold, there came wise men from the east by Jerusalem saying.

(Note the Korean use of presents throughout)

(D)

or of *present action.*

롱부가졈심을먹는다    The farmer (or farmers) is eating his lunch.

ᄋ회가글을닑는다      The boys are reading.

Action going on in the actual present is often expressed by verbal participle with 이오

하인이발셔떠나가요      The servants are already starting.
동리ᄋ회가둙을팔너와요   A village boy is coming to sell chickens.

The **Past.** represents action as past, and may correspond to what is known in Latin grammars as "perfect indefinite" (simple past action) or "perfect definite" (action completed); and thus corresponds to both the "past tense" and "present perfect tense" of later English grammars.

어저씌 셔울 노 왓소.
*He came to Seoul yesterday.*
아춤 먹엇소.
*He has eaten his breakfast.*

The Perfect Past tense, or as Dr. Gale calls it Past Perfect, was not noticed by Korean students until the appearance of Dr. Gale's "Grammatical Notes" and although in frequent use by Koreans has still been almost neglected by foreigners. It is formed by the use of the doubled past tense root and expresses a completed action. The Koreans call it a *"perfected past."* It is often equivalent to the English pluperfect.

| | |
|---|---|
| 우리가인쳔셔써날째에김 쥬스에게뎐보아니ᄒᆞ엿 썻지. | When we left Inchun had we not sent a telegram to Kim Chusa? |
| 자네가내부탁을써날째에 젼연히이졋썻는걸세. | Why! you had absolutely forgotten my commission when you were starting. |
| 그가셔울갓썻소. | In the mean time he has been to Seoul. |
| 그사룸이발셔요젼비에셔 낫썻더이다. | That man had already left on the last boat. |

The Future tense expresses what will take place in future time and corresponds to the simple English future. It is used also in many places where we would use such auxiliaries as "may," "can." At times if desired, an adverb to give the idea of abilty, permission etc., may be used with the future, but this is rare, and the simple future is sufficient. Like so many other distinctions, these are left largely to the context, and it will be noticed, that the potential forms, hereafter to be mentioned in 수 and

만, are in much more common use among foreigners than Koreans. (See P. 222.)

| 부탁ᄒᆞ신대로시힝ᄒᆞ겟슘니다. | I will do as you have commissioned me. |
| 나는영어공부겸며신문을보겟소. | I will read that newspaper and study English at the same time. |
| 여슷히안에그일을능히맛치리다. | I can finish that in six years. |
| 네말대로내ᄒᆞ리라. | I will do as you say. |

The **Future-past tense** may at times coincide with what in English we call the *future-perfect*, and at times with the *potential-past-perfect*. Perhaps the term "past-future" would have better designated it. It represents that an action will or should or would have been done at some time in the past. This tense should not then be confounded with the English *future perfect*, and where the English future perfect refers to an action that *will* be completed, at or before a certain time in the *future*, this tense cannot be used.

At such times, the simple future, with some adverb signifying *entirely*, *completely*, etc., must be employed. The Korean future past will be rendered by such phrases as, "*He must have*," "*He will have*," "*He would have*," when such phrases are used with a present or past time, and refer to some action that is, or has been completed. We consequently often find this in the conclusion of a conditional clause.

| 어제 뎡녕 왓겟소. | "He certainly *must have* come yesterday." |
| 이 ᄯᅢ에 왓겟소. | "He will have come by this time." |

| | |
|---|---|
| 의원 아니 왓더면 발셔 죽엇겟소. | "If the doctor had not come, he would have died long ago. |
| 발셔 업서젓겟소. | "It must have been used up some time ago." |

**135.**—To a certain extent, it will be seen that the compound tenses overlap the simple, and in many cases, as far as the foreigner is concerned, one or other of the simple tenses could be made to replace a compound tense. To the Korean, however, there is always a distinction, and the one cannot properly replace the other, therefore it should be the constant effort of the student to find out, when the one or the other should be used, and to use them accordingly. The following rules for the uses of the compound tenses while not complete in themselves will aid him in this.

The **Progressive tense** represents the action as incomplete, and progressing; and may be either present or past. It is, however, more commonly used in the past tense, and is then exactly equivalent to the imperfect tense of the Greek. With neuter verbs, it is almost restricted to this past tense, but even with these, it may be used in the present.

With active verbs; it may then be rendered into English, by the present participle, with the present or past of the verb "*to be*." With neuter verbs, it may be rendered, by the simple present, or it would be better expressed by the use of the words "*continue to*" or if the past sense is intended, by the *simple past*. It is used for the most part, of what one has seen or experienced or known and is seldom employed in any but the third person.

## THE VERB.

일본에 동빅이만터이다.
"*There were many camelias in Japan.*"
We might add to this sentence the words 지금 (*now*) and it would be—
"*There are now many camelias in Japan*" but it would signify that the speaker had just seen them.

일본은 농ㅅ 잘 ᄒᆞ더라.
"*As for the Japanese they farm well.*"
The speaker knows this for a fact.

아비는 게알너도 아돌은 브지런ᄒᆞ더라.
"*Although the father is lazy, the son is energetic.*"

The **1st Pluperfect tense** represents the action or state, as completed or having existed, at or before, a certain past time, and is exactly equivalent to the English pluperfect, or past perfect tense.

어제 아츰 ᄶᅢ 편지 셋 썻더라.
"*He had written three letters by breakfast yesterday.*"

공의 편지 온 ᄶᅢ에 화륜션 ᄯᅥ낫더이다.
"*When your letter came the steamer had started.*"

비 시작 홀ᄶᅢ 씨 다 심엇더라.
"*He had planted all the seeds when it began to rain.*"

The **2nd Pluperfect tense** of the Korean is formed of the adding of the particle 더 to the doubled past tense root of the Perfect Past tense. In use it is, like the 2nd Pluperfect of the Greek hardly distinguishable from the First Pluperfect. It has been termed a *Continued Perfect Past*. It differs not a little from the English pluperfect. A few sentences will illustrate its use:—

샹년 가을 에는 고양논   Last autumn the harvest
에셔 츄슈가 잘 되얏셧   from the paddy fields of
더이다.                Koyang was excellent.

## THE VERB.

| | |
|---|---|
| 일젼에 국셔방집 학방에 가보니서 이 젼 학 동들은 글들을 쌔 지엿 셧더라. | The other day I went to see the study room at Mr. Kuk's house, certainly the old scholars had written well. |
| 내가어제 갈셔방집 혼인 구경을 갓 셧더니 손이 만히 왓셧더라. | I went to see a wedding at Mr. Kal's yesterday, many guests were there. |

The following illustration of the four past tenses may help to distinguish between them.

| | |
|---|---|
| 지금 사름이 얼마나 왓나냐. | How many have now come? |
| 오날장에 사름이 얼마 왓더냐. | How many came to to-day's market? |
| 어제는 장에 사름이 얼마 왓셧나냐. | How many had come to yesterday's market. |
| 어제는 쟝 에 사름이 얼마나 왓셧더냐. | How many had come to yesterday's market, (and were still there). |

The **Continued Future** as has been stated above, projects the speaker forward into the future, and causes him to view the action from that standpoint.

It refers then, to some action or state that will be in progress, or existing at some future time. It may be rendered into English by the use of the present participle with the future of the verb "to be," or by the colloquial phrase "*going to.*"

엇더케 문드눈지 보랴 ᄒ면 모레 문들겟더라.
"*If you want to see how he makes it, he will be making it the day after to-morrow.*"

### THE VERB.

티일 다 ᄒᆞ겟더라.
"*He is going to finish it to-morrow.*"

오ᄂᆞᆯ은 아니 잡고 모레는 잡겟 더이다.
"*He did not kill to-day; he will be killing the day after to-morrow.*"

What we have termed the **Probable Future Past**, we have thus named, because it has the sense of the future past, given above, but with simply the idea of strong probability. It would not be used of something that is known for a fact, and it represents possibility or contingency with respect to some past action which, it is implied, did not, or may not have occurred. It may be rendered into English by the present participle, with "*He must have been*" or "*He most probably was*" etc., etc.

늙어도 그림을 잘 그리니 젊어셔는 유명ᄒᆞᆫ 화공 잇셧겟더이다.
"*Since in spite of his extreme age he draws so well, when young he was most probably a famous draughtsman.*"

술 집에셔 나왓시니 술 다시 먹엇겟더라.
"*As he has just come out of a wine shop, he must have been drinking again.*"

어제 밤에 비 왓겟더라.
"*It must have rained last night.*"

**136.**—In the Basal Conjugation, we find that the form in 더 is defective, and is not used with what is most commonly known as the ordinary polite termination. It is, however, found in both low and high forms. In addition to this, this form from its very nature, occurs less frequently in the direct indicative form, than when joined with one or other of the conjunctions; and it was this fact, together with the defect in the verb itself, that led the writers of the "Grammaire Coréenne" to classify the form in 더니 as a simple imperfect, or rather as the ending for all of what they termed "Secondary tenses."

The ending 니 is a conjunction, and it is this absence of discrimination between conjunction, and simple termination, that has made the study of the verb, so involved. This distinction must always be made, and when we find that the English word that we have taken to represent a certain conjunction will not hold with certain forms of the verb, we have no right to conclude, that the same form, used in the same way, but after a different mood or tense of the verb is a different conjunction, but simply that the investigations that we have made thus far, have been wrong. From neglect of this rule, and from omitting almost entirely a distinction between termination proper, and true conjunction, a great deal of confusion has arisen. The cause of the want of discrimination has been, that when a conjunction unites itself to a Korean verb, the termination proper is dropped, and in the literal sense of the word, the conjunction becomes the termination. If, however, we desire to arrive at anything like a true conception of the Korean verb, this distinction *must* be made, and held throughout. What, we here denominate "*termination*" or "*termination proper*," *is that part of a verb which ends a direct statement, in an independent sentence*, and in Korean, this varies with the relative positions of the speaker and the one addressed.

In dependent clauses, the dependence is shown in Korean by the use of one or other of the conjunctions, and when this is done, as was just noted, the termination is dropped.

In exclamatory sentences also, the interjection will often be affixed to the verb, and here again the termination is dropped.

**137.**—In considering the terminations then, we find four classes, two obtained from the indicative mood, and two from what we have called the *volitive* mood.

From the Indicative ... {Declarative. Interrogative.

From the Volitive ...... {Propositive. Imperative.

The difference between the termination under each head, is the relative position of the speaker, and the person spoken to. There is also a further difference in Korean verbs, to signify the position of the subject of the act or state.

In the declarative and interrogative terminations, having to do simply with the person speaking, and the person addressed, this consideration has no effect; but in the volitive, where the person addressed and the person speaking, *must* in the one case, and may in the other, be at the same time, the subject of the verb, a change may and generally does occur. For a further understanding of Korean honorifics see Chap. XI, Part 1.

<sub>The old dictionaries show that originally there was an honorific form of the verb 호오 in 호오오, the 오 of the stem of this now obsolete verb still appears affecting both tense root and terminations of honorific forms.</sub>

### DECLARATIVE TERMINATIONS.

**138.**—The declarative terminations as given below are given in the order of their relative use, beginning with the terms for addsessing inferiors.

They are given throughout with the three verbs 호오 (*to do*), 먹소 (*to eat*), and 깁소 (*to be deep*), in the present tense.

<sub>Note.—The first two are active verbs, one with a stem ending in a vowel, the other in a consonant; the second is a neuter verb.</sub>

It will be noticed that in the form used for inferiors, the present tense root 는 of an active verb or a remnant of it, is generally seen. Of course this does not appear in the neuter verb, and when uniting with the other tense roots.

## DECLARATIVE TERMINATIONS.

### PRESENT TENSE.

| | (He does). | (He eats). | (It is deep). | Termination. | |
|---|---|---|---|---|---|
| (1) | 훈다 | 먹는다 | 깁다 | 다 | Used to servants, children, etc. |
| (2) | 훈네 or 훈세 | 먹네 | 깁네 | 에 | Used to intimate friends, aged servants, etc. |
| (3) | 호오 | 먹소 | 깁소 | 오 or 소 | "Half-talk," used among equals and those who are willing to dispense with more polite forms. |
| (4) | 호지오 | 먹지오 | 깁지오 | 지오 | |
| (5) | 훈읍지오 | 먹읍지오 | 깁습지오 | 읍지오 | Honorific terms in the order given. |
| (6) | 훈나이다 | 먹나이다 | 깁나이다 | 나이다 | |
| (7) | 훈압나이다* | 먹압나이다 | 깁삽나이다 | 압나이다 | Honorific term, used generally of positive beliefs. |
| (8) | 호나이다 | 먹나이다 | 깁사나이다 | 사나이다 | |
| (9) | 호도다† | 먹도다 | 깁도다 | 도다 | Exclamatory and poetic. |

\* *Note.*—These are pronounced *ham-ni-da*, *mŏk-sim-nida* and *kip-sim-nida*.
† Changes to 로다 with verb 이오 etc.

These termination for the most part can be used with all the simple tenses, though the future tense in 리 is defective, and as far as terminations are concerned, follows in the line of the compound tenses. In (1) and (2) the 는 or its remnant in ㄴ was seen. This of course disappears with the other tenses and it may also be noted that the terminations

(5) and (7) take the form in 슈 when the verbal stem or tense root to which they are affixed ends in consonants.

Note.—It would be well, right in this place, to notice that the form in 흡 is without doubt a remnant of the old honorific form in 홉 and if we were to write in the ways of the ancients, should be written thus. Time, however has changed this, and to-day 흡 is the form in common use and must then be taken as correct. The old form in 오 is still found in such forms as 하오니 etc.

To illustrate the use of these terminations and their method of affixing themselves to tense roots, we give the following with the past tense.

PAST TENSE.

|   | (He did). | (He ate). | (It was deep). | Termination. |   |
|---|---|---|---|---|---|
| (1) | 흐엿다 | 먹엇다 | 깁엇다 | 다 | To servants children, etc. |
| (2) | 흐엿네 | 먹엇네 | 깁엇네 | 에 | To intimate friends, girl servants, etc. |
| (3) | 흐엿소 | 먹엇소 | 깁엇소 | 소 | Polite form used among equals. |
| (4) | 흐엿지오 | 먹엇지오 | 깁엇지오 | 지오 |   |
| (5) | 흐엿슴지오 | 먹엇슴지오 | 깁엇슴지오 | 슴지오 | Honorifics in the order given. |
| (6) | 흐엿노이다 | 먹엇노이다 | 깁엇노이다 | 노이다 |   |
| (7) | 흐엿슴노이다 | 먹엇슴노이다 | 깁엇슴노이다 | 슴노이다 | Honorific term, used generally of positive beliefs. |
| (8) | 흐엿슴노인다 | 먹엇슴노인다 | 깁엇슴노인다 | 슴노인다 |   |

### THE VERB.

**139.**—The **Terminations** in the Future tense in 리 and the Compound tenses are defective. In the Compound tenses we have only the following forms:—

$$\left.\begin{array}{l}\text{호더라}\\ \text{호데}\end{array}\right\} \ldots\ldots\ldots\ldots\ldots\text{Used to inferiors.}$$

$$\left.\begin{array}{l}\text{호더이다}\ldots\\ \text{호옵더이다}\end{array}\right\} \ldots\ldots\ldots\ldots\text{Used to superiors.}$$

Note.—It will be noticed that in this last 더 becomes part of the termination.

In the Future in 리, we find but three forms:—

$$\left.\begin{array}{lll}\text{호리라} & \text{Used to inferiors}\\ \text{리} & \text{,,  to equals}\\ \text{호리이다} & \text{,, ,, superiors}\end{array}\right\} \ldots\ldots\ldots(I\ will\ do\ it).$$

The 라 used above, is the 라 that ends a statement, but is only used to inferiors and in book language. From this, we also get another form ㄴ니라 which is a decided statement and is much used in books.

We find also the ending 노라 used in much the same way with any one of the tense roots, but restricted to the first person.

Like this also there is the form of assent or agreement in 마 which is joined to the root and has a future sense.

**140.**—The following illustrate the use of these terminations.

모군이 오놀 일 잘 혼다. The coolies are working well to-day.

말 비호랴고 이 칙을 짓네. I am making this book to study the language.

| | |
|---|---|
| 리 보랴고 쟝ᄉ ᄒᆞ오. | In order to make money, I am in business. |
| 벼슬홀 셩각으로 공부 잘 ᄒᆞ엿지오. | Because I desired office I studied hard. |
| 집갑시 만흐니 집이 됴켓 ᄉᆞ옵지오. | As the price was high the house will be a good one. |
| 나라를 위ᄒᆞ야 죽겟ᄂᆞ이다. | I will die for my country. |
| 어제ᄂᆞᆫ 내가 일 만히 ᄒᆞ엿다. | I did a good deal of work yesterday. |
| 그 사ᄅᆞᆷ도 말 잘 비홧네. | That man too has learned to speak well. |
| 아ᄭᅢ 긔챠가 ᄯᅥ낫소. | The train left a little while ago. |
| 발셔 편지 ᄒᆞ엿ᄉᆞ옵지오. | I wrote the letter some time ago. |
| ᄒᆞᆫ둘 젼에 죽엇ᄂᆞ이다. | He died a month ago. |
| 이 칙을 네게 주노라. | I give this book to you. |
| ᄂᆡ일은 내가 가마. | I will go to-morrow. |

## INTERROGATIVE TERMINATIONS.

**141.**—The Interrogative Terminations are almost more numerous than the Declarative. They are given below in the same order and with the same three verbs as the Declarative.

112                    THE VERB.

## INTERROGATIVE TERMINATIONS.
### PRESENT TENSE.

| | (Do you) | (Do you eat?) | (Is it deep). | Termination. | |
|---|---|---|---|---|---|
| (1) | 흐느냐 | 먹느냐 | 깁흐냐 | 느냐 or 으냐 | ⎫ Used to servants and inferiors, the latter is familiar. |
|     | 흐니 | 먹니 | 깁흐니 | 니 or 으니 | ⎭ |
| (2) | 흐뇨 | 먹느뇨 | 깁흐뇨 | 느뇨 or 으뇨 | ⎫ These are called 반 말 or half talk and are used among friends or where one does not desire to be polite. |
| (3) | 흐나† | 먹나 | (Used only with active verbs). 나 | 나 | |
| (4) | 흐지 | 먹지 | 지 | 지 | |
| (5) | 흐노 | 먹노 | (Used only with active verbs). | 노 | ⎭ |
| (6) | 흐오 | 먹소 | 깁소 | 오 or 소 | ⎫ Polite terms among equals. slightly honorific. |
| (7) | 흐지오 | 먹지오 | 깁지오 | 지오 | ⎭ |
| (8) | 흐느잇가 | 먹느잇가 | 깁느잇가 | 느잇가 | ⎫ Honorifics. |
| (9) | 흐옵느잇가* | 먹숩느잇가 | 깁숩느잇가 | 옵느잇가 or 숩느잇가 | ⎭ |

\* Note.—These last are pronounced *hawnika*, *Môksimnika* and *kipsimnika*.
† Note.—In Kyeng Sarg Do both these terms may be employed as terms of respect, and are used to both superiors and inferiors.

## THE VERB.

**142.**—These terminations are even more regular in their use with the other tenses than the Declarative, but to illustrate their use the following table is given.

### PAST TENSE.

| | (Did you do?) | (Did you eat?) | (Was it deep.) | Termination. | |
|---|---|---|---|---|---|
| (1) | {호엿나<br>호엿느냐 | 먹엇나<br>먹엇느냐 | 김헛나<br>김헛느냐 | 나<br>느냐 | Used to servants inferiors etc., the latter is familiar. |
| (2) | 호엿느뇨 | 먹엇느뇨 | 김헛느뇨 | 느뇨 | These are called 반말 and are used among friends or where one does not desire to be polite. |
| (3) | 호엿나 | 먹엇나 {Used only with active verbs. | 김헛나 {Used only with active verbs. | 나 | |
| (4) | 호엿지 | 먹엇지 | 김헛지 | 지 | |
| (5) | 호엿노 | 먹엇노 | 김헛노 | 노 | |
| (6) | 호엿소 | 먹엇소 | 김헛소 | 소 | |
| (7) | 호엿지오 | 먹엇지오 | 김헛지오 | 지오 | Polite terms among equals. |
| (8) | 호엿느닛가 | 먹엇느닛가 | 김헛느닛가 | 느닛가 | |
| (9) | 호엿슴느닛가 | 먹엇슴느닛가 | 김헛슴느닛가 | 슴느닛가 | Honorific. |

114   THE VERB.

**143.**—In the use of the Interrogative terminations, also, the Future in 리, and the Compound tenses are defective.

| (*Was he doing.*) | (*Was it deep.*) | Termination. | |
|---|---|---|---|
| (1) 호더냐 | 깁더냐 | 냐 | To inferiors. |
| (2) 호더뇨 | 깁더뇨 | 뇨 | "Half talk." |
| (3) 호더니잇가 | 깁더니잇가 | 니잇가 | } To superiors. |
| (4) 호옵더니잇가 | 깁스옵더니잇가 | | |

Note.—It will be noticed that in this last, tense root enters and becomes part of the termination.

For the future in 리, we naturally have only the form to a superior.

   호리잇가.   Shall I do it.

Note.—The interrogative particle 가 which properly is an exclamation and can be affixed to any part of the verb, is used for the most part in solilloquies; but can also used in questions. When so used the termination proper is dropped, and it is affixed. It may also be affixed to any of the relative participles.

## PROPOSITIVE TERMINATIONS.

**144.**—What we have termed propositive terminations, are used when the proposition is made, in the doing of which the speaker is to be a party. It can consequently be only of the first person and in the plural. They are joined to the verbal stem and no tense root is used.

They are as follows:—

| (*Let us be doing*). | (*Let ue seize*). | (*Let ue go*). | Termination. | |
|---|---|---|---|---|
| (1) 호자 | 잡자 | 가자 | 자 | { To servants boys, etc. |
| (2) 호세 | 잡세 | 가세 | 세 | { Among equals |
| (3) 호지 | 잡지 | 가지 | 지 | { ("half talk"). |

## THE VERB. 115

(4) $\begin{cases} \text{호옵세다…잡옵세다, 가옵세다, 옵세다} \\ \text{or \quad or \quad or} \\ \text{호옵시다…잡옵시다, 가옵시다, 옵시다} \end{cases}$ Honorific.

(5) 호시옵세다 잡시옵 … 가시옵세다 ……

(6) 홀지어다…잡을지어다…갈지어다 …… Benediction.

Note.—In regard to these terminations, there is a dispute among Koreans; some claiming that (4) and (5) should always end in 시 다, the 시 being the same as in 호시오 and purely honorific. Others, however, claim it an honorific form of (2) and that 세다 should always be used. This last seems the most reasonable, but 시다 is very largely employed.

### IMPERATIVE TERMINATIONS.

**145.**—The Imperative terminations are used when ordering or requesting a person or persons to do something, and are from their nature restricted to the second person and may be singular or plural, that is to say, may command one or more than one.

They are much more numerous than the forgoing and are as follows:—

(*Do or do thou*). (*Seize or seize thou*). Terminations.

호여라………잡아라………어라 or 아라…To inferiors.
호게…………잡게…………게………… { "Half talk to friends, etc.
호소…………잡소…………소…………
호오…………잡으오………오 or 으오…{ Polite among equals.
호시오………잡으시오……시오 or 으시오 { More polite, about like "*please do it.*"
호옵시오……잡으숩시오…옵시오……… } Honorific;
                or
                            으숩시오…… used in entreaties.
호시옵시오…잡으시옵시오, 시옵시오…
호쇼셔………잡으쇼셔………쇼셔…… } Used in
호여지이다…잡어지이다……지이다…… prayers.
   or         or            or
호여지어다…잡어지어다……지어다……

## THE VERB.

### MOODS.

**146.**—In the Basal Conjugation we have but two moods, with Participles, Supine and Bases.

The two moods are the Indicative and the Volitive.

**147.**—The Indicative Mood asserts the action or state expressed by the verb, simply as a fact, or asks whether it is a fact. It is used in dependent as well as independent sentences, but when in dependent clauses the termination is generally replaced by some other word, as a conjunction. It may at times then be rendered by either the indicative, subjunctive or potential mood of the English.

**148.**—What we have here called the Volitive Mood is that mood which expresses the wish of the speaker. It may be either in the form of a proposition to do something, in which act the speaker shall participate, which is then of the first person plural, or it may be in the form of a command, exhortation or entreaty, when it will be of the second person and may be used for either the singular or plural.

Note.—This mood has been called by some the imperative, and the two classes given have been called respectively plural and singular. The *singular* may, however, also be used for the plural, and aside from this fact the first person volitive can never in any sense be called *a command*. Better than this, it would be to call these two distinct moods; but this is hardly necessary, and it seems much better to us, to class both as belonging to the volitive mood, the one in the first person plural, and the other in the second person.

### PARTICIPLES.

**149.**—Like the Greek, Korean presents us with what we have called two classes of participles, the first, which we call Verbal Participles, corresponding in use to

THE VERB. 117

what, in Greek, is commonly known as the "Participle;" and the second, which we call Relative Participles, corresponding almost exactly to the Greek "Verbal Adjective." Most Korean adjectives, being derived from verbs, it has seemed best to us to hold to this division, which was made in the "Grammaire Coreénne," and thus avoid the chance of confusion.

### VERBAL PARTICIPLES.

**150.**—What we here call Verbal Participle, we thus name, because it partakes more of the character of a verb than the Relative Participle as far as its use is concerned.

Without a direct affirmation, it expresses its meaning as an accompanying quality or condition of the subject or object of the principal verb. Of these verbal participles, we do not, like the Greek, have one for each tense, we have only two, a past and a future. That most commonly found is the past and is formed by adding 어 or 야, or a euphonic modification of these to the verbal stem. The Future Verbal Participle is made by adding 게 to the verbal stem.

**151.**—In connection with the Verbal Participle in 야 and 어, there has been much discussion. The attempt has been made by many to prove that the form in 야 is present and that in 어 past. It has arisen from the fact that with not a few verbs both forms are found, and that with these verbs the past indicative, generally forms itself in 었 and not in 얐.

There are, however, great difficulties with this theory. In the first place, in those verbs where there are two forms they are to-day used interchangeably by the Koreans, and only when hard pressed for a distinction by a foreigner will they acknowledge a difference, and state that it is temporal. This, however, is not the main difficulty. If this distinction of present and past holds; we are then presented with the anomaly of a host of verbs, active, neuter and passive which, irrespective of their meaning, have no present verbal participle; and, on the other hand, a multitude with no past verbal participle. We see also that those verbs which (according to this theory) have no past verbal participle, form their *past* indicative in 앗.

152.—In looking at these verbs, however, we find those of a certain form or spelling taking all their verbal participles in 아, and another class with a different form taking them in 어 and between these not a few which may take either. We are left, then, to but one conclusion, that the forms in 아 and 어 do not represent different tenses, but rather the two forms which the same tense, may assume for the sake of Korean euphony.

The general rule is, that all verbs the ultima of whose stems have the sound of 아 or 오, form their past verbal participle in 아 or 아 and all others in 어 or 어.

To this rule there may be a few exceptions.

153.—The Past Verbal Participle is treated by the Koreans in much the same way as a noun, and to it may be affixed postpositions and conjunctions, some of which very much modify its meaning. The postpositions, most commonly, affixed are 셔 (a contraction of 에셔), 야 and 는.

Note.—The 셔 here spoken of, is often written 써 and is supposed to be the verbal part. from 쓰오 (to use). There is no need for this, especially as we find such a tendency among Koreans to contract the postposition 에셔.

These postpositions may or may not be affixed, but if

definitness of expression is desired, they must be employed. When used, they slightly modify the meaning.

| 호여, | "Having done," *or* "doing." |
| 호여셔, | "After" *or* "by having done." |
| 호여셔는, | "As for after having done "=If you do. |
| 호여는, | {"As for doing," *or* as for having done" (rarely used). |
| 호여야, | "Only having done" "only by doing." |
| 호여셔야, | {"Only after having done," "only when you have done." |

154.—The following sentences will illustrate the use of these postpositions.

| 농ᄉ 호여 사는 사ᄅᆷ 이오. | He is a man that lives by farming. |
| 이것 호여 무엇 호겟소. (Lit. This having done, what will do)? | What are you doing this for? |
| 쟝ᄉ 호여셔 부쟈 되엿소. | Having been a merchant, he has become rich. |
| 죠션에 가셔 쟝ᄉ 호 겟소. (Lit. Korea-to having gone, commerce will make). | I will go to Korea and engage in commerce. |
| 아니 먹어 셔는 죽겟소. (Lit. This not having eaten as for, will die). | If you do not eat this, you will die. |
| 그러케 팔아 셔는 밋지 겟소. (Lit. That way having sold as for, will lose). | If you sell in that way, you will lose. |
| 그 약 먹어셔는 낫지 안켓다. (Lit. That medicine taking as for, will not get better). | If you take that medicine, you will not get better. |

오놀 일 다 ᄒᆞ여야 삭  You must finish your work,
주겟다.  if I am to pay you to-day.
(Lit. To-day work all having done only, will I pay you).

은힝소에 가야 돈을 엇 You must go to the bank
겟소.  to get the money.
(Lit. The Bank-to having gone only, money will get).

일본 와셔야 보앗소.  I had to come to Japan to
(Lit. Japan after having come-only, saw).  see it.

죠션 가셔야 알앗소.  I had to go to Korea to make
(Lit. Korea after having gone only, know).  his acquaintance.

155.—Before we turn to the consideration of the Relative Participles a few words on the uses of these Verbal Participles must be given.

We find of course no agreement between it and its subject and it may be used with either the subject or object of the principal verb.

Its main uses are as follows :—

Referring to the subject.

1st. Simply to connect an accompanying, with a main action. When so used the participle and verb may be rendered by two verbs with a conjunction, or sometimes by one English verb containing the two ideas.

Note.—For the difference between a participle so used with a verb, and two verbs united by a conjunction see Part II. Chapter X. Sec. I.

남산 으로 가셔 꼿츨 엇어  Go to Nam San and get
오너라.  some flowers.
(Lit. Nam San-to having gone, flower having got come.)

내가 죠션 으로 가 말 비홧소.  I went to Korea and learned the language.
내가 죠션 약을 가져 왓소.  I brought some Korean medicine.
(Lit. Korean medicine having taken, came).

156.—2nd. To combine this *accompanying* action, with the main action, as the cause, manner or means.

Note.—When so used, it is exactly equivalent to the Ablative Gerund of Latin, and it is rather strange that heretofore this fact should have been overlooked and the Korean Supine, which has none of the force of a gerund, should have been called a gerund.

Cause :—
어제 비 와셔 물이 만소.  There is a great deal of water, because it rained yesterday.
무거워 못 쓰겟소.  It will not do, because it is too heavy.
무엇 ᄒᆞ여 죽 엇소.  Why was he killed?
(Lit. What having done died?)

Means :—
내가 약을 먹어셔 낫소.  I took medicine and am better.
도적질 ᄒᆞ여 사오.  They live by plundering.
비러 먹어 사오.  He lives by begging.

Manner :—
다라나셔 피ᄒᆞ엿소.  They escaped by flight.
담대 ᄒᆞ여 호랑이 잇는 디로 갓소.  He boldly went to the place where the tiger was.

157.—Referring to the object. This Participle is used also in connection with the object of the principal verb, or with a person or thing, mentioned in the sentence. It then conveys some idea of *time, cause condition*; but the relation intended and as a consequence, the true rendering of the participle in English, can only be learned from the nature of the sentence or the connection in which it stands.

When this is done, the object of the principal verb, or the person or thing mentioned to which the participle has reference, is considered as the subject of the verb contained in the participle; and, if a postposition is used, it will be the sign of the nominative. It becomes, then, a dependent clause and in this way, we may at times have a number of nouns with the nominative sign, one after the other.

내가 친구가 병드러셔 가 보왓소.    I went to see my friend, when (or because) he was sick.

옷치 볏치 만흐여셔 잘 피오.    Flowers bloom well, when there is much sunshine.

늙은이 눈이 어두어셔 칙을 잘못 보오.    The old man can not read well, because his eyes are poor.

내가 놈이 량식이 업셔셔 굼는 거슬 불샹이 녁이오.    I pity those who are starving for lack of food.

N.B.—Note the three nominatives in this sentence.

**158.**—This Verbal Participle is also largely used in the making of compound verbs. When such compounds are made, their meaning can always be obtained by translating them as simple verbs.

As:—

가져오오, ("*having taken, to come*") to bring.

가져가오, ("*having taken, to go*") to take away.
먹어보오, ("*having eaten, to see*") to taste.
무러보오. ("*having asked, to see*") to enquire.
여러놋소, ("*having opened, to put*") to leave open.
*올나가오, ("*having mounted, to go*") to mount (in going).
†을녀두오, ("*having elevated, to put*") to put up.

Note.—It will be seen throughout that in many places, the Korean verbal participle past can be rendered in English by the present. This however, does not affect its being a past tense and in all these places, it will be seen that with equal exactness, and generally with more, the past would give the sense, although the English idiom requires the present.

**159.**—The Future Verbal Participle is formed by adding 게 to the verbal stem and is not by any means as often met with as the past.

The most common of its uses are :—

1st. With some particle such as 시리 (*so as to*), when it has the effect of giving us the form of the verb that will be rendered into English by the words "so that it will," "so that it can."

As :—

| 김서방이 오게 시리 ᄒ여라. | Make it *so that* Mr. Kim can come. |
| 이 교의를 잘 흔덕 흔덕 흐게 시리 흐여라. | Make this chair so that it will rock well. |

2nd. Used alone and preceding another verb it generally signifies that for which, the action of the principal verb is done, and may be rendered into English by *that, so that in order that*, to.

---

\* From 오르오, to mount, to climb.
† From 올니오, to elevate, to raise.

| | |
|---|---|
| 이꼿츨 그 ㅇ히 가지게 주오. | Give the flowers to the boy *that* he may take them away. |
| 방이 더웁게 셕탄 만히 너허라. | Put on plenty of coal, *that* the room may be warm. |
| 셔울 가게 교군 엇어라. | Get some chair coolies that we may go to Seoul. |
| 밥 먹게 오너라. | Come to eat. |

3rd. The third and by far the the most common use which is derived from the preceding, is with the verb 호오; giving us, the force of a causative to be rendered into English by "to make to," "to cause to," etc., or it may be used with 호오 much as a sort of imperative.

As :—

| | |
|---|---|
| 그 ㅇ히 가게 호오. | Make that boy go. |
| 이 꼿치 보기 됴흐니 사게 호오. | As these flowers are so pretty, let him buy them. |
| 영어를 알면 텬하에 둔녀도 말을 통홀거시니 잘 비호게 호오. | Since, if you know English, it will be a means of communication even though you travel over the whole world, study hard. |
| 공부를 지금 아니 호면 후회 날 거시니 힘써 호게 호오. | Since, if you do not study now, you will regret it hereafter, you had better take pains to study well. |
| 시간이 느졋스니 밥을 어셔 먹고 가게호오. | As it is already late hurry and give him his supper and let him go. |

# THE VERB.

| | |
|---|---|
| 여긔는 사룸이 만흐니 져리로 오게호오. | As there are a great many here make him come that way. |
| 비가 곱흐니 밥을 사셔 먹게호여라 | As I am hungry, buy some rice and make it so that I can eat. |
| 여긔가 인쳔 뎡거쟝이니 ᄂᆞ리게호여라. | As this is the Inchun station make him get off here. |
| 셔울노 도로 갈터이니 모레 써나게 쥰비호여라. | As I must go back to Seoul get ready to start the day after to morrow. |

## RELATIVE PARTICIPLES.

160.—What we have have called the Relative Participle is rather a verbal adjective derived from the verb. As, however, almost all Korean adjectives are *verbal adjectives* derived from what may be termed "adjectival verbs" to avoid confusion we have held to this term as has been already stated.

In use the Relative Participle always stands as an adjective qualifying some noun and may generally be rendered into English by a relative clause.

As a consequence, it cannot be united to the various postpositions, unless it is first made a noun by the use of such words, as 사룸 (*man*), 것 (*thing*) or one of the pronouns, or, as is often, done by the use of the postposition 이 signifying "*the man.*"

161.—The four Relative Participles most commonly used, may be termed; Present, Past, Future, and Future Past.

The use of the terms *Present* and *Past* is, as will be seen, a little unfortunate and the terms *Active* and *Passive* have been suggested. The same difficulty existing with these latter as with the former, we prefer to retain the former.

162.—What we have termed the Present Participle is formed by adding 는 to the verbal stem.

It will be noticed that the Present Participle follows the lead of the present tense and where in the present tense the stem is slightly modified, this modified form is used in the present participle. This modification for the most part occurs in verbs whose stems end in ㄹ simple. When this is the case the ㄹ is dropped in forming the present, both indicative and participle. In verbs whose stems contain a latent ㅎ, this is not done even though it end in ㄹ. Then the stem is used, though of course the latent ㅎ cannot appear in 는.

Note.—It has been said, and with much reason, that this 는 should rather be called an "active particle" than a "present tense root" for it is only used with *active verbs*; and with *neuter verbs* is never found. However, it always has a *present* sense and can at times be used with almost a passive idea so we prefer to call it simply the *present participle*.

When used, this participle has the effect of designating the person or thing who is now acting, or (though rarely) being acted upon. It may, then, be rendered into English by the relative pronoun with *is* and a present participle, or with the simple present of the verb, or by a new dependent clause.

| | |
|---|---|
| 외국에 가면 아는 사롬이 적소. | If I go to a foreign country, there will be few whom I know. |

비호지 아니 호면 아는 거시 업겟소.   If one does not study, one knows nothing.

지금 호는 사룸 쉬이 굿치겟소.   The man who is working now will soon stop.

163.—What we have termed the Past Participle, is formed by adding 은, (which may undergo a variety of euphonic changes), to the verbal stem. There is little regularity about the special form that this participle shall take; any rules based on the form of the verb will have a number of exceptions.

The following will, however, help :—

1st. All verbs whose stems, end in a vowel, form their Past Relative Participle by simply adding ㄴ. Here we see the 은 contracts, and to uphold the character of the verb, its vowel or combination of vowels is retained.

Thus :—

가오 (to go) ................................ 간 (gone).
오오 (to come) ........................... 온 (come).
보오 (to see) .............................. 본 (seen).
호오 (to do) ............................... 혼 (done).

2nd. Verbs whose stem ends in ㄱ, ㅁ, or ㄴ, form their Past Relative Participle by adding 은 to the verbal stem; in some cases at the same time doubling the final letter of the stem.

Thus :—

죽소 (to die) ...................... 죽은 (dead).
먹소 (to eat) ...................... 먹은 (eaten).
낙소 (to fish) ..................... 낙근 (fished).
숨소 (to hide) .................... 숨은 (hidden).

128  THE VERB.

감소 (to bathe).................감은 (bathed).
안소 (to carry in one's arms)...안은 (carried in arms).
신소 (to put on, of shoes).........신은 (put on).

3rd. Verbs whose stem ends in ㅅ in joining 은 to form their Past Relative Participle ·follow the form of the past verbal participle, and where with this a consonant has been changed in the stem or added in the verbed participial ending they take the same added or changed consonant with 은. After ㅅ, ㅈ, or ㄹ; according to the Korean rules of euphony, this 은 becomes 손, 존 or 른; but in all other cases the vowel 으 is retained.

Thus:—

밧소 (to receive)       V.P. 밧아,   R.P. 밧은 (received).
밋소 (to believe)        ,, ,,  밋어,  ,, ,, 밋은 (believed).
씻소 (to wash)           ,, ,,  씻셔,  ,, ,, 씻손 (washed).
찻소 (to find)           ,, ,,  찻자,  ,, ,, 찻존 (found).
벗소 {to take off clothes.} ,, ,, 벗셔, ,, ,, 벗손 (taken off).
듯소 (to hear)           ,, ,,  드러,  ,, ,, 드룬 (heard).
뭇소 (to ask)            ,, ,,  무러,  ,, ,, 무룬 (asked).
놋소 (to place)          ,, ,,  노하,  ,, ,, 노혼 (placed).
맛소 {to receive in trust.} ,, ,, 맛하, ,, ,, 맛혼 {received in trust.}

4th. Verbs containing a latent ㅎ, form their Past Relative Participle in 혼, irrespective of the final letter of the stem.

Thus:—

갑소 (to pay)..................갑혼 (paid).
덥소 (to cover) .............덥혼 (covered).
일소 (to lose)................일혼 (lost).
알소 (to be sick)............알혼 (sick).

# THE VERB.

5th. Verbs whose stems end in ㅂ form their Past Relative Participle after the form of the verbal participle, those whose past verbal participle is in 워 or 와 form the past relative participle in 운 or 온: all the others in 은 interposing the changed or added consonant of the verbal participle.

| | | | | |
|---|---|---|---|---|
| 업소, | (*to be lacking*) | „ 업서, | „ 업슨, | (*lacking*). |
| 업소, | (*to carry on the back*) | „ 업어, | „ 업은. | (*carried*). |
| 잡소, | (*to seize*) | „ 잡아, | „ 잡은, | (*seized*). |
| 곱소, | (*to be beautiful*) | „ 고하, | „ 고흔, | (*beautiful*). |
| 갓갑소, | (*to be near*) | „ 갓가워, | „ 갓가온 or 운, | (*near*). |
| 가뵈압소, | (*to be light*) | „ 가뵈야워, | „ 가뵈야온 or 운, | (*light*). |
| 아롬답소, | (*to be charming*) | „ 아롬다와, | „ 아롬다온, | (*charming*). |
| 아니쌉소, | (*to be nauseating*) | „ 아니쌔와, | „ 아니쌔온, | (*nauseating*). |

There are several exceptions to each of these rules, and the only safe way for the student is, when he learns a new verb, to learn it with its principal parts.

**164.**—In use, the Past Relative Participle coincides with the present relative participle, except that the past tense is used in rendering it into English. At times, also, it may have a passive sense.

Note.—When this passive sense holds, it is really, because the Koreans do not like to use the passive voice, but in rendering it into English a passive should be used.

| | |
|---|---|
| 네가 밧은 편지 어듸 두엇느냐. | Where have you put the letter you received? |
| 이칼이 네가엇은 거시냐. | Is this the knife that you got? |
| 버슨 옷 쌀내 호오. | Wash the clothes we have taken off. |
| 씻슨 그릇 가져 오너라. | Bring the dishes that have been washed. |

## THE VERB.

| | |
|---|---|
| 니존 말 싱각 못하나냐. | Can not you think of the word you forgot? |
| 져존 옷슨 몰녀라. | Dry the wet clothes. |
| 꽁주를 조츤 사름이 만소. | The followers of Confucious are many. |
| 오놀 못춘 일은 삭 주어라. | Pay him for what he has finished to-day. |
| 어제 드른 말이 거즛 말이오. | What you heard yesterday is false. |
| 아까 무른 말을 쏘 뭇나냐. | Do you again ask the question you just asked? |
| 눔의 맛흔 돈은 쓰지 마라. | Do not use money that you hold in trust for another. |
| 궤에 너흔 칙을 가져 오오. | Bring the book that was put in the box. |

**165.**—The Past Relative Participle of a neuter verb, simply proclaims the existence of the state or condition, and may be rendered by the present or an adjective.

| | | | |
|---|---|---|---|
| 더웁소 | (to be hot)...... | 더운 | (hot or being hot). |
| 깁소 | (to be deep) ... | 깁흔 | (deep or being deep). |
| 무겁소 | (to be heavy)... | 무거온 | (heavy or being heavy). |
| 붉소 | (to be brighty... | 붉은 | (bright or being bright). |
| 늙소 | (to be old)...... | 늙은 | (old or being old). |

**166.**—The Future Relative Participle may be formed from the past by changing ㄴ into ㄹ.

It has the force of *about to*, and may be generally rendered by a relative clause with a future verb. It may be used to express, permission, ability or simple futurity.

일 잘 흘 모군을 불너라. Call coolies who will work well.

# THE VERB. 131

| | |
|---|---|
| 셔울 갈 사롬을 내가 기드리오. | I am waiting for some one who will go to Seoul. |
| 미국셔 올 궤가 아직 아니 왓소. | The box that is coming from America has not yet come. |
| 병들면 음식 먹을 싱각이 아조 업소. | When any one is sick, they have no desire to eat. |
| 됴혼 칙이면 볼 ᄆᆞ음이 만소. | If it is a good book, it will be very popular. |
| 갑시 대단이 비싸 살 ᄆᆞ음 업다. | As the price is so high, I do not want to buy it. |
| 지금 갈 거시오. | You may go now. |

**167.**—The Future Past Relative Participle is formed by adding 실 to the tense root of the indicative past.

It is not nearly as much in use as the three already mentioned; but with 것, 줄, 수 etc. will be rendered by a future or subjunctive perfect. These renderings may be seen and explained in the following:—

| | |
|---|---|
| 편지가 왓실 줄 알앗더니 아니 왓소. | I had thought the letter would have come, but it has not. |
| 어제 늣게 써낫시니 거긔 ᄭᅡ지 아직 밋쳣실수 업섯겟다. | As he started late yesterday, he will not have been able to have reached there yet. |
| 도적 놈이 갓실 거시니 우리 자자. | As the thieves must have gone, let us sleep. |

**168.**—A quite common, and much used Relative Participle, is formed from the progressive tense by adding ᄂ to the tense root.

It gives us then a true Imperfect Relative Participle that generally has a past sense.

| | |
|---|---|
| 어제 왓던 쟝사가 쏘 왓소. | The merchant who came yesterday has come again. |
| 아츰에 먹던 실과 쏘 사 오너라. | Buy some more of the fruit we were eating this morning. |
| 여러히 보고 십던 친구가 오늘 왓소. | The friend whom I had been wanting to see for many years came this morning. |
| 아까 왓던 사름이 누구요. | Who was that who came a little while ago? |

**169.**—In addition to these, relative participles may be formed almost at will by adding 는 to the simple, and ᄂ to the compound tenses of the indicative mood.

This form of the participle is at times found qualifying a noun; but is more often used with particles employed conjunctively or adverbially; such as—지 or 가 meaning "*whether*" or 가 and 고, used in soliloquies, signifying *doubt* etc.

| | |
|---|---|
| 그 사름이 갓는지 알수 업소. | I can not tell whether he has gone. |
| 김 셔방이 왓는가 가 보아라. | Go and see whether Mr. Kim has come. |
| 그 오희가 약을 먹엇 는가 가 보고 오너라. | Go and see whether that boy has taken his medicine, and let me know. |

SUPINE.

**170.**—There is a form of the Basal Conjugation that in use is exactly equivalent to the Former Supine or *Supine*

# THE VERB.

*in um* of the Latin, and we have therefore called it the "Supine."

It is generally formed by adding 러 or 라 to the verbal stem. This form generally follows in the lead of the past verbal participle, taking its stem.

When the stem ends in a consonant, a vowel, either 으 or 오, will be used as a connective.

Note.—Verbal stems ending in ㄹ generally take their supine in 나 or 너. As: 알나 from 아오 (to know). Where, however, there is a ㄹ in the past verbal participle, which is either a changed or added consonant, and which does not appear where the stem precedes a consonant, this same ㄹ appears in the supine; but the connecting consonant must be there, and the Supine is found in 으러. Thus:—듯소 (*to hear*) has 드러 for its past verbal participle, but its future is 듯겟소 and hence we find 드르러 (the 으 following ㄹ becomes 오) for the supine.

The supine is used for the most part with verbs of motion, although we do at times find it with other verbs, to signify the purpose of the act.

| | |
|---|---|
| 뇌일 일흐러 오너라. | Come to-morrow to work. |
| 칙 가질너 왓소. | He has come to get the book. |
| 공부 흐러 왓소. | He has come to study. |

### VERBAL NOUNS.

**171.**—The Korean verb presents us with two verbal nouns, and by some these have been said to be interchangeable. Such is not the case, however, and the distinction made in ¶ 53, should always be observed.

The one is formed by adding ㅁ to the stem. A very simple rule for the formation of this noun, is to replace the ㄴ of the past relative participle by ㅁ.

## THE VERB.

Thus:—

| VERB. | | PAST REL. PART. | | VERBAL NOUN. | |
|---|---|---|---|---|---|
| 밋쇼, | (to trust) | 밋은, | gives us 밋음, | (faith). |
| 닛쇼, | (to forget) | 니존, | „ „ 니좀, | (forgetfulness) |
| 아름답쇼, | (to be beautiful) | 아름다은, | „ „ 아름다음, | (beauty). |

For sentences illustrating its use see ¶ 53.

**172.**—The other verbal noun is formed by the use of 기. In use it it exactly equivalent to the "Latter Supine" or "Supine in u" of Latin.

The most common form in which it is met, is the stem with 기.

Each simple tense may however have its own noun in 기; which is then formed by simply replacing its termination by 기.

Thus we may have:—

호기, 호엿기, 호겟기, & 호엿겟기.

**173.**—This verbal noun, is often used with the various postpositions to express varying ideas such as cause manner, etc.

Most of these will in a moment be apparent from a literal translation, but a few words about the most frequent forms will be in place.

It is very largely used with 는, in phrases and sentences where in English we would simple change the tone. In these sentences, the verbal noun in 기 of the principal verb in the sentence will be used, and immediately precede the verb. It has the effect of showing *lack of interest*, *doubt as to the result*, etc. of the action expressed by the verbs. Its true sense can always be gained, by rendering the verbal noun by the English noun in *ing*, and preceding it by the words, *as for*.

| | |
|---|---|
| 그 집이 됴키는 됴호나 조곰 젹소. (Lit. The house being-good-as-for good although, little small is.) | That house is good but it is a little small. |
| 이 거시 비싸기는 비싸것 마는 보기에 됴소. | This is dear; but it is pretty. |
| 그 시계가 보기는 됴흘 지라도 갑시 비싸오. | As far as the looks of that watch are concerned it is good, but it is high priced. |

**174.**—We find it also used many times with the postposition 에 having then a causal effect.

| | |
|---|---|
| 그 사롬이 의원을 맛낫 기에 살앗소. | That man's life was saved through his meeting the doctor. |
| 도젹놈이 왓기에 큰소릐 호엿소. | I made a great noise because thieves came. |
| 그 하인이 일 잘호엿기에 샹급으로 비단 호필 주엇소. | Because that servant has done his work well I have given him a bolt of satin. |
| 약 먹기에 돈이 만히 업서젓소. | In the taking of medicine I have spent a good deal of money. |
| 그 총이 됴킬네 노로를 만히 잡앗소. | I killed a good many deer because the gun was good. |

Note.—This last, while considered by many a corruption of 기에, is in all probability a contraction of the noun in 기 and some part of the verb 이오 (to be). It is in such general use now that some even call it a causal conjunction.

**175.**—When used with 로 it can often be rendered by the English infinitive.

| | |
|---|---|
| 미국을 릭일 써나기로 작뎡 ᄒᆞ엿소. | I have decided to start for America to-morrow. |
| 약 먹기로 의원의게 말 ᄒᆞ엿소. | I spoke to the doctor about taking some medicine. |
| 집 짓기로 형님의게 긔별 ᄒᆞ엿소. | I have sent word to my brother to build the house. |
| 편지 쓰기로 다른 일 못 ᄒᆞ겟소. | I will be unable to attend to any thing else on account of letter writing. |

BASES.

176.—It remains now but to give the two bases on which verbs of intention, and negatives are formed, and we have the whole of the Basal Conjugation.

The first of these, is what we have termed the "Desiderative Base." It is formed by addtng 러 or 랴 to the verbal stem as it is seen in the past verbal participle; and where this stem ends in a consonant 으 or 으 is interposed as a connective.

It is commonly united with ᄒᆞ오 by 고, as a connective; but this 고 may be dispensed with and then contractions will follow.

It gives us thus a verb signifying—*desire* or *intention of* carrying out the action expressed by the verb. When the verb is thus formed it may be carried through the whole Basal Conjugation.

| | |
|---|---|
| 가랴고ᄒᆞ오 | To intend to go. |
| 주랴고ᄒᆞ오 | To intend to give. |
| 직희랴고ᄒᆞ오 | To intend to guard. |

It may at times be used alone in asking questions, having the sense of "Do you want to," "Do you desire to." This use, however, is not common, and is preeminently colloquial.

| | |
|---|---|
| 굿치 가랴. | Do you want to go along? |
| 어제 가져온 칙 닑으랴. | Do you want to read the book I brought yesterday? |
| 시방 어두웟시니 그만 두랴. | As it is dark, do you desire to stop now? |
| 오날 ᄒᆞ랴고 ᄒᆞ얏더니 손님이 와셔 못힛소. | I had intended doing it to-day but friends came and I could not. |
| 릭일 가랴고 ᄒᆞ얏더니 일이 잇셔 모레나 가겟소. | I had intended going to-morrow but affairs have turned up and I may go the day after. |
| 어제 오랴고 힛지만 비가 와셔 못왓소. | I had intended coming yesterday but it rained and I could not. |
| 학교에 들어가랴고 셔울 을나 왓는듸 집에 일이 잇셔 도로 ᄂᆞ려 가야겟소. | I came up to Seoul intending to enters school but business at home calls me back. |
| 아사 비가 오랴더니 셔풍 이 부러셔 멀니 다라 낫소. | It intended to rain but the west wind blew the clouds away. |

**177.**—A negative idea in Korean, may be expressed either by the use of a simple negative preceding the verb as in English, or a negative verb may be formed. When this is done, what has well been termed a Negative Base is used. This base is formed by affixing 지 to the verbal stem. Strange to say, in many verbs we may have two forms of this base, one formed from the stem as found in the present indicative, and one from that of the future indicative.

This same form of the verb is always used when a negative verb is employed.

For its use and examples see ¶. 206 ff.

**178.**—It will be seen that four principal parts have been given, the Present Indicative, Past Verbal Participle, Future Verbal Participle, and Past Relative Participle. With a knowledge of these any other parts can be formed. In the verb हो ओ the stem is the same throughout, but in many verbs the stem as seen in the first three may differ.

In the forming of the other parts this difference holds and, outside of the supine, desiderative base, verbal noun in ย, and perfect tenses, the general rule may hold that, when the part or parts added to the stem begin with a consonant other than レ, the stem as seen in the future verbal participle will be used; when with a vowel or レ, the stem as seen in the present indicative is followed.

Note.—When the stem ends in a vowel and is followed by a vowel a contraction may take place; when the stem ends in a consonant and is followed by a vowel, sometimes, euphony may require the main consonant to be doubled or another to be inserted.

We find then :—

| | |
|---|---|
| Following the Present Indicative ............ | The Present Participle and those parts of the Volitive Mood whose terminations begin with a vowed. |
| Following the Past Verbal Particle...... | The Past, Fut-Past, Pluperfect and Prob-Fut-Past tenses of the Indicative. The Future Past Particile, the Supine and the Desiderative Base. |
| Following the Fut. Vebal Participle ... | The Future, Progressive and Continued Fut. of the Indicative, those parts of the Volitive Mood whose terminations begin with a consonant: the verval noun in ๆ]; and the Negative Base. |
| Following the Past Relative l'articiple. | The Future Relative Part, and the Verbal Noun in ย. |

## THE VERB.

**179.**—We have, then, following :—

### THE BASAL CONJUGATION.

#### PRINCIPAL PARTS.

| Present Indicative. | Past Verbal Part. | Future Verbal Part. | Past Relative Part. |
|---|---|---|---|
| 호오 | 호여 or 호야 | 호게 | 흔 |

### INDICATIVE MOOD.

#### SIMPLE TENSES.

| Present............... | 호오............. | Do. |
| Past................... | 호엿소.......... | Did. |
| Perfect Past ...... | 호엿셧소...... | Has done. |
| Future ............... | 호겟소........... | Will do. |
| Fut. Past ............ | 호엿겟소...... | Will have done. |

#### COMPOUND TENSES.

| Progressive ......... | 호더이다...... | Am *or* was doing. |
| 1st Pluperfect ...... | 호엿더이다... | Had done. |
| 2nd Pluperfect...... | 호엿셧더이다 | Had done already. |
| Continued Future.. | 호겟더이다... | Will be doing. |
| Probable Fut. Past. | 호엿겟더이다 | Must have done. |

### VOLITIVE MOOD.

| 1st Persons Plural. | | 2nd Person. | |
|---|---|---|---|
| To inferiors, | 호자 ⎫ | To inferiors, | 호여라 ⎫ |
| „ equals, | 호세 ⎬ Let us do. | „ equals, | 호게 ⎬ Do thou. |
| „ superiors, | 호옵세다 ⎭ | „ superiors, | 호옵시오 ⎭ |

### PARTICIPLES.

| Verbal | | Relative | |
|---|---|---|---|
| | | Present, 호는, | Doing. |
| Past, ⎰ 호여 ⎱ or ⎰ 호야 ⎱ having done. | | Past, 흔, | Done. |
| | | Future, 홀, | About to do. |
| Future, 호게, | | Imperfect, 호던, | Were doing. |

Verbal Nouns ........ { 홈, Action.
{ 호기, The doing.
Bases...... { Neg. ...... 호지, To do.
{ Desid. ...... 호랴, Desire to do.
Supine ................ 호러, To do.

Note.—In accordance with the true Korean idea, we have given no person in the indicative mood, and we would remind the student, that any one of the parts there given, may be used with equal correctness for first, second or third persons, singular or plural. We would also call his attention to the fact, that termination 3 in the declarative table, and 6 in the interrogative' coincide, both in form and in use. The forms given in the simple tenses may then be used either affirmatively or interrogatively.

180.—A knowledge of the principal parts of any verb will enable us to carry it through this conjugation. Some of the most common verbs that are a little irregular in forming their principal parts are given at the end of this chapter, and the student is advised to commit them.

By way of illustration the following verbs are conjugated, and as a matter of practise it would be well to take other verbs and in like manner construct paradigms.

The verb. 아오. To know.

1. Principal Parts.

아오, 알아, 알게, 안.

2. Moods, Tenses, etc.

| | INDICATIVE. | VERBAL PART.S. | RELATIVE PART.S. |
|---|---|---|---|
| Pres ........... | 아오... | — | 아는· |
| Past ........... | 알앗소 | 알아 | 안· |
| Perfect Past ... | 알앗셧소 | — | |
| Fut ........... | 알겟소 | 알게 | 알· |

## THE VERB.

Fut. Perf ...... 알앗겟소 ............ — ........ 알앗실·
Prog ........ 알더이다 ............ — ........ 알던·
1st Pluper ... 알앗더이다 ......... — ........ —
2nd Pluper ... 알앗썻더이다 ...... — ........ —
Cont. Fut ... 알겟더이다 ......... — ........ —
Prob. F. P. ... 알앗겟더이다 ...... — ........ —

|  | INF. | EQUALS. | SUP. |
|---|---|---|---|
| Volitive { 1st Pers. Plural. | 알자, | 알세, | 아읍세다· |
| Mood. { 2nd Pers. | 알아라, | 알게, | 아읍시오· |

**VERBAL NOUNS.** **SUPINE.** **BASES.**

암·
알기·       알나       Neg. ...... 알지·
                        Desid. ...... 알냐·

The Verb. 막소 To hinder.

### I.—ACTIVE VOICE.

#### 1. Principal Parts.

막소,    막아,    막게,    막은·

#### 2. Moods, Tenses, etc.

|  | INDICATIVE | VERBAL PART.S. | RELATIVE PART.S. |
|---|---|---|---|
| Pres ............ | 막소 ............ | — ........ | 막눈· |
| Past ............ | 막앗소 ......... | 막아 ........ | 막은· |
| Fut ............ | 막겟소 ......... | 막게 ........ | 막을· |
| Fut. Perf ... | 막앗겟소 ...... | — ........ | 막앗실· |
| Prong. ......... | 막더이다 ...... | — ........ | 막던· |
| 1st. Plup ...... | 막앗더이다 ...... | — ........ | — |
| 2nd Plup ...... | 막앗썻더이다 ... | — ........ | — |
| Cont. Fut ... | 막겟더이다 ...... | — ........ | — |
| Prob. F. P. ... | 막앗겟더이다 ... | — ........ | — |

|  | INF. | EQUALS. | SUP. |
|---|---|---|---|
| Volitive { 1st Pers Plural. | 막자, | 막세, | 막읍세다· |
| Mood. { 2nd Pers. ...... | 막아라, | 막게, | 막읍시오· |

142                    THE VERB.

VERBAL. NOUNS.    SUPINE.         BASES.
막음·                                Neg........... 막지·
막기·              막으러·           Desid ......... 막으랴·

## II.—PASSIVE VOICE. 막히오·

### 1. Principal Parts.

막히오,    막히어,    막히게,    막힌·

### 2. Moods, Tenses, etc.

|  | INDICATIVE. | VERBAL PART.S | RELATIVE PART.S |
|---|---|---|---|
| Pres | 막히오 | — | 막히는· |
| Past | 막히엿소 | 막히어 | 막힌· |
| Perfect Past | 막히엿셧소 | — | — |
| Fut | 막히겟소 | 막히게 | 막힐· |
| F. Perf | 막히엿겟소 | — | 막히엿실· |
| Prog | 막히더이다 | — | 막히던· |
| 1st. Plup | 막히엿더이다 | — | — |
| 2nd Plup | 막히엿셧더이다 | — | — |
| Cont. F. | 막히겟더이다 | — | — |
| Prob. F. P. | 막히엿겟더이다 | — | — |

                          INF.         EQUALS.       SUP.
Volitive ⎰1st Pers. Plur. 막히자, 막히세, 막히옵세다·
Mood.   ⎱2nd Pers. ...... 막히어라, 먹히게, 막히옵시오·

VERBAL NOUNS.     SUPINE.         BASES.
막힐·                              Neg. ...... 막히지·
막히기·            막히러·         Desid. ... 막히러·

### VERBS WITH CONJUNCTIONS.

**181.**—While the matter of conjunctions should properly be left to the chapter on conjunctions; they vary so much in their uniting with the verb, that a few words about them and their use is needed here. In use we find that some unite with the verb in the indicative, some join

THE VERB.   143

themselves to verbal participles, some to relative participles and some directly to the stem.

**182.**—The following list of some of the conjunctions that are most commonly used, divided into these classes should be learned.

1st. Those uniting with the tenses of the Indicative Mood :—

면, 거든............... *If, when;* conditional.
니....................... *Whereas;* causal and concessive.
닛가, 니써, 니가니, 니간드로 etc. ......
매 .......................
죽
죽속 } preceded by ㄴ ...
전대 .....................

*In as much as, seeing that, since, as;* marks the reason.

길너 .................... *Because;* marks the cause.
나 ...................... } *Although, whether;* in part concessive.
디 ......................
거니와 ................
돌 preceded by ㄴ ......

*Although, though;* concessive and in part disjunctive.

마는 .................... *But, however;* disjunctive.
거나 or 거니 ......... *Whether, as though, appears as.*
거놀 .................... } *When after, since;* temporal and causal.
며 ...................... *And.*
고먼, 고만, 고면 ...... } *At the time that, while.* Used in surprise, astonishment, blaming.

Note.—With this last, 는 sometimes is used as a connective.

2nd. Uniting with verbal participles :—

도 ...................... *Though, although;* concessive.

3rd. Uniting with relative participles.

지 ...................... *Whether.*

## THE VERB.

가 ..................... } *Whether*, used also in soliloquies expressive of doubt.

지라도 ............... } *Even though, although, though;* concessive.

듸 ..................... } *When, while, whereas, though at the same time.*

고 ..................... } Used in soliloquies expressive of doubt, or surprise.

진대, 진댄 .......... } In case that, if it should be, under those circumstance.

4th. Uniting with the stem.

고 ..................... *And.*

면셔 .................. } While. Signifies simultaneous action.

There are some adverbs, interjections etc. that, uniting with the indicative tenses in the same way as conjunctions should be mentioned here.

As:—

고나 ......... *Why!* Interjection expressive of surpries.

그리아 ...... *Why!* Interjection expressive of surpries.

Note.—This is used *with* the verbal termination.

다가 ......... *While;* indicates an interruption.

노 ............. { An exclamation of surprise or wonder used in soliloquies.

Note.—This particle is in much more common use in the Province of Kyeng Sang Do. It is there used to either superiors or inferiors in asking questions.

**183.**—As will be noticed, those uniting with the indicative are most numerous. When the conjunction is affixed, as has already been remarked, the termination is dropped. This being done the conjunction unites itself directly with the verb, but euphony may make some changes. With the exception of 마는 conjunctions beginning with ㄴ, ㅁ and ㄷ, cannot unite themselves directly to stems or verbal forms ending in a consonant. A connective is needed and 으 or 이 is quite largely used for this purpose.

With the present indicative, there being no tense root, the conjunction unites directly with the verbal stem and the rule may hold that with all stems ending in a consonant other than ㄹ, ㅅ, or ㅂ, 으 will be used. Of course when there is a latent ㅎ, it will appear before the 으. With those ending in ㅅ or ㅂ, often the final letter may be doubled or another consonant may enter in. The only rule that we can give in this matter is, that all verbs whose stems end in ㅅ and ㅂ take the form of the stem found in the Past Relative Participal and may be formed by dropping the final ㄴ of the Past Relative Participle and adding the conjunction.

Verbs whose stems end in ㄹ are joined to conjunctions beginning with ㅁ directly, without any connective; and when joined to those beginning with ㄴ, the ㄹ is dropped.

As those ending in a vowel :—

오오 (to come), 오면 (if come), 오나 (although come).
자오 (to sleep), 자면 (if sleep), 자나 (although sleep).
주오 (to give), 주면 (if give), 주나 (although give).
쓰오 (to use), 쓰면 (if use), 쓰나 (although use).

Those ending in consonants other than ㅅ, ㅂ or ㄹ :—

먹소 (to eat), 먹으면 (if eat), 막으나 (although eat).
죽소 (to die), 즉으면 (if die). 죽으나 (although die).
숨소 (to hide), 숨으면 (if hide), 숨으나 (although hide).
만소 (to be plentiful). 만흐면 (if plentiful), 만흐나 (although plentiful).

## THE VERB.

Those ending in ㅅ and ㅂ :—

| | | | | | | |
|---|---|---|---|---|---|---|
| 빗쇼 (to receive), | R.P. | 밧은 | then | 밧으면 | (If receive | etc. |
| 맛쇼 (to suit) | ,, | 맛존 | ,, | 맛즈면 | (If suit) | ,, |
| 업쇼 (to be lacking) | ,, | 업슨 | ,, | 업스면 | *(If lacking) | ,, |
| 뭇쇼 (to ask) | ,, | 무른 | ,, | 무르면 | (If ask) | ,, |
| 듯쇼 (to hear) | ,, | 드른 | ,, | 드르면 | (If hear) | ,, |

Those ending in ㄹ :—

아오 (to know)   Stem 알 ; 알면 (If know), 아나 (although know).
부오 (to blow)    ,,  불 ; 불면 (If blow), 부나 (although blow).
ᄂᆞ오 (to fly)    ,,  늘 ; 늘면 (If fly),  ᄂᆞ나 (although fly).
기오 (to be long) ,,  길 ; 길면 (If long), 기나 (although long).

With tenses other than the present, ending in a consonant, the connective is always 시.

As :—

주엇쇼,        주엇시면,         주엇시나,
(he gave).     (if he gave).     (although he gave).

맛잣쇼,        맛잣시면,         맛잣시나,
(it suited).   (if it suited).   (although it suited).

가겟쇼,        가겟시면,         가겟시나,
(he will go).  (if he will go).  (although he will go).

엇겟쇼,        엇겟시면,         엇겟시나,
(he will get). (if he will get). (although he will get).

**184.**—All other conjunctions, etc. unite themselves directly with the form of the verb without the aid of any connective.

As :—

가거든……………… If he go.
듯거든……………… If he hear.
가겟거놀…………… Since he will go.
듯거나……………… Whether he hear.

**185.**—In this place it will be well to give a few words on the

---

* 업시면 is also largely used.

## MEANINGS AND USES.

of some of these conjunctions.

### 면, 거든, 진더, 진던.

면 and 거든. Both these conjunctions have a conditional force.

The first is simply conditional, and is rendered into English by *if*. It may be united with any one of the tenses simple or compound. When united to the simple tenses, we have simple supposition, but when, to the compound, it generally has the idea of supposition contrary to fact.

It is always used when the apodosis expresses a natural or consequential sequence.

It is in regard to the second of these that we find the greatest difficulty. While most rightly acknowledge that 거든 has largely a temporal sense and may be almost always translated as "*when*" or "*as soon as*," this is not found to meet all cases. It is generally found that 면 can replace 거든 without objections but there are many places where 거든 can never take the place of 면. It has been said that 거든 can be used where the apodosis expresses a conditional command (a statement found to be true) but in such places there are many who find a shade of distinction between 면 and 거든. This rule has been widened to 거든 being used where the action in the apodosis is subject to the will of the actor and not a natural sequence of the conditions as expressed above, but it is soon discovered that this rule is not always true and that the exceptions are almost as numerous as the examples. A study of the following examples will it is believed help us to understand the uses of these conditional particles but the rule as given

THE VERB.

above that 거든 cannot be used where the apodosis expresses a natural or consequential sequence always holds.

| | |
|---|---|
| 물을 사면 스인교는 쓸디 업소. | If you buy a horse, there is no need for a chair. |
| 티일 김셔방이 돈 가져 오면 그 집을 사겟소. | If Mr. Kim brings the money to-morrow; I will buy that house. |
| 알는 줄 알앗더면 내가 보러 갓겟소. | If I had known that he was sick I would have gone to see him. |
| 그 약을 먹엇더면 아니 죽엇켓소. | If he had taken that medicine, he would not have died. |
| 내가 알앗더면 못 가게 ᄒ엿겟소. | If I had known, I would have prevented his going. |
| 지금 가더면 나도 가 겟소. | If you were going now, I too would go. |
| 오늘 병이 낫거든 티일 가겟다, | I will go to-morrow if I should get better to-day. |
| 편지 오거든 잘 밧아 두어라. | If a letter should come take care of it. |

면

| | |
|---|---|
| 장연이 됴타 ᄒ여도 일긔가 치우면 나는 됴와 아니ᄒ오 . | Although Chang Yeun is said to be a good place (to live), I don't like it {when / if} the cold weather comes. |
| 그가 글시를 잘써도 바다서 쓰라면 아조 잘 못쓰오. | He can write very well, but {when / if} he is dictated to, he can't write at all. |

## THE VERB. 149

일긔가 치우면 둣거운 옷을 닙어야 ᄒᆞ겟소.  {When / if} it is cold, we have to put on thicker clothes.

만히 먹으면 비가 불너셔 일을 만히 못 ᄒᆞ오.  {When / If} one eats too much, he can not do much work on account of the full stomach.

인쳔 가면 외국 사ᄅᆞᆷ 만히 보겟소.  {When / If} you go to Chemulpo, you will meet a good many foreigners.

### 면, 거든.

비가 드러오 {거든 / 면} 동 힘 ᄒᆞ겟소.  I will accompany you {as soon as / if} the ship comes in.

비가 ᄭᅵ {거든 / 면} 지령 편지 가져 가겟소.  {When / If} it clears up, I will take the letters to Chai Ryung.

비가 오 {거든 / 면} 창문 닷쳐라.  {When / If} it rains shut the windows.

다리 아프 {거든 / 면} 쥬막에셔 쉬여 갑세다.  {When / If} your are tired of walking let us rest a while at the inn.

편지가 아니 오 {거든 / 면} 엇더케 ᄒᆞ리싸.  {When / If} the letter does not come, what am I to do?

ᄯᅡ이 질 {거든 / 면} 나무 신을 신으시오.  {When / If} it is muddy, put on your wooden shoes.

비싸 {거든/면} 사지 마시오  {When/If} it is dear, don't buy it.

물이 약ᄒᆞ {거든/면} 듯지 마시오.  {When/If} your horse is not strong, don't ride her.

진 디 or the same with the postposition 눈, 진 딘 is really a composite conjunction. It means, *in case that, if it should be that* and this thought is simply emphasized by the adding of the Appositive Postposition.

공부 홀진디 부지런히 ᄒᆞ여라.  If you are going to study be diligent about it.

죠션을 갈진디 금강산을 구경ᄒᆞ여라.  If you should go to Korea, visit the "Diamond Mountains."

하인을 보낼진딘 ᄌᆞ셰히 말을 닐너보내라.  If you should send the servant, give him careful instructions.

너 아니홀진딘 놈이나 ᄒᆞ게 두어라.  If you do not do it yourself get somebody else to do it.

**186.—ㄴ.** This conjunction has been the source of much discussion because, at times, it was found giving a simple causal effect; and then, again, without any apparent reason, implying opposition to something that follows, something unexpected.

On examination we find that with the simple tenses the first sense always appears but with the compound the second sense may be found.

(*a*) ㄴ is then exactly equivalent to the English word *whereas*, which may have this dual idea and is used in

## THE VERB. 151

the same connections. With simple tenses, 니 is equivalent to, *considering that, it being the case that, as, since:* with the compound, however, "*when in fact,*" "*while—on the contrary;*" introducing something unexpected or at times introducing a result and marking the cause.

(*b*) A combination of this 니 with 고 (reason) in connection with the relative participle gives us a very common idiomatic expression used to introduce the reason or cause as.

(a)

| | |
|---|---|
| 릭일 공부 호겟시니 일죽 오시오. | Come early to-morrow, as we will study. |
| 쟝ᄉ롤 잘 ᄒ엿시니 부쟈 되엿소. | Since he has been a successful merchant, he is now rich. |
| 셔울을 오ᄂᆞᆯ 가겟더니 비가 외셔 못 갓소. | I was going to Seoul to-day but it rained and I did not. |
| 집을 잘 지엇더니 화지롤 맛낫소. | I built a good house but it took fire. |
| 일본을 가랴고 졔물포 ᄭᆞ지 갓더니 비가 ᄯᅥ 나셔 못 가고 도로 왓소. | Intending to go to Japan I went as far as Chemulpo, but, the boat had gone and I could not, so came back. |
| 공부 잘 ᄒ더니 유명ᄒᆞᆫ 션비가 되엿소. | Because he studied hard he became a renowned scholar. |

152            THE VERB.

| 도적질 ᄒᆞ더니 슌검 의게 잡혓소. | He was arrested by the police because he stole. |

(b)

| 리셔방이 왜 쟝ᄉᆞ를 ᄒᆞ련고 ᄒᆞ니 부쟈가 되기를 목뎍홈이오. | If ycu want to know why Mr. Yi has gone into business it is because he aims to be a rich man. |
| 엇지ᄒᆞ야 김셔방이 오는 월요일에 써나련고ᄒᆞ니 긴ᄒᆞᆫᄉᆞ실이 잇는 서돍이오. | The reason why Mr. Kim intends to start next Monday morning, is because he has some urgent business. |
| 그사ᄅᆞᆷ이 왜 유명ᄒᆞ고ᄒᆞ니 나라에 됴흔 ᄉᆞ업을 만히 ᄒᆞᆫ 서돍이오. | If you want to know why he is renowned, it is because he has served his country well many times. |
| 하인을 급히 왜 보내눈고ᄒᆞ니 그의 친구가 병든 서돍 이오. | The reason why he sent his servant so hurriedly, was because his friend was taken sick. |

NOTE:—It is when the conjunction is used with the compound tenses that we begin to find our difficulties for when added to the tense roots of any of the compound tenses except the *Progressive*, it may be used of all three presons, while most grammars assert that with the *Progressive* tenses it can not be used in the first person.

This latter rule is not quit correct for where there is no causal or concessive sense involved and no definite time expressed, it may be used also of the first person. In other words, of *habitual action*, it may be used of the first person.

If on the other hand, *time, cause,* or *concession* is expressed, it can only be used for the second or third person.

Examples:

| | |
|---|---|
| 내가 이왕에는 거름을 잘 것더니 지금은 잘 못 것소. | I used to be quite a walker, but now I am not. |
| 내가 이왕에는 교인이 아니더니 지금은 진실 흔 교인이 되엿소. | I used to be a non-believer of Christ, but now I am a good Christian. |
| 지난학긔에 공부아니ᄒ더 니 시험에 락뎨ᄒ엿다. | You failed in your examination because you had been idle last term. |
| 그 사ᄅᆞᆷ이 어제는 톱질ᄒ 더니 오놀은 아모것도 아니ᄒᆞᆫ다. | He sawed wood yesterday but he is not doing anything today. |
| 그리스도교를 위ᄒ야 우 리빅셩 의게 일을 만히 ᄒ더니 지금은 뎌희가 그ᄃᆡ를 고마와ᄒ오. | You worked hard among our people for the sake of Christianity and now the people appreciate your service. |
| 아ᄎᆞᆷ에 구름ᄭᅵ더니 지금 비가 오오. | It was very cloudy this morning and now it rains. |

187.—닛가 with its various modifications, 매, 즉 or 즉은 preceded by ㄴ, and 건ᄃᆡ, all mark the reason, or that on account of which something is done.

The strongest of these is 즉 which is about the equivalent of the English word *because*.

| | |
|---|---|
| 그 하인이 일을 잘 ᄒ 닛가 여러 ᄒᆡ 집에 두엇소. | Because that servant works well he has been in this house many years. |
| 아ᄭᅡ 만히 먹엇시닛가 지금 더 못 먹겟소. | As I eat heartily a little while ago, I cannot eat more now. |

길이 멀매 로비가 만흥야 쓰겟소. — As the journey is a long one, the traveling expenses will be heavy.

짐이 무거오매 힘 잇는 삭군을 불너라. — As the load is heavy, call a strong coolie.

갑시 비싼죽 살수 업소. — I can not buy it, because the price is high.

지금은 돈이 만흔 죽 빗 갑흥야 쓰겟다. — As I have plenty of money now, I must pay my debts.

젼디 has a little more of a temporal sense, and may often almost be translated by a conditional clause.

다시 싱각 ᄒ젼디 그 일이 아니 되겟소. — Since I have thought over the matter again, that affair will not succeed.

이 비단을 그 비단에 비ᄒ젼디 이 비단은 대단이 비싸오. — After comparing this satin with that, this is very dear.

죠션 말을 비화 보젼디 대단이 어려올 듯ᄒ오. — Now that I have tried the study of Korean, I think it will be extremely difficult.

쳥젼디 and 원젼디 are used to introduce a petition or request or to express earnest desire.

쳥컨디 대 왕은 기리보 즁 ᄒ시옵소셔. — May your Majesty be long preserved.

쳥컨디 이와 ᄀᆞ치 ᄒ시옵소셔. — I pray you do it this way.

원 컨디 폐하는 그 말을 드르시옵소셔. — My earnest desire is that your Majesty will listen to those words.

| | |
|---|---|
| 원 컨디 저와 굿치 ᄒᆞ시기를 ᄇᆞ라ᄂᆞ이다. | I earnestly hope that you will do it with me. |

**188.**—길ᄂᆡ. This is a contraction of the ending of the verbal noun in 기, with the postposition 에 and a form derived from the verb 이오 (*to be*). It signifies *because*, and shows that the action expressed by the verb that it governs, was the real cause of the action contained in the principal verb of a sentence. It is stronger than any of the conjunctions given in ¶, 186, and 187, as it marks a *result*, following from a cause.

| | |
|---|---|
| 그 놈이 공연이 내게 욕ᄒᆞ길ᄂᆡ 옥에 가도왓소. | Because that fellow insulted me without reason, I had him locked up. |
| 도적이 무셥 길ᄂᆡ 총을 가지고 ᄃᆞ니오.* | Because I am afraid of robbers I carry fire arms. |
| 아ᄭᅡ 비가 오길ᄂᆡ 유삼을 닙엇소. | I put on my water proof, because it was raining a little while ago. |

**189.**—나 is equivalent to *though*, or *although*, and has a concessive force. It is used with verbs of *knowing*, *telling*, etc., where we would use the English word *whether*. Repeated after co-ordinate clauses it is equivalent to *either* —*or*, See 269

| | |
|---|---|
| 말은 잘ᄒᆞ나 일은 잘못ᄒᆞ오. | He talks well enough, but he cannot work well. |
| 갑ᄉᆞᆫ 적으나 보기는 됴소. | Though the price is small, it looks well. |
| 자나 마나 ᄆᆞᄋᆞᆷ 대로ᄒᆞ오. | Sleep or not, suit yourself. |

---

* Literally Because thieves are to be feared I carry fire arms.

이 일은 죽으나 사나 홀    You ought to do this whe-
거시오.    ther you die or live.

190.—거니와, 되 (sometimes written 되), and 둘 preceded by ㄴ, may all be rendered by, *though, although, as though, as if, however*, etc. They generally have a concessive force, but we quite often find them employed where in English we would use a disjunctive.

이 성션을 먹거니와 일홈    Although I eat this fish, I
은 모라겟소.    do not know its name.
총은 노앗거니와 노로는    Though I fired off my gun,
못 잡앗소.    I did not get the deer.
고양이는 만호되 쥐는    Though there are plenty of
아니 잡소.    cats, they do not catch the rats.
키는 크되 발은 젹소.    Though he is tall, his feet are small.
못쓰게 ᄒ는 일은 만히    Even though a man does a
ᄒ들 무엇 ᄒ겟느냐.    host of useless things, of what account is it?
죽은 후에 약을 가져온들    Even though you bring
쓸되 잇느냐.    medicine, after a man is dead, is it any use?

191.—마는. This word, unlike most Korean conjunctions, refers more to what follows, than to what precedes it. It may consequently appear at times, at the beginning of a sentence, and at times we do find it also, standing alone at the end of a sentence. All such sentences are, however, incomplete. It may be rendered into English

# THE VERB. 157

by *but, however*, etc. In its union with the verb, the termination may be retained, or it may be replaced by 것.

Note.—In connection with this word, we should not forget that it is not much used by Koreans. They as a rule, prefer to use one of the concessive particles, and generally transpose the sentence and do so. At times they express the same idea by the use of the verbal noun in 기, with the postposition 는. See ¶ 173. It seems almost as though the Korean prefers to use any other phrase than this, and careful attention, will reveal the fact that 마는 is much more commonly used by foreigners, or Koreans with whom they are associated, than by Koreans generally.

A few illustrations of its use are given:—

| | |
|---|---|
| 됴키는 됴타 마는 갑시 만타. | It is good, but it is dear. |
| 비는 온다 마는 가는 거시 됴켓다. | It is raining, but we had better go. |
| 꿩을 잡으러 가오 마는 잡을넌지 모라겟쇼. | I am going out to get a pheasant, but I do not know whether I shall succeed. |

192.—거나, 거니. This conjunction is generally repeated and may be rendered into English by *whether—or*.

The 거니 form is used quite frequently alone with 호오 expressing appearance and may be translated by *think*.

| | |
|---|---|
| 가거나 말거나 무음대로 호오. | Go or not, do as you wish. |
| 먹거나 굼거나 싱각대로 호오. | Eat or starve, do as you think best. |
| 크거니 적거니 사오. | Whether it is large or small, buy it. |
| 공부호거니호엿시나 작란 호엿고나. | It seemed as though he would study but he frittered away his time. |
| 오거니 싱각호엿쇼. | I thought he was coming. |

193.—거눌 signifying *when, after, since, as,* has both a temporal and causal effect. It is found for the most part in books, but may at times, though very rarely be used in conversation.*

The verb 이오 gives us the form 이어눌.

| | |
|---|---|
| 친구가 죽겟다 흐거눌 엇지 아니 갈수가 잇소리오. | When they say a friend is dying how can one but go? |
| 다른 사롬의 말이 그 칙을 네가 가져 갓다 흐거눌 엇지 네가 아니 가져 갓다 흐겟느냐. | When some one else says that you took the book; how can you say you did not? |

194.—며. This conjunction is simply connective and signifies *and.* Unlike its equivalent 고 which commonly unites directly with the stem, 며 generaly unites with the tenses ar d then replaces the terminations.

While the distinction is not strictly adhered to 며 generaly connects acts that are carried on simultaneously, 고 those that are successive.

| | |
|---|---|
| 밥을 먹으며 공부 홀수 잇느냐. | Can I eat and study (at the same time)? |
| 작란흐며 공부를 엇더케 흐오. | How can you both play and study? |
| 언제 갓스며 언제 왓느냐. | When did you go and when did you come? |
| 어느 시에 써나겟시며 어느 시에 도라올 거슬 주셰히 말흐오. | Tell exactly, what time you will go and at what time you ought to be coming back. |

---

* Some say that 거눌 and 고면 (195) are the same.

# THE VERB.

**195.**—고면, 고만, 고면. These are but three different forms which the same conjunction may assume. They may be rendered into English by—*at the time that, when, while, though at the same time, when in fact,* and are used in expressing surprise, astonishment, and in reproach.

As a rule, they unite directly with the verb, after its termination has been dropped, but 는 may be used as a connective.

| | |
|---|---|
| 지금 비가 오는 고면 아니 온다고 ᄒᆞ느냐. | Even now while the rain is coming down, do you say it does not rain? |
| 네 집에 불 낫고면 아니 가느냐. | When your house is on fire, are you not going? |
| 붓시 됴코먼 언잔타고 ᄒᆞ오. | Though the pencils are good, at the same time, he says they are bad. |
| 김셔방이 잇고면 업다고 ᄒᆞ엿소. | Though Mr. Kim was in he said, he was out. |

**196.**—도. This conjunction signifies, *though, although,* and has a concessive force, but is commonly only found united with the past verbal participle.

| | |
|---|---|
| 지금 가도 그 사름 볼수 는 업소. | Even though you go now you can not see that man. |
| 갑슨 비싸도 내가 사겟소. | Though the price is high, I will buy. |
| 교군군은 왓셔도 아마 못 가겟다. | Even though the chair coolies have come, perhaps he will not go. |
| 그 집을 내가 사고 시버도 돈이 부족ᄒᆞ겟소. | Although I would like to buy that house, I can not afford it. |

**197.**—지, 가 and 고. 지 and 가 are both used with relative participles and signify *whether*, *whether—or*, with verbs of knowing and not knowing, etc. In uniting with the participles, except the future participle in ㄹ, they can unite directly and no connective is needed. With this, however, 넌 is needed as a connective. We find these conjunctions largely in use with those relative participles that are derived from the various simple and compound tenses by affixing 는 and ㄴ. Both these conjunctions are also largely used, (가 more frequently) in soliloquies, expressive of doubt and hesitation and at such times they are joined directly to the Future Relative Participle without the connective 넌.

Sometimes joined direct to the stem 나 becomes 새.

With reference to the word 고, it may be said that it also has this latter sense, and is used in the same way.

| | |
|---|---|
| 오늘 오는지 모라겟소. | I do not know whether he will come to-day. |
| 다 ᄒᆞ엿는지 무러 보아라. | Ascertain whether he has finished. |
| 집에 계신가 알고 오너라. | Go and find out whether he is at home. |
| 어제 왓는가 알수 업소. | I can not tell whether he came yesterday. |
| 릭일 갈넌지 모라겟소. | I do not know whether I shall go to-morrow. |
| 엇더케 ᄒᆞ면 됴흘가. | How had I better do it? |
| 일본 가셔 사면 엇더홀고. | How would it be to go to Japan and buy it? |

**198.**—지라도. This conjunction is found only with the regular future, and future past relative participles. It has the sense of *though, although, even though* etc., and is the strongest of the Korean concessives. With the future participle, it has a present and hence with the future past, a past sense.

| | |
|---|---|
| 다시 오라고 홀지라도 아니 오겟소. | Even though you tell him to come again, he will not. |
| 약 먹을지라도 죽겟소. | Even though you take the medicine, you will die. |
| 어제 갓실지라도 못 맛낫소. | Although I went yesterday, I did not meet him. |

199.—디 is equivalent to *when, while, whereas, though at the same time*, and is joined to relative participles.

| | |
|---|---|
| 비가 오는디 웨 가오. | Why are you going when it is raining? |
| 그 집을 잘 지엇는디 웨 헐나고 ᄒᆞ오. | Whereas they built that house well, why do they want to pull it down? |
| 디일은 손님이 만히 오 겟는디 아모것 디접홀 거슬 사지 아니 ᄒᆞ엿 누냐. | When there are a host of friends coming to-morrow, have you not bought a thing with which to entertain them? |

200.—고. Like 며, this conjunction is, as a rule, simply connective, and may be rendered into English by *and*— See p. 194.

To this the oppositive postposition 는 is often added giving us the effect almost of a conditional.

Note.—This same connective may be affixed to any one of the tenses in the forms ending in 아, and used with ᄒᆞ오; it then gives us the regular form for indirect discourse.

| | |
|---|---|
| 불 쓰고 자거라. | Put out the light and go to sleep. |
| 어제 가고 오놀 쏘 갓소. | He went yesterday and again to-day. |
| 쏫도 피엿고 일긔도 됴흐니 힝긔 ᄒᆞ러 가옵시다. | As both the flowers are out, and the weather is fine, let us take a walk. |
| 티일은 공ᄉᆞ도 오겟고 외부대신 도 오겟시니 됴흔 실과 사 오너라. | As the Minister and the President of the Foreign Office are both coming to-morrow; buy some good fruit. |
| 그리ᄒᆞ고 눈 안되눈 일이 업ᄂᆞ니라. | If you do it that way it cannot but succeed. |
| 너ᄀᆞ치 빗을지고눈 살수 업ᄂᆞ니라. | Nobody can live and be as much in debt as you are. |
| 나잇고눈 네가쉬지 못ᄒᆞᆫ다. | You cannot rest while I am here. |
| 여러훈 충신이 잇고눈 나라가 망ᄒᆞ지 아니ᄒᆞᄂᆞ니라. | If there were such patriots as that the country could not lose. |

201.—고나 and 그리아 are both interjections expressive of surprise, and are used with the indicative tenses. With 고나 the termination is dropped; with 그리아, it is retained. It may be rendered into English by *why!* preceding the clause.

고나 is often contracted with 곤 and we have the constantly used ending ᄒᆞ곤 often pronounced as though is were ᄒᆞ군 and not uncommonly wrongly so written.

| | |
|---|---|
| '비가 어제도 오더니 오놀 도 오눈 고나. | Why! It was raining yesterday and it is raining again to-day. |

## THE VERB. 163

| | |
|---|---|
| 어제 왓던 ᄋ히가 오늘 쏘 왓고나. | Why! The boy who came yesterday, has come again to-day. |
| 오늘 남풍이 죵일 분즉 틱일 쏘 비가 오겟 곤. | Why! It will rain again to-morrow, for the South wind has been blowing all day. |
| 겨울에 ᄭᅩᆺ치 봄과 ᄀᆞᆺᄒᆞ니 이샹ᄒᆞ오 그리아. | Why! It is wonderful that the flowers in winter are like those of spring. |
| 김셔방이 어제 죽엇소 그리아. | Why! Mr. Kim died yesterday. |
| 바롬이 대단 흐즉 큰 화지가 되겟소 그리아. | Since the wind is blowing so hard, it will indeed, be a great conflagration. |

202.—다가. Signifies *while, at the time that when*, and implies an interruption. It is a conjunctive adverb, and may unite with any of the simple tenses of the indicative.

It may at times be rendered by *but*.

| | |
|---|---|
| 셔울 오다가 김셔방을 맛낫소. | I met Mr. Kim when I was was coming to Seoul. |
| 이 병을 일본 가다가 엇엇소. | I got this disease when I was going to Japan. |
| 미국 가랴다가 아니 갓소. | I intended to go to America, but did not. |
| 오늘 공ᄉᆞ를 보랴다가 못 보왓소. | I intended to see the Minister to-day, but did not. |

203.—면셔. This conjunctive adverb also signifies *while*, but it has the sense of simultaneous_action, and indicates that the actions expressed by the dependent, and the principal verbs were carried on at the same time. The Koreans however recognize that the action of the dependent verb may occur at any point during the course of action expressed by the principle verb.

| | |
|---|---|
| 칙 보면서 담비 먹소. | He smokes, while he reads his book. |
| 가 면서 의론 ᄒᆞ옵시다. | Let us consult about it, while we are going. |
| 밥 먹으면서 편지 보겟소. | I will read the letter, while eating. |
| 션ᄉᆡᆼ이 집으로 가랴 ᄯᅥ나면서 학도들을 내게 맛겻소. | The teacher committed the care of the scholars to me, when he was starting for home. |
| 이 집 쥬인이 셔울 가면서 열쇠를 내게 맛겻소. | The owner of this house, committed the key to my keeping, when he went to Seoul. |
| 비 오면서 바람이 부오. | It blows while it rains. |
| 머리가 압ᄒᆞ면서 비가 압ᄒᆞ오. | At the same time that my head aches, my stomach, aches. |

면서 with adverbs of time such as 곳, (*at once*) etc., has also the sense of, *as soon as*. For illustrations of this see Part II. Chap. VII., § II. Sec. 23, 3.

### The Desiderative Verb.

**204.**—The regular desiderative verb is formed by the use of the desiderative base and ᄒᆞ오. generally connected by the connective 고. The 고 may, however, be dispensed with, and then still further contractions may take place.

When such desideratives are formed, they can be carried through the whole basal conjugation. They are equivalent to the English words *to desire to, to intend to, to want to.*

As:—

먹으랴고 호오.................. To intend to eat.
가랴고   호오.................. To intend to go.
자랴고   호오.................. To intend to sleep.

205.—Another from of the desiderative may be obtained by the use of 고저 or 고자 affixed to the verbal stem, with 호오.

In use these two are often interchangeable, and both signify, *desire, intention.*

The true distinction between these, is, that while the form in 려 or 랴 signifies rather *desire, wish,* that in 져 or 쟈 has more the idea of *purpose, intent.*

지금 셔울 잇셔셔 김셔   As I am at Seoul now, I
방을 보고져호오.        purpose seeing Mr. Kim.
미국 잇실때 화륜션을   While I was in America, I
사고져 호엿소.          intended buying a steam-
                        boat.
죠션 공사와 의론 호고져 I intend consulting with the
호오.                   Korean Minister.

Further illustration of both these desiderative forms will be found in Part II. Chap. I, § III. Sec. 13.

### NEGATIVES.

206.—There are in Korean two negatives, 안 or 아니, and 못. Both are simple negatives and may be rendered into English by *not.* 안, however, always brings in the idea of the will of the subject; 못 on the other hand, generally conveys the idea of inability, and is used in negations that were brought about generally, without an act of the will of the subject of the verb. This distinction between 안 and 못 should not only always be recognized when listening to Koreans, but *must always* be observed in speaking. By a lack of discrimination in this matter, the most ludicrous mistakes often occur. These words may be used adverbially when they precede the verb they negate.

On account of the distinction mentioned above, 못 may often be rendered by the English *can not*.

| | |
|---|---|
| 지금 안 자오. | He is not sleeping now. |
| 어제 안 갓소. | He did not go yesterday. |
| 저녁은 안 먹겟소. | I will not take any supper. |
| 오늘 못 써나오. | I can not start to day. |
| 아싸 못 보앗소. | I did see you before. |
| 후에는 못 오겟소. | I can not come afterwards. |

**207.**—These same words may be united with 호오, when they form negative verbs, and still maintain the distinction mentioned above.

When these negative verbs are used, they are preceded by the negative base of the verb they negate. Thus they give us a negative form of the principal verb. From the verb 붉소, we have the negative base 붉지 which joined to the negative verb 아니호오, gives us 붉지 아니 호오. But the 아니 and the 호오 may contract into 안소; the 지 and the 안 into 잔 and we have then 붉잔소 as the negative of the verb 붉소 (*to be bright*).

In like manner from any verb, a negative verb may be formed, which in turn, may be carried through the whole basal conjugation. In forming a negative from the negative base, with 못 ㅎ오, from the nature of the case, contractions cannot occur.

### NEGATIVES.

| | | | | |
|---|---|---|---|---|
| 됴소, | To be good, | 됴치 아니ㅎ오 | or | 됴찬소. |
| 먹소, | To eat, | 먹지 아니ㅎ오 | ,, | 먹잔소. |
| 주오, | To give, | 주지 아니ㅎ오 | ,, | 주잔소. |
| 든니오, | To walk, | 든니지 아니ㅎ오 | ,, | 든니잔소. |
| 성가스럽스, | To be bothersome, | 성가스럽지 아니ㅎ오 | ,, | 성가스럽잔소. |
| 죽스, | To die, | 죽지 아니ㅎ오 | ,, | 죽잔소. |

208.—The negative verb 마오 (*to avoid*) is much more used in Korean than its corresponding word in English. For the most part, it is found in commands, entreaties, exhortations *not* to do something. Like the other negative verbs, it is preceded by the negative base of the verb expressing the action to be avoided.

술 먹지 마오.　　　　Do not take wine.
작란 ㅎ지 마오.　　　 Do not play.
눔 의게 해로온 일을 마오. Avoid injury to others.

209.—Certain verbs have corresponding negative forms, such as, *to want*, and, *to refuse; to know* and *to be ignorant of*; and, where these exist, they are of course used in preference to the negative form that might be derived in the manner described above.

For example :—

됴화ㅎ오. To like.　　　슬희여ㅎ오 To dislike.
아오 ...... To know.　　 모라오 ...... To be ignorant of.
크오 ...... To be big.　　 적소 ......... To be small.
놉소 ...... To be high.　　 눗소 ......... To be low.

잇소 ...... To exist.　|　업소 ......... To be lacking.
먹소 ...... To eat.　|　굼소 ......... To fast.

## AUXILIARY VERBS.

**210.**—There are a number of verbs in Korean, which joining themselves to other verbs or parts of verbs, give not so much a double sense to the new verb thus formed, but a new sense, derived from the union of the two. These verbs have been termed *auxiliary* verbs, and while the term, thus used, does not signify the same as when used in most grammars, we see no reason to make a change.

Many of the verbs thus used as auxiliaries retain their original meaning throughout, and as a rule, a careful study of the auxiliary, and the form of the verb with which it is used will give an accurate understanding of the joint meaning of the two as used together.

In their use, we find that they are joined sometimes, to the verbal participles, sometimes, directly to one or other of the simple tenses, sometimes another particle is interposed, and sometimes they are joined to the relative participle. One and the same verb, may act as auxiliary in all these ways. The greater number, however, are joined to the verbal participles.

**211.**—The following is a list of the most common, divided into classes, according to their method of uniting with the verb :—

1st. Those united to the verbal participle :—

| | | | |
|---|---|---|---|
| 잇소 ............ | To be. | 되오 ............ | To become. |
| 오오 ............ | To come. | 두오 ............ | To leave. |
| 가오 ............ | To go. | 지오 ............ | To grow. |
| 보오 ............ | To see. | 주오 ............ | To give. |
| 족ᄒᆞ오 preceded by ㅁ, | To be worthy. | ᄒᆞ오 ............ | To do. |

# THE VERB.

2nd. Joined to verbal tenses :—

보오, *connected by* 나. (to see).

3rd. Joined to relative participles :—

보오, *connected by* 가, (to see).
십소, *connected by* 가, (to want).

4th. Joined to the stem :—

잇소, *connected by* 고, (to be).
십소, *connected by* 고, (to want).
스럽소, (to be worthy of).
넉이오, (to regard as).

These are but a few of the auxiliaries in common use; and, as has already been said, an exact rendering of them, with the connecting particles and the verb they join, will always give the meaning to be conveyed. A few words, however, about some of them will illustrate this and aid the student.

**212.**—오오, 가오, and 지오. The first two verbs are affixed to verbal participles, and mark the movement, *here* or *there*, as the case may be. 가오 is also affixed to neuter verbs, signifying that the state expressed by the neuter verb is gradually and constantly increasing; and 지오 has this same sense. These verbs then, correspond to what in Latin are known as "*Inceptives.*"

느리오 To lower,    느려오오 To come down,    느려가오 To go down.
오르오 To raise,    올나오오 To come up,    올나가오 To go up.
　붉소 To be bright.    붉아가오 To grow bright.
　검소 To be black.    검어지오 To grow black.
　늙소 To be old,    늙어가오 To grow old.

**213.**—보오 (*to see*) may be found used as an auxiliary, united either with a verbal participle, or with a relative participle, or with a simple tense.

1st. United with a verbal participle; no connective is needed, and the verb 보오 generally then has the sense of, *to try*. But, at times, it and the verb for which it acts as an auxiliary, may be rendered into English by one word.

먹어보오, " Eating try " *to taste*.
무러보오, " Asking see " *to inquire*.
비혀보오, " Cutting try " *to try to cut*.

214.—2nd. United with the relative participles, or with a simple tense, with 가 and 나 respectively as connectives, it signifies *probability, likelihood*. This sense comes naturally from a literal translation, and 간가보오, lit. " *Gone looks*," means " *It looks as though he has gone*," or " *He has probably gone*" Again 비오겟나보오, lit. " *Rain will come though it looks*," means " *It looks as though rain will come*," or " *It will probably rain*."

| | |
|---|---|
| 오놀은 써나는 가 보오. | He probably starts to-day. |
| 셔울셔 왓는 가 보오. | He has probably come from Seoul. |
| 리일은 먹겟는 가 보오. | He will probably eat it to-morrow. |
| 녀롬에 비가 만히 오니 풍년 되겟나 보오 | As there is a good deal of rain this summer, it will probably be a year of plenty. |
| 셕탄이 적으니 불이 써지겟나 보오. | As there is but a little coal the fire will probably go out. |
| 안경 쓰면 그 칙을 보겟나 보오. | If you put on your glasses you can probably read that book. |

**215.**—죽ㅎ오 preceded by ㅁ, is united with the verbal participle, past or future, and signifies, *to be worthy of*—.

This was the original and true meaning of the word, but we find it to-day, used also in the sense of *possibility*, and even *probability*.

Note.—The auxiliary, here used giving what we might call a future sense to the verb with which it is used, may be employed interchangeably with the future or past participle, though the past is the more frequent.

| | |
|---|---|
| 그 음식 몬든 것은 미우 먹암죽 ㅎ오. | That food that has been prepared is tempting. |
| 윤셔방의 동산에 잇는 꼿은 참 보암죽 ㅎ오. | The flowers in Mr. Yun's garden are worth seeing. |

**216.**—스럽소. This auxiliary also has the meaning of "*to be worthy of*"; and is joined with the verbal noun, or any abstract noun. It may also be joined to the preceding auxiliary, replacing ㅎ오. When so used the meaning is unchanged.

| | |
|---|---|
| 오셔방이 사랑 스럽소. | Mr. Oh is a lovable man. |
| 그 병뎡은 미우 소용 스럽소. | That soldier is quite active. |
| 열두시 동안이면 그만치 멀니 감죽 스럽소. | He ought to go that far if he has twelve hours. |
| 오늘은 비가 옴죽 스럽소. | It looks as though it will rain to day. |
| 뛰염죽 스럽소. | He looks as though he could jump. |

## THE VERB.

**217.**—십소 This word may be used either with the verbal stem, or with the relative participle.

    1st. Used with the verbal stem, 고 is interposed as a connective, and 고십소 may then be rendered into English by "*I want to*" "*I desire to.*"

        가고 십소.   To want to go.
        자고 십소.   To want to sleep.
        먹고 십소.   To want to eat.

    2nd. Used with the Relative Participle, 가 or 듯 or 又, must be interposed as a connective.

So used 십소 indicates strong probability, and shows that while the subject of the verb, does not know for a certainty, yet he has strong reason to believe, that the action or state contained in the verb to which 십소 acts as an auxiliary, is a fact.

| | |
|---|---|
| 몸이 대단이 압하 못살 듯 십소. | I am in great pain and probably can not live. |
| 로형이 오지 못홀가 십소. | You will most probably not come. |
| 집이 잘 못 될듯 십소. | I do not think the house will be a good one. |
| 틱일은 갈듯 십소. | I shall probably go tomorrow. |

**218.**—주오 (*to give*) used as an auxiliary, gives the sense of *doing for another*, either as a favor, or in rendering aid. It may often be rendered into English by *let, have, make, get.*

| | |
|---|---|
| 공부 잘 ᄒ게 ᄒ여 주오. | Make it so that I can study well. |
| 병을 곳쳐 주오. | Cure the disease for me. |
| 이 칙을 밧고아 주오. | Change this book for me. |
| 붓 ᄒ나 사 주오. | Buy a pencil for me. |

## THE VERB. 173

**219.**—되오 (*to become*). This auxiliary is seldom used except with the future verbal participle. Used with active verbs it signifies that *circumstances are in a position for the carrying out of the action contained in the verb with which it is used.*

| | |
|---|---|
| 음식이 먹게 되오. | The food is ready for eating. |
| 병이 죽게 되오. | The disease is unto death. |
| 그 사롬이 가게 되오. | That man is so that he can go. |

**220.**—Further modifications of the verb, expressing *probability, possibility, pretension, duty,* etc., are formed by the use of the relative participles qualifying nouns such as 듯 (*reason*), 것 (*thing*), 일 (*work*), 테 (*manner*), together with 호오, 잇소 or 이오. These have come into so general a use, that they have been regarded almost as new verbs. They can, like any other verbs, be carried through the whole conjugation, after the basal form given above. A thorough understanding, however, of the use of each word is sufficient, though in all these we must not forget the distinctive meanings of 호오, 잇소, and 이오.

These three verbs are more used than any others in the changing and modifying of other verbs and in the making of new verbs from nouns, etc.

호오 has the sense of *to do, to make* and is joined to a number of nouns and adjectives which of course then become corresponding verbs. It may at times have the sense of the English *to have*. Its negative will be 아니호오, or 안소, or 못호오.

잇소 which has been commonly considered the equivalent of the English *to be,* has truly the idea of *to exist;*

and may often be rendered by the English *to have, to dwell, to live, to be in*, etc. It is, then, only equivalent to to the "*to be*" of English where it predicates the existence or presence of its subject. Its negative is 업소 *to be lacking*, to be not present, to be non-existent.

이오, on the other hand, predicates something other than "existence" or "presence" of its subject, and is not used independently. It always has another noun or pronoun with it as a predicate and may be rendered by some form of to be, though it can never stand as the equivalent of *to have, to dwell, to live*, or *to be in*. Its negative is 아니오. It is often contracted into 요 and 오.

Examples of the distinctive use of these two will be found in Part II. Chapter I. § I. 1 and 2.

These distinctions must never be lost sight of; it would not only be extremely inelegant to use one where the other ought to be employed, but in the eyes of the Korean, very ludicrous. In not a few cases also a wrong impression would be given.

221.—The following list of the nouns most commonly so used will explain this.

수 (*means*) with 잇소......... ⎫ All signify *ability*.
만 (*ability*) ,, 호오......... ⎬ Rendered into English by
법 (*law*) ,, 잇소......... ⎭ *can, could*, etc.

수 (*means*) with 업소......... ⎫ Signify *inability*. Rendered into English by
만 (*ability*) ,, 못호오...... ⎬ *cannot, could not*, etc.
법 (*law*) ,, 업소......... ⎭

것 (*thing*) ⎫
터 (*place*) ⎬ with 이오  { Signify *duty*. Rendered into English *should ought* etc.
일 (*work*) ⎭

| | | |
|---|---|---|
| 것 (thing)<br>터 (place)<br>일 (work) | with 아니오... | Signify simply that the obligation *does not exist*.\* |
| 것 (thing)<br>일 (work) | with 업소...... | Signifies simply *there is no reason to*. |
| 번 (time) with 호오............ | | Signifies *to be on the point of to just miss*. |
| 테 (semblance) with 호오...... | | Signifies *pretense* and may be rendered into English by, *to pretend, to feign*. |
| 모양 (manner) with 이오...... | | Signifies *appearance*, and may be rendered by, *it seems, it appears*. |
| 듯<br>듯 } with 호오 or 십소......... | | Signify *probability*. |
| 분<br>샤룸 } with 이오 ............... | | These two in use, are exclusive, and may be rendered into English, by, *it is only*. |
| 것 (thing)<br>줄 (affair) | with accus. postpos. and 아오. | Signify certain knowledge. |
| 것 (thing)<br>줄 (affair) | with instru. postpos. and 아오......... | Signify something not known for a fact, but simply an opinion. |

**222.**—A few words on the most important of these, with illustrations of their uses are necessary.

수, 만, and 법 are for the most part, used with the future rel. part. of the verb, to signify *ability*, or *inability*, and a past is generally rendered by the past tense of 호오, or 업소.

*Note.*—The 만 often has the effect of the English terminative, *able* after a verb or noun, meaning *suitable for, fit, worthy of* etc.

---

\* Note.—These cannot then be renered into English by *ought not* and *should not*, which can only be rendered by the negation of the verb which these auxiliaries accompany. For instance—갈것아니오 does not mean "*I should not go*," but that "*I am under* no obligation to go." On the other hand, 아니 갈거 시오 "*I ought not to go.*"

돈이 적은죽 물 살수 업소. As I am short of money I can not buy a horse.
됴회가 업스니 편지 쓸수 업소. As I have no paper, I can not write a letter.
그 글주가 큰죽 볼수잇소. As those characters are large I can see them.
이붓슨 쓸만 호오. I can use this pen.
그 칙이 볼만 호오. That is a readable book.
어제 써낫시니 맛날수 업섯소. As he left yesterday I was not able to meet him.
아써 노래는 드롤만 호엿소. That song of a little while ago, was worth hearing.
비 아니면 바다를 건널 법이 업소. If one does not have a boat, he can not cross the sea.
약이 잇섯더면 그 병을 곳칠 법이 잇섯소. If I had had some medicine I could have cured that disease.

223.—것, 터, and 일, when used to signify *duty*, are generally preceded by the future participle in ㄹ and can be rendered by "*ought to,*" or *should*." The past sense is, strange to say, generally expressed by the use of the past of 잇소, These same auxiliary nouns, preceded by the future past participle, give us the English "*ought to have,*" of strong conviction."

그 칙 내가 볼 거시오. I ought to read that book.
티월에 내가 숑도로 갈 거시오. I ought to go Song Do next month.
그 하인은 진실 홀러히오. That servant ought to be honest.
편지는 로형이 쓸일이오. You ought to write the letter.

| | |
|---|---|
| 비가 어제 졔물포 왓실 거시오. | The boat must have reached Chemulpo yesterday. |
| 열두 시 지낫시니 그 사롬이 갓실 터히오. | As it is past twelve that man must have gone. |
| 어제 부즈런이 ᄒᆞ엿더면 다 되엿실 일이오. | If you had been energetic it would have been finishded yesterday. |

224.—번, This word with ᄒᆞ오 preceded by a future participle, signifies to be on the *point of, to just miss, to almost accomplish* the act of the principal verb.

| | |
|---|---|
| 도적 맛나 죽을번 ᄒᆞ엿소. | I met with thieves and came near losing my life. |
| 가다가 돌에서 너머 질번 ᄒᆞ엿소. | As I was going I almost fell over a stone. |

225.—모양 (*appearance*) may be used with any one of the relative participles and may be rendered into English by "*it appears,*" or "*it seems as though,*" with a present, past, or future verb, as the case may be.

This is sometimes shortened to simple 양 gives us such forms as 흘양으로, or ᄒᆞ량으로; 흘양이면 or ᄒᆞ량이면.

| | |
|---|---|
| 지금 글닑는 모양 이오. | He seems to be reading now. |
| 아쌔 간 모양 이오. | He seems to have gone some little while ago. |
| 릭일 비가 쏘 올 모양 이오. | It seems as though it will rain again to morrow. |
| 그런 험혼 산을 가려훌 양이면 총을 가지고 가거라. | If you should intend to go to such a wild mountain take a gun with you. |

## THE VERB.

| | |
|---|---|
| 쳥국을 유람 ᄒᆞ랴이면 쇼개 편지를 몃쟝 엇 는것이 미우 됴소. | If you should travel in China it would be very well to get several letters of introduction. |
| 미국을 가랴으로 빙표을 엇겟소. | I am going to get a passport as I intend to go to America. |
| 그사뤂이 빗 밧드랴으로 시비 ᄒᆞ오. | He is quarrelling about getting money owed to him. |

듯 and 둣 with ᄒᆞ오 may be used with any one of the relative participles, giving us the sense of *probability*. They may be rendered into English, by adverb *probably*, with a present, future, past, or future-past tense, as the case may be.

| | |
|---|---|
| 지금 쟈는 둣 ᄒᆞ오. | He is probably sleeping now. |
| 발셔 갓실 둣 ᄒᆞ오. | He will probably have gone already. |
| 쟝ᄎᆞ 올 둣 ᄒᆞ오. | He will probably come soon. |

**226.**—The relative participle is also used with certain other words which have an adverbial force, such as 째, 젹, (*time*); 수이, or 시 (*space*); etc., to signify *When, while,* and the like.

| | |
|---|---|
| 편지 쓸 째 손님이 와소. | While I was writing a visitor came. |
| 셔울 잇셧실 째 그 사뤂과 친ᄒᆞ엿소. | While I was living in Seoul I was quite friendly with that man. |

| | |
|---|---|
| 미국 갈 째 훈가지로 가겟소. | When you go to America I will go with you. |
| 칙 볼 적에 써드지 마오. | Do not make a noise while I am reading. |
| 부산 갓실 적에 붓슬 사왓소. | When I went to Fusan I bought the pencils. |
| 공부 훌 적에 쓸 됴희오. | It is paper to be used when studying. |
| 밥 먹을 스이 침방에 도적이 드러왓소. | While we were eating, a thief came into the bed room. |

227.—슈록 and 도록. These two particles as words are often wrongly interchanged. Their distinctive use should always be observed.

슈록 is used with the Future Relative Participle and has the sense of *the more—the more*. It may sometimes be followed by 더욱 adding emphasis.

도록 on the other hand has simply the sense of *up to the point of, up to the completion of, until*, signifying the full attainment of the action of the principle verb. From the Korean standpoint there is but little of a temporal sense in 도록 though we commonly translate it by *until*. It often gives the sense of purpose.

| | |
|---|---|
| 바람이 불 슈록 불이 너러 나오. | The more the wind blows the greater the fire. |
| 됴흔 노래눈 드룰 슈록 듯고 십소. | The more good songs I hear the more I want to hear. |
| 한문은 비훌 슈록 어려워 가오. | The more you study the Chinese character the more difficult it is. |

됴혼 수업은 홀수록 명예가 놉하지는 것이오.  The more you work at a good profession the higher will be your reputation.

그병인이 낫도록 의수는 여긔 잇슬 터히오.  The doctor must stay here till that patient is better.

내가 알도록 셜명하여 주시오.  Explain it to me until I understand it.

내가 오도록 너는 여긔 잇셔라.  Wait here till I come.

더못된 사람은 놈을 망하도록 훈수하야셔 치게 하엿소.  The villain by directing others to their own undoing caused them to be whipped.

불이 죽지 안토록 셕탄을 너어라.  Put coal on so that the fire may not go out.

## The Verb in Indirect Discourse.

**228.**—The verb, *to say, to speak,* is formed from 말 (*speech*) and 하오 (*to make*) but in telling what another has said, both of these words are not commonly used. The 말 is generally dropped, and 하오 alone employed; but joined to the verb, signifying the word spoken, by the conjunction 고. This form however, is only used with tenses of the indicative, ending in 아 when the termination is still retained and 고.하오, simply affixed. In the affirmative, forms, the distinction between the inferior, and superior is almost lost sight of, this distinction being plainly shown by the termination of the 하오 signifying *to say.* Quite often the 고 is elided and then contractions almost unlimited, may follow.

| | |
|---|---|
| 집은 밋하 짓는다고 ᄒᆞ오. | He says that he has contracted to build the house. |
| 이 약을 먹은 후에 효험이 잇섯다고 ᄒᆞ엿소. | He said that after taking this medicine the effect was good. |
| 쉬이 오겟다고 ᄒᆞᆸ더이다. | He said he would come soon. |
| 가겟다고 ᄒᆞ엿것 마는 아니 갓소. | He said he would go but he did not. |

**229.**—By the use of this rule for indirect discourse, an imperative verb has been formed. The low form of the termination of the volitive mood, second person, has been contracted into 라 and 라고ᄒᆞ오 gives us the imperative verb "*to command to*," *to order to*." Here also the 고 may be dropped giving us 라ᄒᆞ오 which may be contracted into 래오.

| | |
|---|---|
| 이 붓ᄎᆡ는 김서방을 주라고 ᄒᆞ오. | Order him to give this fan to Mr. Kim. |
| 평양 갈 ᄯᅢ에 집 잘 보라고 ᄒᆞ엿소. | He ordered his house to be well watched while he was gone to Pyeng Yang. |
| 화덕에 셕탄을 너흐래오. | Tell him to put some coal in the stove. |
| 이 상 못 쓰겟시니 다시 곳치래오. | As this table will not do tell him to make it over again. |

### CONTRACTED AND ELLIPTICAL FORMS.

**230.**—Having seen from the very beginning, the Korean's desire to shorten every thing as much as possible and to use as few words as absence of ambiguity will allow; we are prepared to find that, with a verb that can undergo such changes, and employ such auxiliaries (for in fact almost everything in the whole language can be made to serve the verb), there will be various and numerous contractions and ellipses that have lost almost all resemblance to that from which they have been contracted.

We are also prepared to find that there are idioms p'irases and *bon mots* not to be comprehended at first sight. A careful study of all these should be made.

While no attempt can be made here to give all these contractions, etc. a few words concerning some of the most common will enable the student to see their method of formation, and hereafter to analyze them for himself.

231.—In the following list a few of these are described and their use explained.

The Koreans are very prone to the use of contrasts, and owing to this fact, we find a number of elliptical phrases and contractions arising from the use of the verb 마오 (*to avoid*) in connection with other verbs, active or neuter,.

Various conjunctions are employed and decide the special meaning to be given. Other contractions, etc., are made from the use of other words and conjunctions; and, for the sake of reference to the examples and illustrations given below, we have marked them (*a*), (*b*), (*c*), etc.

(*a*) Forms arising from the use of the conjunction 지 (*whether*), and 마오 (*to avoid*).

Various forms with these two words are derived by the use of the present, past, or future relative participles. They all give us an idea of doubt as to result. With a present participle, it generally signifies that the action expressed by the principal verb, while continuing, and at the time progressing, is progressing, in such a way, that the desired result will not be obtained, or will be obtained to so slight an extent as to be useless.

With a past participle, it conveys the idea, that while the action is completed, the result is such, that it might equally well, have been left undone. With a future participle, it implies, not so much a doubt as to the result, as to what it will be. With 호오, the forms will be :—

> 호논지 마논지.
> 혼지 만지.
> 홀지 말지.

They may or may not be followed by 호오, with no change. That which is here left to be understood is some form or part of the verb 又호오, *to be the same.*

232.—(*b.*) The conjunctions 니 or 고, used with 마오.

Either of these conjunctions affixed to the verbal stem, of the principal verb of the sentence, and immediately followed by the verbal stem of 마오 with the same conjunction, gives the idea of *positive certainty, beyond the shadow of a doubt,* as to the carrying out of the action, or the existence of the state, expressed by the principal verb. The idea seems to be that the state or act being certain, needs no comment and is beyond question.

We have then the forms :—

> 호 니 마 니*⎱ "I will certainly do it."
> 호 고 말 고 ⎰ "Of course I will do it ; "
> (There need be no question about it).

---

\* Note.—The conjunction 니 beginning with ㄴ. when affixed to the verbal stem 마오 which ends in ㄹ, according to the rule already given causes the ㄹ to be dropped, and 말니 become 마니.

놉 고 말 고 "It is undoubtedly high."
(There is no question about its height).

**233.**—(c.) The interrogative particle 가 with 마오.

The particle 가, affixed to the principal verb, and immediately followed by the same form of 마오 with 가, is largely used in soliloquies, and, as will be seen at a glance, implies indecision on the part of the speaker, as to whether the action or state of the principal verb is worth while. It is joined to the Relative Participle and with the Present and Past asserts that the action being carried on or completed is useless ; with the Future that the subject of the verb is undecided as to whether to carry it out or not. It may or may not precede a form of the verb 호오. When it does not precede 호오 it is almost entirely restricted to soliloquies.

호 는 가 마 는 가
혼 가      만 가
홀 가      말 가

**234.**—(d.) The particle 동 used with 마오.

Various forms of the verb are derived from the use of this particle, with a present, past, or future relative participle. At times these forms are used interchangeably with those derived from the conjunction 지 (*whether*), given above ¶ 231. The distinction between the two is, that where 지 expresses doubt, 동 expresses an entire lack of concern or interest, in the result. It may or may not precede an accompanying verb, or a form of 호오.

When 호오 is used, some part of the verb 못호오 (*to be the same*), is understood. With a past participle, it gives the idea of the entire failure of the object. With 호오, the forms are :—

# THE VERB.

ㅎ 는 동   마 는 동
혼 동        만 동
홀 동        말 동

**235.**—(*e.*) Forms resulting from combinations of 나 with 마오.

This form with 호오 is, 홀나 말나 호오, and 나 has been regarded by some, as a separate particle or conjunction, used with the future relative participle. It implies lack of interest or relish of the subject of the principal verb, in the action. He *does a little and stops a little*. It is rather a contraction of the desiderative forms of the principal verb, and 마오, with the adverbial conjunction 다가 which it will be remembered gives the idea of interruption. The full form with 호오 then is:—

호랴 호다가 말냐 호다가, and gives the idea that, at first he did as though he intended to work, and then as though he intended not to work.

The contraction arises, first, by dropping the 호다, and 호랴다가 becomes from euphony 홀냐.

Note.—The ㄴ, following the ㄹ, is but the Korean methods of doubling ㄹ.

**236.**—(*f.*) The form in 고지고.

A much used form of the verb, is derived by affixing 고지고 to the verbal stem. It gives us then the idea of something much desired or longed for, and may be translated by, " would that—," " oh! that—."

**237.**—(*g.*) Exclamation in 나.

An exclamation expressive of fear or danger, and calling out to the one addressed to take care, is derived from the use of the future participle with 나. It may be or may not be followed by some such verb as, to take care. The *idea*, however, of calling upon the party addressed to be careful is always present.

As:—

너머질나, " You will fall ! "

The same form may be used with the verb 보오. (*to see*) implying strong probability.

238.—(*h*). The desiderative form in 라, is we find often changed in the same manner as was seen above under (*e.*), and ᆞ흐라 may become 흘나, and 흐라고 흘나고. Such a form as this, must then be rendered in the same way as the simple desiderative. From this form with the verb 이오 (*to be*), is derived the phrase in 나고요, which for convenience we may then consider formed from the future participle. It may be translated, by, " Do you think that "—" Do you for a moment suppose that—," and signifies a positive negation.

239.—(*i*). The form in 너니.

The phrase derived from the use of the future participle with this, gives the equivalent of the English potential past perfect, with a disjunctive or concessive force. It may, be translated by " would have, but—" " should have, but—" etc.

The full phrase would be.

흘 일 일 너 니.

which is the future relative participle qualifying 일 (*work*), which is the subject of the irregular form of the progressive tense of the verb 이오 (*to be*), to which has been affixed the conjunction 니.

**240.**—(*j.*) The last of these contractions of which we shall speak, are derived from the desiderative base. They are 흐렴, 흐려무냐, and 흐렴 다고냐. They are all used in commands where the person commanding is enraged at the neglect of a former order or well known duty. 흐렴 is a contraction of the colloquial 흐려 (*do you intend to*) and 무엇 (*what*), with some such phrase as "are you doing?" etc., understood. It may be translated by "Do you intend to—" "Why don't you?" etc., 흐려무냐 is a less complete contraction of the same form.

흐렴다고냐 is contraction of.
흐려 무엇 흐다 고냐.
or "*Do you intend to? Why what are you doing.?*"

This last is much stronger than either of the other two, and extremely colloquial. It may be rendered into English by some such phrase as "Why on earth don't you?" "Why under the sun don't you?" All these three phrases are expressive of irritation, annoyance, anger.

**241.**—The following sentences will illustrate these forms, and while the above are not by any means all that might be given, it is hoped that they are sufficient to give the student an insight into them and enable him to make further investigations for himself.

(*a*)

| | |
|---|---|
| 목슈가 돈이 젹다고 일을 흐는지 마는지 흐고 가오. | The carpenter complains that the compensation is small, and is doing his work so that it will be useless. |

| | |
|---|---|
| 졍신 업는 이의게 말을 혼즉 알아 듯는지 마는지 ᄒᆞ옵더이다. | As he told it to a man who had no brains he doubts whether he understood. |
| 오놀은 손님이 만히 와셔 공부를 조꼼 ᄒᆞ엿시니 혼지 만지 ᄒᆞ오. | As we have studied so litttle to-day on account of so many callers, we might as well not have studied at all. |
| 비가 젹게 왓시니 온지 만지 ᄒᆞ오. | As so little rain came, it is of no account. |
| 쟝ᄉᆞ를 혼즉 농ᄉᆞ는 홀지 말지 ᄒᆞ오. | As I have been a merchant, it is doubtful whether I can farm. |

(b)

| | |
|---|---|
| 리가 만ᄒᆞ면 ᄒᆞ니 마니 ᄒᆞ겟소. | If there is plenty of profit, I will certainly do it. |
| 열량 줄 쳑을 스무량을 주엇시니 잘 못 사니 마니. | As you have given twenty nyang for a ten nyang book, you certainly have not bought well. |
| ᄋᆞ희가 어룬의게 욕 ᄒᆞ엿시니 잘 못ᄒᆞ고 말고 말 홀것 업소. | As it was a boy who insulted a man he certainly did wrong; and nothing more need be said about it. |
| 잇흘을 굴멋시니 먹는 거시 됴코 말고. | As I have been fasting for two days, it is certainly good to eat (again). |

(c)

| | |
|---|---|
| 이강은 너무 쟉어셔 션유를 ᄒᆞ는가 마는가 ᄒᆞ오. | This river is too small we can have no pleasure boating here. |

그런 큰소리 가온디는 쟉 은 소릭는 ᄒ는가 마는 가ᄒ오. — In the midst of such a noise a low voice is useless.

이러ᄒᆞᆫ 일은 ᄒᆞᆫ가 만가ᄒᆞ곤. — Why! such work as this is useless.

내말은 ᄒᆞᆫ가 만가ᄒᆞ곤. — Why! What I said is useless.

공부를 ᄒᆞᆫ즉 칙 번역을 ᄒᆞᆯ가 말가 성각 ᄒᆞ오. — As I am studying I am thinking whether to translate the book or not

죠션에 잇스면 ᄒᆞᆯ 일이 만코 미국 가면 불일 젹은즉 갈가 말가 ᄒᆞ오. — As there is plenty of work in Korea, and not much to do in America, I do not know whether to go or not.

이 하인이 일은 잘 ᄒᆞ여도 밀은 잘 아니 드른즉 보낼가 말가? — Though this servant works well, as he does not attend to what is said, shall I discharge him or not?

(d)

올 히는 집 곳치는 일을 ᄒᆞᆯ동 말동 ᄒᆞ오. — I do not care whether I repair the house this year or not.

오늘 비가 만히 온즉 김셔 방이 올동 말동 ᄒᆞ오. — As it is raining hard I doubt whether Mr. Kim will come to-day.

이번 쟝ᄉᆞ에는 리 ᄒᆞᆫ 푼 업시니 ᄒᆞᆫ동 만동 ᄒᆞ오. — As I have not made a penny by this transaction, I might just as well not have done it.

오늘 아ᄎᆞᆷ은 조곰 먹엇 시니 먹은동 만동 ᄒᆞ오. — As I ate only a little this morning it is as though I had eaten noting.

돈이 적어 장ᄉᆞ를 크게 못 ᄒᆞᆯ즉 ᄒᆞ는동 마는동 ᄒᆞ오.   I do not care whether I engage in business or not, as I have but a little money and cannot do so on a large scale.

어제 밤에 일이 만하 반시 동안을 잣더니 잔동 만동 ᄒᆞ오.   As on account of the press of work I only slept for half an hour last night, I mights as well not have slept at all.

(e)

이ᄉᆞ이 몸이 압하 일을 홀낙 말낙 ᄒᆞ오.   Lately on account of pain I work a little and stop a little.
음식이 비위에 합지 아니 ᄒᆞ즉 먹을낙 말낙 ᄒᆞ오.   As the food does not suit I eat without relish.

(f)

그 일을 어셔 ᄒᆞ고 지고.   Would that we could do that work quickly.
병이 급ᄒᆞ니 의원을 급히 보고지고.   As the disease is pressing, would that I could see the doctor soon.

(g)

일을 잘 못 ᄒᆞᆯ나 조심ᄒᆞ여라.   You will not do it well; take care.
가시 목에 걸닐나.   A bone will stick in your throat! Be careful.
목슈가 ᄂᆡ일은 일 ᄒᆞᆯ가 보오.   The carpenter will probably work to-morrow.
약을 만히 먹어도 병이 더ᄒᆞ니 죽을가보오.   Even though I have taken lots of medicine, as the disease is worse I will probably die.

# THE VERB.

(h)

| | |
|---|---|
| 그 거슨 잇다가 훌나고 성각 ᄒ엿소. | I intended to do that later. |
| 이 거슨 너 줄나고 사왓다. | I bought this to give to you. |
| 어제 아니 혼다고 ᄒ엿시니 오ᄂᆞᆯ은 훌 나고요. | When he said he would not do it yesterday, do you think he will do it to-day. |
| 물에 드러 가면 죽을나 고요. | Do you think I want to go into the water and drown? |

(i)

| | |
|---|---|
| 이 일을 잘 훌너니 돈이 부죡ᄒᆞ야 잘 못ᄒ엿소. | I would have done this well, but there was not enough money and I could not. |
| 내 죽을너니 명의를 맛나 살앗소. | I should have died had I not met a renowned doctor who healed me. |

(j)

| | |
|---|---|
| 그ᄉᆞ이 작란 만히 ᄒ엿시니 지금은 공부 좀 ᄒ렴. | As you have played a good while now, do you not intend to study a little? |
| 셔울 가겟시니 교군군을 부르렴. | As I am going to Seoul, why have you not called coolies? |
| 그러케 아니 되거든 이러케 ᄒ려무나. | If it will not do that way, do it this way. |
| 물이 먹기 슬커든 차를 먹으려무나. | If you will not drink water, why do you not take tea? |
| 니져ᄇᆞ리거든 잣고 성각 ᄒ려무나. | If you have forgotten why on earth do you not try and think of it? |
| 일 ᄒ기 슬커든 가려무나. | If you will not work why under the sun do you not go? |

192 THE VERB.

**242.**—The principal parts of some of the verbs most commonly used are given below.

| | Present Indicative. | Past Verbal Part. | Future Verbal Part. | Past Rel. Part. |
|---|---|---|---|---|
| To sit | 안소 | 안자 | 안게 | 안존 |
| To put up | 언소 | 언져 | 언게 | 언존 |
| To be lacking | 업소 | 업서 | 업게 | 업슨 |
| To be | 잇소 | 잇서 | 잇게 | 잇슨 |
| To fit | 맛소 | 마자 | 맛게 | 마존 |
| To complete | 못소 | 못차 | 못게 | 못촌 |
| To forget | 닛소 | 니져 | 닛게 | 니존 |
| To take off | 벗소 | 버서 | 벗게 | 버슨 |
| To wash | 씻소 | 씻서 | 씻게 | 씻슨 |
| To be frequent | 잣소 | 자자 | 잣게 | 자존 |
| To be wet | 젓소 | 져저 | 젓게 | 젓존 |
| To follow after | 좃소 | 좃차 | 좃게 | 좃촌 |
| To drive | 쫏소 | 쫏차 | 쫏게 | 쫏촌 |
| To look for To find | } 찻소 | 차자 | 찻게 | 차존 |
| To be disgusting | 아니꼽소 | 아니꼬와 | 아니꼽게 | 아니꼬온 |
| To be beautiful | 아룸답소 | 아룸다와 | 아룸답게 | 아룸다온 |
| To itch | 가렵소 | 가려워 | 가렵게 | 가려온 |
| To be light | 가븨압소 | 가븨야워 | 가븨압게 | 가븨야온 |
| To be droll | 가쇼롭소 | 가쇼로워 | 가쇼롭게 | 가쇼로온 |
| To be minute | 쌔다롭소 | 쌔다로워 | 쌔다롭게 | 쌔다로온 |
| To be ticklish | 간지럽소 | 간지러워 | 간지럽게 | 간지러온 |
| To be near | 갓갑소 | 갓가워 | 갓갑게 | 갓가온 |
| To be vexatious | 피롭소 | 피로워 | 피롭게 | 피로온 |
| To be heavy | 무겁소 | 무거워 | 무겁게 | 무거온 |
| To be dirty | 더럽소 | 더러워 | 더럽게 | 더러온 |
| To be repugnant | 증그럽소 | 증그러워 | 증그럽게 | 증그러온 |

## THE VERB.

|  | Present Indicative. | Past Verbal Part. | Future Verbal Part. | Past Rel. Part. |
|---|---|---|---|---|
| To mend | 깁소 | 기워 | 깁게 | 기운 |
| To lie down | 눕소 | 누워 | 눕게 | 누운 |
| To deplore | 셟소 | 셜워 | 셟게 | 셜운 |
| To be hot | 더웁소 | 더워 | 더웁게 | 더운 |
| To be cold | 칩소 | 치워 | 칩게 | 치운 |
| To know | 아오 | 알아 | 알게 | 안 |
| To freeze | 어오 | 얼어 | 얼게 | 언 |
| To open | 여오 | 열어 | 열게 | 연 |
| To draw | 잇그오 | 잇그러 | 잇글게 | 잇근 |
| To be lonely | 외싸오 | 외싸러 | 외쌀게 | 외싼 |
| To be dry | 감으오 | 감으러 | 감을게 | 감은 |
| To hang | 거오 | 거러 | 걸게 | 건 |
| To promenade | 건이오 | 건이러 | 건일게 | 건인 |
| To go afoot | 것소 | 거러 | 것게 | 거른 |
| To be long | 기오 | 기러 | 길게 | 진 |
| To raise | 길드오 | 길드러 | 길들게 | 길든 |
| To avoid | 마오 | 말아 | 말게 | 만 |
| To make | 믄드오 | 믄드라 | 믄들게 | 믄든 |
| To be far | 머오 | 머러 | 멀게 | 먼 |
| To stay | 머므오 | 머므러 | 머믈게 | 머믄 |
| To suck | 싸오 | 빨아 | 쌀게 | 싼 |
| To pray | 비오 | 비러 | 빌게 | 빈 |
| To undo | 푸오 | 푸러 | 풀게 | 푼 |
| To load | 싯소 | 시러 | 싯게 | 시른 |
| To make a noise | 떠드오 | 떠드러 | 떠들게 | 떠든 |
| To lift | 드오 | 드러 | 들게 | 든 |
| To hear | 듯소 | 드러 | 듯게 | 드른 |
| To be round | 둥그오 | 둥그러 | 둥글게 | 둥근 |

# CHAPTER VIII.

## THE ADJECTIVE.

243.—Adjectives have been divided into two general classes, Limiting, and Qualifying. Limiting adjectives under the head of Numerals, and Pronominal Adjectives have already been treated. Qualifying adjectives then, alone remain to be considered here. As has already been said, there are very few Korean words that can be termed true adjectives. Those that exist to-day were originally nouns, and by far the greater part, have been derived from the Chinese. Such adjectives always precede the words they qualify, and of course the rule for the use of Sinico-Korean and pure Korean words holds here also. A Sinico-Korean Adjective must qualify a Sinico-Korean noun, and a pure Korean adjective its corresponding noun.

| | | | |
|---|---|---|---|
| 대, | Great. | 대풍, | A great wind. |
| 쇼, | Little. | 쇼인, | A little man, |
| 빅, | White. | 빅마, | A white horse. |
| 황, | Yellow. | 황금, | Yellow Gold. |
| 샹, | Low. | 샹놈, | A low fellow. |

244.—By far the greater number of so called Korean adjectives are neuter verbs, and the past, or perfect relative participle is commonly used as the adjectival form.

## THE ADJECTIVE.

Used predicatively the verbal from will be employed; used attributively the participial. These neuter verbs can be carried through the whole basal conjugation. When the participial form is used, it precedes the noun qualified; when the verbal, the noun qualified, of course, precedes the adjective. The following list of predicative and attributive forms will illustrate this.

| VERB. | | ADJECTIVE. | |
|---|---|---|---|
| 놉소 | To be high. | 놉흔 | High. |
| ➤소 | To be low. | ᄂ즌 | Low. |
| 칩소 | To be cold | 치운 | Cold. |
| 더웁소 | To be hot. | 더운 | Hot. |
| 올소 | To be right. | 올흔 | Right. |
| 그르오 | To be wrong. | 그른 | Wrong. |
| 갓갑소 | To be near. | 갓가온 | Near. |
| 머오 | To be far. | 먼 | Far. |
| 강ᄒ오 | To be hard. | 강흔 | Hard. |
| 유ᄒ오 | To be soft. | 유흔 | Soft. |
| 닉소 | To be ripe. | 닉은 | Ripe. |
| 셔오 | To be unripe. | 션 | Unripe. |
| 어둡소 | To be dark. | 어두온 | Dark. |
| 붉소 | To be light. | 붉은 | Light. |
| 널소 | To be broad. | 너른 | Broad. |
| 좁소 | To be narrow. | 좁은 | Narrow. |

**245.**—The Korean adjective being thus really a verb, admits of a great variety of forms of expression and a number of distinctions unattainable in English. A thorough knowledge of the verb and its forms with their uses will enable any one at a glance to comprehend all these.

## THE ADJECTIVE.

**246.**—In ¶ 211 ff., on auxiliary verbs, several forms which enter into the composition of adjectives of different significations were mentioned. Among these then mentioned were :—

스럽소 joined to nouns, and signifying, *to be worthy of, to have the nature of.*

죽호오, *to be worthy of, to be well worth*, etc., and joined to past verbal participles by the interposition of ㅁ.

만호오. *To be able*, which joined to the future participle in ㄹ, of active verbs gives us the English adjectives in *able.*

지오, *To grow*, or 가오, *to go*, joined to past verbal participles, gives us inceptive adjectival verbs.

| | | | |
|---|---|---|---|
| 사탕스럽소 | To be amiable, | from 사탕 | Love. |
| 원슈스롭소 | To be hostile | „ 원슈 | An enemy. |
| 보암죽호오 | To be worth seeing | „ 보오 | To see. |
| 먹엄죽호오 | To be worth eating | „ 먹소 | To eat. |
| ᄀᄅ칠만호오 | To be teachable | „ ᄀᄅ치오 | To teach. |
| 옴길만호오 | To be moveable | „ 옴기오 | To move. |
| 다스릴만호오 | To be manageable | „ 다스리오 | To rule. |
| 적어가오 | To grow small | „ 적소 | To be small. |
| 커지오 | To grow large | „ 크오 | To be large. |

**247.**—A certain class of adjectival verbs are formed by adding 스럽 to the verbal stem, using a connective. This is almost restricted to colors and gives the idea of *moderately*, or *somewhat*, corresponding to the English termination *ish*.

## THE ADJECTIVE.

| | | | |
|---|---|---|---|
| 붉소 | To be red | 붉으스럼ᄒᆞ오 | To be reddish. |
| 누르오 | To be yellow | 누릇스럼ᄒᆞ오 | ,, yellowish. |
| 푸르오 | To be blue | 푸릇스럼ᄒᆞ오 | ,, blueish. |
| 검소 | To be black | 검으스럼ᄒᆞ오 | ,, blackish. |
| 희오 | To be white | 희웁스럼ᄒᆞ오 | ,, whitish. |

**248.**—A further modification of adjectival verbs of color, is made by a repetition of the stems with ᄒᆞ오, giving us then, the sense of *to be spotted with*, or to be colored in spots.

| | | | | |
|---|---|---|---|---|
| 붉옷붉옷ᄒᆞ오 | To be spotted with red. | | | |
| 누릇누릇ᄒᆞ오 | ,, | ,, | ,, | yellow. |
| 푸릇푸릇ᄒᆞ오 | ,, | ,, | ,, | blue. |
| 검옷검옷ᄒᆞ오 | ,, | ,, | ,, | black. |

**249.**—As in English so also in Korean, but to a much greater extent, nouns are used as adjectives. With many of these we may suppose the insertion of the postposition 의, but as there is no ambiguity if omitted, it is not used.

| | | |
|---|---|---|
| 죠션 | 사름. | A "Korea man" or a Korean. |
| 쥬방 | 소용. | Kitchen utensils. |
| 녀름 | 옷. | Summer clothes. |
| 화로 | 불. | Hibachi fire. |
| 바다 | 물. | Sea water. |

### COMPARISON OF ADJECTIVES.

**250.**—With reference to Korean comparison of adjectives it may be said, that as in all other things, so also here, unless ambiguity would arise without their use, the particles expressing comparison are omitted. In comparing two things then, the Korean as a rule would not use the comparative but the simple positive.

251.—A comparative degree may be formed by the use of the adverb 더 (*more*) preceding the adjective.

| | |
|---|---|
| 오늘 산 궤가 더 됴소. | The box you bought to-day is better. |
| 이 개가 더 사오납소. | This dog is more savage. |
| 이 사룸이 더 늙엇소. | This man is older. |
| 그 물이 더 잘 가오. | That horse goes better. |

252.—In comparing two things, where both are mentioned 보다, sometimes written 보덤, signifying *than*, is affixed to the noun having the quality in the lesser degree, and the adjective is used positively. The use of 보다 together with 더 and the adjective, unless special emphasis is desired, is not common among Koreans, and should be carefully avoided by foreigners.

| | |
|---|---|
| 이 칙 보다 그 칙이 됴소. | That book is better than this. |
| 화륜션 보다 화륜거가 급히 가오. | The steam-car travels faster than the steam-boat. |
| 돌 빗 보다 히빗치 붉소. | Sunlight is brighter than moonlight. |
| 더운 것 보다 치운 거시 됴소. | Cold is better than heat. |

253.—The postposition 에셔 (*from*) may also be used for 보다 in the sense of *than*, to express a comparative degree.

Note.—The use of 브터 and 브덤 for 보다 is wrong, and should be avoided.

# THE ADJECTIVE. 199

| | |
|---|---|
| 이 먹이 뎌 먹에셔 검소. | This ink is blacker than that. |
| 이 물이 그 물에셔 묽소. | This water is clearer than that. |
| 그 물에셔 이 물이 쎨니 가오. | This horse travels faster than that. |
| 쟉년에 한강뎡즈 에셔 피셔 호엿지만 구미포 가 시원훈걸. | Last year we spent the summer at the summer house at Han Kang but Kumipo is cooler. |

**254.**—The superlative degree is expressed by the use of 뎨일 (*the first*) preceding the adjective. However, as was remarked concerning the comparative, even when comparing several, the simple positive is used where the English would require a superlative. Here then we see with regard to both comparative, and superlative, that great care should be exercised by the student, if he desires to speak true Korean and not an Anglicized imitation of it, to as far as possible do away with their use and employ the simple positive.

| | |
|---|---|
| 이 붓시 여럿 즁에 뎨일 됴쇼. | This is the best of several pens. |
| 이 사롬이 킈 뎨일 크오. | This man is the tallest. |
| 네 시계가 뎨일 바로 간다. | Your watch keeps the best time. |
| 죠희치고는 죠션거시 됴쇼. | Korean paper is the best kind of paper. |
| 나라치고는 으로시아가 크다호오. | Among the countries of the world Russia is the largest. |

# CHAPTER IX.

## THE ADVERB.

255.—Korean adverbs may be classified as to their source, and as to their meaning.

Classified as to their source we have Primitive and Derived.

The Primitive Adverbs are few in number, such as:—

| | | | |
|---|---|---|---|
| 지금 | ......... Now. | 아마 | ......... Perhaps. |
| 아쎄 | ......... A little while ago. | 아조 | ......... Entirely. |
| 쏘...<br>다시 } | ......... Again. | 더 | ............ More. |
| 민우 | ......... Very. | 덜 | ............ Less. |
| 오직<br>만...<br>샨... } | ......... Only. | 웨 | ............ Why. |
| | | 아직 | ......... Yet. |
| 얼마 | ......... How much. | 안<br>못 } | ............ Not. |
| 멋... | ......... How many. | | |

256.—Derived adverbs may be divided into two classes, those derived from verbs, and those derived from nouns or pronouns.

The adverb regularly derived from the verb, may be formed by adding 이 or 히 to the verbal stem.

# THE ADVERB.

In adding 이 to the stem, euphonic modifications naturally take place. Verbs in 흐다 change the 흐다 into 히 or sometimes into 이. Verbs whose stems terminate in ㄹ add 니. All other verbs take the form of the stem with its added or changed consonants as found in the past verbal participle, and add 이.

| | | | |
|---|---|---|---|
| 놉소 | To be lofty. | 놉히 | Loftily. |
| 쳔흐오 | To be base. | 쳔히 | Basely. |
| 귀흐오 | To be rare. | 귀히 | Rarely. |
| 갓갑소 | To be near. | 갓가이 | Near. |
| 머오 | To be far. | 멀니 | Far. |
| 널소 | To be wide. | 널니 | Widely. |
| 밧부오 | To be quick. | 밧비 | Quickly. |
| 젹소 | To be little. | 젹이 | Little. |
| 붉소 | To be bright. | 붉이 | Brightly. |
| 쉽소 | To be easy. | 쉬이 | Easily. |
| 깁소 | To be deep. | 깁히 | Deeply. |

257.—The future verbal participle in 게 or 케 is also largely used adverbially.

| | | | |
|---|---|---|---|
| 다르오 | To be different. | 다르게 | Differently. |
| 됴소 | To be good. | 됴케 | Well. |
| 칩소 | To be cold. | 칩게 | Coldly. |

258.—These two classes of adverbs derived from verbs, have been claimed to be identical in signification, and interchangeable, some verbs preferring the from in 게 and some that in 이. Such, however, is not the case, and the distinction made in the "Grammaire Coreénne" always holds. The form in 이 or 히 is in a sense passive, and indicates the manner, not in the object, but in the subject of the verb. The form in 게 is *active*, and indicates the manner, *not in the subject but in the object*. These should in many cases be rendered more properly into English by an adjective. The following sentences will illustrate this difference.

| | |
|---|---|
| 새로혼 칙을 다르게 호엿소. | I have made the new book somewhat different. |
| 일본 비 엇엇소 달니 홀수 업소. | I have obtained a Japanese boat, I cannot do otherwise. |
| 셔울을 쉬이 가겟소. | I will soon go to Seoul. |

259.—The Korean past verbal participle, may also at imes, be rendered into English by an adverb.

| | | | |
|---|---|---|---|
| 누려, | Downward. | 너머, | Too much. |
| 올녀, | Upward. | 건너, | Beyond. |

260.—Adverbs derived from nouns and pronouns, consist for the most part of a noun or a pronoun with one or more postpositions, used adverbially.

| | | | |
|---|---|---|---|
| 안호로 | ......... Inside. | 아춤에 | ... In the morning. |
| 때에 | ............ When. | 후에 | ...... Afterwards. |
| 절노... 스스로 | ......... Naturally. | 낫제 | ...... At noon. |
| | | 젼에 | ...... Before. |
| 임의로 | ......... Willingly. | 별노 | ...... Particularly. |

261.—Comparison in adverbs as with adjectives is not expressed unless the sense demands it. Ofttimes a simple adverb will be used, where we would use a comparative or a superlative. If needed the same particles will be used with the adverb as with the adjective, and in the same way.

집은 더 잘 지오. Build the house better.
노래 룰 더 됴케 ᄒᆞ오. Sing better.
내 몰이 로형의 몰 보다 My horse goes faster than
급히 가오. yours.
죠션 보다 일본셔 비가 In Japan it rains more fre-
자조 오오. quently than in Korea. .

262.—To the primitive adverbs many of the postpositions may be affixed, giving as a result a signification combining the meanings of adverb and postposition, as:—

어듸 (where)   어듸로 (whither).   어듸셔 (whence).
이리 } (here.)   이리로 } (hither).   이리셔 } (hence).
여긔 }           여긔로 }             여긔셔 }

263.—To the ordinal numerals, may be affixed the postposition 은 giving us a form equivalent to the English numeral adverb.

첫재는 (*As for the first*) = Firstly.
둘재는 (*As for the second*) = Secondly.
뎨일은 (*As for the first*) = Firstly.
뎨이는 (*As for the second*) = Secondly.

264.—A long list of all the adverbs is hardly called for in grammatical notes such as these. From a study of the above rules, if they cannot be formed at will, they can be recognized at sight. Of course in their use, they always precede the word they qualify.

265.—Before we close this chapter, a word or two on Korean responsives seem in place.

네 to a superior, and 오냐 to an inferior, correspond to the English *Yes*; while 아니 올시다 and 아닐다 (*it is not*) correspond to *no*.

These words, however, are not as much used as their English equivalents and as a rule, in answering, the verb of the question is repeated, or some such phrases, as "*I don't know,*" "*I know,*" "*It is not,*" "*It is so*" etc., is used.

266.—With reference to answers to negative questions, the Korean idiom, like the Japanese, is the opposite of the English. In such questions, the English regards the facts as they are, and answers "Yes" or "No." The Korean on the other hand regards the *statement implied in the question*, and answers accordingly. The consequence is that we get our answer the very opposite of what we would expect. For instance, in the question "Has he not come?" the Korean regards the statement "He has not come" which is implied in the question, and if he has not come, answers "Yes," meaning that the statement implied in your question is correct, *he has not come*. But if he has come, he will reply "No," meaning that the statement implied in your question is wrong, that he has not, *not* come, *but has come*. This being so directly opposite to the English idiom should be made a subject of great care, for otherwise serious blunders may be committed.

# CHAPTER X.

### THE CONJUNCTION.

**267.**—We divide Korean Conjunctions into two classes, Co-ordinate and Subordinate.

The Co-ordinate, are those which connect words or phrases that are co-ordinate.

The Subordinate, are those which connect dependent with principal clauses. *Some of the most common co-ordinate* conjunctions are—

와 or 과 ..................⎫
밋........................... ⎬ Signifying *and*.
고 or 호고 ............... ⎪
며........................... ⎭

나 or 이나 ............... Signifying *either, or, whether*.

지 ⎫
가 ⎭ Used with verbs ... Signify *whether, or*.

마는........................ { Disjunctive and signifying *but*, etc.

**268.**—와, 밋, 고 and 호고 are all copulatives and may generally be rendered by simple *and*, or with and are *affixed*, like all Korean conjunctions to their words or clauses. 와 affixed to a word ending in a consonant, becomes 과, and where a number of words are united is repeated after all but the last, to which last only, will the postposition governing them all be affixed.

밋 is less frequently used than any of the others, and is restricted almost entirely to books. It is generally prefixed to its word, and as a consequence we may at times find 와 and 밋 used together.

고 and 며 are used to connect verbs. 고 may join itself directly to the stem, and where a series of verbs are connected, the last only will have tense root and termination: this tense root and termination then determines the time and termination of all the preceding verbs connected by 고.

며 is more largely found in books than in the spoken language, and in uniting itself to the verb, the tense root is not necessarily dropped. For illustrations of 고 and 며 with verbs see ¶ 194 and 200 of Part I.

269.—나 or (*affixed to consonants*) 이나, is equivalent to *or*, or *either* of the English. It marks alternatives, only one of which need be expressed, with the others or other understood. It may be joined to verbal tense roots with the same signification.

Joined to numerals and adverbs it signifies *about, in the neighborhood of, almost*.

지 and 가 are used only with verbs and are affixed to relative participles with the same sense. For illustrations of the use of these three conjunctions with verbs, see ¶ 189 and 197 of Part I.

270.—The most common subordinate conjuctions are—

비록, Used independently......  
나 ....................  
듸 or 되 ............. Affixed to verbs...  
거니와 ...............  
=ㄹ (preceded by ㄴ)  
도 ....................

Are all concessive and may be rendered into English by *though, although*.

## CONJUNCTION.

만일, Used independently...... ⎫
면 ⎱ Affixed to verbs ......... ⎬ Are conditional and are rendered by *if*.
거든 ⎰ ⎭

니 ..............................., *Whereas;* both causal and concessive.

닛가 ............... ⎫ ⎫ Mark the reason, and
매 .................. ⎬ Affixed to ⎬ are equivalent to *in-*
즉 (preceded by ㄴ) ⎰ verbs... ⎭ *asmuch as, since, seeing that,* etc.

For illustrations of the use of these conjunctions and their method of uniting with verbs, see in the chapter on verbs. ¶ 181 ff.

Note.—Still further illustrations of Korean conjunctions and their rendering into English will be found in the Chapter on Conjunctions Part II.

There are also a number of phrases that may be rendered into English by conjunctions, however, from the very nature of the case, their true meaning is apparent. A few are as follows, and they can be formed at will.

그러나 ⎱ (*Although that is so*). Becomes ⎰ *notwithstanding,*
그럐도 ⎰ ⎱ *nevertheless.*

그런고로, *For that reason*... ⎱ Becomes *therefore.*
그러므로, *Because that is so* ⎰

그르면, *If that is so* ... ...... Becomes *then, therefore.*

# CHAPTER XI.

### HONORIFICS.

271.—The use of special terms to inferiors and superiors, holds such an important place in Korean, that a special chapter on this subject is thought necessary. Attention has already from time to time been called to this fact, and in various places the terms used to superiors and inferiors have been marked. In the first few sections of Part II. all the sentences, (unless the sense does not allow, and restricts them to one or other class), have been given in three forms, *to inferiors, the polite form to equals,* and *to superiors.* Were these but the three grades with which we have to deal, the subject would be considerably simplified. But in each of these three grades, there are, what we may term sub-grades, and if we desire to be exact, we should have all the proper terminations for even these, at our finger's ends.

These sub-grades are for the most part, determined entirely by the terminations, and a careful study and practice of the lists and terminations given in the Chapter on the verb ¶ 137 ff. will accomplish this. Although the student may not desire to acquaint himself with all these forms, it is absolutely essential if he wishes to be respected by those around him, and to avoid giving

HONORIFICS.

offence to his friends, that he make himself thorough master of the three forms, and their use, given in the first sections of Part II.

**272.**—But not only is the person spoken *to*, to be considered, but in many cases we must also consider the special rank of the person spoken *of*, or the subject of the verb. An honorific of the verb, must then be formed. This honorific is for the most part derived from the simple verb, and formed by the interposition of the particle 시. With verbs whose stems end in vowels, simple 시 is added, but with verbs whose stems end in consonants 으 or ㅇ will be interposed as a connective, and 시 will then unite with the form of the stem, as found in the past verbal participle.

**273.**—The following list of verbs with their honorific forms, will illustrate this.

| Ordinary. | | Honorific. |
|---|---|---|
| 호오 | To do | 호시오. |
| 안소 | To sit | 안지시오. |
| 갓소 | Went | 가셧소. |
| 거럿소 | Walked | 거르셧소. |
| 듯소 | To hear | 드르시오. |
| 눕소 | To lie down | 누으시오. |
| 섯소 | Stood | 서셧소. |
| 싸렷소 | Beaten | 싸리셧소. |
| 찻소 | To look for | 차지시오. |
| 밧고오 | To exchange | 밧고시오. |
| 버섯소 | Took off | 버스셧소. |
| 일헛소 | Lost | 일흐셧소. |

**274.**—We find however in many cases, that there are a number of verbs that have corresponding honorific verbs, and of course where this is the case, it may be used in the place of the honorific form of the simple verb.

The following list of the most common simple verbs, with their corresponding honorifics, should be learned.

| Ordinary. | | Honorific. |
|---|---|---|
| 먹소 | ...To eat | 잡수오. |
| 자오 | ...To sleep | 줌으시오. |
| 죽소 | ...To die | 도라가시오. |
| 잇소 | ...To be | 계시오. |
| 아오 | ...To know | 통촉ᄒ시오. |
| 알소 | ...To be sick | 병환계시오. |
| 평안ᄒ오 | ...To be well | 안녕ᄒ시오. |
| 말ᄒ오 | ...To speak | 말솜ᄒ시오. |
| 오오 | ...To come | 립ᄒ시오. |

275.—There are also certain Korean verbs used to render respect to the person or persons acted upon, or objects of the verb. These are, most of them, honorific verbs from their very nature. For instance you *give* to an inferior, but you simply offer to a superior. A few of these are given below.

| Ordinary. | | Honorific. | |
|---|---|---|---|
| 주오 | ...To give | 드리오 | ...To offer. |
| 뭇소 | ...To ask | 품ᄒ오 | ...To request. |
| 뵈오 | ...To show | 갑쪼오 | ...To show. |
| 다리오 | ...To take with | 뫼시오 | ...To accompany. |
| 닐으오 | ...To tell | 엿주오 | ...To inform. |
| 도라오오 | ...To come back | 환초ᄒ시오 | To return. |

276.—Thus we find that the Korean in speaking considers the rank of the person spoken *of*, as well as the person spoken *to*, and at times this double variation takes place in the same verb. When such is the case we may use an honorific verb with an honorific termination. While at first sight it may seem as though this would involve complications almost unlimited, a careful study *separately*, of the special terminations and of the honorific verbs, will clear away most difficulties.

**277.**—The matter of honorifics, however, does not end with the verbs. It extends to the nouns and even to some postpositions, and is very apparent in the terms used to represent English pronouns. There will be two, and at times even more, sets of words, to designate the same object. The one used in speaking to or of a superior, the other, the common every day word. As has been hinted before, it will be found that Sinico-Korean is the more polite, and hence we find a large number of Sinico-Korean words, acting as the polite terms for pure Korean nouns, pronouns, etc.

**278.**—The following list of some of these nouns should also be learned.

아바지…어루신네, 츈부쟝, 츈쟝, 로친, 가친 부친. Father.
어마니…조당, 훤당, 모친, 대부인………… Mother.
삼촌……완쟝, 아즈씨, 자근아바지 큰아비지…… Uncle.
남편……가쟝, 입조 ……………………………… Husband.
안히……녀샹, 안악 부인………………………… Wife.
아돌……조뎨, 영윤, 영낭…………………………… Son.
쌀………영익, 얼양………………………………… Daughter.
죡하……합씨………………………………………… Nephew.
형………빅씨, 즁씨 ………………………Elder Brother.
아오……계씨……………………………… Younger Brother.
나………년셰, 츈츄………………………………… Age.

212    HONORIFICS.

| | | |
|---|---|---|
| 꼿불...... | 감긔...... | A cold. |
| 니...... | 치아...... | Teeth. |
| 집 ...... | 딕...... | House. |

279.—It must not be forgotten that these honorific terms are not the same throughout the country, and terms used to inferiors in the capital, are in some provinces used to equals or even superiors. This difference, however, is not extensive and can soon be learned, but we mention it here, so that the student shall not only be prepared for some change, but when he is addressed in terms that he has been accustomed to consider degrading, he may first make inquiry as to the usage of the place before he considers himself insulted.

280.—Were it in order in Korea to always use inferior terms of one's self, and to address all others with honorifics the subject would be comparatively easy. We find, however, in Korea that it is important in addressing inferiors to speak of one's self in polite terms, and to address one's servants, children etc., in the terms for inferiors. Unless such a course is pursued one would be considered entirely ignorant of both the distinctions of the language and the rules of propriety.

# CHAPTER XII.

### THE STRUCTURE OF THE SENTENCE.

**281.**—While from time to time, in considering the different words we have attempted to show, not only their meaning, but their use and position in the sentence, a few closing words on the structure of the sentence as a whole are necessary.

In the first place, we may lay it down as a general rule, that the governing word or particle always follows that governed, under these circumstances we consider that the noun governs its adjective, although in Korean there is really no government in this matter.

Or looking at it from another standpoint, we may say, the qualifying word, always precedes the word qualified. Under these circumstances we consider that the action contained in the indefinite verb, at the end of the clause or sentence is qualified or limited by the subject and object which precedes it; that the noun is qualified or limited by the adjective or participle or other noun with postposition that precedes it; that the idea of direction, *to*, or *from* etc., contained in the postposition, which was originally a noun, is qualified or limited, by the word which precedes it.

**282.**—Taking either view of the matter, (the first of which is the clearer and better) we deduce the following.

*Verbs* are always preceded by their subject, object, and the adverb qualifying them, and followed by the conjunctions which connect them with other words or clauses.

The *noun* is preceded by the adjective or participle that qualifies it, and is followed by the postposition which governs, or the conjunction which joins it to another word.

The *adjective*, if in the adjectival form, precedes the noun it qualifies. If in the form of a substantive, it follows the noun with which it stands in apposition. If in the verbal form, it of course, holds the same position as a verb.

The *adverb* precedes the adjective or verb that it qualifies.

The *postposition* always follows the word whose relation it shows to another word in the sentence.

The *conjunction* (except in the case of those used independently, which might well be termed "*intensive*" and are only used in sentences where their corresponding dependent, or subordinate forms are used) always follows the word or clause that it connects with another.

**283.**—As a rule the subject comes first, then the object, then the verb.

In a simple sentence then, we have first, the subject, preceded by its attributes, second the indirect object preceded by its attributes, third the direct object preceded by its attributes, and finally the verb with its adverb or other attributes.

Emphasis, however, may change this, and the emphatic word will generally be found first in the sentence.

The position of the direct, and indirect object of a verb, is immaterial, either may precede the other.

By way of illustration of these rules a careful study of any of the sentences given in Part II. with regard specially to their structure is urged.

284.—When several verbs are to be connected, if they are co-ordinate, the conjunction 고 united to the stem will be used, and only the last verb inflected. If subordinate, however, the past verbal participle of the subordinate verb will be used without a conjunction. For illustrations of this see Part II, Chap. X. Sec. I. 2. (*a*) and (*b*).

285.—What has already been said upon the use of personal pronouns, and of passive constructions, leads us naturally, to notice the extreme indefiniteness as to subject, of a large number of Korean sentences. Not only will no subject be expressed, but none will even be thought of, and under such circumstances, when the context does not plainly show what the subject is, it must be rendered into English, either by an indefinite, such as *some o e, something*, or the phrase must be changed, and a passive construction used.

Indefinite sentences of this kind may be found throughout the book in both parts, and in many cases where definiteness has been expressed by the use of personal pronouns etc., any other subject might have been used.

286.—As in English, so also in Korean, the use of two negatives gives us an affirmative, but this use of two negatives is much more common in Korean than in English.

The following will illustrate this.

| | |
|---|---|
| 미국은 업노 것 업소, | In America they have everything. |
| 이거손 언잔 찬소. | This is good. |
| 그러케 아니하면 못되겟소. | I must do that. |

**237.**—As will be seen from ¶ 230 ff. the Koreans are quite prone to use elliptical forms, and we often hear orders and commands ending in conjunctions, postpositions, etc., but in all cases, some other word is of course, left to be understood. Such phrases would not as a rule be correct in writing, and while allowable in speaking, would not be classed as elegant Korean.

**288.**—In concluding this chapter on the structure of the sentence, we would again remind the student, that postpositions, conjunctions, and verbal modifications, are not to be used as in other languages.

What we understand as minute exactness of speech, is a thing not aimed at by the Korean, his desire is simply to express his idea, in as few words as possible, always remembering his surroundings and circumstances. As a consequence the same sentence taken out of its context might not only be ambiguous, but entirely meaningless, and yet, at the same time considered with its circumstances and surroundings it might be a complete sentence.

**289.**—In almost direct opposition to this, there seems to stand the Korean use of what we have termed conjunctions. The Koreans have no system of punctuation, and where we would use a comma, semicolon, or colon, etc., they would use a cojunction, expressing *cause, manner, means,* etc., as the case might be. Consequent upon this we find that the distinction between sentence and paragraph, does not exist in Korean, each sentence in an English paragraph becomes then, simply a dependent clause, connected by one or other of the conjunctions, and the whole paragraph but one sentence. This becomes much more apparent in the book language, and here is its main difficulty.

**290.**—In closing these "Grammatical Notes" we would say that we have tried but to introduce the student to the study of Korean spoken language. We would repeat that they should not be studied alone, but in connection with Part II. The accuracy of each rule given should be tested by the student, when thus tested they should be put in practice, for in order to gain any language quickly and thoroughly, practice must be combined with theory. Only by so doing can the student ever learn to use the KOREAN SPOKEN LANGUAGE.

# PART II.

# ENGLISH INTO KOREAN

OR THE

## KOREAN SPOKEN LANGUAGE

FROM THE

### ENGLISH STANDPOINT.

# PART II.

# ENGLISH INTO KOREAN.

## CHAPTER I.

### THE VERB.

In the Grammatical Notes, the attempt was made, to approach Korean from the native standpoint; to take Korean idioms, phrases and methods of speech, explain their meanings and uses, and ascertain their equivalents in English. In doing this, we have however, done but little more than half the work that is before us in the study of Korean. We have approached from but one side, and now it remains for us to approach Korean from the English standpoint; to take English phrases, words, and forms of expression, and learn their equivalents in Korean. This has been attempted in the following pages, and while the Korean equivalents, are not by any means claimed to be the only renderings, they are the common and most frequent methods of expressing the ideas they are said to represent In doing this, we have begun with the verb, because here we find the greatest variety of changes. To a great extent what has already been said in the Grammatical Notes, will answer equally well here. This is very true of the verb as well as of the other parts of speech, and there remains under the verb, simply the verbs, *To be* and *To have*, Auxiliaries, The Infinitive, Passive Constructions, and Conditional Sentences. These will be taken up one by one, the rules for rendering them into Korean given, and sentences to illustrate each rule will follow.

## § I.—THE VERB "TO BE."

1 Employed independently, expressing simple existence, *to be* is rendered by 잇소 ; negatively by 업소.

2 Followed by a predicate noun or pronoun, *to be* is rendered by 이오 sometimes contracted into 요 or 오 ; negatively by 아니오.

3 Followed by a predicate adjective, the verb *to be* is united with the adjective. See Chap. VI § I.

4 When equivalent to *become*, the verb *to be*, is rendered by 되오 and negatively by 안되오.

5 For the use of the verb *to be*, as an auxiliary See § III, See. 1 & 2.

### 1.

There are some very high mountains around Seoul.   \* 셔울 일경에 엇던 매우
(*Lit*) *Seoul neighborhood in certain very*
놉흔 산들 잇다,—잇소,
*high mountains·is.*
—잇슙ㄴ이다. †

About how many houses are there in this city?   이 셩 안에 집 얼마
*This city within house how-many*
나 잇ㄴ야,—잇소,—잇슙
*about is?*
ㄴ잇가?

---

\* It will be noticed that for the first few exercises, the sentences are all given in the three forms, for inferiors, equals and superiors, except perhaps in instances where the sentence by its very nature restricts the class to which it is addressed.

† Properly this should be written 잇ㅅ읍ㄴ이다 but pronounced *issimnida*.

Chap. I. § I.        THE VERB.                              223

Is there only one kind of oil in these bottles? 이 여러 병 속에 호 셔워
*This several bottle inside one kind*
기름 샏 잇ᄂᆞ냐,—잇소,
*oil only is?*
—잇습ᄂᆞ잇가?*

About how many soldiers are there in a regiment? 호 진에 군ᄉᆞ가 얼마
*One regiment-in soldier how many*
나잇ᄂᆞ냐,—잇소,—잇습
*about is?*
ᄂᆞ잇가?

There is no telegraph office in Kang Wha. 강화 에 뎐보국 업다,
*Kang Wha in telegraph office is not.*
—업소, 업습ᄂᆞ이다

There is no use in going before breakfast. 아춤 먹기 젼에 갈 것
*Breakfast eating before going thing*
업다, — 업소, — 업습
*is not.*
ᄂᆞ이다.

Is there not any one who can go instead? 아 모 나 디신 갈 사ᄅᆞᆷ
*Any one whatever instead going man*
업ᄂᆞ냐,—업소,—업습
*is not?*
ᄂᆞ잇가?

Was there not any one who knew the way home? 집에 오ᄂᆞᆫ 길을 아ᄂᆞᆫ이가
*House-to coming road knowing one*
업섯ᄂᆞ냐, — 업섯소, —
*was not?*
업섯습ᄂᆞ잇가?

2.

Is that smoke or is it only a cloud? 뎌 거시 연긔 오 구롬
*That thing smoke is? cloud*
샏 이오?
*only is?*

Is that a fox or a dog? 뎌 거시 여호요 개요?
*That thing fox is, dog is?*

Is not that a dog sleeping on the veranda? 뎌 퇴 마루 에 자ᄂᆞᆫ 거시
*That veranda on sleeping thing*
개가 아니냐,—아니오,
*dog is not?*
아니오닛가?

---

* *Properly this should be* 잇ᄉᆞᆸᄂᆞ잇가 *but pronounced isslmnlka.*

| | |
|---|---|
| Was not that an earthquake? | 뎌 거시 디동 ᄒᆞ는 거시, *That thing earthquake making thing* 아니냐—아니오—아니 *was not?* 오닛가? |

3.

| | |
|---|---|
| Our work is very hard. | 우리 일 미우 어렵다,— *Our work very difficult is.* 럽소.—럽습ᄂᆞ이다. |
| The street is very muddy. | 길이 미우 질다, — 지오, *Road very muddy is.* —지오이다. |
| These coolies are not lazy. | 이 일군들이 게으르지 *The coolies lazy* 안타, — 안소, — 안습ᄂᆞ *is not.* 이다. |
| The road from here to Fusan is not good. | 여긔셔 부산으로 가는 *Here from Fusan to going* 길이 됴치안타, — 안소, *road good is not.* — 안습ᄂᆞ이다. |

4.

| | |
|---|---|
| I do not believe it will be much of a fire. | 내 ᄉᆡᆼ각에는 큰 화지는 *My thought in-as-for, big fire-as-for* 아니 되겟다, — 되겟소, *not will become.* —되겟습ᄂᆞ이다. |
| You will never be rich if you are not more thrifty. | 규모를 더 아니 부리 면 *Economy more not employ if,* 부쟈가 아니 되겟다, *rick man not will become.* —되겟소, — 되겟습ᄂᆞ 이다. |
| If this were only mended it would be as good as new. | 이 거슬 곳치기만 ᄒᆞ엿더 *This thing mending only made* 면 젼 과 ᄀᆞᆺ치 잘 *if before as equally well* 되겟다,—되겟소,—되겟 *will become.* 습ᄂᆞ이다. |

## § II.—THE VERB "TO HAVE."

1 Expressing possession or ownership:—
   (a.) By animate beings, *to have* is rendered by the postposition 의게 with 잇소, or by 잇소 alone. Negative, by 업소.
   (b.) By inanimate objects, it is rendered by the postposition 에 with 잇소.

2 Expressing acceptance. This idea does not appeal to the Korean as *accepting* and is therefore variously translated.

3 Expressing *To cause* or *To procure*—By 계ᄒᆞ오 or by 식여 with the appropriate form of the verb.

4 Expressing necessity and followed by the infinitive; it is rendered by the future participle of the verb with 수밧긔업소.

5 For *have*, as an auxiliary see § III. Sec. 4.

### 1 (a).

|  |  |
|---|---|
| Korean noblemen have a great many servants. | 죠션 량반의게 여러 하인이 *Korean nobleman to many servant* 잇다,—잇소,—잇습ᄂᆞ이 *is.* 다. |
| Englishmen often have light hair and blue eyes. | 영국사롬의게 혼이 누론 *Englishman to often yellow* 머리와 푸른 눈이 잇다, *hair and blue eye is.* —잇소,—잇습ᄂᆞ이다. |
| Japanese cats have no tails. | 일본 고양이의게 꼬리 *Japan cat to tail* 업다,—업소,—업습ᄂᆞ *is not.* 이다. |

## 1 (b).

Our house has only five rooms.
우리 집에 다숫 방 만 잇다,—잇소,—잇숩ᄂ이다.
*Our house at five room only is.*

The box has no cover.
케에 두성 업다,—업소—업숩ᄂ이다.
*Box to lid is not.*

This flower has no perfume.
이 꼿이 향내 업다,—업소—업숩ᄂ이다.
*This flower to scent is not.*

## 2.

Will you have five dollars or ten?
오 환 가져가겟소 십 환 가져가겟소?
*Five dollar take will ten dollar take will.*

I will have a cup of tea.
챠 훈 그릇 먹겟다,—먹겟소,—먹겟숩ᄂ이다.
*Tea one cup eat will.*

Will you have a flower?
꼿 한나 가지겟소?
*Flower one take will.*

## 3.

I will have him take it away.
가져 가게 ᄒ겟다,—ᄒ겟소—ᄂ이다.
*Take away make will.*

I will have it done right away.
즉시 ᄒ게ᄒ겟다,—ᄒ겟소,—ᄒ겟숩ᄂ이다.
*At once to do will make.*

We will have these sent up to Seoul.
우리가 이거슬 셔울노 올녀 보내게ᄒ겟다,—ᄒ겟소,—ᄒ겟숩ᄂ이다.
*We these Seoul to up send will make.*

He said he would have the boy bring them.
ᄋ히 싯여 가져 오겟다고 ᄒ엿다,—ᄒ엿소,—ᄒ엿숩ᄂ이다.
*Boy employed will bring said.*

4.

| I will have to go to night. | 오놀 밤에 써날 수 밧긔 |

*To-day night starting way outside*

업다, —업소, —업습ᄂ

*there is not.*

이다.

| If you do not work you will have to starve. | 일ᄒᆞ지 아니ᄒᆞ면 굴물수 |

*Work to do not do if starving way*

밧긔 업다, 업소, 업습

*outside there is not.*

ᄂ이다.

| I have to finish that early to night. | 그거슬 오놀밤, 일쪽 다 |

*That to-day night early all*

홀수 밧긔업다, —업소,

*doing way outside is not.*

—업습ᄂ이다.

## § III.—AUXILIARY VERBS.

### Sec. I.—Am, is, are.

1 Followed by the active participle:—

(a.) Expressing present continued action—either the present indicative or by the present participle with 것 followed by 잇소 or 이오 according to the rules given § I, 1 and 2 of this chapter, or the verbal participle with 이오.

\* Negatively.—either the present indicative preceded by 아니 or by the present participle with 것 followed by 업소 or 아니오 (§ I, 1 & 2), or the verbal participial form of the negative verb with 이오.

See also Part I. ¶ 129 ff. on tenses.

(b) Expressing vivid future.—

As in English so in Korean there is a way of expressing vivid future by the present indicative, and either this or the future indicative may be used. Negatively—present or future indicative with 아니.

---

\* For further use of the negative, see chapter on negative in Part I.

228　THE VERB.　CHAP. I. § III. SEC. 1.

2 followed by passive participle—See passive voice.

### 1. (a).

| A crow is building its nest in the garden. | 화원에 가마귀 보금자리 *Crow garden in nest* 를 짓는다,—지오,—짓숩 *is building.* 누이다. |
|---|---|
| The rats are gnawing a hole somewhere in the ceiling. | 쥐가 어듸던지 텬쟝 에셔 *Rat somewhere ceiling in* 구 멍 을 뚤은것 잇다, *hole gnawing thing is.* —잇소, —잇숩누이다. |
| That is the baby crying. | 뎌거시 아기 우는 거시다, *That thing baby crying thing is.* —이오, —이올시다. |
| Is not the clock striking now? | 죵명죵 지금 치는 거시 *Clock now striking thing* 아니냐, —아니오, —아 *is not?* 니오닛가? |
| It is not raining now. | 지금은 비아니 와—요. *Now as for, rain not coming is.* |
| The carpenters are not working now. | 목슈들이 지금 일 아니ᄒ *Carpenters now work not making is.* 여요. |

### 1. (b).

| I am going home next year. | 내가 릭년 에 본국 으로 *I next year-in own country to* 간다, —가오, —가옵ᄂ *go.* 이다. |
|---|---|
| The German minister to America, is coming back next month. | 미국에 간 덕국공ᄉ *America to gone German minister* 릭월에 도라 오겟다, *next month-in back will come.* —겟소, —겟숩누이다, |
| We are not sending a courier to Chemulpo to-morrow. | 우리가 릭일 졔물포 로 보힝군 아니보닌다, —니오, —닙누이다. |

## Sec. 2.—Was, Were.

1 Followed by the Active Participle:—

(a) Expressing continued action in the past.

The Koreans, prefer the simple past tense, but sometimes render this by the present participle with the past tense of 이오.

See also Part I. ¶ 132 ff.

(b.) Introducing an event happening during the action—다가 with verbal stem.

(c.) Expressing an action intended but not carried out—랴다 or 랴더니 preceded by verbal stem.

2 Followed by passive participle:—

(a.) Of Intransitive verbs—The past tense of verb.

(b.) Of transitive verbs—See Passive Voice.

### 1. (a).

| | |
|---|---|
| We were working all day yesterday. | 어제 죵일 일ᄒ엿다, ᄒ엿소, —ᄒ엿ᄉᆞᆷᄂᆞ이다. |
| Were they laughing or crying? | 웃는거실너냐 우는 거실너냐? |

### 1. (b).

| | |
|---|---|
| * I was going to Chemulpo yesterday, and met fourteen Chinamen. | 어제 졔물포 가다가 쳥인 열넷 맛낫다, — 낫소, —낫ᄉᆞᆷᄂᆞ이다. |

---

\* The Koreans, unless ambiguity would exist, do not use the personal pronouns. The surroundings alone generally determine the subject of the verb. These sentences are taken out of all surroundings, but the student is expected to use them and then circumstances will decide these matters.

He was eating some fish, and a bone stuck in his throat.

성션 먹다가 목에 가시 걸녓다, — 녓소, — 녓숩 ㄴ이다.

1. (c).

Mr. Pak was going to America, but his father died.

박셔방이 미국 가랴다가 아바지가 죽엇다, — 엇소,—엇숩ㄴ이다.

We were coming to see you several times, but we were busy and could not.

여러번 보러 오랴더니 밧바못 왓다, — 왓소, —왓숩ㄴ이다.

2.

He was gone when I got there.

내가 거긔 니룰 째에 발셔 갓다, — 갓소, — 갓숩ㄴ이다.

I went home after nine years, but all my friends were dead.

본국에 아홉히 만에 갓것마는 친구들이 다 죽엇다, — 엇소, — 엇숩ㄴ이다.

SEC. 3.—DO, DID.

1 *Do* and *did* are expressed in Korean by the present and past of the verb.

2 *Do not* and *did not*\* used interrogatively, are expressed either by the interrogative present or past of the verb preceeded by 아니, or by the negative base in 지 followed by interrogative present or past of 아니 ᄒᄋᆞ.

3 *Do not*, used imperatively—by the negative base in

---

\* *Note.*—Interrogative sentences expressed negatively are regarded by Koreans from an opposite standpoint to the English. The Korean, in his answer, considers not the facts of the case, or the thing expected, but the implied statement in the question and when we would answer "Yes" answers "No" and *vice-versa*.

CHAP. I. § III. SEC. 3.   THE VERB.                              231

지 followed by the volitive mood second person of 마오, to avoid.

1.

| Why do you leave the door open? | 웨 문을 열어 두ᄂ냐, *Why door open leave?* —두오,—두옵ᄂ잇가? |
| They do not make it that way any more. | 이스이는 그러케 아니 *Now-a-days as for, that way not* 짓 는다,— 짓소,— 짓숩 *make.* ᄂ이다. |
| Where did you put my umbrelia? | 내 우산 어듸 노핫ᄂ냐, *My umbrella where put.* —핫소,—핫숩ᄂ잇가? |

2.

| * Did not the fans I sent you suit? | 내가 당신씌 보낸 붓치가 *I you to (hon.) sent fan* 합의 치 아니ᄒ엿숩ᄂ *suit did not!* 잇가? |
| Do not the steamers sail twice a month now? | 이스이 화륜션 ᄒᄃᆯ에 *Now-a-day steamer one month in* 두번 식 아니 ᄃᆞ니ᄂ냐, *twice each not ply!* — ᄃᆞ이오,— ᄃᆞ이옵ᄂ 잇가? |
| Why did you not give the coolie the things he came for? | 웨 짐군에게 가질너 온 *Why carrier to, to-take came* 거슬 아니 주엇ᄂ냐,— *thing, not gave!* 엇소,—엇숩ᄂ잇가? |
| Do you not like foreign food? | 외국 음식 됴화 ᄒ지 *Foreign food like to do* 아니ᄒᄂ냐, — ᄒ오, — *not do!* ᄒ옵ᄂ잇가? |

\* For example the question, "Has not the teacher come yet?" expecting in English the answer "yes," will call forth from the Korean the answer "no" if the teacher has come, and "yes" if he has not yet come. See Part I ¶ 266.

3.

| | | |
|---|---|---|
| Do not put on any more coal. | 셕탄 더 넛치 마라,—마오, *Coal more to put-on avoid.* —마옵시오. | |
| Do not take more than you think you will need. | 당신이 쓸 료량에 더 *You needing thought in more* 가져가지 마옵시오. *to take   avoid.* | |
| Please do not tear that newspaper. | 더 신문지를 쎗지 마옵 *That newspaper   to tear avoid.* 시오. (*hon.*). | |
| Do not light the lights yet. | 아직 불 혀지 마라. *As yet light to light avoid.* (*inf.*). | |

### Sec. 4.—Have, has, had.

1 Have :—The auxiliary *have*, is generally expressed in Korean by the regular past tense of the verb.

2 Have been :—

(*a.*) Generally Koreans do not make the distinction between continued past action, and simple past action, but leave it to be decided from the context; hence *have been* in English is largely expressed by the Korean simple past.

(*b.*) The distinction can be made by the use of the present participle with 것 and the past tense of 잇소.

(*c.*) In speaking of the duration of continued action, the participial noun in 지 with the past tense of the verb expressing the extent of time is used.

3 Had :—The Koreans as a rule do not use the pluperfect tense. Such a tense can be formed, and is acknowledged as correct by many, but the great majority prefer

Chap. I. § III. Sec. 4.   THE VERB.   233

to transpose the sentence and use the simple past tense. See Part I on compound tenses ☞ 135.

Had, is then expressed:—

    (a.) In affirmative sentences—either by a complete transposition of the sentence, or by the use of the adverb 발셔 with the past tense.

    (b.) In negative sentences—by either a like complete transposition, or by the use of 아직 with the past tense.

I.

| | |
|---|---|
| Have the coolies brought the freight? | 짐군이 짐 가져 왓숩더니잇가?* |
| Have you heard the news? | 당신이 소문 드럿소? |
| Why haven'nt you brought your dog? | 웨 개 아니 드리고 왓소? |
| The post man has not brought any letters to-day. | 태젼부가 오놀은 아모 편지도 아니 가져 왓수옵더이다. |

2. (a).

| | |
|---|---|
| Your room has not been swept and dusted yet. | 당신 방을 아직 쓸고 훔치지 아니 하엿소. |
| This roof has not been repaired for a couple of years. | 이집 웅을 수년 이나 곳치지 아니 하엿소. ☞ |
| Haven't you repaired your house lately? | 당신이 이수이에 집을 곳치지 아니 하엿소? |
| Have you seen the paper? | 신문지를 보앗소? |

---

\* Note.—Hereafter the three forms referring to inferiors, equals and superiors will not be given with each sentence but only one or the other as the case may demand.

2. (b).

Some body has been sweeping this room.　　*이방 쓰는 이가 잇섯소·

2. (c).

How long have you been living in Sëoul?　　당신이 셔울 잇신지가 얼마 나 되오?

The Sëoul merchants have been selling foreign goods for a long time now.　　지금은 셔울 쟝ᄉ 들이 셔양 물건 을 오래재 푸오·

We have been studying four hours.　　공부 훈지가 네시가 되엿소·

The Japanese have been several years building their railroads.　　일인이 털로 ᄆᆞᆮ는지가 여러 힌 되엿소·

3. (a).

I went to the foreign office but they had all left.　　내가 외아문으로 갓것 마는 발셔 다 갓소·

The coolies had all finished when I got home.　　내가 집에 니르기 젼에 일군들이 일 다ᄒᆞ엿소·

When you left Sëoul, had the Russian legation been begun?　　셔울 쎠나기 젼에 아국 공ᄉ관 짓기를 시작 ᄒᆞ엿소?

I asked him to stop to dinner, but he had dined.　　저녁에 쳥ᄒᆞ엿것 마는 발셔 먹엇소·

3. (b).

When I got to my hotel my letter had not come.　　쥬막에 니롤 째에 내편지 아직 아니 왓소·

I had not heard it when the steamer left.　　화륜션이 쎠나기, 젼에 못드럿 소·

---

* As has been said before, while this is allowable it is not as the Korean would put it, and, unless absolutely necessary, such sentences as this should be avoided.

| Had you not left Séoul before that? | 그쌔 젼에 셔울셔 떠나지 아니 ᄒᆞ엿소? |

## SEC. 5.—SHALL, WILL.

1. Affirmative:—
    (*a.*) Opinion; also in seeking direction and in stating one's purpose or inquiring another's purpose from a third party:—the future of the verb in 리이다: or, interrogatively—in 리잇가.
    (*b.*) Simple future, *certainty*, *determination*, or enquiring another's purpose directly—future in 겟소.
2. Negative:—
    (*a.*) Vividly;—negative present.
    (*b.*) Determination;—negative future.

### 1. (*a*).

| If you do not put in more salt it will spoil. | 소곰 더 넛치 아니 ᄒᆞ면 샹ᄒᆞ리이다. |
| Shall I send word again to Séoul? | 내가 셔울 긔별 쏘 ᄒᆞ리 잇가? |
| Shall I call a jinrikisha on my way to Tchongno? | 죵로에 가다가 인력거 부르리 잇가? |
| I will call again in three or four days. | 삼ᄉᆞ일 간에 다시 오리이다. |
| If you need one I will lend you mine. | 쓸디 잇시면 내 거슬 빌니리이다. |
| Will Mr. Kim go with us? | 김셔방 우리와 ᄀᆞ치 가리잇가? |

### 1. (*b*).

| To day it will close at six o'clock. | 오ᄂᆞᆯ은 여ᄉᆞᆺ시에 닷겟소. |

| | |
|---|---|
| If it rains "cats and dogs" I'll go. | 비가 쏫아져도 가겟소. |
| Mr. Pak will go for it. | 박셔방이 차지러 가겟소. |
| About how long will you stay here? | 얼마 즈음 이나 여긔 잇겟소? |

2. (a).

| | |
|---|---|
| Buddhist priests will not kill even a mosquito. | 즁은 모긔 도 아니 죽이오. |
| I shall not go to-morrow. | 내가 뉘일 안 간다. |

2. (b).

| | |
|---|---|
| I will not give even one cash more. | 내가 한 푼 도 더 주지 안켓소. |
| Not one of these will do. | 이것 한나 도 못쓰겟소. |

### SEC. 6.—SHOULD,—WOULD.

1 In direct clauses—

(a.) Expressing *intention, determination,*—future of the verb. Negatively—future with 안 or 아니.

(b.) Equivalent to *ought,*—see Sec. 11 of this division on Auxiliaries.

(c.) Expressing\* *determination in a past action*—the past tense of the verb; negatively—past tense with 안 or 아니.

2 In indirect clauses—

(a.) Expressing *opinion*—future participle with 줄 아오.

(b.) Expressing *determination, certainty*—form of the future or present used in indirect discourse.

---

\* Note.—In a simple sentence, the idea of determination conveyed by the English "*would,*" cannot be given in Korean except by a circumlocution, unless it is implied by the context. This idea is however in part conveyed by the use of 제가 with the past tense.

CHAP. I. § III. SEC. 6.   THE VERB.                                   237

3 In conditional sentences—

   (a.) In the conditional clause—by the form of the conditional with 면, 거든, etc.
   (b.) In the conclusion—by the future of the verb.

The past tense "*would have*," is rendered by the future perfect.

See also § IV of this chapter, and Chap. X Sec. 8.

1. (a).

| | |
|---|---|
| I would go but I have no passport. | 내가 가겟것 마는 빙표 업소. |
| He would pay but, he has not yet received it from Mr. Yi. | 갑겟것 마는 리셔방 의게셔 아직 돈을 못 밧앗소. |
| I would not give you even a cash to keep you from starving. | 너 굼지 안케 훌, 돈은 훈푼도 안 주겟다. |

1. (c).

| | |
|---|---|
| In spite of all I could do, he would go to the country. | 나는 암만 말녓실 지라도 제가 싀골 노 갓소. |
| He would not listen to reason. | 의리를 안 드럿소. |
| He would squander all his money in spite of all my efforts to stop him. | 말니랴고 암만 의 써도 제가 돈을 다 허비 호엿소. |

2. (a).

| | |
|---|---|
| I thought they would be here by this time. | 이째 넘지 안코 올줄 알앗소. |
| Did you think it would be so dear? | 그러케 비쌀 줄 알앗소? |

2. (b).

| | |
|---|---|
| Mr. Yi said he would send it next week. | 리셔방이 훗 쥬일에 보내 마고 ᄒᆞ엿소. |
| Mrs. Kim said she would come with five other women to-morrow night. | 김셔방되이 릭일 밤에 다른 녀편네 다숫 ᄃᆞ리고 온다고 ᄒᆞ엿소. |

3.

| | |
|---|---|
| If any one should come enquiring for me, say I have gone to the palace. | 누가 날 보러 오거든 대궐 노 갓다고 ᄒᆞ여라. |
| You would have time enough, if you would get up earlier. | 더 일즉 니러나면 ᄯᅢ가 넉넉 ᄒᆞ겟소. |
| If you had been a little more careful, this would never have happened. | 더조심 ᄒᆞ엿더면 이러케 안 되엿 겟소. |
| It would not pay to sell it for less than five dollars. | 오 환 안희 팔면 리 업겟소. |
| If you had gone yesterday, you would have been in plenty of time. | 어제 갓더면 ᄯᅢ 넉넉 ᄒᆞ엿겟소. |

SEC. 7.—CAN, COULD.

*Can* and *could* are commonly rendered in two ways.

1. Affirmatively:—
    (*a.*) By the simple future or past.
    (*b.*) By 수 preceded by the future relative participle, with the present or past of 잇소.
2. Negatively:—
    (*a.*) By 못 with the future or past.
    (*b*) By 수 preceded by the future relative participle with the present or past of 업소.

Chap. I. § III. Sec. 7.   THE VERB.

1. (a).

| If you only know how, you can say anything in Japanese. | 엇더케 홀 줄 만 알면 아모 뜻 이라도 일본 말노 호겟소. |
| If you open the door you can see. | 문 열면 보겟소. |
| He can only hear in one ear. | 호 귀 로 만 듯겟소. |
| Can your dog sit up on his hind legs? | 로형의 개가 뒤 드리로만 안겟소? |
| Can you send any message you please by telegraph? | 아모 말이라도 뎐신 으로 뎐호겟소? |
| When I was a boy I could swim two ri. | 내가 으히째에눈 이리를 헤염 호엿소. |

1. (b).

| When can we see the Kyŏng Pok Kung Palace? | 경복궁 대궐을 언제 구경 홀수 잇겟소? |
| Can we see the inside of the prison if we get a permit? | 문 표지를 엇으면 옥 속을 볼수가 잇소? |
| If you go to the best shops you can get good silk in Korea too. | 큰 젼에 가면 죠션 셔도 됴혼 명쥬 살수 잇소. |
| If I am not sick I can walk more then a hundred ri in one day. | 병 업소면 호로 빅리 더 것겟소. |

2. (a).

| When the fire bell rings I cannot sleep. | 불 낫다고 종 칠 째에 못 자겟소. |
| I went everywhere but could not sell it. | 사방 갓셔도 못 풀앗소. |

| | |
|---|---|
| If you have not government permission you can't sell it. | 정부 허락이 업스면 못 풀겟소. |
| A great noise (of jabbering) arose and we could not hear. | 써드는 소틱가 나셔 못 알아 드럿소. |
| I invited both, but neither of them could come. | 이 두 사름을 쳥ᄒ엿것마는 아모도 못 왓소. |

2. (b).

| | |
|---|---|
| It was dark and we could not see the road. | 어두어 길 볼수 업셧소 |
| I cannot take the accounts to night. | 오늘 밤에 혬 볼수 업소. |
| I cannot go even though he offers me one hundred dollars. | 빅 환 주마고 홀지라도 나는 갈수 업소. |
| He could not get a passport. | 빙표 엇을 수 업셧소. |

SEC 8.—MAY, MIGHT.

1. Possiblity equivalent to *perhaps* :—
    (a.) With present or future—아마 or 혹 with the future.
    (b) With past—아마 or 혹 with the past.
    (c.) Might have—혹 or 아마 with the future past.
2. Ability.—Same as could ; or future participle with 번ᄒ엿소.
3. Permission, liberty—is rendred variously according to the sentence by a transposition.

1. (a).

| | |
|---|---|
| May be there are some mosquitos in the net. | 모긔쟝 안희 아마 모긔가 잇겟소. |
| May be the steamer will be in to-morrow. | 아마 틱일 비 드러오겟소. |

Chap. I. § III. Sec. 8.   THE VERB.   241

| | |
|---|---|
| May be we had better order them from Seoul. | 아마 셔울셔 가져오라면 됴겟소. |
| You might get well if you went to Fusan. | 부산 가면 아마 낫겟소. |
| May be he will not start for a day or two. | 호로 잇흘 동안에는 아마 아니 떠나겟소. |

1. (b).

| | |
|---|---|
| May be he has not heard yet. | 혹 아직 못 드럿소. |
| May be he missed the steamer. | 아마 화륜션을 못 밋쳣소. |
| May be he has been told already. | 아마 발셔 드럿소. |
| May be they have not begun yet. | 아마 아직 시작 아니 호엿소. |

1. (c).

| | |
|---|---|
| If you had risen early perhaps you might have caught the steamer. | 일즉 니러낫더면 아마 비에 밋쳣겟소. |
| If Keuija had not lived, justice might not have been known. | 긔주가 나지 아니 호엿더면 아마 례의가 업섯겟소. |
| If you had only called the doctor sooner, he might not have died. | 의원 더 급히 부르기 만 호엿더면 아마 아니 죽엇겟소. |
| If he had only been honest he might have been a rich man. | 착호기만 호엿더연 아마 부쟈 되엿겟소. |

2.

| | |
|---|---|
| If you had come yesterday, I might have gone to-day. | 공이 어저셔 왓더면 내가 오눌 갈번 호엿소. |

| | |
|---|---|
| If you had only told me, I might have loaned you the money. | 내게 닐녓더면 수일번 흐엿소. |

3.

| | |
|---|---|
| May I go and take a bath? | 내가 목욕흐러 가리잇가? |
| You may put it in the drawer or the bookcase. | 셜합에나 칙상에나 두어도 관계 찬소. |
| I told Sou Pongi he might go to see the Kerdong. | 슈봉이 드려 거동 구경 흐랴면 흐라고 흐엿소. |
| You may stay away from school to-day. | 오놀 학당에 아니 가도 관계 찬소. |
| Did you not say I might borrow your dictionary? | 공이 말흐기를 주뎐 구흐랴면 공의 주뎐 구흐라고 아니 흐엿습ᄂ니잇가? |

SEC. 9.—LET, MAKE, HAVE, GET.

1 The Korean causative form of the verb, may stand for any or all of the above. The distinctive differences between them however, can, if necessary, be expressed by the use of other verbs. *Let,* when it means permission, may be expressed by the additional use of 주오, (*to give*); *get,* by the use of 엇소 (*to obtain*), or 식이오 (*to engage*), etc.

2 "Let us," in a proposition—volitive mood, first person.

1.

| | |
|---|---|
| Soun Yongi has let the lamp smoke. | 순용이가 등을 검게흐엿소. |
| Shall I let the coolies take the freight? | 짐군들 짐을 가져가게 흐오리잇가? |

| | |
|---|---|
| You have eaten enough; now let me have a little. | 당신은 넉넉히 먹엇시니 시방은 나 좀 먹게 ᄒᆞ여 주오. |
| Please don't let the boys come into the rooms with their shoes on. | 학성들이 신 신고는 방에 못 드러 오게 ᄒᆞ여 주시오. |
| Make him wait a little. | 좀 기드리게 ᄒᆞ여라. |
| If those children come in, be sure and make them keep quiet. | 으히 드러 오거든 부듸 죠용이 잇게 ᄒᆞ오. |
| Make the washerman iron these clothes better. | 마젼쟝이 드려 옷슬 좀 낫게 다리게 ᄒᆞ여라. |
| I will have Soun Yongi mail your letters. | 슌용이 식여셔 당신 편지를 우톄국 젼ᄒᆞ게 ᄒᆞ겟소. |
| You had better have the carpenter make it. | 목슈 식여 문들게, ᄒᆞ면 됴켓소. |
| Where did you get this table made? | 이 샹을 어듸셔 식여 문드럿소? |
| You must have your grass cut. | 이 풀을 깍게 ᄒᆞ여야 쓰겟소. |
| Please let the cat go out. | 고양이 나가게 ᄒᆞ여 주시오. |
| Do not let the water run out of the bottle so fast. | 병에서 물을 이러케 급히 ᄯᅩ로지 말게 ᄒᆞ오. |
| I ought to get my watch repaired. | 누구 식여 내 시표를 곳칠 터히오. |

2.

| | |
|---|---|
| Let us go up Nam San to-morrow. | 뉘일 남산에 올나 가옵시다. |
| Let's go by way of Chong-nikol to-morrow. | 뉘일 졍너골 노 가옵시다. |

| | |
|---|---|
| Let's rest and have a smoke. | 쉬고 담비 먹읍시다. |
| Let's pull the cat's tail. | 고양이 꼬리를 잡아 당기자. |

### SEC. 10.—MUST.

1 Expressing necessity :—

(*a*.) Affirmative—past verbal participle with the postposition 야 and future of 호오, or 쓰오.

Sometimes also the same effect is produced by the use of an adverb expressing necessity with the future.

(*b*.) Negative—the negative base in 지 with 말아야 and future of 호오, or 쓰오.

Or, by either a conditional clause, or a relative participle qualifying 것, with 못 and the future of 호오, or 쓰오.

2 Expressing strong probability :—

(*a*.) Must—future, or future participle with 수밧긔업소.

(*b*.) Must have—future perfect.

### 1. (*a*).

| | |
|---|---|
| You must be more careful. | 좀 더 조심 ᄒ여야 쓰겟소. |
| You must make him take it whether he likes it or not. | 됴화 ᄒ던지 아니 ᄒ던지 먹게 ᄒ여야 쓰겟소. |
| You must mind whatever your teacher says. | 무어시던지 션성 ᄒ라는 대로 ᄒ여야 쓰겟소. |
| We must leave the house at twelve o'clock. | 집에셔 열두 시에 써나야 쓰겟소. |
| I must be in Chemulpo by five o'clock to-morrow. | 릭일 오시에 졔물포 잇서야 쓰겟소. |
| I must pay a debt of one hundred dollars to-morrow | 빅환 빗진거슬 릭일 갑하야 쓰겟소. |

CHAP. I. § III. SEC. 11.   THE VERB.                    245

### 1. (b).

| You must not put so much coal on the fire. | 셕탄 그러케 넛치 말아야 쓰겟소. |
| You must not hold the baby so. | 아기 그러케 안는 거시 못 쓰겟소. |
| You must not leave your light burning when you go out. | 어듸 갈 째에 등불 혀두고 가면 못 쓰겟소. |
| I told Soun Yongi, he must not even touch the flowers. | 슌용이 드려 화초 믄지지 말아 야 쓰겟다고 ᄒᆞ엿소. |

### 2. (a).

| It must be so. | 그러케 되겟소. |
| Mr. Song must have more than these. | 송셔방 안테 이 보다 더 되겟소. |
| You must be dreadfully tired. | 대단이 곤홀수 밧긔 업소. |
| He must be wet through in such a rain as this. | 이 비에 흠신 젓겟소. |

### 2. (b).

| You must have seen those books at Sëoul. | 그 칙들을 셔울셔 보앗겟소. |
| *It must have been extremely difficult. | 파히 어려웟겟소. |
| The new place must have been finished before he left Sëoul. | 셔울셔 떠나기 젼에 새 대궐 다 지엇겟소. |

SEC. II.—OUGHT, SHOULD.

1 Obligation, Propriety.

   (a.) Affirmative—future relative participle with 거시오.

(b.) Negative—future relative participle of the negative verb with 거시오.

2 Strong probability.

(a.) Affirmative—future relative participle with 러히오.

(b.) Negative—future relative participle of the negative verb with 러히오 (" Ought to have " takes future past participle).

3 Advice.

(a.) Asking advice,—either future in 리가, or conditional present with 됴켓쇼 or 올켓쇼 or present relative participle with 거시됴켓쇼.

(b.) Giving advice, — either conditional present with 됴켓쇼 or present relative participle with 거시됴켓쇼.

4 Censure, Regret,—conditional past, with future past of 됴쇼 or 됴흘걸그리호엿쇼.

I. (a).

| | |
|---|---|
| The people ought to obey just laws. | 빅셩들이 됴흔 법을 좃칠 거시오. |
| Even an enemy should be forgiven. | 원슈 라도 용셔 홀거시오. |
| Men ought certainly to speak the truth. | 사롬이 맛당이 바른 말을 홀거시오. |
| Every man ought certainly to be vaccinated. | 사롬 마다 맛당이 우두롤 홀거시오. |
| Soun Yongi should certainly be more respectful. | 슌용이가 맛당히 더 공슌 홀거시오. |
| You ought to apologize to the consul. | 공사의 샤죄 홀거시오. |

## 1. (b).

| You ought not to sleep so late. | 그러케 늣도록 자지 아니 홀거시오. |
|---|---|
| Mr. Pak, ought not to be out too late. | 박셔방이 너무 늣게 밧긔 잇지 아니 홀거시오. |
| He ought not to ask so much. | 그러케 만히 아니 달날거시오. |

## 2. (a).

| He ought to be here directly. | 지금 올 터히오. |
|---|---|
| It is already past twelve, the clock ought to have struck. | 발셔 열두 시가 지낫시니 죠명 죵이 첫실 터히오. |
| The dictionary ought to be good, it was written by a scholar. | 이 ᄌ뎐은 박학훈 사롭이 민드럿시니 됴흔 터히오. |
| Oranges ought to be very cheap now. | 지금은 유ᄌ가 미우 싸질 터히오. |

## 2. (b).

| It ought not to have been very cold in Fusan. | 부산셔 미우 칩지 아니 ᄒ엿실 거시오. |
|---|---|
| They ought not to be asleep as early as this. | 이러케 일즉 자지 아니 홀터히오. |
| It was very carefully made, it ought not to be weak. | 이 거슬 ᄆᆞᆷ 드려 민드럿시니 약ᄒ지 아니 홀 터히오. |

## 3. (a).

| Which road should I take? | 어ᄂ 길노 가리잇가? |
|---|---|
| What color ought I to paint this? | 무솜 빗ᄎ로 그리면 됴켓쇼? |

| | |
|---|---|
| How ought I to translate this? | 이거슬 엇더케 번역 ㅎ눈거시 됴켓소? |
| I am going to Chemulpo, about how much ought I to pay the chair coolies? | 내가 제물포를 갈러ᄒᆞᆫ듸 교군군 얼마나 주면 울켓소? |

3. (b).

| | |
|---|---|
| You ought to take an umbrella. | 우산 가지고 가눈거시 됴켓소. |
| You should go. | 로형이 가면 됴켓소. |
| You had better not build a house. | 집 짓지 아니 ᄒᆞ눈거시 됴켓소. |
| You should consult with your father. | 아바지 와 공론ᄒᆞ면 됴켓소. |
| Should you not buy a couple? | ᄒᆞᆫ 두엇 사눈 거시 됴치 안켓ᄂᆞ냐? |

4.

| | |
|---|---|
| Then, you ought to have said so. | 그런즉 그러케 말 ᄒᆞ엿더면 됴핫켓소. |
| You ought to have been more careful. | 더 조심 ᄒᆞ엿 더면 됴핫겟소. |
| I ought not to have said a word about it. | 내가 말 아니 ᄒᆞ엿더면 됴홀걸 그리 ᄒᆞ엿소. |
| I ought to have put on my mangen before. | 망건 진작 썻더면 됴홀 거슬 그리 ᄒᆞ엿소. |

SEC. 12.—THINK, SUPPOSE.

1 Regard as a fact—future participle with 줄노아오, 줄아오.

2 Regard as probable :—

   (a.) Likely to happen—future relative participle with 듯ᄒᆞ오 or 듯십소.

CHAP. I. § III. SEC. 12.   THE VERB.   249

(b.) Likely to have happened—future past participle with 듯ㅎ오 or 듯십소.

Note.—Where we would use the verb "to think," the Koreans, for the most part, use the verb "to know."

"To know" with the accusative postposition, conveys to the Korean the idea of absolute knowledge, but with the postposition 로 the idea of an opinion, merely.

송서방을 아오 means I know Mr. Song but 송서방으로 알앗소 "I knew him (*understood*) for Mr. Song," or "I thought it was Mr. Song."

### 1.

| | |
|---|---|
| I did not think you would come to-day. | 오놀 공이 아니 올줄 알앗소. |
| Some people think that man is crazy. | 엇던 사룸 싱각은 그가 밋친줄 아오. |
| I thought I could go in half an hour. | 내 싱각에는 반시면 갈줄 알앗소. |
| I thought Mr. Song would probably be late. | 내가 송서방이 혹 늣게 올줄 알앗소. |
| When I first saw you I thought you were an old friend. | 로형을 처음 볼 째에 구면으로 알앗소. |

### 2. (a).

| | |
|---|---|
| I do not think you will find any good fresh fish there. | 내싱각에는 조너가 더긔셔 성훈 싱션을 찻지못 홀듯ㅎ리. |
| I do not think you will like Korean food. | 공이 죠션 음식을 됴화 홀가 십지 안소. |
| I suppose there are plenty of fleas in this mat. | 내 싱각에는 이 자리에 벼룩이 만홀듯 ㅎ오. |

### 2. (b).

| | |
|---|---|
| I do not think the minister has arisen yet. | 공ᄉ가 아직 아니 니러나 셧실듯 십소. |

250　　　　　　　THE VERB.　CHAP. I. § III. SEC. 13.

| Do you suppose the steamer has arrived yet? (Addressing an old man). | 어루신너 성각에 화륜션이 드러 왓실듯 십쇼? |
|---|---|
| I suppose the postman passed while I was out. | 나 나간 동안에 톄젼부가 지나갓실듯 십쇼. |
| I suppose the eggs are all gone. | 알 다 썻실듯 호오. |

### SEC. 13.—INTEND.

1 Intend is rendered by the stem of the verb with 랴호오 or 고자호오. These two are really almost interchangeable, but the latter is a little stronger and conveys more the idea of definite purpose, although this distinction cannot always be recognized.

2 Sometimes also the same idea is expressed by the use of the future relative participle with 것.

1.

| I intend to go by the nine o'clock train. . | 아홉시 화륜거에 가랴고 호오. |
|---|---|
| I intended to let you know, but I had no time. | 내가 공씌 알게 호랴고 호엿것 마는 밧바셔 못 호엿쇼. |
| I had not intended to let Mr. Yi know, but he heard it without my knowledge. | 내가 리셔방씌 알니랴는 거슨 아니엿 마는 몰너 듯고 알앗쇼. |
| I had not intended going, but as that person advised it, I went. | 내가 가랴는 거슨 아니엿시나 그 사룸이 권호기에 갓소. |
| I intended building a house, but I could not afford it. | 내가 집을 지랴 호엿시나 저력을 당치 못 호엿쇼. |

| | |
|---|---|
| I intended to use them, but could not. | 쓰랴다가 못 썻소. |
| He intended eating it, but did not. | 먹으랴다가 못 먹엇소, |
| I intended to go, but something came up and I could not. | 가랴 ᄒᆞ엿것 마는 일 잇서 못 갓소. |

2.

| | |
|---|---|
| He says he intended to go, but did not. | 갈 거슬 아니 갓다고 ᄒᆞ옵더이다. |
| I intended to finish the book yesterday, but I was sick and did not. | 그 칙을 어저씌 못칠 거슬 병이 잇서 못 ᄒᆞ엿소. |

### Sec. 14.—Want.

1. Followed by a noun.

   (*a*.) Need, Require—the verb. 쓰오.

   (*b*.) Desire to have—원ᄒᆞ오 or by the use of a verb with 십소 as in number 2.

2. Followed by a verb.

   (*a*.) Desire to do—십소 joined to the verb by the particle 고.

   (*b*.) Wish it to be—밋소 or a circumlocution.

3. Meaning " how about," how would it be."—verb in 랴, 고십소, or conditional present with 엇더ᄒᆞ오.

4. Used independently in questions signifying, *for what purpose*, etc.—a noun or pronoun to signify the thing purposed with the postposition 로.

1. (*a*).

| | |
|---|---|
| Do you want this? | 이것 쓰랴오? |

| | |
|---|---|
| I want a chair to go to Chong No. | 죵로 가기에 보료 쓰겟소. |
| Do you not want some small ones? | 적은 거슨 아니 쓰랴오? |
| I do not think we shall need any crab apples to-day. | 내 셩각에는 오놀 룽금 쓸듸 업슬듯호오. |

1. (b).

| | |
|---|---|
| Sujini wants some grapes. | 슈진이가 포도를 달나고 십소. |
| Do you want a small puppy? | 조굠안 강아지 호나 가지고 십소? |
| I want a Chinese tailor. | 즁국 옷 쟝이 엇고 십소. |
| He said he wanted some foreign cloth. | 셔양목 좀 엇고 십다고 호오. |

2. (a).

| | |
|---|---|
| Mr. Pak wants to borrow a small knife. | 박셔방이 적은 칼 빌고 십소. |
| I wanted to see Yi Cham-pan, but he was out. | 리참판을 보고 십엇시나 츌입 호엿습더이다. |
| Although I did not want to write the letter, as he told me to, I did. | 그 편지를 쓰고 십지 아니 호되 쓰라고 호기에 썻소. |
| I have wanted to give you one for some time. | 발셔 브터 호나 주고 십엇쇼. |
| Do you not want this letter sent to the post office by Soung Yongi? | 이 편지 슌용이 식여셔 우편국에 보내고 십지 아니 호오? |

2. (b).

| | |
|---|---|
| I want it well made. | 잘 만들 기를 밋소. |

CHAP. I. § III. SEC. 15.   THE VERB.                            253

I want it made exactly like this.   똑 이대로 믄둘니고 십소

He wants it pressed well.   잘 눌니면 됴화 ᄒ겟소.

3.

Do you want to change pens?   붓 밧고 랴오?

Do you not want to buy four?   넷슬 사고 십지 안소?

Do you want to go to Nam San this afternoon?   오놀 오후에 남산에 가면 엇더 ᄒ오?

4.

What does he want here?   여긔 무삼 일노 왓소?
What do you want with me?   무삼 일노 나를 불넛소?

SEC. 15.—WISH, HOPE.

1 Desire to do—same as Sec. 14, 2. (*a.*) of this chapter.
2 Hope that a thing is, or will be :—

  (*a.*) Simple desire—verbal noun in 기 with accusative postposition and 보라오 ; or conditional present with future of 됴소.
  (*b*) Coupled with doubt, fear or regret—conditional past with 됴소.

It is also correct to use the conditional past alone as an exclamation, and this practice is much in vogue among Koreans. Sometimes also the past tense of 보라오 is used.

2. (*a*).

I hope to-morrow will be fine too.   뇌일 도 날 됴키를 보라오.

| | |
|---|---|
| I hope that that boy will be a scholar too. | 뎌 ㅇ히 도 션비 되기를 부라오. |
| I hope he will soon recover. | 쉬히 낫기를 부라오. |
| I hope it will be done by the day after tomorrow. | 모레 다 되기를 부라오. |
| I wish you would tell him. | 닐너 주면 됴켓소. |
| I wish it would not rain. | 비가 아니 오면, 됴켓소. |

2. (*b*).

| | |
|---|---|
| I wish I had a little change. | 잔돈 좀 잇섯더면 됴켓소. |
| I wish you had told me sooner. | 더 일쯕 닐넛더면 됴켓소. |
| I wish that dog would'nt bark. | 그 개가 아니 짓주면 됴켓소. |
| I wish we would'nt have any more snow. | 이 후에 눈이 그만 왓시면 됴켓소. |
| I wish I could learn Korean. | 죠션 말 비홀 수가 잇섯더면. |
| I wish I were a little taller. | 좀 더 컷더면. |
| I wish he had come yesterday. | 어저씌 왓더면 됴켓소. |
| I hoped it would be pleasant to-day, but it is doubtful. | 오놀이 됴키를 부랏것마는 엇더홀넌지오. |
| I hoped he would come by that steamer, but he did'nt. | 뎌 화륜션으로 올가 부랏더니 아니 왓소. |

SEC. 16.—NEED.

1. Followed by a noun—Same as Sec. 14, 1 (*a*.) of this chapter *q v.;* or by the use of the past verbal participle with the postposition 야.

2. Followed by a Verb :—
   (a.) Negative—By future relative participle with 것업소.
   (b.) Affirmative—Same as *must* see Sec. 10.

### 1.

| | |
|---|---|
| You need court robes to enter the palace. | 관복 잇서야 대궐에 드러 가겟소. |
| You need a new hat. | 공은 새갓 잇서야 쓰겟소. |
| You need money to build a large house. | 돈 잇서야 큰 집을 짓겟소. |
| You need flour, sugar and eggs to make this cake. | 밀 가로와 사당과 알이 잇서야 이런 사당 떡 문들겟소. |

### 2. (a).

| | |
|---|---|
| You need'nt wait any longer. | 더 기드릴것 업소. |
| You need'nt serve tea before six. | 여섯 시 전에 차 올닐것 업소. |
| You need'nt lock the door when you go out. | 밧긔 나갈 때 문 줌을것 업소. |
| Tell Mr. Kim he need'nt go to Chong Ro to-day. | 김셔방 드려 오늘 종로에 갈것 업다고 후오. |
| As we have a long time yet, we need not go fast. | 아직 시가 머럿시니 급히 갈것 업소. |

### Sec. 17.—Seem, Look.

1 Appearance—the appropriate relative participle and—
  모양이오.
  모양곳소.
  것곳소.
  가보오.
  일이오.
  듯호오.

or appropriate tense of verb with ......... 나보오.

2 Report—the verb, followed by 그리아 or form used in indirect discourse.

1.

| | |
|---|---|
| The fire seems as though it will go out. | 불이 쓰질 모양이오. |
| The fire seems to be going out. | 불이 쓰지는 모양이오. |
| The fire seems to have gone out. | 불이 쓰진 모양이오. |
| When the man came for the shoes he looked a little angry. | 사롬 신 차지러 왓실 째 성 좀 낸것 곳호옵더이다. |
| Those pictures seem to me to be hung a trifle too high. | 내 어림에는 더 그림이 조곰 놉게 걸닌듯호오. |
| When you talk to him he seems to assent. | 말 홀째에는 허락 호는 모양굿소. |
| These mats seem to be dirty. | 이 방석이 더러온 모양이오. |
| This gun seems to be out of order. | 이 총이 병 난것 굿소. |
| It seems wonderful that you can send a telegram to America in four or five hours; does'nt it? | 뎐보로는 소오시 동안이면 미국에 긔별을 보내니 아 춤 이샹훈 일이오 그러치 안소? |
| This pond seems deep. | 이 못시 깁흔것 굿소 |
| This seems the best plan. | 이거시 뎨일 샹척 일듯호오. |
| Mr. Yi looks strong. | 리셔방이 긔운이 미우 센 모양이오. |

| | |
|---|---|
| That man seems to be very clever. | 그사롬 미우 령리혼 모양이옵듸다. |
| That child seems very tired. | 그 ᄋ히가 미우 곤혼 모양이오. |
| It seems to be a fire. | 불 난것 ᄀᆺ소. |
| He looks to me like a thief. | 나 보기는 도젹놈 ᄀᆺ소. |
| The man who came here this morning did'nt look like a Japanese. | 오눌 아춤에 왓던 사롬이 일본 사롬 ᄀᆺ지 아니 ᄒ옵더이다. |
| It looks as though it will rain to-day. | 오눌 비가 올가보오. |
| He had intended to go to see the sights to-day, but it seems as though the rain will prevent it. | 오눌 구경가랴 ᄒ엿더니 엇지면 비가 희방 짓겟 나보오. |
| Last night it seemed as though it would clear. | 어제 져녁에는 날이 길것 ᄀᆺᄒ옵더이다. |
| It does not seem as if there will be much wind. | 바람이 과히 불것 ᄀᆺ지 안소. |
| It does not look like peace. | 태평홀것 ᄀᆺ지 안소. |
| It seems as if this leak is'nt going to stop. | 이 서는거시 긋치지 아닐것 ᄀᆺ소. |

2.

| | |
|---|---|
| It seems there was a fire in Chong Dong yesterday. | 어제 졍동 화지가 낫소 그리아. |
| It seems there is a terrible famine in China. | 지금 즁국에 큰 흉년이 드릿다 ᄒ오. |
| There seems to be no steamer running to Chemulpo now. | 시방은 제물포로 가는 화륜션이 업다 ᄒ오. |
| It seems you've bought a watch. | 시계 삿소 그리아. |

## § IV.—THE INFINITIVE.

In Korean there is no true infinitive; that which the French grammarians denominated the infinitive, is so in no sense of the word. In neuter verbs it is the low form of the indicative present, and in active verbs has little or no use except as a mere designation of the verb, much as we say "the verb to be." There being then no true infinitive and the English infinitive having various senses, it will be rendered therefore in various ways according to circumstances.

1 When it stands as an object or subject of another verb—by the verbal noun in 기, or the relative participle with 것. For this infinitive with auxiliaries, see § III.

2 Signifying the *purpose*, or *object*, with verbs of motion —by the supine in 러 or 라.

3 Signifying *with the intention of*,—the desiderative base with ㄱ or future participle with 나고.*

4 Following the means, instrument or agent—the same as the preceding (3); or, more properly, by the verbal noun in 기 with the postposition 에. (see, Part I. 174).

5 Equivalent to the verbal noun—the verbal noun in 기 or the relative participle, with 것 or 디 etc.

6 Equivalent to "if" and accompanied by "it will" or "it would"—the appropriate tense of the verb with 면.

7 Following verbs of command, direction, or advice,— the imperative verb in 라고 or 라고ᄒᆞ오 sometimes contracted into 래오. (see Part I. ¶ 229).

8 Following verbs of promising, requesting, etc.—the form of indirect narration in 다고.

---

* Note—This last is but a corruption of the desiderative base see Part I. ¶ 238.

CHAP. I. § IV.   THE VERB.   259

1.

| It is wrong to waste time. | 셰월을 허탄이 보내는 거시 그르오. |
| Are you afraid to have your teeth pulled? | 니 쎄기를 무셔워 ᄒᆞ오? |
| The government does not allow foreigners to live in the interior. | 졍부에셔 싀골에 외국 사름 사는 거슬 허락지 아니 ᄒᆞ오. |
| I have decided not to buy a horse. | 물 아니 사기로 결단 ᄒᆞ엿소. |
| Do you want to go to America? | 미국에 가고 십소? |
| You will hardly be able to bring this load alone. | 너 혼자 이짐을 가져올 수 업슬듯ᄒᆞ다. |

2.

| I went to get the vase that we saw the other day, but some one had already bought it. | 젼에 보던 그룻을 사러 갓더니 발셔 누가 사 갓ᄉᆞᆸ더이다. |
| I went to find the children but they had all gone to school. | ᄋᆞ히들 차지러 갓것마는 발셔 다 학당으로 갓소. |
| I went to meet you but you didn't come. | 로형을 맛나러 갓것마는 오지 아니 ᄒᆞ엿소. |
| I came to pay my debts. | 빗 갑흐러 왓소. |

3.

| I raised my hand to strike. | ᄯᅡ리랴고 손을 드럿소. |
| Did you do it to make him angry? | 그 사름 분ᄒᆞ게 홀나고 그러케 ᄒᆞ엿소? |

| | |
|---|---|
| Did you say it to make a fool of him? | 그 사롬 실업는 사롬을 민돌나고 그러케 ᄒᆞ엿소? |
| He bought some arsenic to kill rats, but his child ate it and died. | 쥐를 죽이랴고 비샹을 삿더니 아기가 먹고 죽엇소. |

4.

| | |
|---|---|
| I want a wagon to send this freight to Chemulpo. | 이 짐을 졔물포로 보내 랴고 수래를 엇고 십소. |
| You had better buy a rat trap to catch the rats. | 쥐를 잡기에 쥐 덧슬 사는 거시 됴켓쇼. |
| I must have some nails to mend the box. | 궤를 곳치기에 못슬 엇어 야 쓰겟소. |
| He asks for some money to pay for his supper. | 져녁 밥 갑 주랴고 돈 좀 달나오. |
| I should think it would cost fully a thousand dollars to build such a house. | 내 셩각에는 이런 집은 짓기에 일쳔원 이나 들겟소. |
| How long does it take to send a man to Chemulpo? | 졔물포에 젼인 ᄒᆞ기 몃 시나 되겟소? |
| Call a plasterer to repair the inside of the roof. | 앙로 곳치기에 미쟝이 불너 오너라. |
| Who was appointed to examine the students? | 셩도 샹고 ᄒᆞ기에 누구를 졔슈 ᄒᆞ엿소? |

5.

| | |
|---|---|
| I do not know how much I ought to give, to go on horseback. | 물 틋고 가는디 얼마나 주어야 됴흔지 모르 겟소. |

| | |
|---|---|
| We went down to the beach but the waves were too high to bathe. | 우리가 바다 그호로 갓소 마는 목욕 감기에 물결 이 너무 컷소. |
| How much ought I to give to have my court sodded? | 우리 마당 쎄 닙히는디 돈 얼마나 주면 됴켓소? |
| Did you not have to pay to cross the river? | 강 건너 가기에 돈 안주 엇소? |
| How many chair coolies shall we need to go to Pouk Han? | 북한 가기에 교군군 멋 쓰겟소? |

### 6.

| | |
|---|---|
| It will be a great mistake to wait a month longer. | 혼돌을 더 기드리면 미우 실슈가 되겟소. |
| It will injure the country very much to pass such a law. | 만일 이런 법을 세우면 나라에 미우 욕 되겟소. |
| I don't believe it would pay to publish the "O Ryun Haing Sil" in foreign type. | 내 성각에는 오륜힝실을 양셔로 판각 흐면 리가 못 남겟소. |
| It would be very inconvenient for me to move to Chemulpo. | 졔물포에 이샤 흐면 맛당 찬켓소. |
| It will not be very pleasant to get into debt. | 빗슬 지면 샹쾌 찬켓소. |
| Tell Sou Pongi to serve breakfast. | 슈봉이 드려 아츰 밥을 가져 오라고 흐오. |

### 7.

| | |
|---|---|
| Tell the servant not to forget about the coal. | 하인 드려 셕탄 일을 니져 브리지 말나 흐오. |

262 THE VERB. Chap. I. § V.

| | |
|---|---|
| He told the chair coolies to go to the river in time to meet the steamer. | 교군군 드려 화륜션 맛날 째에 강으로 가라고 ᄒᆞ엿소. |
| Tell the gate-man to go out and get a pack horse. | 문 하인 드려 나가 복마 엇으래라. |
| Didn't the doctor advise you to go to Gensan? | 의원이 공을 원산에 가라고 권치 아니 ᄒᆞ엿 습ᄂᆞ니잇가? |

8.

| | |
|---|---|
| He promised to give me five dollars, but he has not. | 오원 주마고 ᄒᆞ더니 아니 주엇소. |
| He promised to meet us in Chemulpo. | 제물포 에셔 맛나겟다고 샹약 ᄒᆞ옵더이다. |
| I promised to go, but I don't feel well. | 내가 가겟다고 샹약 ᄒᆞ엿시나 편치 못ᄒᆞ오. |
| Shall I go and tell the seamstress to come to get her pay? | 침모 의게 가셔 공젼을 차지러 오라고 닐ᄋᆞ리 잇가? |

### § V.—PASSIVE CONSTRUCTION.

Koreans like most orientals do not find much use for a passive construction. As has been said in the Grammatical Notes, a passive form can be derived from all transitive verbs. In many cases, however, the use of this passive, except in certain sections of the country, is considered inelegant. When, then, the foreigner desires to render a passive construction, there are several ways open to him.

1 In some cases, the use of a passive form with certain

verbs has become so general throughout the whole country that it is not considered inelegant.

2 There are in Korean a number of intransitive verbs, or intransitive forms of expression, that may and do commonly take the place of the English passive.

3 Where neither of the above methods are admissible, the English passive must be rendered into Korean by a change of the form of the sentence. This change of form will of course vary according to the circumstances :—

> (*a.*) When the passive construction can be rendered by the active, with the indefinite "they" the sentence will be translated accordingly.
>
> (*b.*) When the English sentence is simply explanatory it may be rendered by the past and sometimes the present participle, generally with 것.
>
> (*c.*) When the passive clause is the object of another verb, its verb assumes the active form, and is generally, translated by the participle with 것 or 일.
>
> (*d.*) "To be" followed by the passive participle expressing past action still continuing, is rendered sometimes by the simple active construction, as in (*a*); sometimes by the participial form of the verb, with 것잇쇼, or negative, with 업쇼; sometimes by the simple verbal participle with 잇쇼; and sometimes when intransitive verbs are used, by the past form in 더 expressing continued action.

1.

Where were you bitten?  어 듸 룰  물니엿수옵더니 잇가?

| | |
|---|---|
| Soun Yongi has been stung in the finger by a bee. | 슌용이 손가락을 벌의게 쏘이엿습더이다. |
| He was arrested by the police, on the twelfth day of the sixth month. | 륙월 열잇흔 날에 포교 의게 잡혓소. |
| One is open, the other is shut. | 흐나흔 열니고 흐나흔 닷쳣습더이다. |
| At Chemulpo, Fusan and Gensan, trading posts were first opened. | 제물포와 부산과 원산에 쟝ᄉ 항구가 처음 열녓소. |

2.

| | |
|---|---|
| Don't let yourself be cheated. | 속지 마오. |
| Man Chini has been whipped several times, for doing that. | 만진이가 그러케 흐기에 여러 번 믹 마졋소. |
| This child was vaccinated by a Korean doctor, | 죠션 의원 의게셔 이 ᄋ 히가 우두롤 너헛소. |
| A fire arose in Chong Dong, and about half Seoul was burnt. | 졍동셔 화지가 나셔 셔울이 거위 반이나 툿습더이다. |
| About when will the new Pouk Han temple be finished? | 북한 새 졀이 언제나 다 되겟소? |
| It was finished long ago. | 발셔 다 된지 오래오. |
| Not one has been shipwrecked. | 흐나도 파션 흐지 아니 흐엿소. |
| Is much sugar brought to Korea from China every year? | 히 마다 즁국셔 사탕이 죠션에 만히 나오? |

| | |
|---|---|
| This receipt has not yet been signed. | 이 령슈중이 아직 슈결 맛지 아니 호엿소. |
| I thought foreigners would be expelled immediately. | 외국 사룸들이 곳 쏫겨 나갈 줄 알앗소. |
| Has the carpenter been paid for the bookcase? | 목슈가 칙쟝 몬든 갑슬 밧앗소? |
| While I was in Seoul, I was taught by a man from Pyeng Yang. | 셔울 잇슬 적에 평양 사룸의게 비홧소. |

### 3. (a).

| | |
|---|---|
| Has this room been swept? | 방 쓰럿 느냐? |
| Tobacco is used almost everywhere. | 담비롤 거위 스방에셔 쓰오. |
| I understand that in certain countries the criminals are beaten to death with clubs. | 내 드르니 엇던 나라에 셔는 죄인을 곤쟝으로 쏘려 죽인다 ᄒᆞ옵더이다. |
| Diamonds have recently been found in Africa. | 금강셕을 근티 아비리가 에셔 차젓소. |
| At what time is the rice harvested? | 어느 째에 벼를 츄슈 ᄒᆞ오? |
| Where were those oranges put? | 그 유ᄌᆞ를 어디 두엇소? |

### 3. (b).

| | |
|---|---|
| This (boat) ticket was bought for a friend, but he has not yet come. | 이 션표가 친구를 위ᄒᆞ야 산 거시엇 마는 아직 아니 왓소. |
| This certainly was written with a lead pencil. | 이거시 뎡녕이 연필노 쓴 거시오. |

| | |
|---|---|
| Was this letter brought by the Euiju courier? | 이 편지가 의쥬 비지로 가져 온 거시오? |
| Was this cut with a knife or with scissors? | 이 거시 칼노 버힌 거시오 가위로 버힌 거시오? |
| What is kanjang made of, and when is it used? | 간쟝을 무어스로 믄두는 거시며 쏘 언제 쓰는 거시오? |

3. (c).

| | |
|---|---|
| I should like to hear the komengo well played. | 거문고 잘 두는 소리를 드르면 됴켓소. |
| Before I went to America, I had never seen a cannon fired. | 미국에 가기 전에는 대 프 놋는 걸 못 보앗소. |
| Did you ever see a man's head cut off? | 사름의 목 버히는 거슬 흔번 보앗소? |

3. (d).

| | |
|---|---|
| The roof of that house is tiled. | 뎌 집 집웅을 기와로 니엇소. |
| It is in the drawer, wrapped up in paper, and tied with a string. | 설합 속에 드럿 눈디 죠 희로 싸고 노끈 으로 잡아 민 거시오. |
| None of those shoes are well sewed. | 이 신 바누질 잘 흔것 흔나도 업소. |
| This fish is'nt well broiled. | 이 셩션 잘 군 것 아니오. |
| It was hidden under the roots of a pine tree. | 쇼나모 샐희 밋헤 곰초아 잇습더이다. |
| It must certainly be hidden somewhere in the garden. | 어듸 던지 뎡녕이 화원에 곰초인 거시오. |
| Was the lamp lighted in the minister's room? | 공스 방에 불을 혓더냐? |

## § VI.—CONDITIONAL SENTENCES.

We will but consider three classes of conditional sentences in this place.

1st. Simple conditional :—

These are rendered by the simple tenses, present, past, and future, with 면 in the conditional clause; and the future, or sometimes the present, in the conclusion.

2nd. Supposition contrary to fact :—

This class of sentences may be rendered by the compound tenses, or the forms of the verb in 더, with 면 in the conditional clause; and the future perfect in the conclusion. Quite often the conclusion will take the future participle with 번호오.

3rd. Improbable supposition :—

When the supposition contains the idea of doubt, "*if*" may be rendered by 면, with the interposition of a particle expressing doubt or uncertainty as 혹, or by 거든.

Note.—As was remarked in the Grammatical Notes, this particle 거든, has often the idea of time, and may generally be said to give the idea of condition, with the necessary notion of time. In common use to-day, however, it has nearly always, the idea of doubt.

| | |
|---|---|
| If you let the fire out, we shall all take cold. | 불 쓰지게 호면 우리들이 다 감긔 들겟소. |
| If the steamer leaves to-morrow we can't go. | 비가 뇌일 써나면 우리들이 못 가겟소. |
| If he goes I'll go too. | 그가 가면 나도 가겟소. |
| If he has gone we can't help it. | 갓시면 우리가 홀수업소. |
| If he has already sold the books, no matter. | 칙를 발셔 팔앗시면 관계 찬소. |

2.

| If he were going I would go. | 그 사룸 가더면 내가 갓겟소. |
| If you had loaned me fifty dollars then, I could have paid my debt, made a little money myself, and paid you back with interest, in five days. | 그째 로형이 내게 은젼 오십 원을 빌녓더면 젼 빗슬 다갑고 내가 돈 좀 먹고 닷새 만에 로형 의게 빌어 온 돈과 변리를 다 갑핫겟소. |
| If you had told me she was sick, I would have gone there yesterday. | 병 잇셧다고 닐녓더면 어저씌 내가 갈 번 ᄒ엿소. |
| If it were not raining we would all get horses and go to the So Chang Myo. | 비 오지 안터면 우리들이 다 ᄆᆞᆯ 엇고 쇼창묘로 갓겟소. |
| If I were going to do it, I would have done it already. | 그 일 ᄒ겟더면 발셔 ᄒ엿겟소. |

3.

| If it should not be raining at that time let's go. | 그 째 비 오지 아니 ᄒ거든 가옵시다. |
| If he should have gone, bring the letter back. | 갓 거든 편지 도로 가져 오너라. |
| If you should be going to Seoul I wish you would take a letter for me; | 셔울 가겟거든 내편지 ᄒ나 젼ᄒ야 주면 됴겟소. |
| If they should be spoiled he says he will change them. | 샹ᄒ엿 거든 다 밧곤다고 ᄒ오. |

# CHAPTER II.

### THE NOUN.

With reference to the rendering of English nouns in Korean there is little to be said here. For the most part, they are rendered by their exact equivalents in Korean, which can be found in a dictionary. In some instances, (and these from the nature of the case are not a few) where the idea is entirely new to the Korean mind, new words must be formed, either by the use of ideas known to the Korean, or by the bodily introduction of foreign words into the language. This latter course however, except where the use of Korean ideas would make the words altogether too cumbersome for use, is to be deprecated.

In not a few cases where the foreigner would use an abstract noun, the Korean would prefer to transpose the sentence and use a verb.

The heat in this room is very great.   이 방 대단이 더웁소.

Mr. Yi's kindness to me was very great.   리셔방이 내게 대단이 어질게 ᄒᆞ엿소.

It is not necessary here, to give further illustrations of the noun, as these are found in all the sentences.

# CHAPTER III.

### THE ARTICLE.

There are no words in Korean that exactly express the force of the English definite article. As has been stated before, the Koreans are not, for the most part, in the habit of affixing the appropriate postposition to its noun unless it is needed to avoid ambiguity.

The addition of the postposition giving definiteness, has often the effect of the article *the*.

The indefinite article is as a rule not rendered into Korean.

The absence of the proper Korean Postposition generally gives sufficient indefiniteness without any addition. It can however at times be expressed by the use of the Korean numeral 호 (*one*) placed before the noun.

<sub>Note.—The other form of the numeral, 호나, is placed after the noun, emphasizing the fact of there being but *one*, and can never therefore take the place of the English indefinite article.</sub>

Sometimes, this indefiniteness is expressed simply by the absence of any postposition.

The books have come.     칙 들 이 왓쇼.
                                           Books, (plur. nom.) have come.

| | |
|---|---|
| The patient took the medicine, but he died. | 병인이 약은 먹엇시나 죽엇소. |
| A boy came and brought the books. | 훈 ᄋ히 와셔 칙을 가져 왓소. |
| Bring me a pencil. | 연필 가져 오너라. |
| It is a letter from my friend who lives in America. | 이거시 미국 사는 내 친구가 보낸 편지오. |
| He is a famous gentleman among the Chinese. | 그이가 쳥국 사롬중에 유명훈 신사요. |
| Dealing in rice is a profitable business. | 쌀 무역 ᄒ는 거시 크게 유익훈 장사요. |
| I heard the news from a Seoul man, when I was staying with him. | 내가 그 소문을 셔울 사롬의게 드릿 는듸 ᄌᆞ치 떠믈 째에 드릿소. |
| It is very strange how an owl can fly in the night better than in the day. | 올빔이가 낫보다 밤에 잘 ᄂᆞ는 거시 미우 이샹ᄒ오. |

# CHAPTER IV.

PRONOUNS.

## § I.—Personal Pronouns.

As has been said before, the use of the personal pronoun in Korean is very much restricted and on this account we would again urge upon the student the necessity of omitting the pronouns when speaking Korean. At times however, for emphasis, or to avoid ambiguity, and also, sometimes as a matter of politeness the pronouns or words to take their place, are used.

The regular pronouns can be found in the chapter on pronouns in Part I. Other words are often used to take their place, as 쇼인 (*little man*) and 주긔 (*my body*) etc. for I; 로형이 (*elder brother*) 어루신너 (*aged father*), etc. for you.

The English possessive pronouns are formed by affixing the postposition 의 (*of*).

Note.—In many places where we would use the pronoun of the first person singular, the Korean would use the plural, and often for first person plural, they will use the plural 우리 together with the sign of the plural 둘. See Part I. ¶ 60 ff.

| | |
|---|---|
| I brought the box, and the servant carried the bundle. | 그 궤는 내가 가져 오고 보통이는 하인이 들고 왓소. |
| This is different from what I ordered. | 내가 호라는 것과 달소. |
| The ladies rode in chairs, but we walked. | 녀편네들은 교군을 툿시나 우리는 걸엇소. |
| Some of us would like to study history. | 우리 중에 스긔 비호랴 눈이 더러 잇소. |
| Everything I say seems to offend you. | 내 말 마다 로형을 성나게 호는 모양이오. |
| Did you leave the door open? | 뎌 문 네가 열어 노앗 누냐? |
| There was a man here an hour or two ago enquiring for you. | 호 두어 시 젼에 사름이 여긔 와셔 공을 차잣소. |
| That fur hat of yours just fits you. | 공의 털모주가 쪽 맛소 |
| My father died three years ago. | 우리 아바지 삼년 젼에 도라 가셧소. |
| Come out to my house in the country, and spend a month. | 우리 싀골 집으로 와 호둘 머므 시오. |
| You're a little particular. | 당신이 조곰 사다롭소. |
| He's a man of abilility, but he lacks energy. | 저조는 잇시나 브즈런치는 못 호오. |
| Are not these yours? | 이것 공의 거시 아니오? |
| He offered me a hundred dollars but I would not take it. | 날 드려 은젼 빅원 주마고 호엿것 마는 밧지 아니 호엿소. |

SEC. 2.—COMPOUND PERSONAL PRONOUNS.

There is no one word in Korean, that gives exactly the force of the English word "*self*." It must therefore be rendered according to the shade of meaning to be expressed.

1 When it is simply emphatic—simple personal pronoun with the emphatic postposition 눈, or personal pronoun alone.

2 One's self as well as another,—personal pronoun with 도.

3 Signifying one's self as distinguished from others—by the use of 친히, or 조긔, or by the repetition of the pronoun.

4 Signifying alone—by 혼자.

5 Of itself—by 절노.

1.

| | |
|---|---|
| I'll lend it, just as soon as I finish reading it myself. | 나는 다 닑고 곳 빌니리이다. |
| When I would'nt eat it myself, do you think I'd give it to you? | 나는 먹지 아니 하엿는디 네게 줄 줄 아느냐? |

2.

| | |
|---|---|
| I tripped on that sill two or three times myself. | 나도 그 문즁방 에셔 두서너 빈 이나 너머 질번 하엿소. |
| We ourselves could'nt sleep last night, so no wonder you could'nt when you were so near the fire. | 우리도 못 잣는디 공은 불난디 그러케 갓가오니 못 잔거시 이샹 홀것 업소. |

3.

| I'll go myself. | 내가 친히 가겟소. |
| You ought to be able to answer that yourself. | 그거슨 공이 친히 듸답 홀수가 잇슬 거시오. |
| He said that he himself would give five thousand dollars. | 제가 친히 은젼 오쳔원 주마고 ᄒᆞ엿소. |
| I cannot clear myself before God. | 주긔는 주긔를 샹데 압희 발명 홀수 업소. |

4.

| I doubt whether you can do it by yourself. | 공이 혼자 홀가 시부지 안소. |
| He is unable to teach so large a school by himself. | 그러케 큰 학당 혼자 ᄀᆞᄅᆞ칠수 업소? |

5.

| Do you believe the world came into existence by itself? | 공의 싱각에는 세계가 졀노 된듯 십소? |

## § II—RELATIVE PRONOUNS.

Like the Japanese, Korean is without relative pronouns, and the relative clause is rendered by the use of the re-relative participle, which comes before what in English is the antecedent clause, and acts as an adjective governing it. For instance, the Koreans do not say "The man who came yesterday" but, "The yesterday came man," 어졔온사름. It may be well to add that the tense of the relative participle will of cause follow the tense of the relative clause.

When the antecedent is "*it*" or "*that*," either expressed or implied, it is rendered by 것, or of a person by 이.

| Who was that you bowed to just now? | 지금 인사 ㅎ던 이가 누구요? |
| --- | --- |
| Who was that who bowed to you just now? | 공셔 인사 ㅎ던이가 누구요? |
| He is a fellow that used to be a servant of ours. | 젼에 우리게 하인 으로 잇던 놈이오. |
| What is it that crow has in its mouth? | 뎌 가마귀 입에 문 거시 무어시오? |
| Let us see what you have in your hand. | 손에 잇는 것 좀 보옵시다. |
| What the rats don't carry off, the ants eat. | 쥐가 아니 무러간 거슬 개아미가 먹소. |
| Have you done what I told you? | 내가 닐온 것 ㅎ엿느냐? |
| What was the name of the king who used to kill flies when he was a boy? | 어렷실 쎄에 파리 죽이던 님금의 일홈이 무어시오? |
| The horse I gave so much for, is not worth his feed. | 그러케 돈 만히 주고 산 물이 저 먹는 죽 갑 도 못 ㅎ오. |
| Did they take the carpenter who fell off the roof, and sprained his arm to the hospital? | 집웅셔 락샹 ㅎ야 팔 부러진 목슈를 병원 으로 드려 갓소? |
| Who was that woman you met a little while ago with a baby on her back? | 아까 맛나던 우히 업은 계집이 누구요? |
| In which drawer do you keep your lead pencils? | 연필 둔 설합이 어느 거시오? |

| | |
|---|---|
| Is'nt this the book in which you put the letter? | 편지 둔 칙은 이거시 아니오? |
| Where does the clay of which they make these bricks, come from? | 이 벽돌 믄드는 흙이 어듸셔 오오? |
| I can't find the paper in which these books were wrapped. | 이 칙 쌋던 죠희롤 차질 수가 업소. |
| Where is the book that you were going to give me? | 나롤 주랴고 ᄒᆞ던 칙이 어듸 잇슴ᄂᆞ니잇가? |

### § III.—INTERROGATIVE PRONOUNS.

The English interrogatives are translated by their equivalents in Korean, which may be found in Part I. 66 ff.

For convenience and study, however, we will give a few sentences below arranged in the following order.

1. Who, is rendered by 뉘 or 누구, 누, with the appropriate postpositions.

"Whose" used as a substantive is rendered by 뉘것, 뉘히.

Sometimes also *who* may be rendered by the circumlocution, 어ᄂᆞ사롬 (*what man?*).

2. Which:—
   (*a.*) Used substantively,— 어ᄂᆞ것, or 엇던것.
   (*b.*) Used adjectively,— 어ᄂᆞ or 엇던.
3. What:—*

---

* Note.—In many places where we would use "*what*" the Koreans employ some other word. The Koreans would not say "What does Mr. Yi think" but "how does Mr. Yi think." They would not say "At what time" but "At which hour," etc. In many places also where we would use *what* substantively, the Korean uses it adjectively and vice-versa.

(*a.*) Used substantively,—무엇, 무슴것.
(*b.*) Used adjectively,—무슴.
4. What kind of, what sort of,—엇던.

| | |
|---|---|
| Who invented the telegraph? | 누가 뎐신을 발명 하엿소? |
| Of whom have you learned hitherto? | 이 째 까지 뉘게 비홧소? |
| With whom are you living? | 누구 하고 굿치 잇소? |
| Whose shoes are those? | 뎌 신 뉘 희냐? |
| Whose are those apples? | 뎌 룽금 뉘 거시오? |

2 (*a*).

| | |
|---|---|
| Which do you like best? | 엇던 거슬 그즁 됴하 하오? |
| Which of these two books was printed last? | 이 두 칙즁에 어느 거시 그즁 나죵에 박혓소? |
| Which shall I do first? | 엇던 일을 내가 몬져 하리잇가? |

2 (*b*).

| | |
|---|---|
| Which road shall I take? | 어느 길노 가리잇가? |
| Which carpenter shall I call? | 어느 목슈롤 브르리잇가? |
| In which room did you put the new screen? | 새 병풍 엇던 방에 두엇느냐? |

3 (*a*), (*b*); and 4.

| | |
|---|---|
| What are you doing? | 무엇 하느냐? |
| What have you come for? | 무얼노 왓느냐? |

| | |
|---|---|
| What is that? | 뎌거시 무어시오? |
| What is a "pogyo"? | 보쿄가 무어시오? |
| What is Mr. Song's opinion? | 송셔방 성각은 엇덧소? |
| What does Mr. Yi think of it? | 리셔방이 엇더케 녁이오? |
| Please explain to me what is the meaning of this word? | 이 말 뜻시 무어신지 좀 그르쳐 주시오? |
| What flowers do you intend to plant in your garden? | 엇던 화초롤 공의 화원에 십으랴오? |
| By what road did you come? | 어느 길노 왓소? |
| In what neighbourhood does Mr. Kim live? | 김셔방이 어느 동너 사오? |
| At what time does the boat start? | 어느 째에 화륜션 써나오? |
| What is the reason? | 무숨 선둙 이오? |
| What is that man's name? | 그 사름이 셩명이 무어시오? |
| What is the name of this fish? | 이 성션 일홈이 무어시오? |
| What is the name of the place where they get that coal? | 그 셕탄 나는 디 디명이 무어시오? |
| What do they call the river this side of Mapo? | 마포 이편쟉 강 일홈이 무어시라고 호오? |
| In what box did you put it? | 그거슬 어느 궤에 너헛소? |

# CHAPTER V.

PRONOMINAL ADJECTIVES.

Adjectives have been divided into two classes, qualifying, and limiting, the latter have again been divided into articles, pronominal adjectives, and numerals. The few words necessary on articles have already been given, numerals and qualifying adjectives have in part been treated in Part I., and a few additional hints will be given later. There remain therefore for our consideration in this place, pronominal adjectives, or adjectives that are sometimes used to take the place of nouns. Among these are—

| All | Either | Neither | Such. |
| Any | Few | One | Same. |
| Both | Many | Several | That. |
| Each | Much | Some | This etc. |

In the following selection of these words it will be noticed that some not commonly called pronominal adjectives are given. This is because at times they do act as such and take the place of nouns.

[SEC. 1.—THIS, THAT, SUCH.

1 This:—
(a.) Used substantively— 이것.
(b.) Used adjectively— 이.

2 That :—
   (a.) Used substantively—그것, 뎌것.
   (b.) Used adjectively—그, 뎌.
3 Such :—
   (a.) " Like this "—이런.
   (b.) "Like that "—{ 그런.
                        뎌런.

뎌, 뎌것, 뎌런, etc. are used of things near or in sight.

그. 그것, 그런, etc. are used of things more or less remote or out of sight.

Followed by an adjective, and in certain other places where the adverbial form appeals to the Korean, as more proper than the adjective form, the adverbial forms of 이런, 그런, 뎌런 are used.

"Such" used substantively, will be rendered by the adjective form with 것, where it refers to a thing, and with 이 or 사름 when referring to a person.

Note—The remarks made about the use of the plural ending, 들 in the chapter on nouns in Part I. 46 ff. apply equally here, and to all pronouns. Unless then ambiguity would exist without this postposition, we will be safe in omitting it, and in translating "these," "those," etc., as though they were "this," "that." In fact it may be said, that not only are we safe in omitting them, but that we would not be speaking true Korean in using them. In the use of the adjectival forms, we would remind the student that in Korean, there is no agreement either in case or number between the adjective, and its noun. It will also be noticed, that in some places where we would use "this" with a noun, the Koreans would use a noun in which "this" is implied.

### 1. (a).

| | |
|---|---|
| Is this a mosquito bite, or a flea bite ? | 이거시 모긔가 문디요 버록이 문디요 ? |
| This is neither colloquial nor book language. | 이거시 언수도 아니오 문수도 아니오. |

| | |
|---|---|
| This is neither cast iron nor brass. | 이거시 무쇠도 아니오 쥬셕도 아니오. |
| Have you any silk exactly like this? | 꽁셕 이것과 쏙 굿흔 명쥬가 잇소? |
| These are much better than yours. | 이것들이 로형의 것 보다 미우 낫소. |
| Do your trees yield as much fruit as these? | 로형의 과목들이 이것과 굿치 만히 여오? |

1. (b).

| | |
|---|---|
| I have not even yet finished this book. | 이 척 아직도 다 못 보앗소. |
| I want something to put this water in. | 이 물 담을 그릇 한나 차지오. |
| This house is too large for you. | 이 집이 공의게 너무 크오. |
| This is the best day we have had in a long while. | 오래 간 만에 오늘 날이 데일 됴소. |
| This year we have had a bad rice harvest. | 올 히는 화곡 츄슈 잘못 되엇소. |
| In these days Koreans are beginning to regard all the world as brothers. | 이소이는 죠션 사름이 온 셰샹을 형뎨로 녁이는 거슬 시작호오. |
| These apples are all bad. | 이 룽금 다 썩엇소. |

2. (a).

| | |
|---|---|
| What's that (*not seen*)? | 그 거시 무어시오? |
| You wont need as much as that. | 그 처럼 만히 쓸디 업겟소. |
| That is just right. | 그거시 쏙 알맛소. |
| Put these in the box and | 이거슨 궤 속에 너코 |

| | |
|---|---|
| those in the drawer. | 뎌거슨 셜합 속에 너허라. |
| What machine is that? | 뎌거시 무슴 긔계오? |

2. (b).

| | |
|---|---|
| Have you read that book? | 그 척 닑어 보앗소? |
| You had better not eat too many of those cakes. | 그 과즈는 너무 만히 먹지 마는 거시 됴겟소. |
| I have never met either of those two men. | 그 사름은 둘 다 맛난 쎄가 업소. |
| Do you know how long that rope is? | 뎌 줄이 얼마나 긴길 아시오? |
| That dog ought to be killed. | 뎌 개 죽일 거시오. |
| Is'nt that box nailed up yet? | 뎌 궤는 아직 못 박지 아니 ᄒᆞ엿소? |
| That I don't understand (the rest I do). | 그 거슨 나는 몰나. |
| That horse is lame. | 그 몰이 젼다. |
| That boy is the laziest fellow I ever set eyes on. | 그 ᄋᆞ히 내 눈으로 본 놈 즁에 데일 게어른 놈이오. |

3. (a).

| | |
|---|---|
| How much sugar does it take to make such cakes as these? | 이런 과즈 몬들 기에 사탕이 얼마나 드오? |
| I use such a pen (as this) occasionally. | 잇다금 이런 부슬 쓰오. |
| Flowers like these don't grow in Japan. | 그런 화초 일본에 업소. |

| | |
|---|---|
| Such fine weather as this is common in Korea. | 이러개 됴흔 일긔 죠션셔 흔ᄒᆞ오. |

3 (b).

| | |
|---|---|
| How did you make such a mistake? | 엇더케 ᄒᆞ기에 그런 실슈를 ᄒᆞ엿소? |
| Nobody but a fool would say such a thing. | 바삭이 외에는 그런 말ᄒᆞ는 사ᄅᆞᆷ이 업소. |
| Why do you always make such a disagreeable face when you are told to do any thing? | 웨 언제던지 무삼 일을 ᄒᆞ라 ᄒᆞ면 그런 슬중을 내누냐? |
| At such a time one does'nt know what is best to do. | 그런 째는 엇더케 ᄒᆞ여야 됴홀지 모ᄅᆞ겟소. |
| Such talk as that, does more harm than good. | 그런 말은 도로혀 리보다 해가 만소. |
| Why do old Japanese ships have such high sterns? | 일본 녜젼 비는 웨 고물이 그리 놉소? |

SEC. 2.—EITHER, NEITHER, BOTH.

There is no one word in Korean exactly equivalent to any one of these terms and they can only be rendered by the use of several words. Where it is *either* or *neither* of two, if this idea is to be expressed, 둘즁에, (*among two*) with or without one of the demonstrative pronouns 이, 그, or 뎌, must be used in addition to the word used to render *either* or *neither*, as the case may be. Where it is of several, 즁에 with one or other of the demonstrative pronouns is necessary. For example the Korean would not say, " Will either of these do? " but " Of these two, will one do?" "For the rendering then of "either" neither" and "both" we obtain the following rules.

CHAP. V. SEC. 2. PRONOMINAL ADJECTIVES. 285

1. Either :—

(a.) Signifying, one ;—둘즁에 ᄒᆞ나, or 둘즁에 with 것 preceded by the relative participle with or without ᄒᆞ나.

(b.) " One or the other," or " both ;—둘즁에 with 아모나 of persons, and with 아모것 of things, or 아모 with the name of the things repeated.

2. Neither, or Either, with the negative :—The same as No. 1, a. and b. with the negative, or 아모도 with negative may be used.

Note.—Where it is of *several*, of course, 둘 will not be used.

3. Both :—둘다, 량인 or 량, with the noun or its equivalent repeated.

1. (a).

| Is either of these pencils yours ? | 이 붓 ᄒᆞ나흔 로형의 거시오 ? |
| Will either of these suit you ? | 이 즁에 무음 맛는것 ᄒᆞ나 잇소 ? |
| Is either of those men-of-war an iron-clad ? | 그 병션 둘즁에 ᄒᆞ나흔 털갑션 이오니잇가 ? |
| Did either of your sons come here yesterday ? | 로형 아들 둘즁에 어져씌 ᄒᆞ나 여긔 왓슙ᄂᆞ니잇가 ? |

1. (b).

| Either of those will do, hand me one please. | 그 둘즁에 아모 거시나 쓰겟시니 ᄒᆞ나 날 주오. |
| Either of those sticks would be strong enough. | 그 두 막닥이 즁에 아모 거시나 넉넉이 든든 ᄒᆞ오. |

| | |
|---|---|
| Either way will do. | 아모러케나 쓰겟쇼. |
| You will find that character in either dictionary. | 그 글ᄌᆞ 두 ᄌᆞ뎐 즁에 아모 ᄌᆞ뎐에셔나 찻겟쇼. |

2.

| | |
|---|---|
| Neither of those pens is good for anything. | 이 두 붓즁에 하나도 쓸 것 업쇼. |
| I think neither of those houses belongs to Mr. Kim now. | 그 두 집 즁에 지금은 아모 거시나 김셔방의 것 아닌 쥴 아오. |
| I hope neither of you is wounded. | 당신 두분 즁에 아모도 닷치지 안키를 ᄇᆞ라오. |
| Does'nt either of these colors suit you? | 이 두 빗즁에 ᄆᆞ음 맛는 것 업쇼? |
| You must not touch either of these books. | 이 두 칙 아모 거시나 문지지 말아야 쓰겟쇼. |
| You cannot trust either of them. | 그 두 사ᄅᆞᆷ 즁에 아모도 맛을수 업쇼. |
| This character is not in either of the dictionaries. | 이 두 ᄌᆞ뎐 즁에 이 글ᄌᆞ 잇는 ᄌᆞ뎐 업쇼. |
| Did not either of your friends come? | 로형의 친구 둘 즁에 아모도 아니 왓슙ᄂᆞ니잇가? |

3.

| | |
|---|---|
| Both of my flower pots fell off the shelf and were broken. | 내 곳 분이 둘 다 닥ᄌᆞ에셔 ᄂᆞ려져셔 부셔졋쇼. |
| Please lend me both, for a few moments. | 둘 다 잠간 빌녀 주시오. |

| | |
|---|---|
| You must certainly do both. | 둘 다 불가불 ᄒᆞ여야 ᄒᆞ겟소. |
| These ornaments (*for the person*) are both beautiful. | 이 노리기 둘 다 훌륭 ᄒᆞ오. |
| My parents both died while I was a child. | 부모 량친이 나 어렷실 적에 도라가셧소. |
| Bring both the hammer and the screw driver. | 쟝도리 ᄒᆞ고 톱 ᄒᆞ고 둘 다 가져 오너라. |
| Have you looked in both pockets? | 두 쥬머니에 다 차자 보앗소? |
| These chair coolies are both drunk. | 이 교군군이 둘 다 취ᄒᆞ엿소. |

### SEC. 3.—EACH.

1. Signifying every one individually "*each*" may be rendered by 마다 or 각.

2. Signifying apiece—식 or ᄒᆞ나식.

마다 and 식 follow the noun while 각 precedes it.

Note.—Frequently Koreans use "*each*" twice and sometimes oftener, in the same sentence, where we would use it but once. For example where we would say, "I will take three of each sort," the Korean would be very apt to say, "Of each sort, I will take three each." We would note also, that the distinction made above cannot be rigidly adhered to; and as in English "*each*" and "*every*" are at times interchangeable, so ᄒᆞ나식, and 마다, may at times be used, the one for the other.

3. Each other :—서로.

1.

| | |
|---|---|
| Each student lives by himself. | 셩도 마다 각각 거쳐 ᄒᆞ오. |

| | |
|---|---|
| Each soldier had on a different uniform. | 병뎡 마다 다른 군복을 닙엇소. |
| Each man does as he likes. | 각 사름 제 ᄆᆞ음 대로 ᄒᆞ오. |
| Each came up in turn and received his share. | 각 사름이 ᄎᆞ례로 와셔 제 목을 밧앗소. |
| Each horse has its own groom. | 각 물이 제 마부 잇소. |
| Each child recited in turn. | 각 ᄋᆞ히 ᄎᆞ례로 외웟소. |

2.

| | |
|---|---|
| Give one to each child. | ᄋᆞ히들 ᄒᆞ나식 주오. |
| Put a spoonful of tea in each of these cups. | 이 차죵에 차 ᄒᆞᆫ 슈가락식 너히라. |
| Put a stamp on each of these letters, and mail them. | 이 편지에 인지 ᄒᆞ나식 붓치고 우톄국에 두어라. |
| I'll take three of each sort. | 각 식으로 셋식 가지겟소. |
| These lamps have two chimneys each. | 이런 등에는 류리 둘식 잇소. |
| Give each man three of each kind. | 각 사름의게 각식으로 셋식 주어라. |
| You must put three hinges on each door. | 각 문에 경쳡 셋식 두어야 쓰겟소. |

3.

| | |
|---|---|
| Those two men hate each other like cats and dogs. | 그 두 사름 서로 뮈워 ᄒᆞ기를 고양이와 개 ᄀᆞᆺ치 ᄒᆞᆫ다. |

| Men should help each other all they can. | 사롬은 제 힘 대로 서로 도아 줄거시오. |
| Those two men love each other like brothers. | 그 두 사롬 형뎨 ᄀᆞ치 서로 ᄉᆞ랑ᄒᆞ오. |

### Sec. 4.—Some.

As was remarked in Part. I. 66 ff the Korean interrogatives serve equally as well for indefinite pronouns, and hence we get the following rules for rendering "*some*."

1 Somebody—누가, 누구.
2 Something—무엇.
3 Some one of a particular group :—
Here the "*some*" is omitted, and "*one*" only is translated by ᄒᆞ나.
4 When it represents indefinite designation and is equivalent to '*a certain :*"—엇던.
5 Signifying *a part or portion*—도 or 드러. "*Some... some*" becomes 도...도 or 드러...드러.
6 Signifying an indefinite quantity :—
    (*a.*) Used as a substantive—it can only be rendered by some such word as 좀 or 드러는.
    (*b.*) Used as an adjective—it is not rendered.
7 "Some more" ;—
    (*a.*) In addition—더.
    (*b.*) Left—엇히 아직도.

1.

| Somebody is knocking at the door. | 누가 문을 두드리오 |
| I am positive somebody has told it. | 뎡녕 누가 말ᄒᆞᆫ거슬 아오. |

290 PRONOMINAL ADJECTIVES.  CHAP. V. SEC. 4.

Somebody must go to Sëoul to-day to get that money.  
그 돈 차지러 누가 셔울노 오놀 가야 쓰겟소.

Somebody came to see you this afternoon, but refused to leave his card.  
오놀 오후에 누가 로형 보러 왓것 마는 명텹 두기를 슬희여 흐엿소.

2.

You had better plant something here.  
여긔 무엇 심으면 됴켓소.

Something fell down and woke me up at about four this morning.  
오놀 아츰 네시 즈음 무어시 써러져셔 나를 세웟소.

Have you not put something heavy in this drawer?  
무거온것 무엇 이 설합 속에 아니 너헛느냐?

Have you not dropped something?  
무엇 싸지지 아니 흐엿소?

3.

Can you spare me some one of these?  
이 즁에 흐나 날 줄수 잇소?

Will not some one of the coolies from this neighborhood do?  
이 동너 잇는 모군 즁에 흐나 못 쓰겟습ᄂ니 잇가?

4.

Some scholar has written a history in about fifty volumes.  
엇던 문쟝이 오십 권이나 되는 사긔를 지엇소.

Some general with but two or three hundred soldiers defeated the Chinese army last year.  
엇던 대쟝이 쟉년에 이삼 빅명 군ᄉ만 거ᄂ리고 쳔국 군ᄉ를 이긔엿소.

## 5.

| | |
|---|---|
| Some tables have three legs. | 세 드리 샹도 잇소. |
| Some people sympathize with England, and some with Russia. | 영국 편 드는 사룸도 잇고 아라사 편 드는 사룸도 잇소. |
| Some said "go," and some said "don't go." | 가라는 사룸도 잇고 가지 말나는 사룸도 잇섯소. |
| Some among those soldiers were cavalry. | 그 병뎡 즁에 긔병이 더러 잇섯스. |
| Some of the English kings were wise men. | 영국 님금 즁에 더러는 명쳘훈 이가 잇섯소. |
| Most blind men are ignorant, but some are celebrated scholars. | 눈 먼 사룸이 거위 다 무식훈것마는 그즁에 유명훈 문쟝도 잇소. |
| Some of the most celebrated men have been blind. | 데일 유명훈 사룸 즁에 혹 쇼경도 잇섯소. |
| Make some white and some black. | 더러는 희게호고 더러는 검게 호여라. |
| Some of them are better than others. | 그즁에 나흔 것도 잇소. |
| I keep some of my letters, but most of them I burn up. | 내 편지 즁에 더러는 잘 두나 거위 다 틔우오. |
| Song Yongi put some in the bookcase and the rest are still in the box. | 더러는 슌용이가 쳑쟝 속에 너코 놈아지는 궤 속에 그져 잇소. |
| I gave Mr. Song some, ate some myself, and put the rest in the drawer. | 더러는 송셔방 주고 더러는 내가 먹고 놈아 지는 셜합에 너헛소. |

6. (a).

| | |
|---|---|
| Sprinkle some there. | 뎌긔 좀 뿌리오. |
| Some probably dropped out on your way home. | 집에 가는 길에 좀 싸젓실 듯ᄒ오. |
| Take some, to try, and see how you like it. | 더러는 시험으로 가져 가셔 됴화 홀넌지 보아라. |

6. (b).

| | |
|---|---|
| I want to embroider some silk. | 명쥬에 슈롤 노코 십소. |
| Tell the cook to make some Chinese tea. | 슉슈 드려 즁원 차를 문들나고 ᄒ오. |
| I wish I had planted some monthly roses in this garden. | 이 화원에 월계 십엇 더면 됴켓소. |

7. (a).

| | |
|---|---|
| Tell Sujini I must have some more nails. | 슈진이 드려 못시 더 잇서야 쓰겟다고 ᄒ오. |
| Tell the servant to put some more coal on. | 하인 드려 셕탄 더 너라고 닐으오. |
| Please give Mr. Pak some more paper. | 박셔방 의게 죠희 더 주시오. |

7. (b).

| | |
|---|---|
| There are some more in the right hand drawer. | 올흔 편 셜합에 아직도 잇소. |
| Did you say there was some more flour in the house? | 집에 밀 가로 엇히 잇다고 ᄒ엿습ᄂ니잇가? |

SEC. 5.—ANY.

1. Persons:—
   (a.) Somebody—누가, 누구 or the relative clause with 이. Negatively—the same with the negative.

## CHAP. V. SEC. 5. PRONOMINAL ADJECTIVES. 293

    (*b*.) Anybody whatever, no matter who.— 아모나, 누구던지. Negatively— 아무도, 누구던지 with the negative or the relative clause in 이 with 하나도 업소.
2. Things :—
    (*a*.) Something—무엇 or 무삼 with a noun, or the relative participle with 것. Negatively—the same with the negative.
    (*b*.) Anything whatever, no matter what— 아모 거시나, 아모거시라도, 무어시던지, or 무삼 followed by 던지. Negatively—by the same with the negative, except that 아모거시나 becomes 아모 것도. This same negative form is very emphatically rendered by the use of the relative participle with 것하나도 업소.
3. One or more, any at all :—
    (*a*.) In affirmative sentences—not rendered.
    (*b*.) In negative sentences, signifying none at all— 조곰도 or 하나도 with the negative.
4. Any more :—
    (*a*.) In affirmative sentences—엇히 or 더.
    (*b*.) In negative sentences 더 with the negative.

1. (a).

| | |
|---|---|
| Is there anybody in the room? | 방에 누가 잇소? |
| Did anyone ever attempt it before? | 전에 누가 시험하엿소? |
| Did not anyone say anything to you about it? | 누가 아모 말도 아니 하옵더니잇가? |
| If anybody should call, say I can't see them. | 누가 와서 찻거든 못 본다고 하여라. |

| | |
|---|---|
| Cannot anyone translate this? | 이거슬 번역 홀이 업소? |

1. (b).

| | |
|---|---|
| Please call anyone of the soldiers. | 병뎡 ᄒᆞ나 불너주오 누구던지. *or* 병뎡 ᄒᆞ나 누구던지 불너 주오. *or* 아모 병뎡이나 불너 주오. |
| That's a thing that any boy ought to know. | 그거슬 아모 ᄋᆞ히나 알거시오 |
| Anybody who knows Ŏnmun can read that. | 누구던지 언문 아는 사ᄅᆞᆷ은 그거슬 능히 닑으오. |
| Is'nt there any one who can go? | 아모도 갈 사ᄅᆞᆷ 업슴ᄂᆞ니잇가? |
| There is'nt anybody who lives without sin. | 죄 아니 범ᄒᆞ고 사는 이가 ᄒᆞ나도 업소. |
| Nobody came to see me while I was sick. | 병 잇실 적에 아모도 와 보지 아니 ᄒᆞ엿소. |

2. (a).

| | |
|---|---|
| Is there anything in my eye? | 내 눈에 무어시 드럿소? |
| Did Mr. Kim send anything to me? | 김셔방이 내게 무엇 보내옵더니잇가? |
| Have you any business to attend to? | 무슴 볼 일 잇소? |
| Did Mr. Yi tell you any news? | 리셔방 무슴 소문 말ᄒᆞ옵더니잇가? |

CHAP. V. SEC. 5.  PRONOMINAL ADJECTIVES.

| | |
|---|---|
| I wish these boxes had nothing in them. | 이 케를 무엇 안 드럿시면 됴겟소. |
| Did you give anything? | 무엇 주엇슴ᄂ니잇가? |
| Did you say you had nothing to do? | 홀 일 업다고 ᄒ엿ᄂ냐? |

2. (*b*).

| | |
|---|---|
| One can accomplish almost any thing if he is ambitious. | 벽이 잇시면 거위 아모 것도 셩취ᄒ오. |
| Any soft wood will do. | 무솜 나모던지 연ᄒ면 쓰겟소. |
| Any one of those colors will do. | 내 싱각에 이 빗 즁에는 아모 거시나 쓸 듯 ᄒ오. |
| Give me any one of these cups. | 그 차죵 즁에 아모 거시 라도 ᄒ나 주오. |
| Not any one of these toys will please the children. | 이 쟉란 가음 즁에 ᄋ희 ᄆ음에 맛는것 ᄒ나도 업소. |
| There was nothing there that I liked. | 거긔셔 나 됴화ᄒ는 거슨 아모 것도 업섯소. |

3. (*a*).

| | |
|---|---|
| Are there any Chinese characters in that book? | 그 책 안희 진셔가 드럿소? |
| Are there any men-of-war in Chemulpo now? | 제물포에 지금 군함 잇소? |
| Are there any American merchants in Fusan? | 부산에 미국 쟝ᄉ 잇소? |

Are there any schools where English is taught in Pyeng Yang? 평양에 미국 말 ᄀᆞᄅ치는 학당 잇소?

3. (b).

Have'nt you any money? 돈이 조곰도 업소?
Are there no sheep in Korea? 죠션에 양 ᄒ나도 업소?
Don't you have any good fruit in Japan? 일본에 됴흔 실과 ᄒ나도 업슴ᄂᆞ니잇가?
Didn't you see any ducks on the road from Chemulpo? 제물포셔 오는 길에 오리 ᄒ나도 못 보왓소?

4. (a).

Is there any more flour? 엇히 밀 가로 잇소?
Have you any more of the paper I bought the other day? 그젼에 사던 죠희 엇히 잇소?
Have they any more Pyeng Yang coal at Chemulpo? 제물포에 평양 셕탄 엇히 잇소?

4. (b).

Isn't there any more sugar in the house? 집에 사탕이 더 업소?
Do not put in any more. 더 넛치 마오.
Do not put any more ice in the refrigerator until the leak is mended. 어름 궤 샌듸 곳치기 젼에 어름 더 넛치 마라.

SEC. 6.—EVERY

1 Persons :—
　(a.) Everybody, people generally—누구던지.

CHAP. V. SEC. 6. PRONOMINAL ADJECTIVES. 297

    (*b*.) Everybody no matter who, anybody whatever,—
누구라두 or 아모라도.
    (*c*.) Every one of a particular group—모도, 다.
2 Things :—
    (*a*.) Everything, things generally—무어시던지.
    (*b*.) Everything no matter what, anything whatever,—무어시라도, 아모거시라도, 무어시던지
and sometimes by a change in form of the sentence.
    (*c*.) Everyone of a particular group—다, 모도.
" Without exception " is rendered by 이것뎌것업시.

Note.—아모 is more emphatic than 누구. There are also many other ways of expressing these same ideas by a change in the form of the sentence, but enough are given here for all practical purposes.

1. (*a*.)

| | |
|---|---|
| Everybody expected war. | 누구던지 싸홈이 될줄 알앗소. |
| In India everybody has to go to the mountains in summer. | 인도국에는 누구던지 녀름에 산에 갈수밧긔 업소. |
| One ought to be polite to everybody. | 뉘게던지 공슌ᄒᆞ여야 홀 거시오. |

1. (*b*).

| | |
|---|---|
| Everybody can go to see the President. | 아모라도 대통령을 보러 갈수가 잇소. |
| Every Jew had to learn a trade. | 유대 사름은 아모라도 쟝식 일을 비호게 ᄒᆞ엿소. |
| Every Korean must have a top knot. | 죠션 사름은 아모라도 샹투 잇서야 쓰겟소. |

They send every one to the same prison. 아모리도 혼 옥에 보낸다

1. (c).

Please make every one sit down. 다 안게 ᄒᆞ시오.

When I opened the door, everybody said "You must not come in yet." 내가 문 연즉 모도 아직 드러오지 말나고 ᄒᆞ옵되다.

The weather was bad and every one in our house took cold. 일긔가 언잔으니 집에 잇는 사롬들이 모도 감긔 드럿소.

2. (a).

Some people think that everything came into existence of itself. 무어시던지 다 절노 된줄 아는 이가 잇소.

Have you enough of everything, to last till you get to Pyeng Yang? 무어시던지 평양 서지 쓰기가 넉넉ᄒᆞ겟ᄂᆞ냐?

It seems to me you always find fault with everything. 나 보기에 공은 무어시 던지 칙망ᄒᆞ는 모양 이오.

2. (b).

You seem to think you know everything. 공은 아모거시라도 아는 줄 아는 모양이오.

In a little while the Japanese will be able to make everything. 쉬이 일본 사롬이 아모 거시라도 ᄆᆞᆫ돌겟소.

That baby wants everything he sees. 그 어린 ᄋᆞ희는 보는 대로 가지고 십히ᄒᆞ오.

CHAP. V. SEC. 7. PRONOMINAL ADJECTIVES. 299

| You must'nt give the baby everything he wants. | *아기 의게 무어시던지 달나는대로 다 주지 마는거시 올소. |
| They can teach everything at the government college. | 육영공원에셔 아모거시 라도 ᄀᆞᄅᆞ쳐 주겟소. |

2. (c).

| Leave everything as it is. | 다 그대로 두오. |
| Every thing in the house was burnt up. | 집 안에 물건이 모도 ᄯᅡ 부렷소. |
| Have you done every thing as I told you? | 내가 다 닐ᄋᆞ는대로 ᄒᆞ엿느냐? |
| Every one of these bottles is broken. | 이 병들이 모도 ᄭᆡ여 젓소. |
| Every one without exception was broken in two. | 이것 뎌것 업시 다 두 속에 낫소. |

SEC. 7.—NO, NONE, NOBODY.

1 Nobody—업소. with either the relative clause with 이; or 누구도, or 아모도, or 누구던지.

2 Nothing—아모것도 with the negative, or the relative clause with 것 and the negative.

Note.—Sometimes with a relative clause, the repetition of the word will take the place of 것.

3 No :—
   (a.) Not any—negative of verb.

---

\* N. B. In this sentence it would not do to say simply 무어시던지 alone with the negative for this would mean you must not give him anything. If the idea is not to give all 다 with the negative must be used, and in such a sentence as the above, some qualifying clause must be inserted.

(b.) Emphatic—signifying *none at all, not a single one.*—조끔도, 하나도, 도모지, 아조, etc. with the negative.

4 No more—더 with the negative.

1.

| | |
|---|---|
| They looked at one another but nobody said a word. | 서로 다 보기는 하나 아모도 말 하지 아니 하엿소. |
| Nobody can sit up till after twelve o'clock every-night and get up early every morning without breaking down. | 밤마다 밤즁 까지 자지 안코 아참 마다 일쯕 니러나면 힘이 진하지 안는이 도모지 업소. |
| Are none of you wet? | 아모도 옷 져즌이 업소? |
| Nobody expected peace so soon. | 아모도 그러케 쉬이 화친 된줄 몰낫소. |

2.

| | |
|---|---|
| The house caught fire, but nothing was burnt. | 집에 불이 낫시나 튼거슨 업소. |
| I took the cover off, and looked in, and there was nothing there. | 둑겅을 벗겨 본즉 아모 것도 업습더이다. |
| None of those boats is very fast. | 뎌 비 즁에 흔쳑도 샌른 비가 업소. |
| He showed me several, but none of them suited me. | 내게 여러슬 뵈엿것마는 무음에 맛는 것 업섯소. |

3. (a).

| | |
|---|---|
| I've had no fire all day. | 오눌 죵일 불이 업섯소. |

CHAP. V. SEC. 8. PRONOMINAL ADJECTIVES.  301

Are there no snakes in this neighborhood?   이 근쳐 비암은 업소?

I found no mistakes in the essay.   글쟝에 잘못 혼것 못 차젓소.

### 3. (b).

Do you say there is no kerosene in Korea?   죠션에는 도모지 셕유가 업단 말이오?

Are you sure there are no mosquitoes in the net?   모긔쟝 속에 뎡녕 모긔가 혼 마리도 업눈걸 아오?

Are there no strawberries in the garden?   화원에 쌸기 하나도 업소?

Is there no one in this room who will go?   이 방에 갈 사람 도모지 업소?

### 4.

We have no more pears but we have some very nice persimmons.   비는 더 업스나 감은 됴혼 거시 잇소.

We have no more red ones, but have some black ones.   붉은 거슨 더 업스나 검은 거슨 잇소.

I believe I have no more letters to write.   쓸 편지 더 업슬듯 하오.

### SEC. 8.—ALL.

1 Signifying *everyone, the whole number,* or *quantity*— 모도, 다.

2 Signifying *the whole duration* or *extent,*— 온, 온통, 일, 혼, or 다.

302   PRONOMINAL ADJECTIVE.   Chap. V. Sec. 8.

3 Signifying *the last of a thing*,—씬 or 만 may be used.

온, 일, 훈 precede their nouns, the rest follow.

1.

| | |
|---|---|
| You had better throw these all away. | 이것 다 내여 부리면 됴켓소. |
| These letters are all for America. | 이 편지는 모도 미국으로 가는 거시오. |
| The cherry blossoms must have fallen off by now. | 벗나무 꽂촌 모도 떠러 젓실터히오. |
| Put all those needles in the box on the shelf. | 그 바늘을 모도 션반 우희 잇는 케에 너라. |
| Take out all those books, and arrange them well, in sets, on the book shelves. | 케 속에 잇는 칙을 다 쓰어 내여셔 칙장에 질을 차자 잘 싸하라. |
| The hoop broke, and every bit of the water ran out. | 통 테가 끈허져셔 물이 다 쏫 아젓소. |

2.

| | |
|---|---|
| I shall probably be in Sëoul all this winter. | 이 온 겨을 동안은 셔울 잇슬 둣 호오. |
| All next month I must go every day to the palace. | 틱월 훈 둘은 불가불 날마다 대궐에 드러가야 호겟소. |
| From Nam San, they say almost all of Sëoul can be seen. | 남산셔 셔울이 거위 다 뵌다고 호오. |
| There was not a man in all the village that had ever seen a foreigner. | 일촌 즁에 외국 사롬을 본이가 호나도 업소읍 더이다. |

| | |
|---|---|
| Mr. Song has travelled over nearly all the world. | 송셔방은 거위 셰계를 다 돈녓소. |

3.

| | |
|---|---|
| Is this all the tea there is? | 차가 이 섇 이냐? |
| Is this all the flour there is? | 밀가로가 이 섇:이오? |

### SEC. 9.—SEVERAL.

1 Number:—
   (a.) Quite a number,—여러 in its various forms.
   (b.) An indefinite number,—몃.

2 Kind:—식식, 식식이로, 각.
   The distinction made above between 여러 and 몃, is not always adhered to by Koreans. The difficulty with 여러 for "*several*," is that it may mean a large number of almost indefinite proportion, but this is generally expressed, by the strong stress or emphasis, laid upon the word. The English word "*several*" may also be rendered by the Korean words 두서넛, (*two, three, four*) 서너너덧 (*three, four, five.*)

1. (a).

| | |
|---|---|
| There are several pencils in that case. | 이 필통 속에 연필이 여러 자로가 잇소. |
| There were several who declined to go. | 가 기 슬타 는 사 룸이 여러히 잇스옵더이다. |
| I enquired at several shops but there were none. | 여러 젼에 차자 보앗시나 업스옵더이다. |
| I've had several dogs since I came to Seoul. | 셔울 온 후브터 내게 개가 여러히 잇섯소. |
| A fly has several legs. | 파리안틔 발이 여러시 잇소. |

| | |
|---|---|
| | 1. (b). |
| We met a coolie just now carrying several parcels. | 지금 멋 보퉁이 가지고 가는 혼 삭군 맛낫소. |
| He took several boxes to the river this morning. | 오눌 아춤 강으로 몃 케롤 가져갓소. |
| We met several pack ponies laden with cash, on the road. | 즁로 에셔 돈 실은 복마 몃 맛낫소. |
| There seem to be several lame ones among these dogs. | 그 개 즁에 몃치 져는 모양이오. |
| | 2. |
| You have several (kinds) beautiful flowers in your garden. | 공의 화원에 됴은 꼿시 셕셕이 잇소. |
| Birds build their nests in several ways. | 새가 각 모양으로 보금 자리롤 치오. |
| At this hotel, they have several kinds of food. | 이 쥬막에는 음식이 셕셕 이로 잇소. |
| Koreans wear garments of several colors. | 죠션 사룸은 옷슬 셕셕 이로 닙소. |

SEC. 10.—FEW.

1 Few (*not many*)—젹소, 만치안소, which in Korean are verbs, and in rendering *few* can only be used as predicates.

Note.—*To be with a few* is rendered in the same way.

2 A few (*a small number*)—몃 or by some indefinite number as 두서넛, or 서너너덧.

The particle 수 (*number*) prefixed to Sinico-Korean words also conveys this idea.

CHAP. V. SEC. 11. PRONOMINAL ADJECTIVES.

| | |
|---|---|
| Few foreigners speak Korean well. | 죠션 말을 잘ᄒᆞᄂᆞᆫ 외국 사ᄅᆞᆷ이 젹소. |
| There were only a few there last night, but we had a good time. | 어제 밤에 거긔 사ᄅᆞᆷ이 만치 아니나 잘 놀앗소. |
| There were only a few soldiers at the American legation, but they were all brave, and we were not afraid. | 미국 공ᄉᆞ관에 병뎡가 만치 아니 ᄒᆞ엿것마는 다 용밍ᄒᆞ엿시니 걱졍 업섯소. |

2.

| | |
|---|---|
| Go to the garden and bring me a few small stones. | 화원에 가셔 쟌 돌 몃 가져 오너라. |
| Go and buy me a few cigars. | 가셔 엽권연 두세 개 사 오너라. |
| I went to Pouk Han yesterday with a few friends. | 어제 몃 친구 ᄒᆞ고 북한 으로 갓소. |
| A few years ago I was in America. | 수년 젼에 미국에 잇섯소. |
| I will go in a few days. | 수일 후에 가겟소. |

SEC. 11.—ONE, ONES.

One is rendered in Korean by 것.

Note.—It will have already been noticed, that the Korean use of the equivalent for "one" or "ones" is much more frequent than the English, and hence it is found in many places where we least expect it.

| | |
|---|---|
| Either red ones or black ones will do. | 붉은 거시던지 검은 거시던지 쓰겟소. |
| Neither red ones nor black ones will do. | 붉은 거시던지 검은 거시던지 다 못 쓰겟소. |

| | |
|---|---|
| Have not you any (*ones*) a little better? | 좀 더 나흔 거슨 업소? |
| The best ones are all in the godown. | 그 즁 됴흔 거슨 다 광에 드럿쇼. |
| Although even that is good, the one with the cover is better. | 그 것도 됴키는 됴호나 둑겅 잇는 거시 더 됴소. |
| Is this to-day's (*one*)? | 이거시 오놀 거시오? |
| Have you any different (*ones*) from this? | 이 보다 다른 거시 잇소? |

### SEC. 12.—OTHER, ANOTHER.

1 The rest of—이외.
2 Not the same, separate—다른, or by the adverb 달니.
3 Besides—이밧긔, 이외에.
4 One more in addition—더, 호나더.
5 The other one of two—호나, 쏘호나, 다른것, or by a change in the form of the sentence.
" The one...the other "—호나흔...호나흔.
6 People generally as contrasted with one's self—놈.
7 Again—쏘, 다시.

#### 1.

| | |
|---|---|
| See whether the other children don't want some too. | 이외 으히들도 달나 호나 보아라. |
| Please tell the others to come in too. | 이외 사람 드려도 드러오라고 호오. |
| Are the other boxes the same size as this? | 이외 궤들도 크기가 이것 굿소? |
| The other ones will be done in a month. | 이외 거슨 흔돌만 호면 되겟소. |

| | |
|---|---|
| I'll take another newspaper. | 이외 신문지를 보겟소. |
| You had better take these coolies, you may not be able to get the others. | 이외 일군은 혹 엇을 수가 업시니 이들을 쓰는 거시 됴겟소. |

2.

| | |
|---|---|
| I came by another road. | 다른 길노 왓소. |
| That's another matter. | 그거슨 다른 일이오. |
| Another color would probably be better. | 다른 빗치 됴흘둣 호오. |
| As I am a Korean I cannot sit down in any other way. | 죠션 사름 이니 달니는 안질 수가 업소. |
| He really had another reason for going. | 그 사름이 실샹은 다른 일이 잇서셔 간거시오. |

3.

| | |
|---|---|
| I have not another cash. | 이밧긔는 흔푼도 업소. |
| Is'nt there another pencil in that drawer? | 그셜합 속에 연필이 이것 밧긔 업소? |
| If you intend to study Chinese you must get another teacher, (besides the present one). | 한어를 비호시랴면 이외 션싱을 엇어야 홀둣 호오. |

4.

| | |
|---|---|
| This bookcase is a little small, I'll have to get another. | 이 칙쟝이 조곰 젹으니 불가불 호나 더 엇어야 호겟소. |
| It will be all right even though you don't put on another stamp. | 우표 호나 더 붓치지 아니 호여도 됴겟소. |

| | |
|---|---|
| Please order me another copy, of the O Ryun Haing Sil. | 오륜힝실 을 혼질 더 맛초라고 호오. |
| Bring me another pencil. | 연필 호나 더 가져오너라. |
| Bring me another cake of ink. | 먹 혼쟝 더 가져오. |

5.

| | |
|---|---|
| Where is the other hammer? | 맛치 쏘 호나 어듸 잇 느냐? |
| This is too soft you had better take the other one. | 이거슨 너무 연호니 다른 거슬 가져가시오. |
| I gave one to Soun Pogi and one to Eung Whani. | 호나혼 슌복이 주고 호나 혼 응환이 주엇소. |
| I like this house best, but prefer the other location. | 집은 여긔가 됴호나 터는 뎌긔가 됴소. |

6.

| | |
|---|---|
| Don't give too much credit to what others say. | 놈의 말을 너무 고지 듯지 마오. |
| I don't know what others think, and I don't care. | 놈은 엇더케 싱각 홀 넌지 모르나 무어 시라 던지 관계치 안소. |

7.

| | |
|---|---|
| The news has just arrived, of another victory. | 쏘 이긔엿다는 소문 굿 시방 왓소. |
| Did Mr. Pak say that if he went to Fusan he would send another telegram to Seoul? | 박셔방 말이 즈긔가 부산 가면 쏘 셔울노 뎐보 호겟다고 호옵더니잇 가? |

## Sec. 13.—Same.

1. Not different—By the different parts of the verb 굿소 or 굿ᄒ오 (*to be alike*).
2. Not two :—흔, 일.

### 1.

| | |
|---|---|
| Put the same quantity in all the bottles. | 각 병에 굿치 너히라. |
| Those two boys are the same height. | 그 두 ᄋ히 킈가 굿소. |
| Is " Oltarago " the same as " Olsorago ? " | 올타라고와 올소라고와 굿소옵ᄂ니잇가? |
| The meaning is the same, but the letters are a little different. | 뜻손 굿ᄒ나 글ᄌ가 좀 달소. |
| Though you make them of the same material, make them of different colors. | 굿흔 가음으로 ᄒ되 빗츤 다르게 ᄆᄃ러라. |
| Are Buddhist temples all built on the same general plan ? | 졀 짓는 법이 대뎌 다 굿소? |
| I told them both the same thing. | 둘의게 다 굿흔 말을 닐넛소. |
| It is the same as last year's disease. | 작년 병 과 굿소. |

### 2.

| | |
|---|---|
| Were all these prepared by the same man ? | 이거시 다 흔 사름이 진 거시오? |
| Can't you two read out of the same book ? | 흔 칙 가지고 둘이 닑지 못ᄒᄂ냐? |

Let us both stop at the 혼 쥬막에 류호옵시다.
same hotel.

Are you all from the same 다 동향 사롬 이오?
town?

### Sec. 14—Much.

1 In affirmative sentences —the different parts of the verb 만소.
2 In negative sentences—과히 with the negative.
3 Too much—너무, 과히, with and without 만소.
4 So much—그러케 either alone, or with the verb 만소.
5 How much—얼마. About how much—얼마나.
Sometimes also another word such as 대개 will be added. If it is desired to call especial attention to the price the word 갑 will be used. The Koreans use this word 얼마 in places where in English we would use simply *how*.

1.

Is there much money in 뎌 궤에 돈 만히 드럿소?
that box?

Was much rice burned up 젼년에 감을 적에 곡식이
during the drought last 만히 홋소?
year?

Do they import much kero- 셕유가 죠션에 만히 드러
sene into Korea? 오오?

Is there much fruit in Ko- 죠션에 실과 만소?
rea?

2.

I don't have much head- 머리 과히 압흐지 안소.
ache.

## Chap. V. Sec. 14. PRONOMINAL ADJECTIVES.

| | |
|---|---|
| You have'nt taken much pains with your writing. | 글시 쓰기에 되 파히 쓰지 아니 호엿다. |
| I do not like Korean food very much. | 내가 죠션 음식 파히 됴화 호지 아니 호오. |
| To tell the truth I do not feel much like going. | 실샹은 파히 가고 십지 안소. |

### 3.

| | |
|---|---|
| Do not drink too much. | 술 너무 먹지 마오. |
| There is too much sugar in this tea. | 차에 사탕이 너무 만소. |
| You can not sleep if you drink too much tea. | 차를 너무 먹으면 못 자오. |
| This is a little too much. | 이것 좀 너무 만소. |
| You must not spend too much money or you will soon be poor. | 돈 너무 만히 쓰지 말아야 쉬이 가난 찬켓소. |

### 4.

| | |
|---|---|
| If you eat so much candy you will be sick. | 엿 그러케 먹으면 알켓소. |
| I trust him so much that I would lend him whatever he should ask. | 내가 그를 그러케 밋으니 달나는 대로 빌녀 주겟소. |
| You need not take so much pains with that letter. | 그 편지 쓰기에 그러케 되쓸 것 업소. |
| Do not drink so much wine. | 술 그러케 만히 먹지 마오. |
| Do not put on so much coal. | 셕탄 그러케 만히 넛치 마라. |

| | |
|---|---|
| How much for the lot? | 도합이 갑시 얼마요? |
| How much did you give for those pears? | 이 비를 얼마 주고 삿소? |
| About how much salt is there in this water? | 이 물에 소금 얼마나 드럿소? |
| How much vinegar did you say was left? | 초가 얼마 놈앗다고 한 엿소? |
| About how long is that box? | 그 궤 길기가 대개 얼마나 되오? |
| How much silk shall I get? | 명쥬 얼마 사리잇가? |
| How much is the annual income of the government? | 정부에 일년 슈입 대개 얼마나 되오? |

SEC. 15.—MANY.

The Koreans do not make the distinction between *many* and *much*, that we do. Sometimes it can be done by the interposition of the word 수 (*number*) and 수가 만소, "*the number is much*" means "*there are many.*" As a general rule however, the simple use of the verb 만소 will answer all purposes and the context will tell whether it is quantity or number that is referred to. There is a difference between *how much* and *how many*.

We find then the following rules.

1 In affirmative sentences—the different parts of the verb 만소; and in negative sentences—the same with the negative.

2 A good many—The word "*good*" is not rendered, 만소 alone is used.

CHAP. V. SEC. 15.  PRONOMINAL ADJECTIVES. 313

3 A great many—미우 or 대단이 etc. with 만소.
The English phrase "a great deal" is also rendered in the same way.

4 Too many—너무, 과히, etc. with 만소. As was said with regard to "*too much*," 만소 may be omitted.

5 How many—멋. About how many 멋치나.

### 1.

| Confucius has many disciples. | 공즈는 데즈가 만소. |
| Many of the Americans have blue eyes. | 미국 사름이 눈 푸른 이가 만소. |
| Formerly there were not many ironclads in the American navy. | 이젼에 미국 히군에 털갑 션이 만치 안소. |
| Many Korean flowers have a very sweet odor. | 죠션 못 됴흔 향내 나는 것 만소. |
| There are not many sheep in Korea. | 죠션에 양 만치 안소. |
| I didn't buy many, because they were dear. | 비싸 만히 사지 아니 ᄒ엿소. |

### 2.

| A good many Japanese seem to wear glasses. | 일본 사름에는 안경 쓴 이가 만흔 모양 이오. |
| It seems a good many farmers made money this year. | 올 히는 돈 눕진 농군이 만흔 모양 이오. |

### 3.

| A great many fishing smacks pass here every morning. | 아츰 마다 어션이 이리 미우 만히 지나 둔니오. |

| | |
|---|---|
| The fire last night destroyed a great many houses. | 어제 밤 화지가 대단이 만혼 집을 망케 ᄒᆞ엿소. |
| We've used a great deal of coal this year. | 올히 셕탄 대단이 만히 썻소. |

### 4.

| | |
|---|---|
| There are too many books in that bookcase. | 그 칙쟝에 칙이 너무 만소. |
| There are too many people on that boat, I'm afraid it will sink in such a sea as this. | 그 비에 사람이 너무 만호니 그런 바다에 쌔질가 념려요. |
| There are too many chairs in this room, there is no place for the table. | 이 방에 교의가 너무 만호니 상 둘ᄃᆡ 업소. |
| There are too many windows in this room, there is no place for a wardrobe. | 이 방에 문이 너무 만호니 의쟝 둘ᄃᆡ 업소. |

### 5.

| | |
|---|---|
| How many pears shall I buy? | 비 멋치나 사리잇가? |
| About how many bottles are left? | 병이 멋치나 놈왓소? |
| How many days are there in a month? | 멋 날이 훈 돌이오? |
| How many chickens did you order? | 병아리 멋 사리잇가? |
| How many servants do you keep? | 공이 멋 하인 둠ᄂᆞ잇가? |

| | |
|---|---|
| How many sons has Mr. Kim? | 김셔방이 아돌 몃치오? |

## SEC. 16.—MORE.

More is rendered into Korean by 더. Quite often 좀 (*a little*) will be used with it.

| | |
|---|---|
| When are you going to put on more men? | 언제브터 일군을 더 두랴오? |
| If you don't put on more coal, the fire will go out. | 셕탄 더 넛치 아니 ᄒᆞ면 불 ᄭᅳ지 겟소. |
| I wish I had bought more of this tea. | 이 차를 좀 더 삿더면 됴흘번 ᄒᆞ엿소. |
| You can get a good article if you will pay more. | 돈 더 주면 됴흔 거슬 엇을 수가 잇소. |
| Which costs the more? | 엇던 거시 갑시 더 들겟소? |
| I have not a bit more. | 내게 조곰도 업소. |
| Go and get some more ice. | 가셔 어름 더 엇어 오너라 |

## SEC. 17.—MOST.

1. Nearly all—거위 다.
2. The greatest of several quantities:—

The Koreans, commonly do not make the distinction between "*more*" and "*most*." The common way of expressing "*most*" would be by 더 with or without 만소. Sometimes however, when they wish to be accurate they will use 예일 instead of 더.

For the superlative degree, see Part II. Chapter VI. § II. Sec. 2., and Part I. ¶ 254.

1.

| | |
|---|---|
| Most foreigners dislike a native chair. | 외국 사롬들 거위 다 보료를 슬희여 ᄒᆞ오. |

| | |
|---|---|
| Most of you have heard this I suppose. | 공들은 거위 다 이거슬 드럿실듯 ᄒᆞ오. |
| Although some of them have not yet been told, most of them probably know it. | 그 즁에 아직 닐 ᄋ 지 아닌 사롬도 잇시나 거위 다 알듯 ᄒᆞ오. |
| I gave most of them five hundred cash each, but some of them left early and did not receive it. | 내가 거위 다 닷 냥식 주엇시나 더러는 일쪽 나갓시니 밧지 아니 ᄒᆞ엿소. |

2.

| | |
|---|---|
| Which box holds the most? | 어ᄂᆞ 궤 만히 들겟소? 어ᄂᆞ 궤 더 만히 들겟소? 어ᄂᆞ 궤 뎨일 만히 들겟소? |
| Then I will have the most. | 그러면 내가 더 만히 가지오. 그러면 내가 뎨일 만히 가지오. |

SEC. 18.—ENOUGH.

In rendering the pronominal adjective, *Enough*, the various parts of the verbs 넉넉ᄒᆞ오, 족족ᄒᆞ오, 자라오, etc., verbs meaning, " to be sufficient " should properly be used. The Koreans, often, however, use other words or phrases to express the same idea. As, they will say "That much will do," " That is much " etc. When we use the word *enough* in English, we do not always have the idea of " sufficient for a purpose," we often mean "*plenty*," "*a good deal*," and the Koreans in

CHAP. V. SEC. 18. PRONOMINAL ADJECTIVES.

this respect are almost more exact than we. Remembering these facts, we obtain the following rules.

1 Signifying a sufficiency, and without the verb "*to be,*" either as simple adjective qualifying a noun, substantively, or as an adverb we may render " *enough,*" by 넉넉히, 족족히, 만히.

2. To be enough—넉넉ᄒ오, 족족ᄒ오, 자라오, etc. or we can use 그만, (*that only*), or 그만콤 (*that much*) with the future of such a verb 쓰오. Negatively—the same with the negative, or a negative verb, as 부족ᄒ오 may be used.

3. To do a thing *enough*.
   (*a.*) In affirmative sentences—the adverbial form of the verbs.
   (*b.*) In negative sentences—the same with the negative, or 덜 without the negative.

4. Enough to,—future participle of verb, or fut. past. with 만콤, or 것 ; negatively, the same with the negative. 자라오 may be used.

1.

| | |
|---|---|
| Thanks, I've had enough already. | 곰압소 마는 만히 먹엇소. |
| How many nails shall I bring? Bring enough. | 못 멋출 가져 오리잇가? 넉넉히 가져 오너라. |
| Be sure and put enough sugar in. | 일뎡 사탕 넉넉히 너라. |

2.

| | |
|---|---|
| Is there enough sugar? | 사탕이 넉넉 ᄒ오? |
| There is not quite enough sugar in this cake. | 이 과즈에 사탕이 조곰 부족 ᄒ오. |

| | |
|---|---|
| Is this enough? | 이 거시 넉넉호오? |
| Six inches will be wide enough. | 광이 여슷 치 넉넉 호오. |
| That's enough. | 그 만콤 쓰겟소. |
| This won't be enough. | 이것 못 자라겟소. |
| Was there enough coal? | 셕탄 넉넉 호엿소? |

3. (a).

| | |
|---|---|
| We've walked enough now, let's go back. | 지금은 넉넉히 운동 호엿시니 도라 갑시다. |
| You've read enough now, that will do. | 인제 넉넉히 닑엇시니 그만 두오. |
| As the coolies have rested long enough, let us hurry on. | 일군 그만 쉬엇시니 어셔 갑시다. |

3. (b).

| | |
|---|---|
| Haven't you had enough to eat yet? | 아직 넉넉히 먹지 아니 호엿소? |
| These potatoes are not boiled enough yet. | 이 감자롤 아직 덜 삷엇소. |
| You have'nt taken enough medicine yet. | 약 아직 덜 먹엇소. |

4.

| | |
|---|---|
| Have you enough stamps to put on that letter? | 그 편지 붓칠만콤 우례표 잇소? |
| Have we coal enough to last till next spring? | 틔년 봄 ᄭᆞ지 쓸 셕탄 잇소? |
| Have you studied into the subject enough to really understand it? | 실샹 그 일을 알 만콤 샹고 호엿소? |

| | |
|---|---|
| We had enough plums to send some to all our friends. | 우리게 즈도는 각 친구의게 보낼 만큼 잇셧소. |
| We went to see them and instead of finding them starving, we found they had enough rice, stored away in bags to last them a whole month. | 우리가 보러 간죽 굼지 아니 호고 오히려 혼돌 쓸 쌀이 셤에 넌것 잇는 거슬 차졋소. |

# CHAPTER VI.

### THE ADJECTIVE.

### § I.

The previous chapter having treated of pronominal adjectives, there remains for us here, simply qualifying, or descriptive adjectives. As will be seen in Part I, Korean has but few true descriptive adjectives, and as a consequence, in translating English into Korean, adjectives must be variously rendered.

1 Used attributively—either a simple adjective will be used, or a past relative participle, which will then, as in English precede the noun it qualifies.

2 Used predicatively—the verbal form in the appropriate tense will be used.

Note.—When two or more adjectives qualify the same word, they will be rendered by the stems of the adjectival verb with 고, and the last only will be inflected. It must also be remembered that often where we use the attributive, the Korean uses the predicative form, and vice versa.

1.

This is a rainy day.    오늘 비오는 날 이오.
Those are very pretty flowers.    그 것 미우 묘흔 쏫 치오
My sister has dark eyes.    우리 누님은 눈알이 검소.

## THE ADJECTIVE.

| | |
|---|---|
| That is a large house. | 그 거시 큰 집이오. |
| Koreans wear black hats and white coats. | 죠션 사룸은 검은 갓 쓰고 흰 옷 닙고. |
| You will need a thick overcoat. | 둣거온 두루막이 잇 셔야 쓰겟소. |
| Koreans like bright colors. | 죠션 사룸 환훈 빗 됴화 ᄒᆞ오. |
| That is a good fire. | 그 것 됴흔 불이오. |
| There is a large white dog in the garden. | 화원에 훈 크고 흰 개 잇소. |
| He wears a heavy gold chain. | 무거온 금 ᄉᆞ슬을 찻소. |
| My mother sent me a silver cup. | 우리 어마니가 훈 은 잔 을 보내엿소. |

### 2.

| | |
|---|---|
| Japanese are very small. | 일본 사룸 미우 적소. |
| American women are tall. | 미국 녀인이 킈 크오. |
| The road was very muddy. | 길은 대단이 질엇소. |
| Good coal is plentiful in Korea. | 됴흔 셕탄 죠션에 만소. |
| Those chairs are very strong, but they are very heavy. | 그 교의는 미우 든든 ᄒᆞ것마는 무겁소. |
| That dress is very pretty. | 그 옷시 미우 묘ᄒᆞ오. |
| That overcoat is thick. | 그 두루막이 둣겁소. |
| Most Korean colors are bright. | 죠션 물식은 거위 다 광치가 잇소. |
| That fire is good. | 그 불이 됴쇼. |

| | |
|---|---|
| That gold chain is heavy. | 그 금 수술 무겁소. |
| He was a tall, strong, handsome man. | 킈 크고 힘 세고 어엿분 사롬 이엿소. |
| I had a large, gentle, and fleet Chinese pony. | 내게 큰 크고 슌 ᄒ고 ᄲᆞᄅᆞᆫ 즁국 ᄆᆞᆯ 잇셧소. |

## § II.—COMPARISON OF ADJECTIVES AND ADVERBS.

### Sec. 1.—The Comparative Degree.

As was seen in Part I. in the chapter on adjectives, the idea of comparison is expressed largely by Koreans by the use of the simple positive. If there are a number, and it is desired to know which is the best, the Korean picking out simply one, and saying "This is good," will mean that it is the best. Similarly where there are only two "Of these two this is good" means, *This is the better*. There are however, cases where the expression of the comparative or superlative degree is necessary to the sense.

The comparative degree may be expressed by such words as 더 (*more*) 낫소 (*to be better*), 보다 (*than*)에셔 (*from*). In connection with the use of these words, we must always remember, that in Korean the governing word always follows the word it governs, and the 보다 or 에셔, will refer then to the word which precedes it and not to the word that follows. 더 being an adverb, precedes the adjective or verb it qualifies, and we should remember that as a rule Koreans do not use 더 with 보다 or 에셔, either one alone, being sufficient. For the rendering of the English comparative degree we obtain then the following rules:—

1 Signifying in a greater degree—더 preceding the adjective or neuter verb.

2 When two different objects are compared :—
   (a) When *than* is expressed—보다 or 에서 affixed to the noun having the quality in the lesser degree; and the adjective in the positive.
   (b) When *than* is not expressed—the postposition 는 may be affixed to one or both of the nouns, or 즁에 (*among*) may be used with the positive: or 더 may be affixed to the adjective.

3 *The more—the more*, marking the introduction of two correlative clauses, may be rendered into Korean, by 사록.

1.

| | |
|---|---|
| Would it not be well to tie that bundle tighter? | 그 보퉁이를 더 든든이 미는 거시 됴치 안켓소? |
| You must be more energetic. | 더 부즈런 ᄒ여야 ᄒ겟소. |
| I wish you had waked me a little earlier. | 좀 더 일즉 끼왓더면 됴왓지오. |
| They are pretty well made, but I wish they were a little smaller. | 꽤 잘 믄든 듯 ᄒ나 좀 더 적엇더면 됴왓 지오. |

2. (a).

| | |
|---|---|
| Fusan is hotter than Söul. | 부산이 셔울 보다 더워. |
| The days are a good deal longer in summer than in winter. | 녀름 에는 히가 겨울 보다 미우 기오. |
| He is a good deal taller than his wife. | 안히 보다 키 미우 크오. |
| Chairs are easier than jinrikshas. | 교군이 인력거 보다 편ᄒ오. |
| I am about three years older than my brother. | 내가 동셩 보다 삼년 우히오. |

2. (b.)

| This is the prettier but the other is the cheaper. | 이 거슨 묘훈것 마는 그 거슨 싸오. |
|---|---|
| Of these two houses, the one nearer here is the higher. | 그 두집 즁에 갓가온 집이 놉소. |
| Mine is the stronger horse. | 내 물이 힘 세오. |
| This is the better pen. | 이 붓시 낫소. |
| Mine was the greater fault. | 내 허물 더 크오 |
| My sister is the prettier. | 우리 누님 더 묘호오. |

3.

| The quicker the better. | 새를 수록 됴쇼. |
|---|---|
| The more the better. | 만흘 수록 됴소. |
| The more one gets, the more he wants. | 더 엇을 수록 더 가지고 십소. |
| The more I study, the less I seem to myself to know. | 공부를 홀 수록 성각에 더 무식훈 듯 호오. |

SEC. 2.—THE SUPERLATIVE DEGREE.

As was noticed above, unless the sense requires it, Koreans do not employ the superlative, the positive answering all the purposes. If it is necessary, it may be rendered by the ordinal 뎨일 (*the first*), prefixed to the adjective.

| Which is the best hotel in Seoul? | 셔울에 어느 쥬막이 뎨일 됴소? |
|---|---|
| The first plan seems to me the best. | 처음 계교가 내 성각에 뎨일 인듯 호오. |

| | |
|---|---|
| He is the richest man in America. | 미국에 데일 부쟈요. |
| He was the bravest soldier in the regiment. | 진 즁에 데일 담대 훈 사룸이 엇소. |
| Of all these books which is the best. | 이 모든 칙즁에 어느거시 됴소. |
| Is not the lion the most fearful of all animals? | 즘싱 즁에는 샤즈가 무셥지오? |
| Of all clothes foreign clothes are the easiest to wear. | 모든 의복 즁에 닙기 경편훈 거슨 양복 이오. |

# CHAPTER VII.

### THE ADVERB.

English adverbs may be rendered into Korean in various ways. Methods for forming adverbs from adjectives, with their various distinctions, may be found in the chapter on Adverbs, in the "Grammatical Notes." We have not here then to deal with these, but will simply consider how a few of the English adverbs of *place, time, manner,* etc., are rendered into Korean.

### § I.—ADVERBS OF PLACE.

To Korean primitive adverbs, the various postpositions can be affixed.

SEC. 1.—HERE.

1 Signifying this place—여긔, 이리, 이곳 etc.
2 Signifying this neighborhood—이근쳐.

1.

| | |
|---|---|
| Here it is. | 여긔 잇소. |
| Here is where I lost my watch. | 여긔가 내 시계 일허 부리던 듸요. |
| Here is where Son Doli fell into the river. | 여긔가 손돌이 강에 싸지던 듸요. |

CHAP. VII. § I. SEC. 2.  THE ADVERB.    327

| | |
|---|---|
| Is the book you bought yesterday here? | 어제 산 칙이 여긔 잇소? |
| Sou Dongi and Sou Jini were here just now. | 슈동이 ᄒᆞ고 슈진이 ᄒᆞ고 죽금 여긔 왓다 갓소. |
| Do they make pottery here? | 여긔셔 사긔 굽소? |
| Do they generally drill the soldiers here? | 병뎡들을 대테 여긔셔 조련 ᄒᆞ오? |
| Has'nt some one been writing here? | 여긔셔 누가 쓰지 아니 ᄒᆞ엿소? |
| Bring it here! | 이리 가져 오너라. |
| Come here with the baby! | 어린: 오히 이리 드러오 너라. |
| Tell Nomi to come here. | 놈이 드려 이리 오라고 ᄒᆞ오. |
| Then we must certainly ride in chairs from here. | 그러ᄒᆞ니 여긔셔 불가불 교군을 ᄒᆞ야 쓰겟소. |
| How far is it from here to the next hotel? | 여긔셔 이다음 쥬막 ᄭᅡ지 얼마나 머오? |

2.

| | |
|---|---|
| Are there any deer about here nowadays? | 이 근쳐에 이스이도 사ᄉᆞᆷ이 잇소? |
| Do they not have a flower show here to-night? | 오늘 밤에 이 근쳐에 꼿 져주 버리지 안소? |

SEC. 2.—THERE.

There—뎌긔, 뎌리, 거긔, 그리. The difference between 뎌 and 그 noticed in Part I. ¶ 72 extends to these adverbs.

| | |
|---|---|
| There's a man with a dog and a gun. | 뎌긔 총 가지고 개두리고 잇는 사름 잇쇼. |
| There have been fires there, very many times this year. | 뎌긔 금년에 불이 미우 여러번 낫셧쇼. |
| I hope Mr. Chyeng will wait there till we come. | 우리 오기 ᄭᅡ지 뎡셔방 거긔셔 기두리면 됴켓쇼. |
| Do they make much kanchang there? | 거긔셔 간쟝 만히 ᄆᆞᆫ두오? |
| What kind of a ship is that they are building there? | 뎌긔셔 ᄆᆞᆫ두는 거시 무슴 비오? |
| That's all right. Put it down there. | 관계치 안쇼 거긔 노하 두오. |
| I think most of the silk thread comes from there. | 내 ᄉᆡᆼ각에는 대데 명듀실 모도 거긔셔 나오는 줄 아오. |

SEC. 3.—WHERE.

1 Interrogative—어듸, 어느곳.
2 Relative—듸 with relative participle.
3 Somewhere—어듸, 어듸던지, 어듸션지.
4 Everywhere, wherever,—by 던지 with the relative participle; by two negatives; or by such words as ᄉᆞ방 (*four sides*), 곳곳, 쳐쳐 etc.
5 Anywhere—아모듸나, 아모듸던지, 어듸던지.
6 Nowhere—아모듸도 with negative.

1.

| | |
|---|---|
| Where does the washerwoman live? | 마젼 집이 어듸오? |

| | |
|---|---|
| Where was it that you met Mr. Kim this morning? | 오늘 아츰에 김셔방 맛나던 되가 어디오? |
| Where is this flower pot cracked? | 이 꼿분이 어디가 금이 갓소? |
| Where is Mr. Yi? | 리셔방 어디 잇소? |
| Where is the spoon I left on the table? | 상 우희 논 슈가락 어디 잇소? |
| Where is the shirt I sent to the wash? | 빨너 보낸 속 젹삼 어디 잇소? |
| Where did you buy this fish? | 이 싱션은 어디셔 삿소? |
| Do you know where these grapes were grown? | 이 포도가 어디셔 자란지 암니가? |
| Where's my dictionary gone? | 내 주뎐이 어디 갓소? |
| Where were you going when I met you yesterday? | 어제 맛날 째에 어디 가는 길이엇소? |
| Where does the best rice come from? | 뎨일 됴흔 쌀이 어디셔 나오? |

2.

| | |
|---|---|
| Is this where we take the boat? | 여긔가 비 드는 디요? |
| Here's where we have to show our passports. | 여긔셔 빙표 뵈논 디요. |
| Sit where you can hear. | 들닐 디로 안지오. |

3.

| | |
|---|---|
| Isn't there a bridge somewhere on the river? | 어디 던지 강에 드리 업소? |

| | |
|---|---|
| Are there not fireworks somewhere to-night? | 오늘 밤에 어듸 던지 불노름 ᄒ지 안소? |
| It seems to me I saw a second hand one at some book store on the main street. | 어듸 션지 큰 길 쳑샤에셔 늙은 거슬 본 둣ᄒ오. |
| He has gone somewhere. | 어듸 갓소. |
| He put the book somewhere, and has forgotten where it is. | 칙은 어듸 노코 논듸를 니젓소. |

4.

| | |
|---|---|
| He smokes tobacco wherever he goes. | 어듸를 가던지 담비는 먹소. |
| He makes friends wherever he goes. | 어듸를 가던지 친구가 성기오. |
| Mosquitoes are everywhere in Japan. | 일본셔 모긔가 업는듸 업소. |
| Steamboats go everywhere now. | 지금은 화륜션이 곳곳이 가오. |
| There are plenty of merchants everywhere. | 쳐쳐에 쟝ᄉ가 만소. |
| The cat has looked everywhere for her kittens. | 고양이가 삿기를 ᄉ면으로 차잣소. |
| I am lonely wherever I go. | 아모듸 가던지 심심ᄒ오. |

5.

| | |
|---|---|
| I can't find my handkerchief anywhere. | 내 슈건 아모 듸셔 던지 차질수 업소. |
| Of course water runs down hill anywhere. | 본티 물은 어듸 던지 누즌 듸로 흐르오. |

| | |
|---|---|
| You can travel anywhere in Japan without a passport. | 빙표 업시 일본에 아모 듸 던지 돈니겟소. |

6.

| | |
|---|---|
| He is nowhere in the house. | 집에는 아모 듸도 업소. |
| There were no fish anywhere this morning. | 오늘 아츰에는 성션이 아모 듸도 업섯소. |
| Foreigners could live nowhere except in the open ports. | 외국 사롬은 통샹 항구 외에는 아모 듸도 못 사랏소. |

## § II.—ADVERBS OF TIME.

### SEC. 1.—ALWAYS.

1 Invariably—언제던지.
2 Continually—늘, 느루.
3 From the beginning—본틱 with or without 지금 ᄭ지.
4 At all times—흥샹, 일샹.
5 Signifying *all*—다.

1.

| | |
|---|---|
| Is June always rainy? | 륙월은 언제 던지 쟝마오? |
| Does the king always have a guard? | 님금 씌는 언제 던지 호위병이 뫼시고 잇소? |
| I suppose the waves are not always as high as this. | 내 성각에는 풍랑이 언제 던지 이 ᄭ치 놉지 아닐 듯 호오. |
| Do you always put out your light before you get in bed? | 언제 던지 침상에 들기 젼에 불 ᄭ오? |

## 2.

| | |
|---|---|
| Are you always in pain? | 느루 압흐오? |
| Is the earth always in motion? | 쌍이 늘 동흐오? |
| Before you had the smallpox were you always well? | 역질노 알키 젼에눈 늘 평안 흐엿소? |
| Is a bird always on her nest when she is hatching her young? | 새가 샷기 칠 쌔에는 느루 그 보금자리에 잇소? |
| Is a sentinel always walking when he is on guard? | 슌경 군이 슌경 돌 쌔에 는 느루 것소? |

## 3.

| | |
|---|---|
| Have you always lived in Seoul? | 본릭 셔울셔 지금 ᄭ지 살앗소? |
| The English have always been good sailors. | 영국 사룸 본릭 사공 노릇 잘 흐오. |
| Have there always been eight provinces in Korea? | 본릭 죠션에 팔도가 잇 섯소? |

## 4.

| | |
|---|---|
| God is always the same. | 샹뎨는 일샹 흔 모양 이오. |
| It is always best to do right. | 올케 ᄒ는 거슨 흥샹 됴소. |
| I am always glad to see that man. | 그 사름 보기 흥샹 반갑소. |
| He is always telling lies. | 일샹 거줏 말 흐오· |
| That baby is always crying. | 그 어린 것 흥샹 울더라. |

CHAP. VII. § II. SEC. 2. THE ADVERB. 333

Although the Koreans are always eating rice, they never refuse it.    죠션 사룸 일샹 밥 먹으디 훈번도 슬치 안소.

5.

Are crows always black?    가마귀는 다 검소?
Do mapoos always wear felt hats?    마부는 다 벙거지 쓰오?

### SEC. 2.—WHENEVER,

1 At whatever time—언제던지 or 어느때던지.

2 Every time—때마다 with the relative participle. The above may also be used, but this is the better.

1.

I'll start whenever it is convenient to you.    어느 때 던지 당신의 뎍당훈 때에 써나겟소.

Can I borrow your dictionary whenever I send for it?    어느 때 던지 가질너 보내면 조뎐을 빌수 잇겟소?

We must go on board whenever the ship comes in.    어느 때던지 비가 드러 오거든 득야 항겟소.

Be ready whenever Mr. Yi comes.    어느 때 오게 되던지 리셔방 예비호여 두어라.

2.

Whenever I go to Chemulpo it rains.    제물포 가는 때 마다 비가 오오.

He gets angry whenever he argues.    론난홀 때 마다 셩이 나오.

Every time I read it, it seems harder.    닑을 때 마다 더 어려온 모양 이오.

I have a headache whenever
I smoke.    담비 먹을 째 마다
            두통이 잇소.

### SEC. 3.—GENERALLY, USUALLY.

Generally, usually—혼이, 대개, 대뎌, 힝용.

What kind of a pen do you generally use?    혼이 무솜 붓슬 쓰오?

Cholera generally comes in the summer.    쥐통이 혼이 녀롬에 잇소.

We generally have tiffin at one.    힝용 훈 시에 뎜심을 먹소.

We generally take a walk in the afternoon.    우리돌이 대개 오후에 힝기 호오.

It generally rains a good deal in July.    양력 칠월에 대뎌 비가 만히 오오.

We do not usually have much snow in Southern Korea.    죠션 남편에논 혼이 눈 만히 오지 안소.

### SEC. 4.—OFTEN, FREQUENTLY.

Often, frequently—자조, 잣고.

I often have headache.    두통이 잣고 나오.

Come and see me often, when you come to Seoul.    셔울 오거든 자조 와 보시오.

We often read together.    자조 굿치 닑소.

### SEC. 5.—SOMETIMES.

1 Occasionally, now and then, once in a while—
잇다금, 갓금, 째로.

2 On certain occasions, at particular times—엇던째논.

3 Indefinite,—째 with relative participle.

## 1.

| | |
|---|---|
| Even the wisest plans sometimes fail. | 암만 됴흔 계교 라도 잇다 금 실슈가 잇소. |
| Do you still go to the palace sometimes? | 이 수이도 잇다금 대궐에 드러가오? |
| Why do you not let me hear from you sometimes? | 웨 갓금 편지도 아니 ᄒᆞ오? |
| I meet him sometimes, but not very often. | ᄉᆡ로 맛나 나 잣지는 안소. |
| You may go occasionally. | 잇다금 이나 가오. |
| Once in a while I take a nap in the day time. | 잇다금 낫잠 자오. |

## 2.

| | |
|---|---|
| Sometimes one does not know what to do. | 엇던 ᄯᆡ는 엇더케 ᄒᆞ여야 됴흘 넌지 모르오. |
| Sometimes she sings even better than she did tonight. | 엇던 ᄯᆡ는 오ᄂᆞᆯ 밤 보다 노래를 도 더 잘 ᄒᆞ오. |
| Sometimes I half suspect we have made a mistake. | 엇던 ᄯᆡ는 내 성각에 우리 들이 실슈 ᄒᆞᆫ듯 ᄒᆞ오. |
| When we were in Japan last year, it sometimes rained for four or five days in succession. | 샹년에 일본 잇슬 ᄯᆡ 엇던ᄯᆡ에는 닷시를 날마다 비 왓소. |

## 3.

| | |
|---|---|
| I eat rice sometimes. | 밥 먹는 ᄯᆡ 잇소. |
| He comes sometimes in the mornings. | 아ᄎᆞᆷ에 오는 ᄯᆡ 잇소. |

| | |
|---|---|
| Sometimes I cannot sleep all night. | 밤 시도록 안 자는 째 잇소. |
| Sometimes not one of the boys knows his lesson. | 날 마다 비호 는 거슬 아는 ㅇ히가 하나도 업 는 째 잇소. |

### SEC. 6.—SELDOM.

Seldom—별노 followed by the negative.

| | |
|---|---|
| I seldom have a cold. | 나는 감긔가 별노 아니 드오. |
| I seldom smoke in the house. | 나는 집에셔 담비 별노 아니 먹소. |
| I have seldom seen him of late. | 이스이는 그 사룸을 별노 맛나지 못 ᄒ엿소. |

### SEC. 7.—NEVER, EVER.

1 Temporal:—

  (*a.*) On no occasion, not once—제 or 째 with the relative participle. If emphatic, 훈 번도 may be used.

  (*b.*) Invariably not—언제던지, followed by the negative.

  (*c*) At no future time—아모 째 이라도 with the negative.

  (*d.*) Never before—그젼 에 는 with the negative.

2 Emphatic:—

  (*a.*) Not at all—아조, 도모지, with the negative.

  (*b.*) Positively not—일뎡코, 쟉뎡코, with the negative.

  (*c.*) Under no circumstances whatever:—세샹 업서 도, 암만 ᄒ여 도 and the like with the negative.

Chap. VII. § II. Sec. 7.   THE ADVERB.    357

### 1. (a).

| | |
|---|---|
| I never had toothache till I was twenty. | 갓 스 물 되 기 ᄭᅡ지 ᄂᆞᆫ 치통이 ᄒᆞᆫ번도 업섯소. |
| I have never ridden in a chair. | 보교 ᄒᆞᆫ번도 아니 ᄐᆞᆺ소. |
| This grass has never been cut. | 이 플은 ᄶᅡ가 본제가 업소. |
| Does small-pox ever prevail in Korea? | 죠션에도 역질이 셩ᄒᆞᆫ ᄶᅢ가 잇소? |
| Have you ever been robbed? | 도적 마자 본제가 잇소? |
| Had you ever been to Sëoul befere you met me? | 나 맛나기 젼에 셔울 와 본제가 잇섯소? |

### 1. (b).

| | |
|---|---|
| Some people never get up till seven or eight o'clock. | 언졔 던지 칠팔 시 젼에 ᄂᆞᆫ 니러나지 안ᄂᆞᆫ 사ᄅᆞᆷ 도 잇소. |
| Do you never take sugar in your tea? | 언졔 던지 차에 사탕 노코 안잡수오? |
| I never take wine. | 언졔던 지 술 안 먹소. |

### 1. (c).

| | |
|---|---|
| Will murderers who have escaped by bribery never be punished? | 돈 드리고 도망ᄒᆞᆫ 살인 죄인은 아모 ᄶᅢ 라도 잡지 안켓소? |
| I will never see him again. | 아모 ᄶᅢ· 라도 다시 안 보 겟소. |
| The soul can never die. | 령혼이 아모 ᄶᅢ 라도 죽 지못 ᄒᆞ겟쇼. |

1. (d).

| | |
|---|---|
| I never saw such flowers before. | 그 젼에는 그런 옷 못 보앗소. |
| Did you never understand it before? | 그 젼에는 몰낫소? |

2. (a).

| | |
|---|---|
| Are diamonds never found in Korea? | 죠션 셔는 금강셕이 도모지 아니 나오? |
| I never see him now. | 지금 도모지 못 보오. |
| Korean ladies never go out. | 죠션 부인 들이 도모지 출입 아니 호오. |

2. (b).

| | |
|---|---|
| I shall never love any one so much again. | 내가 쟉뎡코 아모 사롬 이라도 다시 그러케 스랑 호지 안겟소. |
| I will never give him another cash. | 다시는 쟉뎡코 혼 푼도 아니 주 겟소. |
| Never do a thing like that again. | 다시는 일뎡코 그런 일 마라. |
| I can never consent to such a thing as that. | 그런 일은 일뎡코 허락홀 수 업소. |

2. (c).

| | |
|---|---|
| He can never study Japanese. | 셰샹 업서도 일본 말 공부홀 수 업겟소. |
| He can never live unless he takes medicine. | 약먹기 젼에는 셰샹 업서 도 살수 업소. |
| I believe I'll never be able to learn Korean. | 나는 암만 호여도 조션 말을 비홀수 업술 것 굿소. |

| | |
|---|---|
| You'll never find it without a light. | 불 업시는 암만 ᄒᆞ여도 차질 수 업ᄉᆞ리이다. |
| Can you never forgive him? | 암만 ᄒᆞ여도 용셔 ᄒᆞᆯ수 업소? |

### SEC. 8.—AGAIN.

1 Another time—쏘 or 다시.
2 Once more—쏘 ᄒᆞᆫ번.
3 To do over again—새로 or 곳쳐.

**1.**

| | |
|---|---|
| I'll call again. | 쏘 오리이다. |
| Be sure and call again. | 부듸 쏘 오시오. |
| Do not do that again. | 다시 그 것 ᄒᆞ지 마라. |
| It just stopped raining, and it is raining again. | 비가 긋쳣다가 쏘 오오. |

**2.**

| | |
|---|---|
| Sing that song again. | 쏘 ᄒᆞᆫ번 그 노래 ᄒᆞ시오. |
| If you don't understand I will explain it again. | 모ᄅᆞ시면 쏘 ᄒᆞᆫ번 닐너 드리리이다. |

**3.**

| | |
|---|---|
| You will have to do it over again. | 새로 ᄒᆞ여야 쓰겟소. |
| You will have to iron these clothes again. | 그 옷을 곳쳐 다루리 질 ᄒᆞ여야 쓰겟소. |
| The legs of this table are not alike, you must make it over again. | 이 상 ᄃᆞ리가 ᄀᆞᆺ지 아니 ᄒᆞ니 곳쳐 ᄆᆞᆫᄃᆞ라야 쓰겟소. |

### SEC. 9.—WHEN.

1 Interrogative :—
   (*a.*) At what time—언제, 어ᄂᆞ째.

(b.) Until what time—언제서지, 어느째서지.
How long—얼마.
(c.) About when—언제나, 어느째즈음.
(d.) At what hour—어느시.

2 Relative :—

(a.) At the time—째 or 젹 with relative participle.
(b.) By the time—째밋처셔 with relative participle.
(c.) After the time—후 with relative participle; sometimes 거든 will be used with one of the simple tenses.

1. (a).

| When did you write this letter? | 이편지를 언제 썻소? |
| When do you intend going to Chemulpo? | 제물포 에 어느째 가랴고 호오? |
| When would you like it to be done? | 언제 호면 공의 무음에 맛 겟소? |
| When was that? | 그 것 언제 일 이오? |
| When did foreigners come to Korea? | 언 제 브터 외국 사룸이 죠션에 왓소? |
| When did Keuija live? | 긔즈가 어느째 사룸 이오? |

1. (b).

| Till when can you wait? | 어느째 서지 기드리겟소? |
| How much longer can you wait? | 어느째 서지나 더 기드리 겟소? |
| About how much longer do you intend to be in Seöul? | 셔울 얼마나 더 계실 경 영이오? |

1. (c).

About when will it be done? 언제나 되겟소?

CHAP. VII. § II. SEC. 9.   THE ADVERB.                    341

About when does the rainy      쟝마가 어느째 즈음 시쟉
  season begin?                  호오?

                    1. (d).

When shall I wake you          어느시에 씨여 드리오리
  Sir?                           잇가?
When do you retire?            어느시에 긔침 호시누니
                                 잇가?
When do you tiffin?            어느시에 뎜심 잡수시
                                 누니 잇가?

                    2. (a).

Which of the boys was it       부롤적에 디답 호던 으
  that answered when you        히가 누구요?
  called?
I will send word when I        졔물포 편지 홀째에 긔별
  write to Chemulpo?             호겟소?
When the Japanese am-          일본 대신이 드러 올째
  bassador comes will he         대군쥬를 뵈오러 가
  go to see the King?            겟소?
He broke it just when it       막 다 될만호 째에 써트
  was about done.                렷소.
What did he say when he        잡혓실 째에 무어시라고
  was arrested?                  호옵더니잇가?

                    2. (b).

It will certainly be done      오실 째 밋처서 뎡녕 다
  when you come.                 되 겟소.
The letters must all be        톄젼부 올째 밋처서 편
  written by the time the        지를 다 써 두어야
  postman comes.                 쓰겟소.

## 2. (c).

| | |
|---|---|
| When you have swept and dusted the room shut the door. | 방을 다 쓸고 홈친 후에 문 닷아라. |
| When Sou Dongi comes back, tell him to put these jars in the box. | 슈동이 온 후에 이 항아리 들을 케에 너라고 ᄒᆞ오. |
| When this sugar is gone I will buy more. | 이 사탕이 다 업거든 더 사겟소. |

### Sec. 10.—While.

While—동안에, 소이에, 적에.

| | |
|---|---|
| While the chair coolies were eating we climbed the mountain. | 보교군이 밥 먹을 동안에 우리가 산에 올나 갓소. |
| While I was in the country I studied hard. | 싀골 잇슬 적에 공부 만히 ᄒᆞ엿소. |
| Please do not talk just now while I am writing a letter. | 지금 나 편지 쓸 적에 잔소티 말아 주오. |
| While I was standing in front of the monastery, a priest came out. | 절 압헤 섯실 동안에 즁이 나왓 소옵더이다. |
| A while ago, while we were coming it was very cold. | 아싸 올 적에 미우 칩소 옵더이다. |
| While you are studying do not play. | 공부 홀적에 작란 ᄒᆞ지 마오. |

### Sec. 11.—As.

1 When—, 적에, 제, ᄯᅢ에.

2 Indicating simultaneous action— 면서 affixed to verbal stem.

3 Taking advantage of the opportunity—길에 with relative participle.

4 On the way—다가 with verbal stem. 길에 may also be used here. 다가 indicates an interruption and often something unexpected.

### 1.

| | |
|---|---|
| Do the men-of-war always fire a salute as they leave port? | 군함이 항구에 나갈 제마다 레포를 놋소? |
| We got home just as it began to rain. | 비가 막 올쌔에 집에 도라 왓소. |
| The postman came just as I was finishing my letter. | 편지를 다 막 못칠 쌔에 톄젼부 왓사옵더이다. |

### 2.

| | |
|---|---|
| I will read as I ride. | 물 트고 가면서 보겟소. |
| As you read, notice carefully the writing of the characters. | 닑으면서 글즈 쓴 거슬 즈셰히 보겟소. |
| According to Korean custom they do not talk as they eat. | 죠션 법에는 밥 먹으면서 말 아니 ᄒᆞ오. |

### 3.

| | |
|---|---|
| As you are going to Chong No, call chair coolies. | 죵로 가는 길에 교군 불너라. |
| As you are mending it, you had better put in a new lock. | 곳치는 길에 새 잠을쇠 사지 두면 됴켓다. |
| As you are going home, please call there. | 딕에 가는 길에 거긔 좀 둔녀 가오. |

| | |
|---|---|
| As we sailed up the river we stopped at Samkai. | 강에 올나 가다가 삼키셔 지쳬 흐엿소. |
| He told me that story as we went to Song Do. | 송도 가다가 그 니야기 흐엿소. |
| As I was going to the palace I met Mr. Yi at Chong No. | 대궐 가다가 종로에서 리셔방을 맛낫소. |
| As I was coming up to Seoul I stopped at Oricole. | 셔울 올나 오다가 오리 골셔 머물녓소. |

### Sec. 12.—Then.

1. At that time,—그째, 그째에, 그째는.
2. Till that time,—그째ᄭᅡ지.
3. By that time,—그째에, (*indefinite*) 그째즈음.
4. After that time,—그후 or 그째브터.
5. At that point,—그다음.

#### 1.

| | |
|---|---|
| Will you be here then? | 그 째에 여긔 잇겟소? |
| Then there were Buddhist Monasteries in all the provinces. | 그 째에는 졀이 팔도에 잇섯소. |
| The people paid their taxes in rice then. | 그 째에 빅셩 들이 구실을 쌀노 밧쳣소. |

#### 2.

| | |
|---|---|
| Leave it here till then. | 그 째ᄭᅡ지 여긔 두오. |
| I will be at home till then. | 그 째ᄭᅡ지 집에 잇겟소. |
| We had better give it up till then. | 그 째ᄭᅡ지 그만 두는 거시 됴켓소. |

CHAP. VII. § II. SEC. 13. THE ADVERB. 315

3.

| Then the boys will be old enough to work for themselves. | 그 째에 ㅇ히가 제 손으로 버러 먹을 만콤 크겟소. |
| Then there will be railroads. | 그째 즈음 텰로가 잇겟소. |
| Will you be ready then? | 그 째 즈음 다 쥰비가 되겟소? |

4.

| Then the wind blew so hard, we could not go and came back. | 그 후는 바람이 대단히 여셔 가지 못ᄒ고 도라왓소. |
| Then we got in a boat and went to see the fire works. | 그 후에 비를 트고 승긔젼 구경 ᄒ러 갓셧소. |
| Then I will go to the palace. | 그 후에 대궐에 드러 가겟소. |
| Then I studied. | 그 후 브텀 내가 공부 ᄒ엿소. |
| From then on I stayed here. | 그 후 브텀 여긔 잇섯소. |

5.

| What did you say then? | 그 다음 무어시 라고 ᄒ엿소? |
| Then I asked him another question. | 그 다음 다른 말을 무러 보앗소. |

SEC. 13.—NOW.

1. At the present time:
   (*a.*) Definite, 시방, 지금.

(b.) Indefinite, 근뢰, 근일, 이스이, 요스이.
2, Now as opposed to formerly—the same with 는.
3. By this time already,—인제.
4. Next,—이 다음에.
5. Than before,—젼보다 or 아샤보다.

### 1. (a).

| | |
|---|---|
| Is not Mr. Song in Korea now? | 지금 송셔방이 죠션에 업소? |
| He is out at present, Sir. | 지금 츌입 ᄒᆞ엿 스읍ᄂ이다. |
| We are just out of it now. | 시방 못츔 다 썻소. |
| Kerosene is very high now. | 시방 셕유가 미우 비싸오 |

### 1. (b).

| | |
|---|---|
| There are a good many mad dogs about now. | 근뢰 밋친 개가 만혼 모양이오. |
| Nobody seems to make much money now. | 근일에는 누구 던지 리 남기지 못 ᄒᆞ는 모양이오. |
| It is very dear now. | 요스이 대단이 비싸오 |

### 2.

| | |
|---|---|
| Nowadays Koreans don't wear the large hat. | 이스이는 죠션 사름이 큰 갓슬 쓰지 아니 ᄒᆞ오. |
| The Japanese government tolerates Christianity nowadays. | 이스이는 일본 정부에셔 예수교 ᄒᆞ는 거슬 모르는 테ᄒᆞ오. |

### 3.

| | |
|---|---|
| Most of them will have been sold by this time. | 인제 거위 다 팔앗 겟소 |

| | |
|---|---|
| Your house must be about done now. | 공의 집 역亽는 인제 다 못찻실 듯 호오. |
| It's too late now. | 인제 느젓소. |
| It would be useless to send for the doctor now. | 의원 부르러 보내여 도 인제 쓸디 업소. |
| You had better apologize now. | 인제는 샤죄 호는 거시 올켓소. |
| They will probably be here directly now. | 인제 곳 올듯 호오. |
| It is boiled enough now. | 인제 다 삷엇 겟다. |
| Tea will be ready directly now. | 인제 차가 곳 다 되겟소. |

4.

| | |
|---|---|
| Son Pongi will recite now. | 이 다음에 슈봉이 외오 겟소. |
| We will read Chinese now. | 우리들이 이 다음에 진셔 비호겟소. |

5.

| | |
|---|---|
| The tide is running out more rapidly now. | 아샤 보다 죠슈가 더 샏르게 나가오. |
| I am in much better health now. | 젼 보다 내 몸이 더 편 호오. |
| We are having less rain now. | 젼보다 비 덜 오오. |

SEC. 14.—ALREADY.

1. At the time spoken of,—임의. 발셔.
2. Prior to the time spoken of,—이왕.
3. Equivalent to *so soon* expressive of surprise,— 어느스이.

Note.—With this last 발셔 also may be used.

1.

| The wind has already begun to blow. | 발셔 바롬이 불기 시작 ᄒᆞ엿소. |
| --- | --- |
| I have already applied for a passport. | 입의 빙표를 쳥구ᄒᆞ 엿소. |
| He says he has been waiting for about an hour already. | 발셔 ᄒᆞ시 동안 이나 기 드렷다고 ᄒᆞ옵더이다. |
| I was going to give the shoemaker a blowing up, but they were already done. | 갓밧치를 수지지랴고 ᄒᆞ 엿더니 발셔 다 ᄆᆞᆫ드럿 소옵더이다. |
| I have had plenty already. | 발셔 그만 먹엇소. |

2.

| As I have already explained several times. | 이왕 여러번 닐넛 거니와. |
| --- | --- |
| He has already declined two or three times. | 이왕 이삼ᄎᆞ나 슬타고 ᄒᆞ옵더이다. |

3.

| Have you finished already? | 어느 수이 다 ᄒᆞ엿소? |
| --- | --- |
| Have they come already? | 어느 수이 왓소? |
| Are the cherry trees in blossom already? | 어느 수이 벗 ᄭᅩᆺ치 피 엿소? |

### SEC. 15.—FORMERLY, USED TO.

Formerly, used to—근본, 젼에, 더거번에.

| Formerly all ships were made of wood. | 근본 비를 다 나모로 ᄆᆞᆫ드럿소 |
| --- | --- |
| There used to be no jinrikshas in Korea. | 죠션에 근본은 인력거가 업섯소. |

CHAP. VII. § II. SEC. 16-17-18. THE ADVERB. 349

| | |
|---|---|
| It used to be thought that the sun went round the earth. | 젼에 히가 쌍을 도눈 줄 알앗소. |
| There used to be a temple here. | 뎌거번에 여긔 졀이 잇섯소. |
| Formerly foreigners could not live in Seoul. | 이젼 에는 외국 사롬들이 셔울셔 살지 못ᄒ엿소. |

### SEC. 16.—HITHERTO.

Hitherto— 이쌔ᄭ지, 지금ᄭ지.

| | |
|---|---|
| Where have you lived hitherto? | 이쌔 ᄭ지 어듸셔 살 앗소? |
| What have you studied hitherto? | 이쌔 ᄭ지 무어슬 공부 ᄒ엿소? |
| As I have lived without eating meat hitherto, I will not eat it now. | 지금 ᄭ지 고기 안 먹고 살앗시니 안 먹겟소. |

### SEC. 17.—RECENTLY, OF LATE.

Recently, of late,— 이ᄉ이, 근틱, 졉쌔.

| | |
|---|---|
| Have you read any new books lately? | 근틱 무솜 새칙 이나 닑엇소? |
| The government has recently built a new custom house. | 졍부 에셔 이ᄉ이 새로 히관을 지엇소. |
| Did I not see you lately in Japan? | 졉쌔 일본셔 보지 아니 ᄒ엿소? |
| The king has not come out lately. | 이ᄉ이는 님금 거동 아니 ᄒ엿소. |

### SEC. 18.—AGO.

I. Ago— 젼, 젼에.

2. Long ago,— 오래젼. The Koreans generally, however, render this by the relative participle of the verb,

with 지 or 제 followed by the verb 오라오, *to be long* (*temporal*).

3. Several days ago,— 일젼에.
4. A little while ago,— 아까.
5. Just a minute ago,— 인제, 지금, 시방.

1.

| | |
|---|---|
| He died three years ago. | 삼년 젼에 죽엇소. |
| I wish I had written a month ago. | 훈 돌 젼에 편지를 ᄒ엿더면 됴홀 번 ᄒ엿소. |
| How many years ago was Sëoul built? | 셔울이 몃히 젼에 되엿소? |

2.

| | |
|---|---|
| I saw him a long while ago. | 오래 젼에 보앗소. |
| It was made long ago. | 믄든 제가 오라오. |
| He promised to lend it long ago. | 발셔 빌니 마고 샹약 훈 제가 오라오. |
| I knew it long ago. | 안 지가 오라오. |

3.

| | |
|---|---|
| There was a dealer here the other day with some very pretty fans. | 일젼에 쟝수가 고흔 붓체 를 가지고 왓소. |

4.

| | |
|---|---|
| I sent him to the office a while ago to mail the letters. | 아까 편지를 보내라고 우톄국 에 보내 엿소. |
| Mr. Kim was here an hour or two ago with his nephew. | 아까 김셔방이 그 족하 ᄒ고 왓스옵더이다. |

5.

| | |
|---|---|
| As I told you a minute ago. | 인제 말솜 훈 대로. |

CHAP. VII. § II. SEC. 19-20-21. THE ADVERB. 351

I saw him ride by here a few minutes ago.    지금 이리 듯고 지나 가는 거슬 보앗소.

### SEC. 19.—JUST NOW.

Just now—끗, 끗시방, 시방, 금방 etc.

I have just been seeing some dancing girls perform.    끗지금 기성이 춤 추는 거슬 보고 왓소.

The clock has just struck.    조명종이 금방 첫소.

When I've just given him one nyang will he ask more?    금방 혼량 주엇 는듸 쏘 달나 ᄒᆞ오?

### SEC. 20.—TILL, YET.

Still, yet—그져, 아직, 아직도.

Are you still sick?    그져 편치 안소?

This pail isn't full yet.    이 통이 아직 도 차지 아니 ᄒᆞ엿소.

Is'nt dinner ready yet?    져녁 아직 도 (그져) 안 되엿소?

### SEC. 21.—TILL, UNTIL.

1 Time:—

(a.) Up to—ᄭᅡ지.

(b.) Before—젼에는.

2 Degree—도록 with the verbal stem.

#### 1. (a).

Wait till he comes.    오기 ᄭᅡ지 기드리오.

I read till dark.    어둡기 ᄭᅡ지 닑엇소.

I must wait till twenty five minutes of five.    네시 삼십오분 ᄭᅡ지 기드리여야 쓰겟소.

1. (b).

| I can't go until ten minutes past five. | 오시 십분 젼에는 가지 못 ᄒ겟소. |
| --- | --- |
| I can't leave home until the middle of next month. | 릭월 보롬 즈음 젼에는 집에셔 써날 수 업소. |

2.

| I read till I was tired, | 곤ᄒ 도록 닑엇소. |
| --- | --- |
| Don't bend it till it breaks. | 부러지 도록 휘지 마오. |
| He pulled the cat's tail till she bit him. | 물니 도록 고양이 쇠리를 잡아 드렷소. |

SEC. 22.—BY AND BY.

By and by—잇다가 with future tense for future, and past tense for past time.

| By and by bring me some hot water. | 잇다가 더운 물 가져 오너라. |
| --- | --- |
| By and by go to the post-office for me. | 잇다가 우테국에 둔녀 주오. |
| By and by let's study. | 잇다가 공부 ᄒ옵시다. |
| By and by we met a chair. | 좀 잇다가 교군을 맛낫소. |
| There were no chair coolies in Chemulpo, and as it was hard to walk up, by and by having met a jinriksha on the way, I rode up. | 졔물포에 교군이 업서셔 거러 올나 오기에 미우 어렵더니 좀 잇다가 길에셔 인력거를 맛나셔 ᄐ고 올나 왓소. |

SEC. 23.—SOON.

1. 쉬 or 쉬이 or some such phrase as 일간, 오라 지 아니 ᄒ여, 얼마 아니 ᄒ여 etc.

2. As soon as :—The verbal stem with 면셔, followed by such a word as 곳, 즉시, etc. Whether past, present

or future, the verbal stem is used, and the time marked by the tense of the principal verb. The same effect will be produced by the use of the copulative conjunctions, in the same way. This idea may also be expressed by use of the relative participle with 대로.

1.

| | |
|---|---|
| They say there will soon be a railroad to Sëoul. | 쉬이 셔울 사지 털로를 싼다 ᄒᆞᆸ더이다. |
| The steamer will be in soon. | 일간 화륜션이 드러 오겟소. |
| We must start soon. | 쉬 떠나야 ᄒᆞ겟소. |
| It will stop raining very soon. | 비가 곳 긋치겟소. |
| The rain came down in torrents and soon the roof began to leak. | 비가 급히 쏫아지더니 얼마 아니 ᄒᆞ여셔 집웅이 시기 시작 ᄒᆞ엿소. |
| Supper will soon be ready. | 오라지 아니 ᄒᆞ여셔 져녁 다 되겟소. |
| I will soon go to America to study. | 오라지 아니 ᄒᆞ여셔 미국으로 공부 ᄒᆞ러 드러가겟소. |

2.

| | |
|---|---|
| I take a bath as soon as I get up. | 니러나 면셔 즉시 목욕 ᄒᆞᆫ다. |
| As soon as they get on board they begin to smoke. | 화륜션에 오른 면셔 즉시 담비 먹기를 시작 ᄒᆞ오. |
| He died as soon as he heard it. | 드른 면셔 곳 죽엇소. |
| As soon as he took the medicine he got better. | 약 먹으면셔 즉시 나엇소. |

I'll go as soon as I have  저녁 먹고 곳 자겟소.
dined.
I'll have a bath as soon as  목욕 물이 다 되는 대로
it's ready.  곳 오겟소.

### SEC. 24.—DIRECTLY, AT ONCE.

Presently—지금. 시방, etc., may be used : immediately
—즉시, 곳, 곳지금 etc., will be needed.

I'll come directly.  지금 오겟소.
The bell will ring directly.  인제 인경 치겟소.
Let me know what he says  그 사롬이 무어시 라고
immediately.  ᄒᆞ는 거슬 곳 긔별 ᄒᆞ오
Serve breakfast at once.  아춤 곳 올녀라.
Send that man away at  그 사롬 즉시 내여 보
once.  내라.

### SEC. 25.—BEFORE.

전에. The same word is used with nouns or verbs, but the English verb limited by *before*, takes the form of the verbal noun in 기.

#### 1.

We must start before ten.  열시 젼에 떠나야 ᄒᆞ겟소.
Let us have tiffin before we  떠나기 젼에 뎜심 먹읍
go.  시다.
I can't start for the country  우편 편지가 오기 젼에
before the mail comes in.  싀골 떠나지 못 ᄒᆞ겟소.
I want to speak to him be-  저즈에 가기 젼에 말 좀
fore he goes to market.  ᄒᆞ고 십소.

### SEC 26.—AFTER, SINCE.

1 With a verb or noun—후에. The verb limited by *after*, takes the form of the past relative participle and

CHAP. VII. § II. SEC. 26. THE ADVERB.   355

precedes 후에. Quite often this same idea is expressed by the simple verbal stem, with the conjunction 고.

2 Afterwards may be expressed by 후에는, 그후에 etc.
3 Signifying *past*—by a from of the verb 지나오 (*to pass*).

### 1.

| | |
|---|---|
| It began to rain after we passed Oricole. | 오리골 지난 후에 비가 시작 호엿소. |
| After the war was over, most of the troops returned to China. | 싸홈이 지난 후에 군스 들이 거위 다 즁국 으로 도라 갓소. |
| After you've seen to all the doors, put out the light. | 문 다 슬피 본 후에 불을 쓰오. |
| Four or five days after I came to Seoul I was taken sick. | 셔울 올나 온 후 스오 일에 병이 낫소. |
| The road dried an hour after the rain stopped. | 비가 긋친지 흔 시 후에 길이 물낫소. |
| Everything looks beautiful after the rain. | 비 후에는 무어시 던지 다 묘호오. |
| I can not go after the last of the month. | 금음 후에 못 가겟소. |
| I will come after I have written the letter. | 편지를 쓰고 오리이다. |
| I will come after dinner. | 뎜심 먹고 가리이다. |

### 2.

| | |
|---|---|
| Afterwards we moved to Pyeng Yang. | 후 에는 평양 으로 이스 호엿소. |
| He was better for a while, but afterwards he became worse. | 좀 낫다가 후에는 더호 엿소. |

3.

| | |
|---|---|
| It is already after twelve. | 발셔 십이 시가 지낫소. |
| I can not go till after four. | 네시 지나 기 젼에는 못 가겟소. |
| He started a little after three. | 세 시 좀 지나셔 떠낫소. |

SEC. 27.—LONG TIME, LONG.

1. Long time, long,—오래, or a form of the verb 오라오 (*to be long*).

2. A long time before:—

   (*a.*) A long time requisite,—오라지안코셔는 followed by the negative.

   (*b.*) Where the idea of necessity is absent.—The clause qualified by *before*, is put negatively in the substantive form followed by the verb 오라오 to be long. Sometimes the sentence is transposed and the equivalent of the English relative, *when*, used.

1.

| | |
|---|---|
| The hot weather seems to last a long while this year. | 금년에는 더위가 미우 오란 모양이오. |
| I cannot wait long. | 오래 못 기드리겟소. |
| I will not wait long. | 오래 아니 기드리겟소. |
| I have'nt seen your father for a long time. | 어루신너씌 오래 뵈읍지 못 호엿소. |
| He has been sick for a long time. | 오래 병이 드럿소. |
| I have been studying Korean for a long time. | 죠션 말 비혼지가 오 랏소. |

CHAP. VII. § II. SEC. 28. THE ADVERB.   357

| | |
|---|---|
| I did'nt understand that for a long while. | 그 거슬 모른지가 오랏소. |

2. (a).

| | |
|---|---|
| It will be a long time before you can talk like a Korean. | 오라지 안코 셔는 죠션 사름 처럼 말 못 호오 리이다. |
| It will be a long time before a railroad will be laid to Ham Heung. | 오라 지 안코 셔는 함흥 싯지 털로가 쌀니지 못 홀 듯호오. |

2. (b).

| | |
|---|---|
| It was a long while before we went home. | 우리가 집에 안 도라 간 지가 오랏소. |
| It was a long while before we became friends. | 우리들이 친구 안 된 지가 오랏소. |
| Was it a long while before foreigners could travel anywhere in the interior of Japan? | 외국 사름이 일본 싀골 아모 듸라도 돈니지 못훈 제가 오랏 수읍ᄂ 니잇가? |
| It was long before the country recovered from the effects of the war. | 그 나라 란리가 뎡돈 되지 아닌 지가 미우 오랏소. |
| It was a long while before I recovered completely. | 병이 쾌차 ᄒ지 아닌 지가 미우 오랏소. |
| Was it a long while before you could talk with Koreans? | 죠션 사름과 말ᄒ지 못훈 지가 오랏 수읍ᄂ니 잇가? |
| He died long before you were born. | 로형 날째에 그 사름 죽은 지는 오랏소. |

SEC. 28.—SOME TIME.

The Korean interrogatives being at the same time

indefinites, *some time* will be rendered by 얼마, and the context alone shows whether it is interrogative or indefinite.

| | |
|---|---|
| Will you be in Seoul for some time? | 셔울 얼마 계시 겟소? |
| I shall probably not see you for some time now. | 인제 얼마 못 뵈올 듯 ᄒ오. |
| It will take some time to finish it. | 그 것 다 못치기에 얼마 더 가겟소. |
| I waited some time, but nobody came. | 얼마 기드렷 것 마는 아모도 아니왓소. |

SEC. 29.—A LITTLE WHILE.

A little while—잠간, 조끔, 조끔동안에, etc.

| | |
|---|---|
| You need'nt go for a little while yet. | 아직 조끔 동안에 갈것 업소. |
| Wait a minute. | 조끔 기드리오. |
| Tell him to wait a little. | 잠간 기드리라고 ᄒ여라. |

SEC. 29.—FINALLY, AT LAST.

Finally, at last—나죵에, 양죰에, 필경. 나죵 means simply *in the end*, while 필경 refers to *delay*, and something happening after much waiting.

| | |
|---|---|
| At last the chair men came. | 나죵에야 교군군이 왓소. |
| Finally we got to the top. | 나죵에 꼭닥이에 올 나갓소. |
| At last, little by little I came to understand. | 필경 조끔식 조끔식 알아 내엿소. |
| Finally he consented. | 필경허락 ᄒ엿소. |
| At last the Italians were victorious. | 필경 이다리가 이긔 읍더이다. |
| We walked everywhere and finally went to Chong No | 소면 두니 다가 나죵에 죵로에 갓소. |

| | |
|---|---|
| At last he got angry. | 나죵에 (양죵에) 셩이 낫소. |

## § III.—ADVERBS OF CAUSE, MANNER AND DEGREE.

Adverbs of manner derived from adjectives etc. are not treated of here.

### SEC. 1.—WHY.

Why—웨, 엇지호여 or by some circumlocution.

| | |
|---|---|
| Why are the Japanese leaving Sëoul? | 웨 일본 사롬이 셔울을 써나오? |
| Why does wood float and iron sink? | 웨 나모는 쓰고 쇠는 갈아 안소? |
| Then why do not you tell him to do it again? | 그러호면 웨 다시 호라고 닐ㅇ지 안소? |
| Why did you pick those roses? | 엇지 호여 뎌 월계 꼿츨 쌋소? |
| Why do Korean women when they go out cover their faces with the green coat? | 엇지 호여셔 죠션 샹녀편 네 들이 츌입 훌젹에 쟝옷 스로 얼곤을 ᄀ리 우오? |
| Why do not you build your house of wood? | 무솜 셔돍 으로 집을 나모로 짓지 아니 호오? |
| Why did he say he wouldn't go? | 무솜 셔돍에 가지 안켓 다고 호옵더니잇가? |

### SEC. 2.—ACCORDINGLY, CONSEQUENTLY, THEREFORE.

These are rendered by—그런고로, 그리호여셔, 그씨돌에, 이러호기에, etc.

| | |
|---|---|
| Accordingly I did so. | 그런 고로 그리 호엿소 |
| Accordingly he went to the Kyeng Ou Kung. | 그리 호여셔 경우궁 오로 갓소. |

| | |
|---|---|
| Consequently they changed the law. | 그 사둙에 법을 곳첫소. |
| It rained for three days without stopping, and consequently all the bridges were swept away. | 사흘을 비가 줄 곳 오기에 드리가 다 업서 젓소. |
| Breakfast was fifteen minutes earlier than usual today, and consequently we couldn't eat together. | 오놀 아츰이 그 젼 보다 일은 사둙 으로 우리가 밋쳐 참예 ᄒ지 못ᄒ 엿소. |

SEC. 3.—How.

1. Interrogative,—엇더케 or some form of the verb 엇더ᄒ오.

2. The way in which,—participle with 것.

Note.—How, with verbs of *knowing*, etc., may often be rendered into Korean by the future participle with 줄아오.

1 & 2.

| | |
|---|---|
| How is the road from here to Eui Ju? | 여긔셔 의쥬 가기 ᄭᆞ지 길이 엇덧ᄉᆞ옵더니 잇가. |
| How do they make Kanchang? | 간쟝을 엇더케 ᄆᆞᆫ드오. |
| Do you know how they print photographs? | 사진을 엇더케 박는 줄 아오. |
| Did you hear how your friend was killed? | 내 친구가 엇더케 죽엇단 말 드럿소. |
| Before he came to Seoul he did not even know how to hold a pen. | 셔울 오기 젼에 붓도 잡을 줄 몰낫소. |
| Does that carpenter know | 목슈가 ᄉᆞ덕ᄉᆞ덕 ᄒᆞ는 |

| | |
|---|---|
| how to make rocking chairs? | 교의 문들줄 아오? |
| He knows how to construct a sentence, but he does not know the pronunciation. | 말 마듸는 엇더케 문들 줄 알것 마는 음은 몰나. |
| It is very strange how a snake crawls. | 비암이 긔는 거시 미우 이샹 호오. |
| Please teach me how to hold my pen. | 붓 잡는 거슬 좀 그르쳐 주오. |

### SEC. 4.—So.

1 Manner:—

    (*a.*) In this manner—이러호오.

    (*b.*) In that manner—{그러호오. / 뎌러호오.

2 Degree:—

    (*a*) In this degree—이러게.

    (*b.*) In that degree—{그러게. / 뎌뎌게.

Note.—For the distinctive difference, between 뎌 and 그, see Part I ¶71 ff.

3 So that, so—as,—도록, and the forms of the verb 又소 with 와.

#### 1.

| | |
|---|---|
| Be sure and not do it so, do it so. | 부듸 그러케 말고 이러케 호오. |
| If that's your opinion, why do not you say so? | 만일 성각이 그러 호면 웨 말 호지 안소? |
| That's so. | 그러 호오. |
| I thought so. | 그린 줄 알앗소. |

2.

| | |
|---|---|
| Tell that man not to make the shelves so high. | 그 사름 드려 탁즈룰 그러케 놉히 문둘지 말나고 ᄒᆞ오. |
| It would have been well if you had not been quite so hasty. | 그러케 셩급ᄒᆞ게 아니ᄒᆞ엿더면 됴홧지오. |

3.

| | |
|---|---|
| It is so bright that it hurts my eyes. | 빗치 눈이 압흐 도록 붉소. |
| It was so hot that the grass withered. | 풀이 무르 도록 더웟소. |
| He is so tall that he looks awkward. | 보기 실 토록 커 크오. |
| That is not as good as this. | 그것 이것 과 굿치 됴치 아니 ᄒᆞ오. |
| I don't go to Chemulpo as often as I used to. | 젼과 굿치 자조 졔물포 아니 간다. |

SEC. 5.—LIKE, AS.

1 Manner :—
   (a.) In a similar way,—처럼 or 굿치.
   (b.) In the way,—대로.
   (c.) To be like; and like used as an adjective will be rendered by 굿ᄒᆞ오 in its various forms. 굿흔 prefixed to 처럼 has the force of *exactly*, and 쏙 also has this effect.
      *Like this* is 이런, *like that* 그런 or 뎌런.
2 Degree—처럼 or 와굿치.

1. (a).

| | |
|---|---|
| If I could do as you do, I would be glad. | 나도 군 처럼 ᄒᆞ엿 시면 됴켓소. |

| | |
|---|---|
| I should hate to work like a coolie. | 일군 처럼 일 ᄒᆞ기는 슬소. |
| He lives like a king. | 님금 처럼 사옵ᄂᆞ이다. |
| He dresses like a Chinaman but he talks like a Japanese. | 즁국 사름 처럼 옷슬 닙엇 것만는 일본 사름 처럼 말ᄒᆞ오. |

### 1. (b.)

| | |
|---|---|
| As I have already said. | 내가 발셔 브터 말ᄒᆞ는 대로. |
| Try and repeat the conversation just as you heard it. | 드룬대로 말을 옴겨보오. |
| Why didn't you put out your light last night as you were told? | 웨 닐온 대로 밤에 불을 ᄭᅳ지 아니 ᄒᆞ엿ᄂᆞ냐? |
| Make it round like this. | 이대로 동굴게 ᄆᆡᆫ두오. |
| Just like this. | ᅉᅩᆨ 이 대로. |

### 1. (c).

| | |
|---|---|
| Are the Japanese iron-clads exactly like the English? | 일본 털갑션 도 영길리 것 과 ᅉᅩᆨ ᄀᆞᆺ소? |
| Have you any silk like this? | 이런 명듀 잇소. |
| Have you any silk exactly like this? | 이 것 과 ᅉᅩᆨ ᄀᆞᆺᄒᆞᆫ 명듀가 잇소? |
| Pens like this are useless. | 이 것과 ᄀᆞᆺᄒᆞᆫ 붓 쓸 ᄃᆡ 업소. |

### 2.

| | |
|---|---|
| When one is thirsty there is nothing like water. | 목 ᄆᆞ룰 ᄯᅢ에 물 처럼 됴흔 것 업소 |
| Is Nam San as high as Sam Kak San? | 남산이 삼각 산 과 ᄀᆞᆺ치 놉소? |

| Go as quick as you can to the house and tell Son Dongi to go for the doctor. | 아모 조록 섈니 집에 가셔 슌동이 드려 의원을 쳥ᄒ라고 닐너라. |

### Sec. 6.—Very.

1 In affirmative sentences,— 미우, 대단이, 과히, 금 직이, 십히, etc.

2 In negative sentences except when interrogative,— 그리.

1.

| This pen is very bad. | 이 붓시 미우 피악 ᄒ오. |
| I will be very busy in the morning | 릭일 아쵬에는 미우 밧부겟소. |
| He was very sick but he is better now. | 대단이 알러니 지금은 좀 낫소. |
| It is very cold. | 대단이 칩소. |
| It is very dear. | 과히 비싸오. |

2.

| The sky is not very clear to-day. | 오놀 하놀이 그리 쳥명치 못ᄒ오. |
| It is not very good. | 그리 됴치 안소. |
| They do not like each other very much. | 그리 됴흔 ᄉ이 아니오. |
| That fan was not very dear. | 그 붓쳐가 그리 비싸지 아니 ᄒ옵더이다. |
| It is not very cold in Seoul in winter, | 셔울이 겨울에 그리 칩지 안소. |

### Sec. 7.—Only.

1 Only—만, 샏. 오직, 단, 다만.
2 Preceded by if,—만 with the conditional.
3 Not later than, yet,—아직 ; 밧긔 with negative.
4 Not until,—계우.

CHAP. VII. § III. SEC. 7. THE ADVERB.  365

1.

| | |
|---|---|
| It's only a dog barking. | 개가 지질 분일다. |
| As I only came as company for you, why do you want to quarrel with me? | 동힘 으로 올 분 인디 웨 나ᄒᆞ고 싸호랴고 ᄒᆞ오? |
| I go to Chemulpo only once or twice a month. | ᄒᆞᆫ 둘에 졔물포 가기는 ᄒᆞᆫ 두번 분이오. |
| He not only wears a sword but he knows how to use it. | 다만 칼 찻실분 아니라 쓸 줄 도 아오. |
| How is it this jinriksha has only one wheel? | 이 인력거가 웨 박휘 ᄒᆞ나 분이오? |
| Only half the number I ordered have come. | 맛초인 수에 다만 반만 왓소. |
| Mr. Kim has only one brother. | 김셔방 단 형뎨 분이오. |
| I expected only twenty, but about forty came. | 이십 명 만 올줄 알앗더니 ᄉᆞ십 명 왓소. |

2.

| | |
|---|---|
| If we only had a good cat, we could catch these rats | 됴흔 고양이 만 잇더면 이 쥐를 잡앗겟소. |
| If you only use moderation, there will probably be no difficulty. | 알맛게 만 ᄒᆞ면 어려울 것 업 술듯 ᄒᆞ오. |

3.

| | |
|---|---|
| To-day is only the fifth. | 오놀 닷시 밧긔 아니 되엇소. |
| Why it's only three o'clock. | 무얼 아직 세 시오. |
| He's only a child. | 아직 어린거 시오. |
| Your letter reached me only yesterday. | 공의 편지가 어져ᄭᅴ 계우 왓소. |

4.

## SEC. 8.—TOO.

1 Too— 너무, 과히, etc., with the adjective.
2 Too...to— 너무 with the past verbal participle followed by the negative.

1.

| | |
|---|---|
| This pencil is too soft. | 이 연필 과히 (너무) 연호오. |
| This bottle is too small. | 이 병 과히 (너무) 적소. |
| Are not your ceilings a little too high? | 면쟝이 과히 놉지 안소. |
| This is a little too much. | 이 거시 좀 과호오. |

2.

| | |
|---|---|
| These clothes are too dirty to wear. | 이 옷시 너무 더러워셔 닙을 수 업소. |
| Pine is too brittle to make a cane. | 쇼나모는 너무 연호여셔 집힝이 홀 수 업소. |
| His talk is too low to hear. | 말 소틱가 너무 ᄌᄂ러셔 드를 수 업소. |

## SEC. 9.— EVEN.

1 Even— 도, or more strongly 이라도 affixed to its word.
2 Signifying, *even including*,—사지.

1.

| | |
|---|---|
| Even a child can do that. | 어린 ᄋ히 라도 그 거슨 호오. |
| Even Soun Yongi can read Chinese pretty well. | 슌용이 라도 계법 진셔를 볼 줄 아오. |
| Even to-morrow will do. | 릭일 이라도 ᄒ겟소. |

CHAP. VII. § III. SEC. 10. THE ADVERB. 367

| He hasn't even eaten rice to-day. | 오 늘 밥 도 아니 먹으웁 더이다. |
| Soun Yongi didn't even sweep the room this morning. | 오 늘 식젼 에는 슌 용이가 방을 쓸지 도 아니 ᄒᆞ 엿소. |
| If I walk even one ri I get very tired. | 일 리 라도 거러 가면 대단이 곤ᄒᆞ오. |

2.

| They killed even the children. | 어린 으ᄒᆡ ᄭᅡ지 도 죽 이엿소. |

SEC. 10.—ALMOST.

1 Nearly—거위.
2 Nearly all, the most of—거위 다 거반, 거반다.

1.

| It's almost twelve o'clock. | 거위 십이 시오. |
| It's almost a year since I went to Pyeng Yang. | 평양 갓다 온지가 거위 일년 이오. |
| My horse stumbled, and I almost fell off. | ᄆᆞᆯ이 압 드리를 ᄭᅮ러셔 거위 써러젓소. |

2.

| The rain water is almost gone. | 비 물이 거반 업서 젓소. |
| Almost every one in the house has a cold. | 집 안 사ᄅᆞᆷ 거반 다 감긔 드럿소. |
| Almost all the apples were rotten. | 사과가 거위 다 썩엇소. |
| Nearly all our sugar was stolen. | 우리 사탕 거위 다 도젹 마잣오. |
| I am home almost every afternoon. | 오후 ᄒᆞ면 거위 항샹 집 에 잇소. |

## Sec. 11.—About

Approximately—훈 preceding the quantity or number, or 즈음 sometimes contracted into 좀, or 나 following it. At times both these may be used, the one preceding and the other following the quantity referred to.

| | |
|---|---|
| About how much will it cost? | 얼마 나 된 듯 ᄒᆞ오? |
| You had better put in about ten pounds and boil it about half an hour. | 훈 열근 너코 반시 간 즈음 쓰리는 거시 됴켓다. |
| I waited about half an hour, and then called a chair and went home. | 훈 반시 간 기드리 다가 교군을 불너 투고 집으로 갓소. |
| He is about five feet high and weighs about a hundred pounds. | 그가 크는 훈 오척되고 무게는 빅근 즈음 되오. |
| It's about twice as large as ours. | 우리 것 보다 훈 곱절 되엿소 |

# CHAPTER VIII.

## NUMERALS.

With reference to numerals little need here be said. In treating of them from the Korean, they have virtually at the same time, been considered from the foreign standpoint. We then saw that Korean numerals might be either adjectives or substantives. When used substantively they stand in apposition to the noun they limit, and consequently hold a position much more emphatic, than when used adjectively. Hence, if, when using English numerals, the *number* is the special thing to which attention is to be called, it must be rendered into Korean by the use of the substantive form. If on the other hand, the number is simply secondary, and only mentioned incidentally, and its noun is the principal thought, the adjective form will be used, and it will precede its noun.

In rendering English into Korean, we should also remember, the Korean constant use of " Specific Classifiers." Many of these cannot be rendered into English and consequently when we render English into Korean, if we would speak idiomatic Korean, the proper classifier must be introduced. A careful study of these classifiers must then be made.

It has been noticed, that there are two classes of numerals, pure Korean, and Sinico-Korean, and while they may be used interchangeably, it must not be forgotten, that where a Sinico-Korean numeral is used a corresponding Sinico-Korean noun must also accompany it.

While the importance of this rule may not at first sight appear to the student, its neglect is altogether wrong, grates upon Korean ears, and will cause the offender to be regarded as ignorant of one of the fundamental rules of Korean etymology. With reference to ordinals and fractions, enough has already been said in Part I.

Right in this place, we should speak of the method of addressing a letter. In this matter, the Korean is more logical than the foreigner; his plan is the reverse of ours, for instance, he would begin with the country then the province, city, ward, street, and end with the name of the party addressed.

> As sentences illustrating the use of the numerals, occur everywhere throughout the book, none need be given here.

# CHAPTER IX.

### THE PREPOSITION.

The English prepositions may be rendered into Korean generally by Korean postpositions, simple or composite; verbal participles; phrases; or, where the sense is clear without, they need not be rendered. From this it will be seen that the Korean equivalent of an English preposition, will always follow the word it governs.

### Sec. 1.—At.

1 Signifying place:—
   (*a*.) With a verb of situation—에.
   (*b*.) With a verb of action—에셔 or simply 셔.
2 Referring to time—에.

#### 1. (*a*).

| | |
|---|---|
| There used to be temples at Seoul. | 셔울에 근본 졀이 잇섯소 |
| Are there no tombs of the Whang dynasty at Song Do? | 왕씨 째 룽이 숑도에 업소? |
| I wish there were no mosquitoes at Pouk Han. | 북한에 모긔가 업섯 더면 됴켓소. |

#### 1. (*b*).

| | |
|---|---|
| We buy our vegetables at that shop. | 뎌 젼 에셔 치쇼는 사오. |

We stopped at Pyeng Yang 평양셔 사흘 류 ᄒᆞ엿소·
three days.
We rested at Oricole. 오리골셔 쉬엿소·

2.

I got up at half past four 오ᄂᆞᆯ 식젼 에는 네시
this morning. 반에 니러 낫소·
Wake me at sunrise to- 뇌일 히 돗기 에 ᄭᆡ워라.
morrow.

SEC. 2.—IN.

1 With verbs of situation,—에 which is often used with 도오.

2 With verbs of action,—에셔 which may contract into 셔 or 에.

3 Inside of, within, during,—속에, 안희, 에 or 동안·

1.

Is there a good hotel in 셔울에 됴흔 쥬막이 잇소?
Seoul?
There are two or three fine 죠션에 됴흔 폭포가 두
water-falls in Korea. 서너 곳 잇소·
Is there anything in the 집 안에 무엇 잇소?
house?
Don't sit in a draught. 바람 :모지에 안지
마라.
What is in that box? 그 궤에 무엇 드럿ᄂᆞ냐?
Is there a hole in this tea- 이 차관에 구멍 잇소?
pot?

2.

He probably died at Tokio. 동경셔 죽은 듯 ᄒᆞ오·
I must have dropped it at 뎡녕 죵로 에셔 ᄯᅥ러
Chong No. 트린 듯 ᄒᆞ오·

| | |
|---|---|
| How much wine do you suppose is drunk in Sëoul in a year? | 일년에 셔울셔 술이 얼마나 먹힐 둣 ᄒᆞ오? |
| You can't get good chairs in the country. | 싀골 셔는 됴흔 교군을 엇을수가 업소. |
| Which is the longest street in Sëoul? | 셔울 셔는 어느 길이 그 즁 기오? |
| Which is the largest island in the world? | 텬하에 읻던 셤이 그즁 크오? |
| It's in the leather trunk, wrapped in paper. | 가쥭 샹ᄌᆞ 속에 됴희로 싸 너헛소. |
| I saw a fox in the woods. | 수풀 안희 여호를 보앗소. |
| You can go to Chong No in twenty minutes. | 이십 분 동안 에 죵로에 가오. |
| You probably put it in your pocket. | 쥬먼이에 너헛 실 둣 ᄒᆞ오. |

### Sec. 3.—On.

1 On—에.

2 On the top of, on the surface of,—우희.

| | |
|---|---|
| Please write "Mr. Kim" on this envelope. | 이 피봉에 김셔방 이라고 써주오. |
| There's a stain on my handkerchief. | 내 슈건에 어룽이 젓소. |
| There's a fly on the celling. | 텬쟝에 파리가 잇소. |
| You went home on the first. | 초 ᄒᆞ로에 집에 갓소. |

2.

| | |
|---|---|
| Is not that a dog sleeping on the floor? | 뎌 마루 우희 자는 거시 개가 아니오? |
| My hat is on the table. | 내 갓 샹 우희 잇소. |
| I dropped a stone on my foot. | 발 우희 돌을 ᄯᅥ러트렷소. |

## SEC. 4.—TO.

1 With animate objects—의게, 안테, or 씌, which last is honorific.

2 With inanimate objects—에 or 로; ofttimes also the simple accusative postposition 을 will be used.

3 As far as—셔지. (See Part I. 107).

Note.—With the indirect object, the postposition is frequently omitted.

1.

| | |
|---|---|
| Give something to the dog. | 개 무엇 좀 주오. |
| Don't lend it to anyone. | 그거슬 뉘게 던지 빌니지 마오. |
| What did you say to Mr. Song? | 송셔방씌 무솜 말ᄒᆞ엿소? |
| Give ten nyang to Mr. Pak. | 열량 박셔방안테 주오. |

2.

| | |
|---|---|
| He has gone to Song Do. | 송도로 갓소. |
| In order to see the sights, we are going by boats to Kang Wha to-morrow. | 뒤일 경쳐롤 보랴고 비 등고 강화롤 가오. |
| Would you like to take a walk to Nam San? | 남산에 힝긔 ᄒᆞ는 거시 엇더겟소? |

3.

| | |
|---|---|
| How much is it to An Dong and back? | 안동 셔지 안밧 얼 마나? |
| I went to Pak Dong but I did'nt meet him. | 박동 셔지 갓시나 맛나지 못 ᄒᆞ엿소. |

SEC. 5.—FROM, OUT OF, OFF.

1 Preceding a noun,—브터, 에셔.

2 Preceding a verbal noun,—the negative with future verbal participle and 호오.

3 With verbs of receiving accepting, etc., equivalent to *at the hand of*—의게 or 안테 will be used.

4 *Off*, in the sense of *detached from*, is generally expressed by some form of the verb.

5 *Off shore*—압회 or 압회셔 dependent upon whether there the accompanying verb is one of situation or action.

1.

| | |
|---|---|
| About how far is it from here to that tree? | 여긔셔 뎌 나모 ᄭᅡ지 얼마 나 되오? |
| Hang it from the fourth nail on the right. | 올흔 편 넷재 못셋셔 거오. |
| I rode steadily from six in the morning, till six in the evening. | 아춤 륙시 브터 져녁 륙시 ᄭᅡ지 믈을 늘 ᄒᆞᆺ소. |
| Can you borrow one from next door? | 니웃 집에셔 빌수 잇소? |
| Take a pound of sugar out of that box. | 뎌 케에셔 사탕 훈근 내여라. |
| Empty it out of this bottle and pour it into that. | 이 병 에셔 ᄯᅡ라셔 뎌 병에 부어라. |
| Take the books off this table. | 칙을 이 상 에셔 갓다 노하라. |
| I fell off my horse and sprained my foot. | 내 ᄆᆞᆯ 에셔 ᄯᅥ러져셔 발을 쎄엿소. |

2.

| | |
|---|---|
| Is there any way of keeping things from moulding? | 곰팡 아니 나게 훌 수가 잇소? |

| | |
|---|---|
| Be careful, and keep the children from taking cold. | 오히 감긔를 지안케 ᄒᆞ오. |

3.

| | |
|---|---|
| I received fifteen dollars from Mr. Pak. | 박셔방 안테 은젼 열 다ᄉᆞᆺ 개 밧앗소. |
| I got a passport from the minister. | 공ᄉᆞ 의게 빙표 엇엇소. |
| I obtained permission to go to the eastern palace from the president of the foreign office. | 동판 대궐 드러 갈 허락을 독판 안테 엇엇소. |

4.

| | |
|---|---|
| The leg is off the table. | 뎌 상 ᄃᆞ리가 ᄲᅡ젓소. |
| The tiles are off the roof. | 뎌 집웅에 긔와가 버셔 젓소. |
| He took off his clothes. | 옷슬 버셧소 |

5.

| | |
|---|---|
| Two large whales were killed off Fusan. | 부산 압회셔 큰 고래 둘 잡앗소. |
| Two Chinese men-of-war have been off Chemulpo for over a month. | 졔물포 압희 즁국 병션 둘이 ᄒᆞᆫ 둘 넘 도록 잇소. |

SEC. 6.—BY, THROUGH.

1 Of the agent—의게, 안테, 에. (see Part I. ¶ 101 ff.)

2 Of the instrument, by means of—로 or 으로 ; or 셔 문에 which, if the English preposition it represents governs a verbal noun, is preceded by the participle, or verbal noun in 기 of the appropriate verb.

CHAP. IX. SEC. 6.   THE PREPOSITION.   377

3 Beside—엽희.
4 Of time—에, or more exactly 넘지안코.
5 From end to end of—통ᄒᆞ야, 통과ᄒᆞ야.

### 1.

| | |
|---|---|
| I had it made by a blacksmith. | 내가 대쟝 안테 몬드럿쇼. |
| This book was written by a Korean. | 이책 죠션 사ᄅᆞᆷ 안테 썻쇼. |
| I was struck by a stone. | 내가 돌 안테 마잣쇼. |
| I was cut by a knife. | 내가 칼노 버히엿쇼. |

### 2.

| | |
|---|---|
| He went to Tokio by rail. | 텰로로 동경 갓쇼. |
| Let me know by telegraph immediately. | 뎐신으로 곳 내게 알게 ᄒᆞ여 주오. |
| Were you not awakened by the earthquake last night? | 어제 밤에 디동으로 아니 ᄭᅢ엿쇼? |
| I could'nt sleep all night through his crying. | 우는 ᄭᅥ문에 밤시 도록 못 잣쇼. |
| I lost fifty dollars through Mr. Kim. | 김셔방 ᄭᅥ문에 오십원 일 헛쇼. |
| He lost his whole fortune through the burning of his house. | 집 ᄐᆞ는 ᄭᅥ문에 잇는 저물 다 일허 ᄇᆞ렷쇼. |
| He avoided such a mishap by riding on a horse. | 몰ᄐᆞ고 가기ᄭᅥ문에 그런 봉패가 업썻쇼. |

### 3.

| | |
|---|---|
| Did you ever stand by a water-fall? | 폭포슈 엽희 섯서읍더니 잇가. |

| | |
|---|---|
| Let's see, you live in the house by the bridge? | 로형이 드리 엽희 집에셔 살지오 그랴? |
| This brook runs by our house. | 이 내 우리 집 엽희 느러 가오. |

#### 4.

| | |
|---|---|
| It will be ready by noon. | 열 두시 에 다 되겟소. |
| It may possibly stop raining by evening. | 혹 져녁 째에 비가 긋칠 듯 ㅎ오. |
| The chair must be here by four o'clock. | 네시 넘지 안코 보교 여긔 잇셔야 쓰겟소. |
| I must start for home by the last of the month. | 금음 넘지안코 집에 가 기로 써나야 쓰겟소. |

#### 5.

| | |
|---|---|
| I ran through the house. | 내가 집을 통ㅎ야 드라 왓소. |
| I rode through a crowd in a jinrikisha. | 인력거를 듯고 사룸 모힌 듸를 통파 ㅎ엿소. |

### Sec. 7.—With

1 Of the instrument,—로 or 으로.

2 Together with, in company with,—ㅎ고; 훈가지로; ᄀᆺ치; 홈ᄭᅴ, 더브러.

3 Belonging to, connected with,—에 or often not rendered.

#### 1.

| | |
|---|---|
| You'd better tie that parcel with a string. | 뎌 짐을 노ᄉᆫ으로 미면 됴치오. |
| Wipe it with a cloth. | 슈건으로 씻셔라. |
| That man writes with his left hand. | 그 사룸 왼손으로 쓰오. |

CHAP. IX. SEC. 7.   THE PREPOSITION.                379

### 2.

| | |
|---|---|
| I argued with that man for about an hour. | 그 사롬 ᄒ고 ᄒ시나 힐난 ᄒ엿소. |
| Send the pears along, with the grapes. | 포도롤 비 ᄒ고 보내오. |
| I put it in the corner with the umbrella. | 구셕에 우산 ᄒ고 두엇소. |
| Then I'll go with you. | 그리 ᄒ면 조녀와 훔ᄭ 가겟너. |
| That which is called "Ojunhoiem" is the king meeting with all the officials to consider affairs of state. | 어젼 회의라 ᄒᄂᆫ 것은 군쥬가 모든 관리로 더부러 국ᄉ를 의론ᄒᄂᆫ거시오. |
| That old man passes the time each day with his many grandchildren. | 뎌로인은 미일 조긔의 여러 손조들노 더브러 소일ᄒ오. |
| I came with a Chinaman. | 쳥국사롬 파ᄭ치 왓소. |
| Do you expect to get breakfast and study with me. | 나ᄒ고 ᄭ치 공부 ᄒ게 죠반 먹고 오려나. |
| When I went with Mr. Yi, to engage in trade I saw such sights. | 리셔방과 훈가지로 무역 ᄒ러 갓다가 그런 구경 ᄒ엿소. |
| Don't you want to go to Tokyo with me. | 나와 훈가지로 동경가지 아ᄂ려나. |

### 3.

| | |
|---|---|
| Is there no key with this watch? | 이 시계 트리기 업소? |
| Is there not is a wick with this new lamp? | 이 새등 십지가 업소? |
| Was there not a letter with this box? | 이 궤에 편지 업섯소? |

## Sec. 8.—Without.

1 Preceding a noun :—
 (*a*.) Not having—업시 affixed to the noun.
 (*b*.) Unless one has—업스면.

2 Preceding a verbal noun.—the verbal stem preceded by a negative, connected with the accompanying verb by 고 ; or, the negative base with 안코, and the accompanying verb. Emphasis is added by the use of 는 after 고 or 코.

### 1. (*a*).

| | |
|---|---|
| This letter came without a stamp. | 이 편지가 우표 업시 왓소. |
| Why did you make it without handles ? | 웨 손 잡이 업시 몬드럿쇼? |
| These sulphur matches burn without any smell. | 이 석류황이 내암새 업시 틋오. |
| Don't go without permission. | 허락 업시 가지 마라. |

### 1 (*b*).

| | |
|---|---|
| You can't open it without a key. | 열쇠 업스면 열수 업소 |
| Mr. Kim can't read anything without glasses. | 안경 업스면 김셔방이 아모 글즈 도 못 보겟소. |

### 2.

| | |
|---|---|
| I suppose it wouldn't do for us to go in without taking off our shoes. | 아마 신 아니 벗고 집에 드러 가면 됴치 안치오 |
| You must not go without letting me know. | 나를 알게 흐지 아니 흐고는 가지 마라. |

CHAP. IX SEC. 9.   THE PREPOSITION.                381

| | |
|---|---|
| Don't buy sugar without weighing it. | 근수를 달지 안코는 사탕을 사지 마라. |
| He went without (*taking*) an umbrella. | 우산 아니 가지고 갓쇼· |
| Bring me the lamp without (*putting on*) the chimney. | 등피씨우지 말고 등을 가져 오오. |
| I'll go without (*eating*) supper. | 져녁 아니 먹고 가겟쇼 |
| Will you go without (*taking*) a guide? | 인도 ᄒᆞᄂᆞᆫ 사름 아니 ᄃᆞ리고 가겟쇼? |

SEC. 9.—OF.

1 Possession,—의 if expressed, but more generally not expressed.

2 Apposition,—not rendered.

3 Partitive :—

  (*a.*) Some of a group as contrasted with the remainder, or emphasized, (hence frequently accompanied by a pronominal adjective)— 그 즁에, 에.

  (*b.*) When no contrast or special emphasis is expressed the *of*, is not rendered.

4 Made of,—로.

1.

| | |
|---|---|
| The nails were rotten and the bottom of the box fell out. | 못시 다 삭아셔 궤 밋치 째젓쇼· |
| Don't you like the smell of a good cigar? | 됴흔 엽권연 내암새 됴화 아니 ᄒᆞ오? |
| Don't handle the property of others. | 남의 지물 몬지지 마라. |

2.

| | |
|---|---|
| In the province of Chyella there are some fine houses. | 젼라 도에 됴흔 집 잇소. |
| In the city of Song Do they raise a great deal of Ginseng. | 송도 셩 안회 인삼 만히 기르오. |

3. (a).

| | |
|---|---|
| Some of us would like to study history. | 우리 즁에 엇던 사롬이 ᄉᆞ긔를 비호고 시비 ᄒᆞ오. |
| Many of the Japanese dress in foreign clothes. | 일본 사롬 즁에 양 복 닙는 이가 만소. |
| Many of them don't know how to read or write. | 그 즁에 글 닑지 못ᄒᆞ고 글시 쓸 줄 모르는 이가 만소. |
| Many of the Japanese speak English. | 일본사롬 즁에 영어 ᄒᆞ는 이가 만소. |
| Few of the chair bearers live to be fifty. | 교군 군에 오십 ᄉᆞ지 사는 이가 만치 아니 ᄒᆞ오. |

3. (b).

| | |
|---|---|
| Please hand me one of those pens. | 그 붓 ᄒᆞ나 주오. |
| One of Mr. Kim's daughters was married yesterday. | 김셔방 ᄯᅡᆯ이 어저씌 ᄒᆞ나 싀집 갓소. |

4.

| | |
|---|---|
| Make it of pine. | 쇼나모로 ᄆᆞᆫ드러라. |
| It's made of flour, eggs, and sugar. | 밀 가로와 사탕파 알노 ᄆᆞᆫ드럿소. |

CHAP. IX. SEC. 10.   THE PREPOSITION.                        383

Do you intend to build the 집 벽돌노 지랴고 ᄒᆞ옵
house of brick?            ᄂᆞ니잇가?

### SEC. 10.—FOR.

1 For the sake of,—위ᄒᆞ야.
2 Instead of,—디신.
3 To serve as, to be used for,—로 or 으로.
4 Considering that,—로ᄂᆞᆫ, 으로ᄂᆞᆫ.
5 To be delivered to,—의게 with a participle of some such verb as 젼ᄒᆞ오 or 주오.
6 To be used *with, on, by*—에쓸.
7 Addressed to,—의게 or 셔.
8 To fetch, to get,—가질너, 차지러.
9 To call,—부르러.
10 Price,—으러, or 에.
11 Courtesy, usually of a favor for a third party,—the verbal participle with 주오.

#### 1.

He died for his country.        나라 위ᄒᆞ야 샹ᄉᆞ 나셧소.
The doctor to-day recom-        오눌 의원이 날 회츈 ᄒᆞ기
  mended me to go to the        위ᄒᆞ야 싀꼴노 가라고
  country for my health.        권ᄒᆞ엿소.

#### 2.

Do not use scissors for a       칼 디신 으로 가위를 쓰지
  knife.                        마오.

#### 3.

What are those boards           뎌 널판지 무어 ᄉᆞ로
  for?                          쓰겟소.
That wont do for a pillow.      뎌 거시 목침 으로 못
                                쓰겟소.

| | |
|---|---|
| He will do well for a teacher. | 션싱 으로 잘 될듯 ㅎ오. |
| I bought it for a thing to put pens in. | 붓 시질 거스로 삿소. |

**4.**

| | |
|---|---|
| He speaks very well for a foreigner. | 외국 사롬 으로논 말 잘 ㅎ오. |
| He runs very well for a child. | 으히 로논 잘 드라 나오. |
| It was very badly done for him. | 그 사롬으로논 잘 못 ㅎ엿소. |
| Isn't this hot weather for Seoul? | 지금 일긔가 셔울노논 더웁지 안소? |

**5.**

| | |
|---|---|
| Mr. Kim has a letter for you. | 김셔방이 로형씌 젼홀 편지 잇소. |
| Yesterday I gave him a letter for Mr. Song. | 어저씌 송셔방 의게 젼홀 편지 주엇소. |
| Mr. Choi received some money for you. | 최셔방이 로형씌 줄 돈 밧 앗소. |

**6.**

| | |
|---|---|
| I want a key for this box. | 이 궤에 쓸 열쇠 ㅎ나 엇으랴고 그리 ㅎ오. |
| Have you a cork for this bottle? | 이 병에 쓸 막이 ㅎ나 잇소? |
| Get another chimney for this lamp. | 이 등에 쓸 등피 또ㅎ나 사 오너라. |

**7.**

| | |
|---|---|
| Did any freight come for me a little while ago? | 아ᄭᅡ 내게 오논 짐 왓ᄉ 읍더니잇가? |
| A letter has come for you. | 로형씌 편지 왓소. |

CHAP. IX. SEC. 10.   THE PREPOSITION.                    385

### 8.

| | |
|---|---|
| Soun Yongi has gone for my watch. | 슌용이가 우리 시계가질너 갓소 |
| Send Soun Yongi for it. | 슌용이 차지러 보내오. |
| Have you written to Japan for that money? | 그 돈 차지러 일본 편지 썻소? |

### 9.

| | |
|---|---|
| I went for the doctor, but he was out. | 의원 부르러 갓것 마는 업섯소 |
| Some time or other to-day, you must go for the carpenter. | 오늘 어느 때 던지 목슈 불르러 가야 쓰겟소. |
| You had better go for four more chair coolies. | 교군 넷 더 부르러 가면 됴켓다. |

### 10.

| | |
|---|---|
| I don't think you can buy one for ten yen. | 내 성각에 열원 으로 못 살듯 호오. |
| I bought it for five dollars and sold it for six. | 오원 으로 사셔 륙원 으로 팔앗소. |
| He sold it for five thousand dollars and got the money. | 은젼 오쳔 원에 팔고 돈다 밧앗소. |
| I'll go for two nyang. | 두량 에 가겟소. |

### 11.

| | |
|---|---|
| Please sharpen both ends of this pencil for me. | 이 연필 량 끗 싹가 주시오. |
| Buy some toys for the children. | 으히 작란 ᄀ음 사주시오. |
| Wont you buy a horse for me? | 나를 몰 안 사 주겟소? |

I want you to write two letters for me. 공이 나를 편지 둘 써 주면 됴 켓소.

## SEC. 11.—ACROSS, OVER, BEYOND.

1 On the other side—건너 or 넘어. When it is simply *across*, it is 건너 ; when it has gone *over*, it is 넘어.

2 Further on than :—지나.

### 1.

| | |
|---|---|
| Who is that over there? | 뎌 건너 잇는 이가 누구요? |
| What's that house across the canal? | 기쳔 건너 뎌 집이 무슴 집이오. |
| The kite went over the house. | 연이 집 넘어로 넘어 갓소. |
| There is another temple beyond Sam Kak San. | 삼각산 넘어 가셔 쏘 졀 ᄒᆞ나 잇소. |

### 2.

| | |
|---|---|
| It's a little beyond the Kwang Chung bridge. | 광츙 ᄃᆞ리 조곰 지나 잇소. |
| He lives just beyond the American legation. | 미국 공ᄉᆞ관 좀 지나 산다. |

## SEC. 12.—AMONG.

Among—즁에.

| | |
|---|---|
| I think you'll find it among the tools. | 연쟝 즁에 차질 듯ᄒᆞ오. |
| Who among us will obtain office first? | 우리 즁에 누가 몬져 벼슬 ᄒᆞ겟소? |
| Is there an Ok Pyen among them? | 그 즁에 옥편 잇소? |

## SEC. 13.—AMONG.

1 On all sides 에워.
2 About and round 도라, 두루.

### 1 and 2.

| | |
|---|---|
| There was a crowd of policemen standing around the house. | 훈 무리 슌검이 집을 에워 싸고 셧소. |
| Let's put some flowers around the fruit. | 실과를 꼿츠로 에워 싸옵시다. |
| He walked three times around the city. | 성을 세번 두루 돈녓소. |
| The rats ran all round the kitchen every night. | 밤 마다 쥐들이 쥬방으로 도라 돈니오. |

## SEC. 14.—BEFORE.

In front of—압희, 압희셔.

| | |
|---|---|
| He stood before the king. | 대군쥬 압희 셧소. |
| He planted a tree before the house. | 집 압희 나모를 심엇소. |

## SEC. 15.—BEHIND.

Behind—뒤희.

| | |
|---|---|
| There's a well behind the house. | 집 뒤희 우물이 잇소. |
| The key has fallen down behind the clock. | 조명종 뒤희 트리기 써러졋소. |
| Please hand me that book behind you. | 뒤희 칙 좀 집어 주시오. |
| The troops marched behind the king. | 대군쥬 뒤희 병뎡가 따라가옵더이다. |
| You go first and I'll come after. | 형은 몬져 가고 나는 뒤희 가겟소. |

## Sec. 15.—Between.

Between—스이에.

| | |
|---|---|
| There's a well between the doctor's house and mine. | 의원의 집과 우리 집 스이에 우물이 잇소. |
| It has fallen down between the bookcase and the wall. | 벽호고 칙쟝 스이에 써러 졋소. |

## Sec. 16.—During.

During 스이, 동안 with or without the postposition 에.

| | |
|---|---|
| He died during the night. | 밤 스이에 죽엇소. |
| How were you during the night? | 밤 스이 엇더 호시오? |
| He worked very hard during the whole year. | 일년 스이에 미우 힘썻소. |
| The children played during the teacher's absence. | 션싱 업슬 동안에 오희들 작란 호엿소. |
| If any one should come during dinner tell him I can't see him. | 뎜심 먹을 스이에 누가 오면 못본다고 호여라. |

## Sec. 17.—Except, besides, but.

1 Excepting, besides—밧긔.
2 Only—만, 뿐, etc., or 밧긔 with the negative.

### 1.

| | |
|---|---|
| I have nothing except a foreign dollar. | 양은젼 밧긔 업소. |
| Didn't you go anywhere but to the house? | 집 밧긔 다른 듸 아니 갓더냐? |
| Everything except this is perfectly plain. | 이 말 밧긔는 다 붉소. |
| Haven't you any pens besides this? | 이 붓 밧긔 업소? |

CHAP. IX. SEC. 18-19. THE PREPOSITION. 389

| He has taken two himself, and has n't given me but one. | 뎌는 둘 가지고 나는 ᄒᆞ나 만 주엇소. |
| He didn't send but half a pound. | { ᄒᆞᆫ 반근만 보내 엿소. *or* 반근 밧긔 아니 보 내엿소. |
| I wont give but a little more. | 조곰 만 더 주겟소. |
| He did n't wait but a little while. | 조곰 밧긔 아니 기드렷소. |

## SEC. 19.—INSTEAD OF.

1 Before a noun,—디신.
2 Before a verbal noun,—the verbal stem with 안코 or the verbal stem preceded by a negative with 고.

### 1.

| Did n't you put in salt instead of sugar? | 사탕 디신 소금 안 너헛 누냐? |
| They arrested the father instead of the son. | 아들 디신 아비가 잡 혓소. |
| Bring Korean money instead of dollars. | 양 은젼 디신에 죠션 돈 가져 오너라. |
| If you go instead of him it will be well. | 그 사롭 디신 가면 됴 켓소. |

### 2.

| Instead of going to Chemulpo he went to Fusan. | 졔물포 안 가고 부산 으로 갓소. |
| He sleeps all day instead of doing his work. | 일 ᄒᆞ지 안코 죵일 자오. |
| I think I'll build instead of buying. | 집 사지 안코 짓듯 ᄒᆞ오. |

## Sec. 19.—Over, Above.

Over, above... 우희, 우호로.

| | |
|---|---|
| There's a sign over that door. | 뎌문 우희 현판 잇소. |
| It's hanging over the shelf. | 탁즈 우희 걸엇소. |
| There are a lot of buzzards flying about over that mountain. | 뎌 산 우호로 소리개 여러히 놀나 가오. |

## Sec. 20.—Under, Below.

Under, below—밋희.

| | |
|---|---|
| The books are under the shelf. | 탁즈 밋희 칙이 잇소. |
| Go and put it under the table. | 상 밋희 갓다 두어라. |
| There is a dog under the verandah gnawing a bone. | 뎌 마루 밋희 쎠를 서무러 뜻는 개 잇소. |

## Sec. 21.—According to, in accordance with.

1 Dependent on, regulated by—대로, 써라.
2 Of opinions, teachings, etc.—으로는.
3 Of statements etc.,—말대로, 말노 or 대로.
4 In harmony with,—와합호오.

### 1.

| | |
|---|---|
| The rate differs according to the number of characters. | 글즈수 대로 갑시 다르오. |
| The postage differs according to the weight of the letter. | 편지 무게 대로 우세가 다르오. |
| I change my clothes according to the weather. | 일긔를 써라 옷을 밧고아 닙소. |

| | |
|---|---|
| They're arranged according to color. | 빗 대로 버려 노핫소. |
| I may go or not according to circumstances. | 갈넌지 안 갈넌지 일 되는 대로 하겟소. |

### 2.

| | |
|---|---|
| According to the opinion of some, this is a mistake. | 엇던 사롬의 싱각 으로는 이거시 그르오. |
| According to my opinion this book is not worth much. | 내 싱각 으로는 이칙 쓸디 별노 업소. |

### 3.

| | |
|---|---|
| According to the doctor, he has the small-pox. | 의원 말노는 역질 이라 홉더이다. |
| According to the doctor's, orders the patient was taken to the country. | 의원 하라는 대로 병인을 싀골노 드려 갓소. |

### 4.

| | |
|---|---|
| Is that in accordance with Japanese custom? | 그것 일본 풍쇽 과 합 하오? |
| Your view is not in accordance with the treaty. | 공의 싱각이 약됴 와 합지 안소. |
| That's not in accordance with your agreement. | 이 거시 로형의 샹약 과 합지 안소. |

---

## CHAPTER X.

### THE CONJUNCTION.

English conjunctions are variously rendered into the Korean by particles, verbal moods, and the participial forms of adjectives and verbs.

Sec. 1.—AND.

1 Connecting nouns—by 호고 (*repeated after the last noun*), or 과 becoming 와 after a vowel.

2 Connecting verbs and adjectives. When the sentences and clauses connected are :—

(*a.*) Co-ordinate—by the verbal root with 고 or 며 the final verb only being inflected.

For distinction difference between 고 and 며 see Part I. 194, 200.

(*b.*) Subordinate—by the participial form of the verb of the subordinate clause.

3 Equivalent to, "*but*" "*yet*" "*because*" "*when*" "*if*" *etc.*—it is translated accordingly.

4 "*And-so-forth*" is translated by—와...와...다.

1.

| | |
|---|---|
| Please buy some pens, paper and books for the children. | 오히룰 붓 호고 됴회 호고 칙 호고 좀 사 주오. |
| For breakfast we will have rice, tea, and bread. | 조반에눈 밥 과 차와 쎡을 먹겟소. |

2. (*a*).

| | |
|---|---|
| The chairmen put down the chair and went into the saloon. | 교군군들이 보교룰 누려 노코 술막으로 드러 갓소. |

| | |
|---|---|
| I dreamed the house was on fire and woke up with a start. | 쑴에 집 불이 난 거슬 보고 놀나 셔엿소. |
| I met Mr. Kim before breakfast and proposed that we study together. | 식젼에 김셔방을 보고 又치 공부 ᄒ자고 ᄒ엿소. |

2. (b).

| | |
|---|---|
| I intended to cross the river and go to a hotel. | 강을 건너 가셔 쥬막에 들냐고 ᄒ엿소. |
| The ball went over the fence and we cannot find it. | 공이 담을 넘어가셔 차질 수가 업소. |
| It rained and we could not start. | 비가 와셔 써나지 못 ᄒ엿소. |

3.

| | |
|---|---|
| I told Mr. Yi what you told me some time ago, and he said it was not so. | 일젼에 ᄒ시던 말을 리셔방ᄭ의 ᄒ엿더니 그러치 안타고 ᄒ엿소. |
| This roof was newly thatched barely a month ago, and it has begun to leak again. | 이 집움은 계유 ᄒ 둘 젼에 새로 니어도 ᄯᅩ 새기 시쟉ᄒ오. |
| Sou Dongi did not put on much coal and the fire went out. | 슈동이가 셕탄을 만히 넛치 아니ᄒ셔 불이 ᄭᅥ젓소. |
| Put them in the sun and they will dry directly. | 볏희 내여 노면 곳 ᄆᆞ르겟소. |
| Everybody else gets them, and why can not you. | 다른 사름은 다 엇어 가지는듸 웨 공은 못 ᄒ오. |

4.

| | |
|---|---|
| He has pens, paper, ink, etc. | 붓과 됴희 와 먹과 다 잇소. |

SEC. 2.—BOTH...AND.

1 Usually the verb is repeated with 도...도.
2 With adjectives, simple 고 following the roof of the first adjective is often used.

1.

| | |
|---|---|
| There seem to be plenty of both roses and camelias in your garden. | 공의 화원 에는 월계 꼿 도 만코 동빅꼿 도 만흔 모양이오. |
| It both rained and snowed to-day. | 오늘은 눈도 오고 비도 왓소. |

2.

| | |
|---|---|
| There are many things that are both useful and ornamental. | 곱고 긴한 물건 만소. |

SEC. 3.—TOO, ALSO.

Too, also—도.

| | |
|---|---|
| Bring a spoon too. | 슈가락 도 가져오너라. |
| They have a custom like that in Korea, too. | 죠션도 그런 풍쇽이잇소. |
| Does your right eye pain you also? | 올흔 편 눈도 압흐오? |
| Did you forget to speak about that too? | 그말도 니져버렷소? |

SEC. 4.—BUT.

1 A disjunctive is much less frequently used by Koreans than by English, the former preferring a transposition, and the use of the concessive.

2 It may however be rendered by its Korean equivalent 마는, or 만셔도, which may be joined directly to any one of the indicative tenses without the elision of its termination ; or connected by 것 to any indicative form, when 것

replaces its termination : or to any participle, and then the participle qualifies 것.

1.

| | |
|---|---|
| It is good enough but the price is high. | 됴ᄒᆞ나 갑시 만소. |
| The screen is old, but it is well painted. | 이 병풍이 늙기는 늙엇 시되 그림은 잘 그렷소. |
| That ring is good but it is a little small. | 그 가락지가 됴키는 됴ᄒᆞ 되 좀 젹소. |

2.

| | |
|---|---|
| It will probably rain but I must go. | 비 올 듯 ᄒᆞ것 마는 갈수 밧긔 업소. |
| If you want to go, go, but come back early. | 가랴면 가거라 마는 일즉 도라 오너라. |
| I tried to get him to write for me but he would n't. | 편지 써 주도록ᄒᆞ여보앗 것마는 아니 썻소. |
| I tried to sleep, but it thundered so I could n't. | 미우 자랴고 ᄒᆞ엿것 마는 련동이 대단ᄒᆞ야 못 잣소. |
| My brother likes Korean food, but I cannot eat it. | 형님은 죠션 음식을 됴화 ᄒᆞ것 만셔도 나는 못 먹겟소. |

### SEC. 5.—THOUGH, ALTHOUGH, STILL.

**1** Although may be rendered into Korean by any one of the concessive conjunctions,—나, 도, 거니와, etc., and a stronger, form (*even though*) may be rendered by 지라도 with a relative participle.

**2** Even so, and yet,—그러컷 마는, 그러ᄒᆞ여도, etc., may be used.

1.

| | |
|---|---|
| Although he is still very sick he will probably get well. | 아직도 미우 편치 못ᄒᆞ 나 나흘 듯 ᄒᆞ오. |

| | |
|---|---|
| I suppose we'll have to take it, although it doesn't suit. | 모음에 아니 드러도 엇지 홀수 업소. |
| Though he's a rice man he will not give a cent. | 부쟈 되여도 훈푼 도 안 주겟소. |
| He wont give up smoking, though it's injuring him. | 담빅가 몸에 해롭 거니와 긋 치지 아니훙읍더이다. |
| He's getting pretty old, but he is strong yet. | 좀 늙어졋 거니와 아직도 건쟝 호오. |

2.

| | |
|---|---|
| Still, you had better apologize. | 그러컷 마는 샤죄 호는 거시 낫겟소. |
| Still, it will cost a thousand nyang. | 그러호여도 천량은 드려야 호겟소. |
| Still, it would be better not to stop. | 그러 호여 도 쉬지 말고 호는 거시 됴켓소. |
| Still, he can't possibly be here for some time yet. | 그러 호여 도 오랴면 아직도 멀엇소. |

SEC. 6.—EITHER, OR, WHETHER.

1 One or the other.
   (*a.*) In simple sentences—나.
   (*b.*) In direct questions connected by *or*, Koreans ask two questions without *or*.
   (*c.*) In indirect questions containing *whether*, followed by *or*—the verb is repeated with 지 or 가, sometimes by 나.

2 Either one or the other, no matter which—던지...던지.

3 Either with a negative, and equivalent to *any more*, or *any bether*,—도.

CHAP. X. SEC. 6.   THE CONJUNCTION.   397

### 1. (a).

| | |
|---|---|
| To-day must be about the third or fourth of the month. | 오늘이 뎡녕 사흘 이나 나흘 즈음 되오. |
| Let me know by letter or by messenger. | 편지 로나 사룸 으로 긔별 ᄒ기를 ᄇ라오. |

### 1. (b).

| | |
|---|---|
| Is this black or red? | 이거시 검소 붉소? |
| Is to-day the fifth or the sixth? | 오늘이 닷셔오 엿셔오? |
| Will you need a jinrikisha or not? | 인력거를 ᄃ랴오 아니 ᄃ랴오? |
| Were you speaking to him, or about him? | 그 사룸 드려 말 ᄒ엿소 그 사룸을 말ᄒ엿소? |

### 1. (c).

| | |
|---|---|
| I don't know whether that is silk or cotton. | 그 거시 명쥬 인지 무명 인지 모르겟소 |
| Please ask whether the bath is ready. | 목욕 물이 다 되엿나 무러 보아 주시오. |
| I don't know whether it will rain or not. | 비가 올는지 아니 올는지 알수 업소. |
| Do you know whether the steamer goes to-day or to-morrow? | 화륜션 오늘 ᄯ어나는지 ᄅ일 ᄯ어나는지 알으시오? |

### 2.

| | |
|---|---|
| Either take a chair or walk. | 교군을 ᄐ던지 것던지 ᄒ오. |
| Tell him to come either to-day or to-morrow. | ᄅ일 오던지 모레 오던지 ᄒ라고 ᄒ오. |

THE CONJUNCTION.

| | |
|---|---|
| I told the carpenter he might make it round or square. | 목슈 드려 그 거슬 둥글게 ᄒ던지 모지게 ᄒ던지 ᄒ라고 ᄒ엿소. |
| I don't care whether it rains or not. | 비가 오던지 아니 오던지 관계치 안소. |
| It is no matter to me whether he stays or not. | 류ᄒ 던지 아니 ᄒ던지 샹관 업소. |
| It does n't make any difference whether it's bamboo or not. | 대나모 던지 아니 던지 관계치 안소. |

3.

| | |
|---|---|
| That wont do either. | 그 것도 못 쓰겟소. |
| There now, see that! You can't do it either. | 자 그것 보오 당신도 ᄒ지 못 ᄒ리이다. |
| You mustn't leave your light burning at night either. | 즈너 도 밤에 불혀 두지 말게. |
| You can't go either. | 너 도 가지 못ᄒ다. |
| He did n't say a word about that either. | 그 것도 아모 말도 아니 ᄒ옵더 이다. |
| They don't say that either. | 그러라고 도 아니ᄒ옵더이다. |

SEC. 7 NEITHER-NOR.

Neither...nor—도...도 with the negative.

| | |
|---|---|
| It is neither a flea nor a mosquito. | 벼록 도 아니오 모긔 도 아니오. |
| There is neither a table nor a chair. | 교위 도 업고 샹 도 업ᄉ 읍더 이다. |
| It neither rained nor snowed for a month. | 흔 돌 동안은 비 도 아니 오고 눈 도 아니 오오. |

| Hereafter I will neither borrow nor lend. | 이 후 브러는 빌지 도 안코 빌니지 도 안켓소 |
| He can neither read nor write. | 칙 보지 도 못 ᄒᆞ고 글ᄌᆞ 쓰지도 못 ᄒᆞ오. |

### SEC. 8.—IF, UNLESS.

1 If—면.

   (*a.*) In simple supposition—면 with one or other of the simple tenses.

   (*b.*) Supposition contrary to fact—면 with one or other of the compound tenses.

2 When "if" introduces a future effect or consequence (sometimes expressed in English by '*and*') it is frequently rendered by the verbal stem and 고는.

3 Mere supposition, equivalent to "in case," "supposing that" if that was the case," etc., it may be rendered by 디경이면, 진대, 거든.

4 Even if.—relative participle with 지라도 or verbal participle with 도.

Unless, is rendered the same as, *if not*.

### 1. (*a*).

| If it is on the main road we can find it directly. | 큰 길에 잇ᄉᆞ면 곳 차질 수 잇소. |
| Do not go out if it is raining. | 비가 오면 나가지 마오. |
| He will probably go if he is not otherwise engaged. | 다른 일이 업ᄉᆞ면 갈 듯 ᄒᆞ오. |
| Unless he is in a hurry he will probably stop at Oricole. | 밧부지 아니 ᄒᆞ면 오리골 셔 지체홀 듯 ᄒᆞ오. |
| If it does n't suit you, you need n't pay for it. | ᄆᆞ음에 맛지 아니 ᄒᆞ면 갑슨 그만 두오. |

| | |
|---|---|
| You'd better not buy them unless they are cheap and good. | 싸고 쓰 됴흔거시 아니면 사지 아니ᄒᆞ는 거시 됴켓소. |
| You must keep quiet if you come in here. | 여긔 드러 오면 종용ᄒᆞ 여야 ᄒᆞ겟소. |
| If you will lend me your penknife I will make you a kite. | 쥬먼이 칼을 빌니면 연 ᄆᆞᆫ드러 주리이다. |
| If he hasn't got up yet shall I call him? | 아직 니러나지 아니 ᄒᆞ엿 시면 ᄭᆡ우리잇가? |
| If you haven't put it in the room, where have you put it? | 방에 두지 아니 ᄒᆞ엿시면 어듸 두엇소? |
| If the bridges haven't been carried away they probably got along without difficulty. | ᄃᆞ리가 ᄯᅥ라나지 아니 ᄒᆞ엿시면 걱정 업시 지낫실 돗 ᄒᆞ오. |
| If he is out what shall I do? | 출입 ᄒᆞ엿시면 엇더케 ᄒᆞ리잇가? |
| If it is past twelve, we must start immediately. | 십이 시 지낫 시면 곳 ᄯᅥ나야 ᄒᆞ겟소. |
| What shall I do if the passport has not come? | 빙표가 아니왓시면 엇더케 ᄒᆞ오? |

1. (b).

| | |
|---|---|
| What should we have done if the bridges had all been carried away? | ᄃᆞ리가 ᄯᅥ 나갓더면 엇 더케 지나갓실고? |
| If I had not had a horse, how could I have come? | ᄆᆞᆯ이 업섯 더면 엇더케 왓겟소? |
| How could I have studied unless I had a teacher? | 션ᄉᆡᆼ이 업섯 더면 엇더케 글을 비홧실고? |

CHAP. X. SEC. 8.   THE CONJUNCTION.               401

| If I had studied at once, it would have been well. | 공부를 진죽 ᄒᆞ엿더면 됴홧겟소. |
| If he had come yesterday I would have seen him. | 어저씌 왓더면 보앗지오. |
| If I had gone yesterday I would have come back. | 어저씌 갓더면 도라왓겟소. |
| If you let him have it, he'll spoil it. | 가져가게 ᄒᆞ면 샹ᄒᆞ리다. |

### 2.

| If you are going to-morrow, you must get coolies. | 틱일 가랴 고는 교군을 엇어야 겟소. |
| If you go to Chemulpo to-morrow you can't come here. | 틱일 제물포로 가고는 여긔는 못 오겟소. |
| If you don't take care, you will break it. | 조심 아니 ᄒᆞ고는 부러트리리이다. |
| You'll get wet if you don't take an umbrella. | 우산이 업고는 옷슬 적시리이다. |
| You can't stay here if you cry. | 울 고는 여긔 잇슬 수가 업다. |
| You'll be late if you don't hurry. | 어셔 ᄒᆞ지 아니 ᄒᆞ고는 늣겟소. |

### 3.

| If he won't sell it for a thousand cash, give him two thousand. | 열량에 팔지 아니 ᄒᆞ거든 스무 량을 주오. |
| If you've rested sufficiently, begin to study. | 다 쉬엿거든 공부 시작 ᄒᆞ시오. |
| Well, if your head aches, go and lie down. | 머리 압흐거든 가 누오. |

| If you don't want to never mind. | 슬커든 그만 두오. |
| --- | --- |
| If it suits you, take it. | 무음에 맛거든 가지오. |
| Take this letter, and in case the man has gone, bring it back. | 이 편지 가지고 가셔 만일 그사룸 써난 디경 이면 도로 가지고 오오. |
| If he is busy never mind. | 밧불진틴 그만 두오. |

4.

| Even if he had known how to swim, he probably would not have been saved. | 헤염을 홀줄 알앗실 지라도 살지 못 ᄒ엿실 듯 ᄒ오. |
| --- | --- |
| Even if I explain it he probably will not understand it. | 닐너 주어 도 알지 못 홀듯 ᄒ오. |
| He probably wont come, even if he said he would. | 온다고 ᄒ엿 셔도 오지 아니 홀 듯 ᄒ오. |

## SEC. 9.—BECAUSE.

Because, may be rendered by any one of the Korean conjunctions having a causal effect. It is quite often, however, expressed, by the use of the verbal noun in 기 with the postposition 에 ; or by the use of a noun such as 서돔 or 고, expressing reason or cause, with a postposition 에 or 로.

| I perfer Kumipo because it's cool. | 구미포가 셔늘 ᄒ기에 됴화 ᄒ오. |
| --- | --- |
| I waited because I thought it would clear. | 날이 긔일줄 안 서돔에 기드렷소. |
| He went because he had to. | 불가불 갈 터힌 고로 갓소. |

It's colder to-day because it has snowed.　오늘은 눈이 오는고로 더 칩소.

## SEC, 10.—THEN.

In that case—그러면, 그런즉, 그러커든.

Then I don't think you will will find one in Sëoul.　그러면 셔울셔 ᄒᆞ나도 못 엇을 듯 ᄒᆞ오.

Then he may get well.　그런 즉 날 듯 ᄒᆞ오.

Then you must give up smoking.　그러 커든 담비를 ᄭᅳᆫ히야 ᄒᆞ겟소.

Then don't go.　그러 커든 가지 마오.

## SEC. 11.—THAT.

1 Introducing a statement—고 ᄒᆞ오.
See Part I. 228. ff.

2 So that, in order that,—future verbal participle.

### 1.

I told Mr. Kim that it would be all right for him to read it.　김셔방 드려 보아도 무방 ᄒᆞ다고 ᄒᆞ엿소.

Did not the doctor say that he would have to try the hot springs, to get well?　의원이 온쳔을 ᄒᆞ여야 됴 타고 아니 ᄒᆞ옵 더니 잇가?

I heard from Mr. Pak that some foreigner wrote that letter.　그 편지ᄂᆞᆫ 엇던 외국 사ᄅᆞᆷ이 셧다 고 박셔방 안헤 드럿소.

### 2.

Open the door so that I can see out.　밧 겻 잘 내다 보게 문을 여오.

Please open the door so that the air can come in.　바람이 드러 오게 문 좀 열어 주오.

| | |
|---|---|
| Roll up your sleeves so that they wont get wet. | 젓지 안케 소미를 것으오. |
| Please arrange the net well so that the mosquitoes wont get in. | 모긔 드러오지 못 하게 모긔 장을 잘 치오. |
| Take care that you don't slip. | 밋그러지 잔케 조심 하여라. |

SEC. 12.—THAN.

1 With the Comparative Degree,—보다, 에셔. See also Part 1. ¶ 250 ff. & Part II. Chap. VI § II.

2 Rather than,—츨하리 or the verb 낫소 may be used.

3 More than, (of *quantity or number*).—

(*a*.) In affirmative sentences—넘어.

(*b*.) In negative sentences—밧긔.

1.

| | |
|---|---|
| A mule is stronger than a horse. | 로새가 물 보다 세오. |
| Korea is more healthy than Japan. | 죠션이 일본 보다 슈로가 됴소. |
| It rains more frequently in Japan than in Korea. | 죠션 보다 일본은 비가 자조 오오. |

2.

| | |
|---|---|
| I had rather walk than ride. | 트는것 보다 츨하리 것겟소. |
| I had rather write to him than tell him to his face. | 보고 말하는 것 보다 츨하리 편지로 하겟소. |
| I had rather smoke cigars than cigarettes. | 지권연 보다 츨하리 엽권연 먹겟소. |
| I had rather die than go to see the doctor. | 의원을 보러 가는 것 보다 츨하리 죽는 거시 낫겟소. |

CHAP. X. SEC. 12.  THE CONJUNCTION.  405

| That fellow had rather starve than work. | 그 놈은 일 ᄒ기 보다 굼는 거시 나흔 줄노 아오. |
| I had rather live in Korea than Japan. | 일본 보다 출하리 죠션 살겟소. |

### 3. (a.)

| It will cost more than fifty nyang. | 오십 량 넘져시 쓰겟소. |
| I have waited more than an hour for you. | ᄒ시간 넘어 기드렷소. |
| We have more than an hour yet. | 아직 도 ᄒ시 간 넘어 놉 앗소. |
| You must put in more than a handful. | ᄒ 줌 넘어 너허야 ᄒ 겟소. |
| There were more than a hundred there. | 거긔 빅명 넘어 잇스 옵더이다. |
| That book has more than a hundred pages. | 그 칙에 빅장 넘어잇소. |
| It is more than eighty ri to Chemulpo. | 졔물포 ᄭ지 팔십 리 넘어 되오. |
| I want more than ten pounds. | 열 근 넘어 쓰겟소. |

### 3. (b).

| I shall not want more than ten pounds. | 열근 밧긔 는 아니 쓰 겟소. |
| It will probably not cost more than two or three nyang. | 이삼 량 밧긔 는 아니 될 듯ᄒ오. |
| You must not put in more than a handful. | ᄒ 줌 밧긔 더 넛치 마오. |

| There are not more than ten ships in the harbor at present. | 지금 항구에 비가 열밧 긔업소. |
| --- | --- |
| I can't stop more than two or three days. | 이삼 일 밧긔 잇슬 수 업소. |
| There are not more than four. | 넷 밧긔 업소. |
| Here are no more sentences than are necessary to a thorough knowledge of Korean. | 여긔 잇는 말 마디 가죠션 말 주세 히 비호 기에 쓸 만콤 밧긔 업소. |

*THE END.*

# APPENDIX A.

## PHONETICS.

### I KOREAN PHONETICS.

#### INTRODUCTION. DEFINITIONS AND NOTES.

**1.** Phonetics. Phonetics is the science of position, movement, tension and action in speech sounds, and the art of making these sounds.

**2.** The ground tone. The ground tone is made by the vocal cords—the overtone by the cavities above, viz. pharynx, mouth, and nasal passages.

**3.** A consonant is a speech sound made by a complete or partial closure of the oral passage at one or more points.

**4.** A vowel is a voiced sound made through a fixed oral passage.

**5.** Syllables. A syllable is the least measure of speech, and is produced by a single impulse. A close syllable is one that ends in a consonant, and an open syllable is one ending in a vowel. It is a matter of some difficulty to know where one syllable begins and another ends, especially in English. English often makes a syllable with consonants l, m, and n, and these are consequently called "syllabic" consonants, but there do not seem to be any syllables in Korean words without vowels. It is worthy of note that the syllabification of the Korean spelling does not always seem to coincide with that of pronunciation.

**6.** Recoil. This, the recoil of the organs from close contact, as in English, pop, tip, (use your mirror) is a very important element in the pronunciation of English final stop consonants, but is not heard in Korean single words as 밥, 집, etc. However when these words occur in sentences they usually end in a vowel, so that the recoil must of necessity take place. The glottal catch, which is the very opposite of a recoil is frequently heard in the midst of Korean sentences.

The glottis is the "mouth" between the vocal cords; we close it in straining, and in coughing. If one will lay the fingers of one hand on the side of the throat about the larynx and snap against the finger nails with those of the other hand as he breathes, it will be noted that the sound is rather dead. Now inhale and "catch" the breath, and then snap. At once there is a change in the sound. The pent-up air, held by the shut glottis, has made the difference. One must learn to control this at will, and in combination with the stops p, t, and k. It occurs also with l, n, ng and between vowels, as 니러낫다 안젓소 (I rose and sat down).

7. Glide. If you pronounce the English vowels o, oo, as you look in the mirror, you will see the lips move slightly to a closer position at the end. This is called the *w* glide. At the end of the English "long" a and e, there is the *y* glide. Perhaps this is why we spell *day* and *they* and *bow*, and wrongly explain the *y* and *w* as "silent." It is difficult for English speaking people to pronounce a vowel without a glide.

8. Personal and National Difficulties.—Occasionally a person comes to the foreign field who is tongue-tied. Such an impediment must seriously interfere with ease and excellence of articulation. Inability to run one's tongue well down on to the lower lip may lead one to suspect this

defect. If so, a surgeon can easily remedy it. There are some who are accustomed to slur over their " r ' s ", and consequently inclined to import this same pronunciation into Korean but perhaps the greatest difficulty comes from assuming that the Korean letters are the same as the corresponding sounds in English. Almost no Korean letter has the identical sound of the corresponding English letter. Special attention should be given to the point of contact for forming l, and to the shape of the rest of the tongue, during its formation. This will remove the difficulty that many Koreans have in understanding foreigners when they use words ending in l. Our American l has a glide in it that is very confusing to Koreans.

9. Analysis of Sounds.—It is very important that these suggestions as to the manner in which sounds are formed be reviewed again and again, and the sounds thoroughly analysed. To go from the analysis of the known English sounds to the unknown Korean sounds is the only practical way to accomplish this. Whispering Korean sounds will often lay bare the secret of their formation. Or it may be better to sing them with a (ah) before and after the consonant. A half-inch stick between the jaw teeth of the teacher will often facilitate the investigation. Sometimes the best way to discover the difference between the Korean sounds and our own is to make up a sentence in which the sound under investigation is prominent, and then get a Korean who knows no English to repeat these words. His departure from the normal English pronunciation will reveal to you the degree in which you ought to conform your pronunciation to his that you may speak Korean acceptably.

10. Intonation —Intonation is the peculiar melody which forms an integral part of a language, and may differ in different localities, even where the language is the same. Korean intonation in some sentences seems very much like English, and again it is absolutely different. It might be called the language "tune," and the mastery of it is more important than the correct pronunciation of an individual sound. It is never learned by those who follow the book, or the word method. It exists only in sentences in nature, and should be watched for at such times as you have opportunity to listen to the Koreans as they talk among themselves. Failure to give the proper intonation makes the foreigner always remain a foreigner in speech, and his best efforts may cause the soul-saddening remark, "We do not understand English." It is because our fellow countrymen retain our own melody that we are able to understand their Korean so much easier than that of the native; and for the like reason when the native speaks English to us, we often mistake, and think he is speaking his own tongue.

11. Articulation.—Articulation is the uniting of consonants and vowels, so as to give to each its proper value. Many students of Korean will need to cultivate a better articulation in Korean than they have in their mother tongue. A valuable exercise to this end is the reading in a whisper, in either language, to some one at a distance of twenty-five or thirty feet, with such distinctness that they can understand what is read. To do this well and easily, one must know the exact position to be taken for each sound and then assume such positions clearly and as soon as the sound is made, release the position just as clearly and decidedly.

## APPENDIX A.

## PHONETIC ANALYSIS.

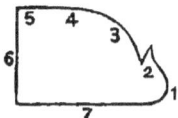 The various positions of the lips, tongue and other parts of the vocal organs, may be represented by the above diagram. No. 1, represents the lip in contact, No. 2, the teeth ; Nos. 3, 4, and 5, the roof of the mouth; No. 6, represents the posterior portion of the mouth closed ; and No. 7, the floor of the mouth. If the sound is a surd, i, e, unaccompanied by a vibration of the vocal cords, this line (No. 7) is a light line, if a sonant, i. e. accompanied with a vibration of the vocal cords, the line is heavy, thus ———.

The position of the tongue is indicated by a line to any point where the tongue may be in contact. If the tongue lies in the floor of the mouth it is not indicated in the diagram. A mirror should be used for determining the various positions.

Let us first indicate

### THE ENGLISH CONSONANTS.

Which must always precede an intelligent study of the corresponding Korean sounds.

The labial position is a cardinal position in English and is represented in the following ways.

The letter p being a stop sound, the lips are (1) in contact, the posterior portion of the mouth (2) is closed and there is no vibration of the vocal cords.

B differs from p only in that it is a sonant or in other words there is a vibration of the vocal cords and is therefore represented by the heavy line.

P' aspirated is represented the same as the unaspirated with the addition of the dotted line to show the explosive factor in producing the sound.

## A.—PHONETIC TABLE ENGLISH.

| | Stop. | Aspirate. | Combination of Stop and Continuant. Nasal. | Continuant. | | |
|---|---|---|---|---|---|---|
| | | | | Central. | Lateral. | Flap or Trill. |
| Labial | p  b | p' | m  m° | wh  w | | |
| Dental | | | | | th  dh  l  l° | r  r°  r  r° |
| Dental Labial | | | | | | |
| Pre-Palatal | t  d | t' | n | s  z | | r  r° |
| Blade-Palatal | ch  j | ch' | ñ | sh  zh | | r  r° |
| Velar | k  g | k' | ng | | | |
| Glottal | | | | h | | |

412 APPENDIX A.

## APPENDIX A.

M° voiceless is uncommon but is found in the final m of word *rheumatism*.

M is a nasal sound being a combination of a stop and continuant. The lips are closed but the posterior part of the mouth is open enough to allow the current of air to go through the nasal passages. With this there is a vibration of the vocal cords which is represented by a heavy base line.

The common expression that a person talks through his nose when he has a cold is not the true statement of fact, for it is just the opposite. The air in such a case does not go through the nasal passages and the *m* becomes a *b*. For example we say "good bordik" for "good morning." *m* becomes *b*, *n* becomes *d* and *ng* becomes *k*.

The *wh* and *w* are made by a continuous current of air coming through the rounded lips and back of the mouth, *wh* being voiceless while *w* is a vibrating sound.

The dental position is uncommon in English being represented only in *th* and *dh* and by some persons in the letter *r*.

In "*th*" the tongue is against the teeth the current of air coming out at the sides of the tongue. A vibration of the vocal cords in the same position produces *dh*.

The *r* is formed by a flap or trill with the tongue against the teeth and the sides rounded out. There is occasionally a voiceless *r* as *prey*, but usually it has the accompanying vibration of the vocal cords.

*f* and *v* are the only consonants in the dental labial position. They are made by placing the lower lip in contact with the edge of the upper teeth and allow the current of air to escape at either side. The *f* has no vibration of the vocal cords while the *v* has such vibration.

The prepalatal position is a cardinal position.

T is made with open lips. The tip of the tongue in the prepalatal region i. e. there is a break in the middle of the tongue, and the throat closed. It is a voiceless sound.

D is made in the same way with the addition of a vibration of the vocal cords.

T' The aspirated *t* is indicated by the curved dotted line.

N is a nasal sound being a combination of a stop and a continuant. The lips are open the tongue having its tip in the prepalatal region forms the anterior stop. The posterior position is partially open so that the current of air goes through the nose as indicated by the arrow. There is at the same time a vibration of the vocal cords.

S is a central continuant made by having both the lips and posterior position of the mouth open, as the current of air comes out it is forced through centrally because the edges of the tongue are in contact with the roof of the mouth at the prepalatal region.

Z is produced in the same manner with the addition of a vibration of the vocal cords.

The voiceless *l*° is uncommon—as in *ply*.

The usual *l* is produced with the tongue in the prepalatal region but with its tip in contact and the current of air coming out at either side—represented by an arrow. It is accompanied with a vibration of the vocal cords.

APPENDIX A.   415

The voiceless and voiced 'r' are made as above indicated except in this position the tongue is further back, i. e. in the prepalatal position.

In the blade palatal position we have first the stop *ch*. This is produced with the lips open, the posterior position of the mouth closed and the tongue arched so that it is in contact with the palate. It may be noticed here that while in the letter *t* there is a break in the middle of the tongue in *ch* there is no break. This is a voiceless sound.

*J* is produced in the same way with the addition of vibration of the vocal cords.

*Ch* aspirated is indicated by a dotted curved line.

*Ñ*. This sound may be represented by *ny*. It is the *ñ* in *cañon* or *oñion*. The position is the same as *ch* except that the posterior position is open enough to permit the air to pass through the nose.

*Sh* is a voiceless sound made by a continuous current of air. The sides of the arched tongue being in contact with the palate the air comes out centrally.

*Zh* is produced in the same way with the addition of the vibration of the vocal cords.

*r* in this position is made as the *r* in the prepalatal and dental except the tongue is further back.

The velar position is represented by,

*K* is a voiceless sound. The lips are open and the tongue is pressed against the posterior position of the mouth.

G is produced in the same way with the addition of vibration of the vocal cords.

K Aspirated is represented the same as the voiceless k except for the addition of dotted curved line to show the explosive quality of the sound.

Ng is the nasal correspondent of the velar stop. It is produced as indicated in diagram by leaving a position of the posterior part of the mouth open so as to allow the air to pass through the nose.

H is a glottal voiceless sound produced by a continuous current of air passing out through the rounded portion of the posterior part of the mouth.

---

Let us next consider
The Korean Consonants.

The labial position is a cardinal position in Korean as well as in English.

ㅂ is a voiceless sound i. e. there is no vibration of the vocal cords. The lips and the posterior position of the mouth are closed. It is the same as the unaspirated English p and many make the mistake of giving it the same sound as the English aspirated p.* There is no recoil to the lips when it is the final letter. To demonstrate this, watch the lips in a mirror and pronounce the English word "pop" and the Korean word 밥.

ㅃ is produced with the same position of the lips as ㅂ except there is more tension of the lips which we may represent by a heavy line. It is

---

* The same criticism applies to all the stop sounds which beginners are liable to give as aspirated.

## B.—PHONETIC TABLE KOREAN.

| | Stop. | Aspirate. | Combination of Stop and Continuant Nasal. | Continuant. | | |
|---|---|---|---|---|---|---|
| | | | | Central. | Lateral. | Flap or Trill. |
| Labial | ㅂ b | ㅍ p | ㅁ m | 하 ⸱o | | |
| Dental | ㄷ d | ㅌ t | ㄴ n and Initial ㄹ | | ㄹ Final | ㄹ Medial |
| Dental Labial | | | | ㅅ s | | |
| Pre-Palatal | | | | ㅈ ⸱ | | |
| Blade-Palatal | ㅈ j | ㅊ ch | 샤 | | | |
| Velar | ㄱ g | ㅋ k | ㆁ ng | | | |
| Glottal | | ㅎ h | | | | |

418   APPENDIX A.

not made with a vibration of the vocal cords as is the English *b*.\*

ㅍ differs from the unaspirated ㅂ in that there is more tension of lips and it is immediately followed by a sound originating in the glottis and is made much like a roughened *h* sound in English. This we represent by the curving forward of the posterior line ).

ㅁ is formed in the same way as the English *m* except there is less vibration of the vocal cords. It has much the sound of the final *m* of the word *rheumatism*.   ㅁ final has no recoil to the lips before a vowel.

ㅊ before the vowel 아 is like the Englsh *wh* except for a slight roughening of the sound. Korean has no equivalent of *w* because he does not vibrate the vocal cords.

ㄷ final ㅅ. The lips are open and the tongue slightly raised posteriorly with its tip against the teeth and the posterior of the mouth closed.  ㅅ final has no recoil.

ㅈ is formed in the same way as ㄷ except there is more pressure of the tongue against the teeth and more tension of the tongue, which we may represent by the dark marking. No vibration of vocal cords.

ㅌ is made in the same position as ㄷ with more tension to the tongue with the addition of the roughened *h* sound explained above.

Initial ㄹ is formed the same as the English *n* except the tip of the tongue is against the teeth and there is no vibration of the vocal cords, being a

---

\* There is no exact equivalent of the English *b* in Korean.

voiceless sound it is sometimes not pronounced at all or may have the consonantal *y*, sound as in 리.

Final ㄹ is formed by having the lips and the posterior position of the mouth open and the tip of the tongue against or just behind the upper teeth— the current of air coming out on either side.

It differs from the English final *l* as follows:

(1) With the English *l*, the tip of the tongue is in the prepalatal region, whereas in Korean the tip of the tongue is as above indicated against or just above the upper teeth.

(2) The English final *l* has a recoil whilst the Korean has not.

(3) The English final *l* is usually accompanied with vibration of the vocal cords while the Korean final has little if any vibration.

ㄹ medial is produced by placing the tip of the tongue against or just above the upper teeth and with the sides of the tongue not as full out as the English *r* in this same position and making a flap, i. e. bringing the tongue down to the floor of the mouth. Occasionally there is a slight trill instead of a flap. The sound is not accompanied by a distinct vibration of the vocal cords as is usual in English.

It may be noted by the above table that the Korean has no consonant sounds in the dental labial or prepalatal positions. The change of the prepalatal position in English to the dental position in Korean is one of the most striking changes.

The consonant ㅅ (except when final see above) occupies a position midway between the prepalatal and blade palatal positions.

It is made by a continuous current of air coming centrally through a space left by the edges of the tongue coming in contact with the roof of the mouth at the midway point above mentioned.

This point may be ascertained with considerable exactness by pronouncing in English the following, *sin, syin* and *shin*. In other words in the Korean the tongue is midway between the English *s* and *sh* and has somewhat the *sy* sound.

Furthermore, it should be noted that the Korean is more subdued than the usual English *s*.

ㅆ The position of the organs are the same as in ㅅ but there is more tension. There is not however the vibration of the vocal cords which would give the English *z* sound.

ㅈ is in the blade palatal position, It is a voiceless sound made by the arched portion of the tongue coming in contact with the roof of the mouth at the point indicated in the diagram. The lips are open and the posterior portion closed.

ㅉ is produced in the same manner except there is more tension of the tongue. It has not the distinct vibration of the vocal cords as the English *j*.

ㅊ is produced in the same way as ㅈ with addition of roughened *h*. It is nearly like the English *ch*.

There is in Korean an *ny* sound which is the same position as ㅈ except that there is an opening posteriorly allowing the air to go through the nose. This sound is not accompanied by the distinct vibration of the vocal cords, in other words the ㄴ is almost voiceless. This probably accounts for the differences in pronunciation in some parts of the country the ㄴ being distinct, and in other parts it is left out entirely. e. g. 녀related.

ㄱ occupies the velar position. The lips are opened the posterior part of the mouth is closed off by an arching back of the tongue as indicated. It is a voiceless sound. There is no recoil to the final ㄱ.

ㄲ is produced in the same way as ㄱ with the exception of more tension of the tongue. It is not accompanied by as distinct a vibration of the vocal cords as is the English *g*.

ㅋ differs from ㄱ only in more tension of the tongue and the roughened *h* sound following.

ㅇ is produced with the same position as ㄱ except there is an opening posteriorly indicated by arrow allowing the current of air to go through the nose. There is also a less distinct vibration of the vocal cords than is found in English *ng*.

There is no recoil to this consonant in Korean.

The ㅎ sound in Korean is unlike the *h* in English in that it is more of an aspirate made with tongue raised at the back and a roughened sound of glottis, while the English *h* is a continuant sound and voiceless.

## PHONETIC CHANGES.

The above table of Korean consonants is of value not only as an aid to producing the sounds but also as an aid in understanding the so-called euphonic changes.

For example it is stated in books that ㄱ before ㄴ, ㄹ, and ㅁ becomes ㅇ, but no reason or explanation is given.

By referring to the Table it will be noted that ㄱ is a velar, stop, voiceless sound and to change from this consonant to ㄴ would require two movements, viz. opening the posterior portion to allow the air to go through the nose and placing the tip of the tongue against the teeth. ㅇ is in the velar position, but is a nasal sound and requires but one change, namely the changing of the tongue to become ㄴ. Therefore to facilitate the ease of speaking ㄱ becomes ㅇ because one change is easier to make than two, i. e. euphony is ease of utterance.

As nasal sounds are stronger than stops so the laterals as ㄹ (medial) are stronger than nasals.

The change of *l* to *r* between two vowels is because the position of the Korean tongue makes it easier to say *r* than *l*. Phonetic changes are not infrequently a good clue to the organic positions.

## NORMAL POSE.

As a preliminary to the discussion of the vowels it will be well to note what is meant by the term, normal pose, or, as it is sometimes called, "organic basis," or "basis of articulation." These all refer to that characteristic attitude of the vocal organs, as produced by their positions and tensions, which prevails among any given race, while they are in the act of speaking their language. It might be termed the musical "key" of the language. The points to be observed in determining this are, whether the lips are forward, back, or neutral, whether the throat is open or rather shut, the tongue high or low, front or back, and whether the organs are tense or lax.

The imitation of the involuntary grunt, "uh," which occurs between the words of an unready speaker, is the best key to his normal pose. So too, if one will make a Korean open his mouth and give with open jaw the vowels 아, 어, 오, and compare the position of the tongue in saying the English " a " (ah), it will be a great help to securing the correct normal pose. The high back tongue and shut throat which is, with high tension, so characteristic of Korean speech, makes one wonder that any one can speak Korean without getting a " preacher's sore throat."

## VOWEL MODIFICATIONS.

These arise from the changes in the oral cavity, made by the varying shapes and tensions of the softer organs, as when the lips are spread or passive or rounded ; when the tongue is highest at back, mid, front, or tip ; or when the velum, the soft palate, is open, neutrally shut, or rounded. Further, all these organs may be lax or tense, which are also termed " wide " or " narrow."

Rounding. Rounding is the making of the oral passage round at one or more points. It is distinguished as outer, between the lips ; inner, between the back of tongue and the velum ; and medial, between the front of the tongue and the hard palate. English has only inner and outer rounding, while Korean, with French and German, has all three.

*Vowels Triangles.* Korean has two complete triangles, though one or two of the vowels are not found everywhere in the peninsula. It has but one or two diphthongs.

Triangle " A " is formed, where the lips are either spread or neutral, and " B " is composed of rounded vowels. If you take any of the Arabic numbered vowels, and round it, you get the corres-

# VOWEL TRIANGLES.

## A

- Front. III 의 ü
- II 애 ö
- I Low 아 a
- IV 오 o
- V Back. 우 u
- High.

## B

- Front. 이 i
- 3
- 2 에 e
- 1 Low 아 a
- 4 어 ŭ
- 5 Back. 으 ŭ
- High.

ponding Roman number, unless it be for I. If to these ten vowels we add the one unclassified vowel short a ㅐ, not written in the diagram, you get eleven, the number of vowel signs in King Se-jong's alphabet. It raises the question as to whether the symbols, constant in number, may not have changed in signification, as have the vowel symbols of English. Vowel III 위 is pronounced in some places as 3 이, and in some as a consonant and vowel, *wi*. The symbol 의, *ui*, is often pronounced as 3, 이. It offers a field for investigation especially if any old rhymed poetry might be available to help to determine what the older sounds really were.

As we take up the A vowels and say ㅐ *ă* ㅔ *e* ㅣ *i* we note how the tongue comes to the front of the mouth and raises higher and higher toward the back. The tongue positions of the B triangle cannot be observed by the mirror, owing to the closed position of the lips.

While both *a*'s 오 and 아 are now sounded alike, yet it may be they had this same difference of rounding, as in our English *a*, in father, and *a*, in all. If so the triangles would be complete at the apex; and if the pronunciation of the German ü, as now heard in Southern Korea, is the original sound of the symbol 위, then the whole triangle agree, part for part.

The vowels frequently have two pronunciations, one a long, which occurs in syllables that have the stress; and the short, which occurs in both stressed and unstressed syllables. This short sound may differ in quality from the long, but it often differs only in quantity, that is, sometimes you may hear a short i, as in the word 집, *house*, where the vowel is not the same as our English short i. but a short *e* sound. So it may be with short *a*, *e. o* and *u*, Short *a* is often like the final a in "America."

The chief difference between the sounds e and i, as distinguished from English ey (long a, so called) and i (long e) is in the final glide that is characteristic of all our English long vowels. Take a mirror and say *a, e, i, o, u,* (ah, ey, ee, o, oo) and note the movement of the organs, as the sound comes to its finish. That is the "glide." Have a Korean give the similar sounds and you will see how immobile his lips are, and how his glide, if he does make one, is in his throat. In speech he really makes none though in giving the syllabary he frequently does.

The easiest way to learn the sounds *ö* and *ü* is by unrounding Korean *o* and *u*. They are also a trifle more lax than the rounded sounds. It is for this reason partly that I have concluded that the Roman symbols short *o* and *u* had best be used to designate them. Another reason, however, is that the symbols *ö* and *ü* in German have these same values, and as many study German before they come out it would seem better to retain these symbols with their former signification. The differences in sound of the two are all made by rounding the vowels of the corresponding position in triangle I, save the bottom vowel, *a*, A rounded throat, and the lip give an *o*, ㅗ from an *ŏ* ㅓ, and a rounded throat and lip give an *u*, ㅜ from an *ŭ*,—while rounded throat, lip and tongue give *ö ü* from *e* and *i*.

Any difficulty in mastering the sound *ö* will arise from failure to hold the front of the tongue in rounded shape against the hard palate. Difficulty in mastering the sound

## APPENDIX A.

*u*, misnamed French *eu*, arises in failure to unround the organs as they are in position to say *u*. The fact that the symbol *u*, 으, has different sounds in words now written with this vowel, only shows phonetic decay, and means Korean like English should have a reform in spelling. Careful copying of the teacher's organic attitude and action in the pronounciation of these vowels will enable one to reproduce the sounds. Like begets like.

To unround 오 or 우, 으 or *u*, prolong the sound and at the same time insert the little fingers in the mouth and pull the lips toward the corners.

The study of phonetics is now recognized as an integral part of the study of any language and we had hoped to have been able possibly to add a Part III to this book that would have dealt very thoroughly with this subject. This however, being impossible we are very glad that the above digest of what Prof. Cummings prepared for the student of Korean is able to be presented at this time. It is due to Dr. A. I. Ludlow, to say that he kindly consented to undertake its preparation and we sincerely hope and trust that either he or others interested in the subject will elaborate the same so that a student of Korean may be enabled the more speedily to attain a good working knowledge of this language.

There have also been those who have desired that something on the line of English phonetics for the use of Korean students of English should be prepared and Mr. Sangkyu Pack, Ph. B. of Brown University, U. S. A. has kindly prepared Part II for such purposes.

## II ENGLISH-KOREAN PHONETICS.
## 鮮英音對照
### 母音

**A**

에이  此字는九種의各音이有ᄒᆞ니

(1) ā 에이 āte=에이트
(2) ă 에 sĕn'ăte=센/쎈}에트
　　　此는上節音에揚音이有홈으로因ᄒᆞ야生홈
(3) ạ 「오」及「어」의間音이니
　　　 all=오ㅣㄹ(올)
(4) a=ŏ 「어」及「아」의間音이니
　　　 was 우{어/아}쓰
(5) ä 아 ärm=아ᅟᅳᆷ(암)
(6) à 「아」分「이」의間音
　　　 àsk=｛아/이｝쓰크
(7) â=ê 애~ câre=캐~
(8) ă 애 ăt=애트
(9) ạ 어 (不分明)此는 ä 와或 à 가有ᄒᆞᆫ節音에揚音이업는境遇에生ᄒᆞᄂᆞ니
　　　 about=어싸우트
　　　 ăn'mạl=에네멀

**E**

이ㅣ  下의七音이有ᄒᆞ니
(1) ē=ï 이ㅣ Hē=히ㅣ
(2) ē 이 此는下節音에揚音이有홈을因ᄒᆞᆷ이니
　　　 Rēmāin'=리멘

APPENDIX A.   429

(3)  e=ā     에이      Eight=에이트
(4)  ê=â     애~       whêre=왜~
(5)  ẽ=ī=û   어~       Hĕr=허~
(6)  ĕ       에(短)     Mĕn=멘
(7)  ẹ       어        (不分明)此는上節音에揚音이有
                      홈으로生ᄒᄂ니
                      Mŏ'mẹnt=모ㅣ먼트

## I

아이 四種의 音이 有ᄒ니

(1)  ī=ȳ     아이      īce=아이쓰
(2)  Ĭ=y̆     이        ĭn=인
(3)  ï=ē     이ㅣ      Pŏlice=폴리ㅣ쓰
(4)  î=ê=û   어~       Bîrd=뻐~드

## O

오우 八種의 音이 有ᄒ니

(1)  ō       오우      ōld=오울드
(2)  ȯ       오        上節音에揚音이有홈을因ᄒ야 ō
                      와 如히 長音이 되지 못ᄒᄂ니
(3)  ô       오어      Hŭ'rô=히ㅣ로
                      Fôr=ᅙ포~
(4)  ŏ=ạ     「어」와「오」의 間音이라
                      nŏt=낫}트
                           넛
(5)  ọ       어        (不分明) 下節音에揚音이有
                      홈으로「어」音又ᄒ되 不分明
                      ᄒᄂ니라 cọnsūme'=컨수ㅣ메
(6)  ȯ=ŭ     어        cȯme=컴 (俗爾캄)
(7)  ọ=ụ=ōō  우ㅣ      dọ=두
(8)  ọ=ụ=ŏŏ  우        gŏŏd=우드

## U

유ㅣ 七種의音이有호니

- (1) ū 유ㅣ ūse=유ㅣ쓰
- (2) ŭ 유 dŭra'tion=두레ㅣ슌
- (3) ŭ=ŏ 어 ŭs=어스
- (4) ṳ 「아」와「어」의 間音이니 上節音에 有호 揚音으로 因호야 生호는 바이라 dā'tṳm=쎄ㅣ텀
- (5) û=ī=ē 으어 ûrn=으언
- (6) ṳ=ọ 우ㅣ rṳde=루ㅣ드
- (7) ṳ=ọ 우 Put=풋트

## W

떠블뉴  此字는音이 ōō=ṳ=우ㅣ니 恒常 他 母音字나 子音字와 倂合호여 發音이 되느니라

## Y

와이 二種의 音이 有호니

- (1) y̆=ĭ 이 cĭ'ty̆=씻티
- (2) ȳ=ī 아이 bȳ=빠이

oi=oy 오이 Boy=샏이
ou=ow 아우 Out=아우트

# 子音

## B

쎄ㅣ 我諺文에「ㅂ」와「ㅃ」의 間音이니 例호건티

Boy=샏이
Combĭnā'tion=캄/컴}빈네슌

APPENDIX A. 431

**C**

씨ㅣ 　此字는二音이有ᄒᆞ니
(1) 我諺文애「ㅋ」와「ㄱ」의間音되는境遇니即「K」字와同ᄒᆞ니라
　　Căn=킨
　　mū′sĭc=무ㅣ시크
(2) 「ㅅ」와「외」의間音이니
　　Cŏntĕr=센}러~
　　　　　썬
　　Āce=에이스

**Ch** 「C」와「H」의 二字가結合ᄒᆞ야三種의音을成ᄒᆞᄂᆞ니
(1) 上에論ᄒᆞᆫ C=K 와同ᄒᆞᆫ境遇
　　Chĕmistry=케미스추리
　　Christ=크라이스트
(2) 「ㅊ」音이有ᄒᆞᆫ境遇
　　Chĕss=체스
　　Child=차일드
(3) 「Sh」字音과同ᄒᆞᆫ境遇니此字의音은我諺文으로表示키難ᄒᆞ기로「ㅎ」로表홈
　　Chĕrōōt′=허우~트
　　Măchīne′=메허인

**D**

씨ㅣ 「ㅅㄷ」音도되고「ㄷ」音도되ᄂᆞ니例ᄒᆞ면
　　Do=ᄯ두ㅣ
　　Gŏd=까ㅣ드

**F**

에ᅘᅲ 　此字의音과仿佛ᄒᆞᆫ거슨我諺文에는업는지라此音을發코저홀진되上齒를下唇內애接付ᄒᆞ고

APPENDIX A.

「氣音」이有호「ㅍ」音을前齒間으
로出發호면此音을得호지니라
France=흐프란스
Beef=쎄ㅣ흐프

**G**

지ㅣ

此字논「ㅅㄱ」와「ㄱ」의間音이니
Gŏd=싸ㅣ드
或時논「ㅆ」와「ㅈ」의間音도되ᄂᆞ니
Gĕrmăny̆=쩌 } 민네
저

**Gh**

F 字의 音과 同홈
Enough=이너흐푸

**H**

에이취

此논英音의所謂「氣音」이라稱ᄒᆞ
논音이니我의「ㅎ」와相當ᄒᆞ니
라
He=히ㅣ
「H」字논 「C」「G」「P」「S」「T」「W」
字等과連合ᄒᆞ야各種의音을成
ᄒᆞᄂᆞ니以上에「Ch」及「Gh」논
論훈바여니와「Ph」「Sh」「Th」
「Wh」논「P」「S」「T」「W」字下
에見ᄒᆞ라

**J**

쩌

此音은上에論ᄒᆞᆫ바「G」字第二音
과同ᄒᆞ야「ㅆ」와「ㅈ」의間音이니
例훌진되
Jew={쭈ㅣ
　　　주ㅣ
Jăck={쎅
　　　젹

## APPENDIX A.

**K**
케
此字는二音이有하니
(1) 「ㅌ」字와同하야「ㅋ」와「ㄱ」의間音이有흔境遇라
Kōréa=고리ㅣ아
King=킹
(2) 或時는「ㄱ」와相當하느니
Handkerchief=힝거취ᅌᅵ후
「K」가「N」上에在흔境遇에는「K」는發音되지 아니홈은原則이라 홀지라

**L**
엘
此字는二音이有하니
(1) 빗침「ㄹ」와同흔境遇
All=올
(2) 「L」의音을發코져하면舌端을口蓋 (上顎) 에付하며同時에「氣音」이有흔듯흔「ㄹ」音을發하느니라此音의表는「ㄹㄹ」로定흠
Lace=레ㅣ스

**M**
엠
「ㅁ」와同하니라
Man=만
Ham=함 (밧침의「ㅁ」)

**N**
엔
(1) 「ㄴ」와同하느니
Name=네임
Man=만 (밧침의「ㄴ」)
(2) 밧침「ㅇ」와同흔境遇도有하니
Linger=링거~

## APPENDIX A.

**Ng** 　　「N) 라 「G」의 二字가合ᄒᆞ야밧침
　　　　「ㆁ」이되ᄂᆞ니
　　　　　Sing=씽
　　　　　Singer=씽어~

**P**

피 ㅣ 　　此字ᄂᆞᆫ兩音이有ᄒᆞ니字頭에在ᄒᆞᆫ
　　　　時ᄂᆞᆫ恒常氣音이有ᄒᆞ고로「ㅍ」
　　　　音이有ᄒᆞ고他에在ᄒᆞᆫ境遇에ᄂᆞᆫ
　　　　「ㅂ」가되ᄂᆞ니例를擧ᄒᆞ건ᄃᆡ
　　　　　Pie=파이
　　　　　Map=맵
　　　　「P」가字頭에在ᄒᆞ며「n」「s」「t」字
　　　　前에잇ᄂᆞᆫ境遇에ᄂᆞᆫ「P」ᄂᆞᆫ이恒
　　　　常默音이되ᄂᆞ니라

**Ph** 　　「F」와同ᄒᆞᆷ

**Q**

큐 ㅣ 　　此字ᄂᆞᆫ無音ᄒᆞ고恒常「u」字와結
　　　　合ᄒᆞ야二音을成ᄒᆞᄂᆞ니
　(1)　「K」字와同ᄒᆞᆷ
　　　　　Liquor=리커~
　　　　　Piqu'ant=피칸트
　(2)　「Kw」의 音 卽 「ㄲ」「콰」「궈」「궈」의
　　　　音이有ᄒᆞᄂᆞ니例를擧ᄒᆞ건ᄃᆡ
　　　　　Quail=퀘ㅣㄹ

**R**

아[ㄹ] 　　兩種의音이有ᄒᆞ니
　(1)　「ㄹ」相當
　　　　　Mary=메리
　(2)　字頭에在ᄒᆞ든지字末에在ᄒᆞ야ᄂᆞᆫ
　　　　「애」의音이有ᄒᆞᆫ듯ᄒᆞᆫ「ㄹ」音을

發ᄒᆞ야得ᄒᆞᄂᆞ니라
Right=～라잇트

## S
애스
(1) 「ㅆ」와同ᄒᆞᆫ境遇
　　Sŭn=썬
(2) 氣音이有ᄒᆞᆫ「ㅅ」音이니(此ᄂᆞᆫ「ㅎㅅ」로表홈)
　　Is=이ᄊᆞ
(3) 「솨」「쉬」의音과同ᄒᆞᆫ境遇니「Sh」와同ᄒᆞ니라
　　Sūre=슈～
　　Leisūre=레ㅣ슈～

## Sh
「Ch」即「솨」「쉬」와 同ᄒᆞᆫ境遇
　　Shē=쇠ㅣ
　　Shīne=솨인

## T
티ㅣ
此字은三種의音이有ᄒᆞ니
(1) 氣音이有ᄒᆞᆫ境遇即「ㅌ」와同ᄒᆞᆫ境遇가是라
　　It=잇트
　　to=투
(2) 「U」字와「R」字의前에在ᄒᆞ야ᄂᆞᆫ「T」ᄂᆞᆫ「大」音이有ᄒᆞᆫ듯ᄒᆞ니라
　　Natūre=네ㅣ츄～
(3) 「I」字前에在ᄒᆞ야氣音이有ᄒᆞᆫ「ㅅ」即「ㅎ」音이有ᄒᆞ니라
　　Nation=네ㅣ쑨

## Th
此付合은兩字中에一字의音도업고他音이有ᄒᆞ니
(1) 舌端을上下齒間애置ᄒᆞ고氣音이有ᄒᆞᆫ「ㄷ」音을發ᄒᆞᄂᆞᆫ듯ᄒᆞᄂᆞ니

Thick=띡크
Thin=띤

(2) 舌端을上下齒間에置ᄒᆞ고氣音이
有ᄒᆞᆫ「ㄷ」音을發ᄒᆞᄂᆞᆫ듯ᄒᆞᄂᆞ니
The=듸ㅣ
Thine=ᄃᆞ인

### V

에ㅣ 　此音을發코져ᄒᆞ면上齒를下脣內
에付ᄒᆞ고齒間으로「ㅂ」을發ᄒᆞ
면其音을得ᄒᆞᄂᆞ니라
Vās =에ㅣᄡᅳ

### Wh

此付合의音은「Hw」니「화」「훠」
의音과相當ᄒᆞ니
Whăt=훠ㅣ트
What=화ㅣ트

### X

此字의音은「G」와「Z」의結合ᄒᆞᆫ
것即「ㄱ」와「ㅅ」의間音 과氣
音이有ᄒᆞᆫ「ㅅ」ᄡᅳ「라」라相當
ᄒᆞ니라
Āxle=읰흘
Ĕxămpl =엑햄불

(2) 「K」字와「S」字結合即「ㄱ」와「ㅅ」
의音으로도發音되ᄂᆞ니
Fŏx=학}ㅅ
　　핵

### Z

씨ㅣ 上論ᄒᆞᆫ氣音을帶ᄒᆞᆫ「S」即「ᄡᅳ」相
當이니
Zōne=ᄌᆞᆫ

# APPENDIX B.
## PECULIAR FORMS.

While we have given in the book itself rules from which we believe almost every form of the spoken language can be derived there are certain forms that have come over at times from the book language and also other forms derived from the now obsolete verbs and also certain other forms that are almost restricted to Korean poetry.

While it is impossible to enter into a discussion of all these forms at this point a few words may possibly aid the student in the study of the same. We will therefore, consider briefly a few of these under three heads :—

I. Peculiar forms.
II. Poetic usage.
III. Book forms.

I. Peculiar forms.

There were originally in Korean a number of honorific forms of the verb in which in a peculiar way the subject of the verb was honored by the use of the same. These verbs in most of their forms are now obsolete so that the dictionary will hardly record them and consequently there may be, naturally, difficulty in finding certain forms still remaining over from the now obsolete verb. Notably among these we would mention 흐읍다 (already referred to in the body of the book) 듯좁다 for 듯다 *to hear.* 밧좁다 for 밧다 *to receive.*

The following forms may be derived from these: 흐오이다, 흐외다 흐도소이다, 이로소이다, 이올시다,

which are all declarative; 호샤이다, imperative; 돗자와' a verbal participle, and 밧줍지, a negative base.

This might be carried out almost indefinitely but the above will show how such forms are derived.

II. Poetic forms.

In Korean poetry which has at times both rhyme and rhythm and which to no small extent inclines to what might almost be termed Oriental Antiphonies; many of the regular forms will be found with slight divergencies from common usages. In the desire for rhythm the form in 에 marked No. 2, in both the declarative and propositive terminations is very largely used and when so used the fact that it is not a polite form is lost sight of entirely. Thus in poetry 호네 (declarative) 호게 (imperative) 호세 (propositive) will be freely used and implies no inferiority at all, in the person addressed or spoken of.

In their antiphonies the verbal noun in 홈 with 이여 in the first part and 이로다 in the second part will be very common. Verse after verse of their poetry will continue down with 홈이여 for the end of the first half of the verse, and 홈이로다 for the second half.

Questions and soliloquies are poetically put with forms of 호논고, 홀고 and the ending in 가. Exclamations are not unfrequently given with the forms 인뎌 and 진뎌.

It is a pity that in most of our hymnology next to no attention has been paid to proper poetical forms, but this of course, will come in time. It should also be borne in mind that Korean poetry does not commonly follow the foreign plans of four lines following each other but as a rule has two lines each, two lines above, and two lines below. Whether this should be introduced in our hymnology time alone will show but it is to be hoped that some of the students of Korean will make a special study of the poetic forms.

III. Book forms.

It may possibly be in the book forms that the student will find his greatest difficulty especially as he will have considerable to do with these in his reading and preparation of Korean books. One of the greatest difficulties in the reading of Korean is the lack of punctuation points, capitalization or any thing whatever, to mark the breaks in speech and consequently, as we pick up Korean novels or other books that record conversations and describe scenes we are constantly met with what seems to us an absolutely unnecessary repetition of "he said" and "said he," etc, etc through the whole book. It seems almost necessary for the Korean.

Attempts are being made to introduce into Korean certain forms of punctuation, capitalization, etc, etc ; to enable us to have a more intelligent idea of the page of printed matter almost at a glance than can be obtained now. While there are those that claim that there is no punctuation in Korean it should be noticed that the verbal endings of the paragraphs may be said to be the equivalents of punctuation.

The endings 니, 거놀 are said by some to be the equivalent of commas ; 하는지라 and 헌지라 may be said to be the equivalents of a colon or semi-colon, while 하느니라 and 하더라 mark a complete ending.

When there is a series of quotations marking answers back and forth in a conversation 하니 and 하거놀 are very commonly used alternately making the statement and the reply.

The honorific verb in 시 gives us quite often in book

form the verbal participle in 샤 which naturally is the honorific form of a participle in 호여.

The following list of book forms should therefore be carefully studied with the teacher:—호더라 호니라 호더시다 호노라 이로라 이러라 all of which are declarative, and may mark the ending of a complete sentence. In addition to these we should also make a careful study of such forms as these; 호거놀, 호니 일가보냐, 인뎌, 호노니, 호샤, 이닛고, 이니이다, 호니이다, etc.

IV. Letter writing.

In the matter of Korean letter writing all students should endeavor to attain efficiency and the following forms have been prepared and a careful study of the same will we believe be of considerable benefit to the student.

# APPENDIX C.

년 월 일  부답

사룸을 권호여 농ᄉᆞ나 혹 실시 아니 되게호고 공부를 근간히 호여라 이만 긋친다
경영호는 일이 뜻과 굿지못호여 오래 되니 답답호다 졈졈 농시는 집안
나는 디중에 무고호고 쥬인의 후디와 일긔의 온화홈으로 디리 한고의 피로음은 업스나
셔난지 오래 되여 굼굼 무궁호더니 글시보니 무양호고 혼솔이 무고호다호니 다힝이다

## 답 가오셔

년월일 조모 샹셔

무고호오니 복힝이오며 속히 환초호시기 ᄇᆞ라옵고 이만 알외옵ᄂᆞ이다
모 간졀이외이다 쇼ᄌᆞ는 침식이 무양호옵고 어마님씌셔도 안녕히 계시옵고
디즁 귀후 만강호옵시고 보시는 일은 뜻과굿치 잘 되옵고 어ᄂᆞ날즘 환초 호옵실ᄂᆞ지 복
힝ᄎᆞ옵신지 돌포 되오나 문 안 듯잡지 못호와 하졍 답답호오이다 츈일이 부됴호온디

## 아바님 젼 샹셔

아들이 집에 잇셔 부친꾀 호는것

APPENDIX C.

모가 아들 공부간ᄃᆡ

ᄋᆞ희의게

네가 집을 써난지 루일에 무수히 가셔 무양히 잇눈지 쇼식 진시 못 드러 굼굼 갑갑
다 돌포 ᄉᆞ이 ᄃᆡ즁 신샹이 평길ᄒᆞ고 학교 시험에 멋년 급이나 되엿스며 날마다 샹학ᄒᆞ
양ᄒᆞ니 다힝ᄒᆞ다 그리온 회포 무궁ᄒᆞ나 ᄇᆞ라눈거슨 네가 공부를 독실히 ᄒᆞ야 속속히 졸
업ᄒᆞ고 도라와 일반 쳥년의 ᄉᆞ표 되기를 간졀히 ᄇᆞ란다 ᄉᆞ연 무궁ᄒᆞ나 로망으로 이만
굿치니 희외 풍셜에 몸을 조심 보호ᄒᆞ고 근면ᄒᆞ여 공부ᄒᆞ기를 ᄇᆞ란다

년 월 일 조모 평신

손ᄌᆞ가 외국 류학ᄒᆞ눈ᄃᆡ

손ᄋᆞ의게

너를 유치 ᄋᆞ희로 알고 일시라도 눈 압헤 업스면 천금을 일흔듯ᄒᆞ던 바로 히외에 분리
ᄒᆞ니 창결훈 심회를 지밀노다 그록 못ᄒᆞ겟다 멀고 먼 슈로에 무ᄉᆞ 득달ᄒᆞ야 희풍에
샹훈 즁셰나 업스며 려관 슉식에 음식이 덕구 ᄒᆞ지 스려 만만일다 나눈 병은 업스나 네
가 집에 업슨 후로 쥬야 실혼ᄒᆞ듯ᄒᆞ다 너의 조무쎠셔 안강ᄒᆞ시고 너의 부모 형뎨도 무

APPENDIX C.    443

년 월 일 쥬 (아모)    샹셔

그리 강녕 ㅎ옵시기를 축슈 ㅎ옵ᄂ이다

레를 폐ㅎ옵고 가스를 불고 ㅎ오니 하졀에 죄송 ㅎ와이다 이만 알외오며 리리

극난ㅎ울듯 쥬야 근심이오며 졔몸의 공부를 위ㅎ와 년만ㅎ신 조부모와 양당에 신혼의

무탈ㅎ옵고 학교 시험에 드러와 민일 샹학ㅎ오나 과졍이 다단ㅎ와 둔질 용지로 졸업이

각 집이 균안ㅎ시며 동성 쇼으들도 무양ㅎ오니 복힝이오며 무스도 착ㅎ와 침식이

시즁 긔후 만강ㅎ옵시고 할아바님 두분 톄졀이 만강ㅎ옵시며 아바님 긔톄 강왕ㅎ시고

무러 온지 돌포 되와 하회 셥셥ㅎ옵더니 하셔 밧자와 복회 만만이오며 이 동안

## 어마님젼 샹답셔

년 월 일 모    평신

아니ㅎ다 너는 가루 념려는 말고 공부를 독실히ㅎ기 밋고 브란다

쇠셔도 만안ㅎ시고 가너가 다 무고ㅎ며 으히들도 충실ㅎ니 만힝일다 대쇼 가스의 말은

눈지 여러 가지로 굼굼ㅎ다 여긔는 할아바님 두분 침슈 만안ㅎ시고 너의 대인(아바지)

년 월 일 　모

를 부란다

긔 효셩이 업슬듯ᄒᆞ다 심요 이만 긋치니 릭릭 시봉 평길ᄒᆞ고 삼가 조심ᄒᆞ여 잘지내기

다 민일 근간히 조심ᄒᆞ야 효봉 슝슌ᄒᆞ여 싀가의 칭예를 듯는다ᄒᆞ는 말을 드르면 이 밧

이 간절ᄒᆞ야 닛지 못ᄒᆞ는중 미진훈 인ᄉᆞ로 구당의 걱정이나 아니 듯는지 ᄉᆞ려 만단일

ᄒᆞ시고 너의 대인 지(아바) 안강ᄒᆞ시고 으히들이 무양ᄒᆞ나 다힝ᄒᆞ나 나는 쥬쇼간에 네 셩각

ᄒᆞ시며 각되이 일안들ᄒᆞ시냐 향념 무궁ᄒᆞ다 시솔(시하면 셩솔이나 / 시솔이라 칭홈) 무고ᄒᆞ고 할아바님 안녕

시봉(조부 ᄒᆞ시봉이라 홈) ᄒᆞ시며 신샹이 평길ᄒᆞ고 량 대 존후 만강ᄒᆞ시며 셔탕 형뎨 남미 분도 평안

ᄉᆞ며 그후 돌포 되여 굼굼ᄒᆞ기 우편으로 두어 ᄌᆞ 붓친다 근일 일긔(그ᄉᆡ 일긔 대로 홀것 부됴훈되)

홀쳐 보낸후 즐연 셥셥ᄒᆞ기 지필노 다 긔록 못ᄒᆞ겟다 하인 회편에 글시 보고 ᄀᆞ득 반것

아모집 보아라(식집 셩대로 아모 / 집이나 실이 라홈)

모가 ᄯᆞᆯ의게

## APPENDIX C.

지남셕이 바늘을 쓰으는거슨 네브러 지덕이 겸비ᄒᆞᆫ쟈라야 감당ᄒᆞᄂᆞᆫ 바오 실노 대와 것

놈이 나를 쳔거홈을 샤례 평교의게

무를 속히 쳥쟝ᄒᆞ고 도라가 ᄒᆞᆫ가지로 양로ᄒᆞ기를 성각ᄒᆞ노라 이만 긋친다

니 봉양지 졀이야 범연ᄒᆞ랴 샤형은 긱디 범빅이 신산ᄒᆞ나 엇지 피롭다ᄒᆞ겟ᄂᆞ 대뎌 슈

량당 태후 안강ᄒᆞ시다 ᄒᆞ니 만힝이오 가즁이 무고ᄒᆞ니 깃브다 내가 업셔도 네가 잇스

분리ᄒᆞᆫ지 오래 되여 심히 챵연ᄒᆞᆫ 즁 글을 보니 위션 흔회ᄒᆞ며 시즁 신샹이 태평ᄒᆞ고

　　년 월 일 샤형　　답셔

## 답 샤뎨셔

　　년 월 일 샤뎨 (아모)　　샹셔

오며 이만 샹달 ᄒᆞᄂᆞ이다

오래 계심으로 량당의 우려ᄒᆞ심이 김흐시오니 민망ᄒᆞ와이다 속히 환츄 ᄒᆞ옵시기를 브라

이다 샤메는 량당 긔력 뭇잡지 안코 각졀 일안 ᄒᆞ시오니 다힝이오나 형님씌셔 긱디에

긔후 만안 ᄒᆞ옵시고 경영ᄒᆞ시ᄂᆞᆫ 일은 예산과 굿치 될듯ᄒᆞ오닛가 두루 복념 간졀 ᄒᆞ와

써나신 후로 풍일이 불슌ᄒᆞ온뒤 엇더케 득달ᄒᆞ셧스며 쎄치시ᄂᆞᆫ즁에

## 형님젼 샹셔

　　남ᄌᆞ 형뎨간

# 샹셔

## ᄉ데간 왕복

그 태후 만안ᄒᆞ읍신지 복모 간절ᄒᆞ오며 대죠는 친후가 셔즁으로 여러 날 미녕ᄒᆞ시와 초
방학시 하직ᄒᆞ온 후 문안 모로와 하회 셥셥ᄒᆞ오며 로염(老炎)이 심ᄒᆞ온디 이째

### 년월일 대(아모) 비

기두리오 이와ᄀᆞᆺ치 파도ᄒᆞᆫ 칭예를 밧으오니 붓그럽슙ᄂᆞ이다
째ᄉᆞ지 침톄ᄒᆞ심을 사름마다 미우 가셕히 아는 바여늘 엇지 다만 대의 구구ᄒᆞᆫ 포양을
빅옥이 엇지 영영 흠에 뭇치고 ᄡᅳ이는 바― 되지아니ᄒᆞ리오 형의 넉넉ᄒᆞ신 포부로 이

### 답

### 년월일 대(아모) 비

지닛ᄉᆞ 오릿가 죵ᄎᆞ 가셔 뵈오려니와 위션 두어 쥬로 치사ᄒᆞ옵ᄂᆞ이다
감당을 눈지 두렵ᄉᆞ온즁 이로 좃차 흉업의 긔초를 셰움이 만힘이와다 몽민 즁인들 엇
산파ᄀᆞᆺ치 놉고 바다ᄀᆞᆺ치 깁혼지라 엇지 다 감샤ᄒᆞᆼ오릿가 그러나 형의 념려대로 가히
치 용렬ᄒᆞᆫ 쟈의 닐을 바는 아니어늘 형이 놋비아지 아니ᄒᆞ시고 과도히 쳔망ᄒᆞ신 은혜

APPENDIX C.

르오니 하정에 황송ᄒᆞᆫ 말솜 다 알외올수업ᄉᆞ오며 로양 여에 련ᄒᆞᆸ업셔 힝초ᄒᆞᆸ신지 둘이 지내ᄋᆞᆸ도록 샹셔치 못ᄒᆞᆸ고 하셔도 밧잡지 못ᄒᆞ와 이ᄶᅢᄉᆞ지 문안모

## 부쥬젼 샹빅시
### 아ᄃᆞᆯ이 긱리에 계신 부친ᄭᅴᄒᆞᄂᆞᆫ 셔식

년 월 일 졍말 (셩명) 돈

지내 노라
도 셤셤ᄒᆞ도다 졍말(情末)은 아직 ᄒᆞᆫ 모양이나 학교 법빅이 여의치 못ᄒᆞ야 날노 슈란이
이로다 슈유는 긔별대로 허ᄒᆞ야 주나 긔학 시에 궐셕ᄒᆞᆷ도 민망ᄒᆞ고 진시 맛나지 못ᄒᆞᆷ
친환으로 초민히 지내시는 일 듯기 너머 놀나오며 무슨 약이나 써 드리는지 소ᄒᆞᆫ 향념
심훈 더위에 성각이 민양 간졀ᄒᆞ더니 졍찰 보고 깃부나

### 답

년 월 일 며ᄌ (셩명) 샹셔
쳥유ᄒᆞ오니 하량ᄒᆞ오셔 일쥬일 슈유를 주시와 친환을 구호케 ᄒᆞᆸ시기 ᄇᆞ라ᄂᆞ이다
민훈온 졍ᄉᆞ가 겻흘 써날 길이 업ᄉᆞ옴으로 츄긔 긔학에 진시 참예치 못ᄒᆞ올듯 ᄒᆞᆸ기

답 가온셔

년 월 일 조 모 샹셔

로가 불가흐야 우금수지 음식이 슌하치 못흠으로 병이 절노 싱기눈즁 불일이 헛튼 머
흐니 이보다 더 즐거온 일이 쏘 어듸 잇겟누냐 이제는 모음이 노힌다 부는 이 곳에 슈
대방 제졀이 안녕ᄒ옵시며 네 주당쯰셔도 범졀이 일안ᄒ시고 너의 형데 남미도 츙건ᄒ다
업ᄂᆫ즁에
흐즈도 못붓쳐 조민흔 심회를 진뎡치 못ᄒ던 초에 네 슈셔를 밧아 보니 반갑기 측량
집을 써난지 수쟉이 갓갑도록 총요흔 일에 억미여 잠시도 한목을 엇지 못흠으로 편지
ᄒ셔로 조쳐ᄒ게 ᄒᆞ교ᄒ옵 심을 복망ᄒ옵ᄂᆞ이다 여불비샹달
파ᄒ을 도리를 차리겟숩ᄂᆞ이다 세쇄흔 말솜은 협지에 모다 알외오니 하감ᄒ옵신 후 곳
니 복힝이외다 조모님 긔톄와 주친쯰옵셔 제졀이 젼졍이 군졸 ᄒ오니 속히 분부를 무러야 됴
ᄒ셩이외다 근일 곡가가 졈졈ᄒ옵고
긔톄후 안녕ᄒ옵시고 보시옵ᄂᆞᆫ 일이 신속히 타협이 나겟숩ᄂᆞᆺ가 복모 원념ᄒ와 불임

APPENDIX C.    449

못ᄒᆞᆫ이쌔에

솝ᄂᆞ이다 못ᄎᆞᆷ 신편이 잇습기 두어즈 알외오며 가을 긔운은 졈졈 놉ᄉᆞ온뒤 슬피옵지

알겟습ᄂᆞ잇가 샹셔나 붓치려ᄒᆞ온들 먼 길에 인편이 간단ᄒᆞ오니 억울ᄒᆞᆫ 수졍도 펼수업

당ᄒᆞ오매 미양 문을 셔난 회포를 견듸지 못ᄒᆞ와 비감ᄒᆞ 눈물이 옷깃슬 젹시 눈줄 누가

아바님 슬하를 써나 외로히 이곳에 와셔 잇ᄉᆞ온지 거연히 츈하를 다 지내옵고 이 ᄶᆡ를

## 츌가ᄒᆞᆫ ᄯᆞᆯ이 친뎡 부친ᄭᅴ ᄒᆞ는 셔식

년 월 일 부   답셔

방심말고 아비 도라갈 ᄯᆡ를 기두려라 놈은 말은 총요ᄒᆞ여 이만긋친다

거던 김 아모의게 가셔 말ᄒᆞ면 얼마 던지 뒤여주리라 내가 써난 ᄯᆡ에 부탁ᄒᆞ엿다 부듸

대방에 효셩을 극진히ᄒᆞ야 아모됴록 병환 나지아니시게 ᄒᆞ여라 량도와 용젼이 부족ᄒᆞ

내가 어ᄂᆞᄶᆡ 도라 가던지 그동안 여젼히 집을 보젼ᄒᆞ고 불초ᄒᆞᆫ 아비디신

더기 두려 귀덩이 나지 아니ᄒᆞᆯ 모양이면 소세 박부득이 다 물니처 ᄇᆞ리고 갈밧긔 업다

리 못ᄒᆞ야 취셔가 망연ᄒᆞᆫ즉 집에 도라갈 긔한이 부지하셰월이다 아모리 싱각ᄒᆞ여도 좀

## 쌀의게 답셔

년 월 일 녀식 샹빅시

(지면에는 아바님젼 샹술)이라고 쓰는법

안후나 알게ᄒ시옵쇼셔

이만 알외오니 회편에 하셔나 곳 븟치시와 위션

량당 슬하에 환요ᄒ옵ᄂᆞᆫ 즐거옴 엇기를 쳔만 북망ᄒ옵ᄂᆞ이다 븟슬 잡을 겨를이 업소와

하촉ᄒ시옵쇼셔 어셔 밧비 가셔 여러 남미로 더브러

친뎡 부모씌옵셔 싀가 구고씌 보내 주시기 쳥ᄒ옵ᄂᆞᆫ 왕복이 잇서야 되겟ᄉᆞ오니 일직

틱이 오며 어ᄂᆞ 째에나 드려 가시랴 ᄒ심ᄂᆞᆫ잇가 일일이 삼츄 ᄀᆞᆺ ᄉᆞ오니 친가 근힝ᄒ옵기는

복력 불이옵ᄂᆞ이다 녀식은 존당 텨후 일안ᄒ시고 혼도가 균길ᄒ오니 하념ᄒ옵시ᄂᆞᆫ 덕

그태후 일형만안ᄒ옵시고 어마님 졔졀 강건ᄒ옵시며 오라비와 동성들이 무양ᄒ오닛가

# APPENDIX C.

아바님젼 샹술이
쥬부가 친뎡에셔 싀부께 샹셔ᄒᆞᄂᆞᆫ 셔식

긔톄후 만안ᄒᆞ옵시고 어마님 졔졀 안녕ᄒᆞ옵시며 대도가 즁길ᄒᆞ시오닛가 복모 불이옵
알외오며 츈일이 화창ᄒᆞ온되 련ᄒᆞ옵셔
우톄가 머너 잇고 인편이 간단ᄒᆞ와 오래 샹셔치 못ᄒᆞ니 하졍에 죄송ᄒᆞ온 말솜 엇지다

년 월 일 친부 답셔

편지 볼 ᄉᆞ이도 업슬듯ᄒᆞ기에 이만 긋친다
슨니 힝이나 너의 모친이 너를 보고 십허 더욱 셩화ᄒᆞ니 오기는 속히 와야 ᄒᆞ겟다 지리히
둔녀 가셔 효양 부모ᄒᆞ고 승슌 군쥬ᄒᆞ야 부도를 극진히ᄒᆞ여라 친가에셔는 아직 별고 업
실수 업는고로 드리러 보내겟다마는 친가에 와셔 오래 잇는 법도 업는거시니 잠시
모가 네 부모요 친뎡 부모는 다 쓸디 업ᄂᆞ니라 출가ᄒᆞᆫ 후 친뎡에 근친 멧번
거시니 그러나 녀ᄌᆞ가 되여 나셔 출가ᄒᆞ매 싀가이 네 집이오 싀부
시보니 반갑기 츙냥 업다 이 회편에 너의 싀부의 편지 곳 붓치고 멧철 후에 드리러 보낼
라 청ᄒᆞᆫ 후에 곳 뒤좃차 두고 올거슬 초려 보내라 ᄒᆞ엿더니 못ᄎᆞᆷ 신편이 잇기 무고ᄒᆞᆫ 글

년 월 일 식부 답셔

다 총요ᄒᆞ야 다 못 젹는다

병환도 나ᄒᆞ시겟다 부듸 속히 오게ᄒᆞ여라 너의 친뎡 어루신네씌도 셔ᄌᆞ로 말슴 엿주엇

민망ᄒᆞ다 네가 어셔 와셔 졔반ᄉᆞ를 모도 솔펴야 집안 살님 모양도 되고 너의 어마

아직 혼솔이 무고ᄒᆞ니 힘이나 너의 싀모ᄭᅴ셔 속 병으로 다일 피로히 지내시니 보기에

십혼 ᄉᆡᆼ각 진뎡키 어렵던 ᄎᆞ에 무고히 잇셔 친당 시봉 일안ᄒᆞᆫ일 흔위 무량일다 시부는

네가 귀뎡ᄒᆞᆫ지 ᄌᆞ못 날이 오래매 아릿ᄃᆞ온 용모가 눈 가온듸 미여 잇셔 쥬소로 보고

## 답 ᄌᆞ부셔

년 월 일 ᄌᆞ부 샹술이

그 뒤후 강건ᄒᆞ옵심 쳔만 복망 ᄒᆞ옵ᄂᆞ니다

외오며 뒤뒤

ᄒᆞ오니 익휼ᄒᆞ심을 더ᄒᆞ옵셔 불효의 허믈을 용셔ᄒᆞ시옵쇼셔 인젼이 총총ᄒᆞ와 뇟비 알

와 뎡셩을 팡궐ᄒᆞ오니 불효 막대 ᄒᆞ온지라 녀름 날이 되기 젼에 다시 나아가셔 뫼시랴

지 못ᄒᆞ옵ᄂᆞ이다 ᄌᆞ부는 친뎡 졔졀이 태평 ᄒᆞ시오니 ᄉᆞ힝이오나 몸이 친가에 오래 류ᄒᆞ

# ENGLISH INDEX.

N.B.—Numbers in ordinary types refer to Paragraphs in Part I. Heavy faced types refer to Part II.

## A

Ability, Expressed by............ —
  수, 법 with 이쇼 ............... 222
  만 with 호오 .................... 222
  **Chap. I. ? III., Sec. 7.**
About ....................................
  **Chap. VII. ? III. Sec. 11.**
Above, over ........................... 113
  **Chap. IX. Sec. 2 and 20.**
Abstract, nouns in 흠 ............ 53
  **Chap. II.**
According to, in accordance with —
  **Chap. IX. Sec. 22.**
Accordingly ........................... —
  **Chap. VII. ? III. Sec. 2.**
Across ................................... 113
  **Chap. IX. Sec. 11.**
Adjectives .........Chap. VIII.
  **Chap. VI.**
  Comparison of ...................250ff
    **Chap. VI. ? II.**
  Avoidance of...................... 250
    **Chap. VI. ? II. Sec. 1.**
  Comparative ........ 251, 252, 253
    **Chap. VI. ? II. Sec. 1.**
  Superlative ...................... 254
    **Chap. VI. ? II. Sec. 2.**
  Classification of.................. 243
    **Chap. V.**
  Neuter verbs...................... 244
  Nouns as adjectives ............ 249
  Position in Sentence ......... 282
    **Chap. VI. ? I. Sec. I.**

  Predicate form of .........244, 245
    **Chap. VI. ? I. Sec. 2.**
  Pronominal......................59ff
    **Chap. V.**
  Sinico-Korean .................... 243
  Use of 보다, 보덤, 에서 in
    comparison ............252, 253
    **Chap. VI. ? II. Sec. 1.**
  Wrong use of 브터, 보텀 ... 233
Adverbs ...............Chap. IX. 255
  **Chap. VII.**
  Classification of................... 255
  Comparison of ................... 261
    **Chap. VI. ? II.**
  Derived.
    ,,   from Verbs...256, 257, 258
    ,,   in 게 and 이............ 258
    ,,   from Nouns............ 260
  Position in Sentence ......... 282
  Primitive ................. 255, 262
  Responsives ............... 265, 266
  Verbal Participle used as ... 259
After, Since .................. 111, 260
  **Chap. VII. ? II. Sec. 26.**
Again .................................... 255
  **Chap. VII. ? II. Sec. 8.**
Agency, Nouns of.................... 52
Ago ..................................... 255
  **Chap. VII. ? II. Sec. 18.**
All ........................................ 70
  **Chap. V. Sec. 8.**
Almost ................................. 224

## ENGLISH INDEX.

**Chap. VII. & III. Sec. 10.**
Alphabet, Korean ............... 13ff
Consonants ............... 14, 28, 38
„  Aspirated ......... 39
„  Names of ......... 40
Sounds; its ..................... 15ff
Vowels ....................... 14-22
Already ........................... —
**Chap. VII. & II. Sec. 14.**
Also, too ..................... 267
**Chap. X. Sec. 3.**
Although..182, 189, 190, 196, 198, 270
**Chap. X. Sec. 5.**
Always ........................... —
**Chap. VII. & II. Sec. 1.**
Am, are ........................... —
**Chap. I. & III. Sec. 1.**
Among............................. —
**Chap. IX. Sec. 12.**
And............ 182, 194, 200, 267, 268
**Chap. X. Sec. 1.**
Another, other ................... 70

Any ............................... 69
**Chap. V. Sec. 5.**
Around | ........................... —
**Chap. IX. Sec. 13.**
Article:
  Definite ..................... 43
  **Chap. III.**
  Indefinite ................... —
  **Chap. III.**
As ............................... —
**Chap. VII. & II. Sec. 11.**
As, like ........................... —
**Chap. VII. & III. Sec. 5.**
At ............ 94, 99, 101, 104, 111
**Chap. IX. Sec. 1.**
At once, directly ................. —
**Chap. VII. & II. Sec. 24.**
Auxiliary Verbs ............ 210, 219
**Chap. I. & III.**

**Chap. V. Sec. 12.**

## B

Basal conjugation............ 127, 179
Bases.
  „  Desiderative ......... 176
  „  Negative ............ 177
Be, to, Verb.
  Auxiliary ..................... 211
  **Chap I. & I.**
Because ...... 111, 113, 182, 186, 187, 188, 270
**Chap. X. Sec. 9.**
Before (place) .............. 111, 112
**Chap. IX. Sec. 15.**
Before (time) ............. 111, 260
**Chap. VII. & II. Sec. 25.**

Behind ............................ 111
**Chap. IX. Sec. 15.**
Below ....................... 111, 112
**Chap. IX. Sec. 21.**
Besides ........................... —
**Chap. IX. Sec. 18.**
Between ........................... —
**Chap. IX. Sec. 16.**
Beyond ..................... 113, 259
**Chap. IX. Sec. 11.**
Book Language.
  Diff. Verbal Termination of. 6
  **Appendix B. III.**
Both, either, neither ............ —
**Chap. V. Sec. 2.**

ENGLISH INDEX.       455

*Both, and* (conj.) .................. 267
   **Chap. X. Sec. 2.**
*But* (conj.) ............ 182, 191, 267
   **Chap. X. Sec. 4.**
*But* (prep.)................................ 94
   **Chap. IX. Sec. 18.**

*By and by* ............................ 202
   **Chap. VII. ¿ II. Sec. 22.**
*By, through* ............... 94, 101, 102
   **Chap. IX. Sec. 6.**

# C

*Can, could* ................. 221, 222
   **Chap. I. ¿ III. Sec. 7.**
*Cardinal Numbers* ................. 76
Case Endings.
  „ Lack of ...................... 42
  „ Postpositions as ............ 44
   **Chap. IX.**
Causative voice ...... 121, 122, 123
Chinese, Relation to Korean ... 7
Classifiers, specific ............... 77
   **Chap. VII.**
Comparison of adjectives ...... 251
   **Chap. VI. ¿ II.**
Comparison of adverbs ......... 261
Composite Postpositions... 111, 112
   **Chap. IX.**
Compound Nouns.................. 51
Compound Verbs................... 158
Conciseness ....................... 10
Conditional Sentences ............ 183
   **Chap. I. ¿ VI. Chap. X.**
   **Sec. 8.**
  „ 을 with verbal participle 105
Conjugation, Basal ........ 127, 179
Conjunctions ............ Chap. X.
   **Chap. X.**

Classification of ............... 267
Co-ordinate ......... 267, 268, 269
   **Chap. X. Sec. 1, 2a.**
Distributive use, of 고, 며... 184,
                                   200, 268
   **Chap. X.**
Phrases as ....................... 270
Position in Sentence ......... 282
   **Chap. X.**
Conjunctions (Cont.)
Subordinate ..................... 270
   **Chap. X.**
With verbs ..................... 181ff
   **Chap. X.**
Meaning and uses with verbs
  see verbs with conj.
*Consequently.*
   **Chap. VII. ¿ III. Sec. 2.**
Consonants.......................... 14
 „ Aspirated ......... 28-39
 „ Doubled ............... 28
 „ Euphonic Changes in 29
 „ Names of ............... 40
 „ Pronunciation of... 30-39
Continued future tense ......... 135
Contraction of verbs......... 230-241

# D

Days of month.................. 83, 84
Declarative Terminations ...... 138,
                             139, 140

Declension, lack of ......... 42, 44
 „ a form of ......................
 „ for nouns ............... 44

456 ENGLISH INDEX.

a form for pronouns ......... 62
Demonstrative pronouns ... 71, 72
 Chap. V. Sec. 1.
Derived adverbs.
 „ from Nouns............. 260
 „ from Verbs ...... 256-259
Desiderative Base ............... 176
Dipthongs ....................... 23-27

Directly, at once.
 Chap. VII. § II. Sec. 24.
Distributive Pronouns ...... 69, 70
 Chap. V. Sec. 2ff.
Do, did ................................. 211
 Chap. I. § III. Sec. 3.
During.
 Chap. IX. Sec. 17.

## E

Each .............................. 65, 70
 Chap. V. Sec. 3.
Either, neither, both.
 Chap. V. Sec. 2.
Either, or (conj.). 182, 189, 192, 267
 Chap. X. Sec. 6.
Elliptical forms ............ 230ff 287
Emphasis.
 „ Change of Order, by. 283
 „ Postposition ᄂ by
 use of ........................... 105
Enough. .................................. —
 Chap. V. Sec. 18.
Eromun.
 (see önmun).
Euphony ............................... —

Appendix "A" on Phonetics.
 „ Adverbial changes ... 256
 „ Consonantal ......... 89
 „ Postpositions, effect on.............................. 42
Euphong Pronominal changes. 29
Even ..................................... —
 Chap. VII. § III. Sec. 9.
Ever, never ........................... —
 Chap. VII. § II Sec. 7.
Every ................................. 70
 Chap. V. Sec. 6.
Except ................................. —
 Chap. IX. Sec. 18.

## F

Few ...................................... —
 Chap. V. Sec. 10.
Finally, at last ...................... —
 Chap. VII. § II. Sec. 29.
For ......... 94, 102, 111, 112, 113
 Chap. IX. Sec. 10.
Formerly, used to .................. —
 Chap. VII. § II. Sec. 15.

Fractions ............................. 86
Frequently, often ................. —
 Chap. VII. § II Sec. 4.
From, out of, off ......... 94, 104, 106
 Chap. IX. Sec. 5.
Future past tense................. 134
Future tense................. 134, 140
 Chap. I. § III. Sec. 5.

# G

Gender ..................... 45
  „ Exactness, lack of ... 43
  „ Expressed by Specific Particles ...................... 45

Generally, usually ................. —
  Chap. VII. § II. Sec. 3.
Get........................................ —
  „ Causative ............... —
  Chap. I. § III. Sec. 9.

# H

Half-talk ... 138, 140, 141, 144, 145
Have to, Verb ..................... —
  Chap. I. § II.
  As Auxiliary ................... —
  Chap. I. § III. Sec. 4.
Causative sense.................... —
  { Chap. I. § III. Sec. 9.
  { Chap. I. § II.
Here ................................. 262
  Chap. VII. § I Sec. 1.
Hitherto ............................. —
  Chap. VII. § II. Sec. 16.
Honorifics 12............. Chap. XI.
  „ Construction of Hon. Verbs ............ 272, 273

Honorifics, Importance of Use of ..................... 271. 280
  „ Specific Hon. Nouns 278
  „ Specific Hon. Verbs. 274, 275
  „ Terminations... 138ff 276
  „ Terms for Servants etc. ........................... 280
Honorifics Verbs Honoring Object ....................... 275
Honorifics Verbs Honoring Subject ....................... 274
Honorifics Two Combined ...... 276
Hope, wish ..................... 217
  Chap. I. § III. Sec. 15.
How ................................. —
  Chap. VII. § III. Sec. 3.

# I

If, unless ............ 182, 185, 267
  Chap. X. Sec. 8.
Imperative ....................... 148
  „ terminations ......... 145
  „ verb .................... 229
Impersonality of Verb ......... 115
In ........................... 94, 101
  Chap. IX. Sec. 2.
Indefiniteness of Speech ... 10, 285, 288
Indefinite Pronouns. 66, 67, 68, 69
  Chap. V.

Indicative Mood ... 147, 179, 180
Indirect Discourse ............... —
  „ Verbs in ......... 228, 229
Infinitive ........................... —
  Chap. I. § IV.
Instead of ................... 111, 112
  Chap. IX. Sec. 19.
Intend ............................. —
  Chap. I. § III. Sec. 13.
Interrogative Pronouns...... 66, 67, 68, 69, 70
  Chap. IV. § III.

# ENGLISH INDEX.

## J

Just now ............................................. —
    Chap. VII. § II. Sec. 19.

## K

Korean, Adjectives ............... 243
Korean, Calendar......... 82, 83, 84
Korean, Money ............... 79, 80
Korean, Relation to Chinese ... 7

## L

Last at; finally ..................... —
    Chap. VII. § II. Sec. 29.
Late of; recently ................. —
    Chap. VII. § II. Sec. 17.
Let ..................................... 144
    Chap. I. § III. Sec. 9.
Like, as ............................... —
    Chap. VII. § III. Sec. 5.

Little while, a ........................ —
    Chap. VII. § II. Sec. 29.
Long time, long ..................... —
    Chap. VII. § II. Sec. 27.
Look, seem ............... 221, 225, 226
    Chap. I. § III. Sec. 17.

## M

Make (causative) ..................... —
    Chap. I. § III. Sec. 9.
Many ................................... —
    Chap. V. Sec. 15.
May, might ........................... —
    Chap. I. § III. Sec. 8.
Measures ........................ 90, 91
Memorizing, necessity of......... 5
Money, Korean ............... 78, 80
Moods................................... —
    Indicative ......... 147, 179, 180
    Volitive ...... 117, 148, 179, 180

Months, names of............... 82
More ............ 231, 232, 253, 261
    Chap. V. Sec. 16.
More—the more .................. 227
Most ................................... 254
    Chap. V. Sec. 17.
Much ................................... —
    Chap. V. Sec. 14.
Multiples ................ 87, 88, 89
Must ........................... 153, 154
    Chap. I. § III. Sec. 10.

## N

Names, plurality of............... 55
Native, grammarians ............ 11
Need ................................... —
    Chap. I. § III. Sec. 16.

Negative.
    „   Base ............... 177
    „   Difference between 안
       and 못 ........................ 206

# ENGLISH INDEX.

Negative Formation of Neg.
Verb. .................................. 207
Negative Response to Neg.
Quest. .................................. 265
Negative Use of Double Neg.... 286
„ Verb 마오 ............ 208
*Note.*—For negatives of English anxiliaries see desired verb under *auxiliary Verbs*.
    **Part II. Chap. I. § III.**
*Neither, either, both* (adj.) ......... —
    **Chap. V. Sec. 2.**
*Neither, nor* (conj.)..................... —
    **Chap. IX. Sec. 7.**
*Never, ever* ............................ —
    **Chap. VII. § II. Sec. 7.**
Neuter .................................. —
  „ Verbs as Adj... 119, 120, 244
    **Chap. VI. § I. Sec. 1, 2.**
*No, none, nobody*..................... —
    **Chap. V. Sec. 7.**
Nouns .................................. 42
    **Chap. II.**
Nouns Abstract in ㅁ ............ 53
    **Chap. II.**
Nouns As Adjectives ............ 249
  „ Agency, of ............ 52
  „ Compound ............ 51
  „ Gender, in ............ 45
  „ Indeclinable ......... 42
Nouns (cont.).
  „ Number ............... 43
  „ Position in Sentence. 282

Nouns (cont.).
  „ Proper ............... 54, 55
  „ Reduplication ...... 48
  „ Verbal in 흠 ...... 53, 171
  „ „ in 기... 33, 172
  „ „ with p.p. 는.. 173
  „ „ with p.p. 에.. 174
  „ „ with p.p. 로.. 175
*Now* .................................. 255
    **Chap. VII. § II. Sec. 13.**
Number .................. 43, 46, 47
  „ Distinction, lack of... 43
  „ Specific Words for Plural ............................ 50
Numeral Adverbs..................... 263
Numerals ........................... 74 ff
    **Chap. VIII.**
Numerals Adjectives, as ......... 74
  „ Cardinal ............ 76
  „ Classifiers, Specific. 75, 77
    **Chap. VIII.**
Numerals Fractions ............... 86
  „ Korean ......... 74, 76
    **Chap. VIII.**
  „ Measures ......... 90, 91
  „ Money ......... 79, 80
  „ Multiples ...... 87, 88, 89
  „ Ordinal............... 81
  „ Sinico-Korean...... 74, 76
    **Chap VIII.**
Numerals Substantives as ...... 74
  .. Times and Season ... 8
        82, 83, 84, 85
Weights..................................... 91

# O

*Of* ........................... 94, 98
    **Chap. IX. Sec. 9.**
*Off, out of, from* ......... 94, 104, 106
    **Chap. IX. Sec. 5.**

*Often, frequently*..................... —
    **Chap. VII. § II. Sec. 4.**
*On* ......... 94, 101, 111, 112, 113
    **Chap. IX. Sec. 3.**

*One, ones* ........................... —
    Chap. V. Sec. 2.
*Only* ..................... 94, 108, 255
    Chap. VII. ¿ III. Sec. 7.
Önmum ............................ 7, 8
Ordinal Numbers ................. 81
*Other, another* ..................... 70
    Chap. V. Sec. 12.

*Ought, should* ............... 221, 223
    Chap. I. ¿ III. Sec. 11.
*Out of, off, from* ........ 94, 104, 106
    Chap. IX. Sec. 5.
*Over, across* ...................... 113
    Chap. IX. Sec. 11.
*Over, above* ......................... 111
    Chap. IX. Sec. 20.

## P

Paradigm .................. 179, 180
Participles.
  Classification of ............ 146
  Distinction between part, in
  어 and 아 non-existent ... 151
Participles Relative ......... 160-169
  ,,  Verbal ............ 150-158
  ,,  ,,  with post-
positions ................. 153, 154
Particle ............................. —
  ,,  Progressive, in 더 ... 132
Parts of Speech.
  ,,  Classification of ............ 11
Passive, construction.
    Chap. I. ¿ V.
Passive, voice ............... 121, 122
    Chap. I. ¿ V.
Passive Avoidance of ............ 124
    Chap. I. ¿ V.
Past tense ......................... 134
Perfected Past tense ............ 134
Persons in verb.
  ,,  forms in 노라, 마 ... 118
  ,,  non-existence ......... 115
Phrases as Conjunctions ......... 270
Pluperfect tense ................. 135
Possessive .................... 94, 98
    Chap. IX. Sec. 9.
Postpositions .................. 93*ff*
    Chap. IX.

Postpositions Case endings as. 44, 94
  ,,  Classification of ...... 93
  ,,  Composite ...... 111, 112
  ,,  Euphonic changes in. 95
  ,,  는 with verbs giving
Condition ........................ 105
Postpositions Position in Sen-
tence ............................ 282
    Chap. IX. Introduction.
Postpositions Simple ... 94. 96-110
  Verbal ........................ 113
Prepositions ....................... —
    Chap. IX.
Present tense .................... 134
Primitive Adverbs ......... 255, 262
    Chap. VII.
Principal parts of verb ... 178, 242
Probable fut.-past tense ......... 135
Probably ......................... 226
Progressive tense ................. 135
Pronominal Adj. ................. 243
    Chap. V.
Pronouns ........................ 59*ff*
    Chap. IV. V.
  Classification of ............ 59
  Demonstrative ........... 71, 72
    Chap. V.
  Distributive ............. 69, 70
    Chap. V.

Euphonic Changes in ......... 62
Indefinite ........................ 66ff
Chap. V.
Interrogative ..................... 66ff
Chap. IV. § III.
Personal ............ 60, 61. 62, 63
Chap. IV. § I.
Personal 1st Person............ 60
,,   2nd   ,,   ...... 61, 62
,,   3rd   ,,   ......... 63
Pronouns (cont.). .................. —
Reflexive ........................ 65
Chap. IV. § I. Sec. 2.

Recently ; of Late.
Chap. VII. § II. Sec. 17.
Reduplication ..................... —
,,    Effects of ............... 43
Reflexive Pronouns ............... 65
Chap. IV. § I. Sec. 2.
Relative Pronouns ............... 73
Chap. IV. § II.
Responsives .................. 265, 266

## S

Same ................................. —
Chap. V. Sec. 13.
Seem, look ................... 221, 225
Chap. I. § III. Sec. 17.
Seldom............................... —
Chap. VII. § II. Sec. 6.
Sentence Structure ............. 281ff
Several ........................... 70
Chap. V. Sec. 9.
Shall, will ................ 134, 140
Chap. I. § III. Sec. 5.
Should, ought ..................... —
,,   obligation ...... 221, 223
Chap. I. § III. Sec. 11.

Relative ................... 73, 164
Chap. IV. § II.
Restricted use of ............... 64
Third Pers. Untranslatable... 63
Pronunciation ..................... —
of Consonants.............. 30-40
of Diphthongs............. 23, 28
To be learned from native... 2
of Vowels ............... 15-22
Proper Nouns ............. 54, 55
Propositive Termination ...... 144

## R

Should, would ..................... —
Chap. I. § VI. Sec. 6.
Should (conditional) ............ 185
Chap. I. § VI.
Simple Postposition...... 94, 96-110
Since, after ...................... —
Chap. VII. § II. Sec. 26.
Sinico-Korean .............. 7, 243
Sinico-Korean adj. ............ 243
So................................... —
Chap. VII. § III. Sec. 4.
Some ...................... 66, 70
Chap. V. Sec. 4.
Sometime ........................... —
Chap. VII. § II. Sec. 28.
Sometimes .......................... —
Chap. VII § II. Sec. 5.
Soon............................ 253
Chap. VII. § II. Sec. 23.
Specific Classifiers................ 77
Specific Honorific Nouns ...... 278
Specific Honorific Verbs... 274, 278
Still... 182, 189, 190, 196, 198, 270
Chap. X. Sec. 5.

# ENGLISH INDEX.

Still, yet (adv.) .................. 255
   **Chap. VII. § II. Sec. 20.**
Subordinate Conjunctions ...... 270
Such, this, that ..................... —
   **Chap. V. Sec. 1.**
Superlative degree ............... —
Superlative of Adjectives ...... 254

   **Chap. VI. § II. Sec. 2.**
  ,, of Adverbs ............ 261
   **Chap. VI. § II. Sec. 2.**
Supine ........................... 170
Suppose, think.
   **Chap. I. § III. Sec. 12.**

## T

Teacher .............................. 2
Tenses ................................ —
  ,, Classification of ............ 133
  ,, Definition of ......... 134, 135
Tense roots ................... 129, 133
Terminations.
  ,, Classification of ...... 137
  ,, Declarative .......... 138, 139, 140
  ,, Definition of ......... 136
  ,, Imperative ............ 145
  ,, Interrogative ......... 141, 142, 143
  ,, Propositive ............ 144
Terms for servants etc. .......... 280
Than ................................... 250
  {**Chap. VI. § II.**
   **Chap. X. Sec. 12.**
That ................................... 270
   **Chap. X. Sec. 11.**
Then (adv.) ............................ —
   **Chap. VII. § II. Sec. 12.**
Then (conj.) ........................... 270
   **Chap. X. Sec. 10.**

There ................................... 72
   **Chap. VII. § I. Sec. 2.**
Therefore ............................. —
   **Chap. VII. § III. Sec. 2.**
Think, suppose ...................... —
   **Chap. I. § III. Sec. 12.**
This, that, such ..................... 71
   **Chap. V. Sec. 1.**
Through, by ............ 94, 101, 102
   **Chap. IX. Sec. 6.**
Times and Seasons ... 82, 83, 84, 85
Till, until, ......................... 107
   **Chap. VII. § II. Sec. 21.**
Titles ................................. 56
To ...... 94, 99, 100, 101, 102, 107
   **Chap. IX. Sec. 4.**
Too (adv.) ........................... 259
   **Chap. VII. § III. Sec. 8.**
Too (conj.) also ................... 267
   **Chap. X. Sec. 3.**

## U

Under ....................... 111, 112
   **Chap. IX. Sec. 21.**
Unless, if ............ 267, 112, 185
   **Chap. IX. Sec. 8.**

Untill, till ......................... 107
   **Chap. VII. § II. Sec. 21.**
Used to, formerly ................. —
   **Chap. VII. § II. Sec. 15.**

# ENGLISH INDEX.

*Usually, generally* ..................... —
    **Chap. VII. § II. Sec. 3.**
Verb ...................... Chap. VII.
    **Chap. I.**
Active............................. 119
Auxiliary ................. 210-219
Bases ............................... —
  Desiderative ..................... 176
  Negative.......................... 177
Volitive .......................... 177
Causative ............ 121, 122, 123
Compound ....................... 158
Conjugation of .................. —
  Basal .................. 127, 179
  Stem ........................... 128
  Tense Roots ............ 129-133
  Future ......................... 131
  Past............................. 130
Conjunctions with ............ 131*ff*
Euphonic changes ............. 183
Meanings and uses of.......... 183*ff*
  도 196; 더 199; 다가 202; 지 197; 지라도 198; 가 197; 거나 192; 거늘 193; 거든 185; 거니와 190; 고만, 고면, 고면 195; 고 200; 고나, 고리오 201; 길너 188; 마는 191; 면 185; 면셔 203; 나 189; 니 186; 닛가 187; 머 194.
Contractions of ............ 234-241
  ᄒᆞ오, 잇쇼, 이오 with certain nouns............... 222, 227
  List of above nouns......... 221
Half-talk ................. 138, 140, 141, 144, 145
Imperative........................ 115
Impersonality of ......... 228, 229
Indirect Discourse; in ...... 146*ff*

Verbs (cont.)....................... —
Moods............................... —
  Indicative ...... 147, 179, 180
  Volitive... 117, 148, 179, 180
  Neuter ................... 119, 120
  Paradigm ............... 179, 180
Particle, progressive in 더 132
Participles ..................... —
  Classification of............... 149
  No distinction between participles in 어 and 아. 151
  Relative ......... 160, 161, 169
  Future ......................... 166
  Future past .................. 167
  Imperfect ..................... 168
  Past ............. 163, 164, 165
  Present ........................ 162
  Verbal..................... 150-154
  Future.......................... 159
  Past ...................... 155, 158
Postpositions with....... 153, 154
Passive ..................... 121, 122
    **Chap. I. § V.**
  Avoidance of.................. 124
    **Chap. I. § V.**
Persons in ........................ —
  found in 노라, 마 ............. 118
  lack of ......................... 115
Position in Sentence ......... 282
Principle Parts ........ 178, 242
Supine ............................ 170
Verbs (cont.).
Tenses............................... —
  Classification of ............ 133
  Continued-Fut. ............... 135
  Future ......................... 134
  Future-Past .................. 134
  Past ............................. —
  Pluperfect .................... 135

Present ............... 134
Probable-Fut.-Past ......... 135
Progressive ............... 135
Tense roots ......... 129-133
Terminations............... —
  Classification of......... 137
  Definition of ............ 136
  Declarative ...... 138, 139, 140
  Imperative............... 145
  Interrogative..... 141, 142, 143

Propositive ............... 144
Verbal Noun.
  „ in 기 ......... 53, 172, 173
  „ with pp. 는 ............ 173
  „  „ pp. 에 ............ 174
  „  „ pp. 로 ............ 175
  „ 홀 ............ 53, 171
Verbal Postposition............... 113
Very ............... 255
  Chap. VII. § III. Sec. 6.

# W

Want ............... 211, 217
  Chap. I. § III. Sec. 14.
Was, were ............... 211
  Chap. I. § III. Sec. 14.
Weights ............... 91
When ............... 260
  Chap. VII. § II. Sec. 9.
Whenever............... —
  Chap. VII. § II. Sec. 2.
Where ............... 262
  Chap. VII. § I. Sec. 3.
Whether ... 182, 189, 192, 197, 267
  Chap. V. Sec. 6.

While ............ 182, 202, 203, 227
  Chap. VII. § II. Sec. 10.
Why ............... 255
  Chap. VII. § III. Sec. 1.
Will, shall ............... 134, 140
  Chap. I. § III. Sec. 5.
Wish, hope ............... —
  Chap. I. § III. Sec. 15.
With ............ 94, 101, 102
  Chap. IX. Sec. 7.
Without ............... —
  Chap. IX. Sec. 8.
Would, should............... —
  Chap. I § III. Sec. 5.

# Y

Yet. still............... —
  Chap. VII. § II. Sec. 20.

# INDEX OF VERBAL FORMS.

Numbers in ordinary type refer to paragraphs in Part I. The heavy faced type refers to Part II.

| | | | |
|---|---|---|---|
| 흐엿거든 | 134, 185 | 흐엿겟느뇨 | 134, 141 (2) |
| 흐야, Verbal Participle | 150ff | 흐엿겟는가 | 134, 109 |
| 흐얌즉흐다 | 215 | 흐엿겟는고 | 134, 197 |
| 흐야셔 | 153 | 흐엿겟는지 | 134, 197 |
| 흐야도 | 196 | 흐엿겟네 | 134, 141 (2) |
| 흐여, Verbal Participle | 150ff | 흐엿겟노 | 134, 141 (5) |
| 흐여야 | 153 | 흐엿겟숩니다 | 134, 138 (7) |
| 흐여이다, Appen. B. I. | — | 흐엿겟슙느잇가 | 134, 141 (8) |
| 흐여가다 | 212 | 흐엿겟스면 | 134, 185 |
| 흐염즉흐온, Hon. rel. part. of verb | 215 | 흐엿겟스닛가 | 134, 141 (8) |
| 흐염즉흐, rel. part. | 215 | 흐엿겟쇼 | 134, 138 (3) |
| 흐염즉흐다 | 215 | 흐엿겟과 | 134, 138 (1) |
| 흐염즉스러온 〉 흐염즉스럽다 ∫ | 215, 216 | 흐엿겟다마는 | 134, 191 |
| 흐여눈 | 153 | 흐엿겟메 | 135 |
| 흐여보아라 〉 흐여보다 〉 흐여보지 ∫ | 213 | probable future past | 138 (2) |
| | | 흐엿겟더이다 | 135, 138 (6) |
| | | 흐엿겟더면 | 135, 185 |
| | | 흐엿겟더냐 | 135, 141 (1) |
| | | 흐엿겟더니 | 135, 186 |
| 흐여라 | 145 | 흐엿겟던잇가 | 135, 141 (8) |
| 흐여서 | 153 | 흐엿겟더뇨 | 135, 141 (2) |
| 흐여서야 | 153 | 흐엿겟던가 | 135, 141, 269 and 197 |
| 흐여셔는 | 153 | 흐엿겟던고 | 135, 197 |
| 흐여든 | 153 | 흐엿겟더라 | 135, 138 |
| 흐여도 | 196 | 흐엿겟지 | 135, 141 (4) |
| 흐엿겟거든... 134 (future-past) | 185 | 흐엿겟지오 | 135, 138 (4) |
| 흐엿겟기에 | 172, 173 | 흐엿겟지마는 | 135, 191 |
| 흐엿겟나 | 134, 189 | 흐엿거나 | 134 (past) 192 |
| 흐엿겟느이다 | 134, 138 (7) | 흐엿거늘 | 134, 193 |
| 흐엿겟느잇가 | 134, 141 (8) | 흐엿거니와 | 134, 190 |
| 흐엿겟느냐 | 134, 141 (1) | 흐엿것마는, =흐엿것마 는 | 134, 191 |

## INDEX OF VERBAL FORMS.

호엿겟느니 ................... 134, 186
호엿겟느닛가 .......... 134, 141 (8)
호엿기 ............................... 172ﬀ
호엿기에 ........................... 174
호엿기가 ........................... 173
호엿기는 ........................... 173
호엿기를 ........................... 173
호엿기로 ........................... 175
호엿길닉 ....................... 134, 188
호엿고나 ..................... 134, 201
호엿나 ......................... 134, 189
호엿나보다 ............ 134, 211, 214
호엿누이다 ............... 134, 138 (7)
호엿누잇가 ............... 134, 141 (8)
호엿누냐 ................... 134, 141 (1)
호엿누니 ................... 134, 141 (1)
호엿누니라 ..................... 134, 140
호엿는잇가=호엿누닛가, q.v. —
호엿누뇨 ................... 134, 141 (2)
호엿는가 ..................... 134, 197
호엿는고 ..................... 134, 197
호엿는고나 ................... 134, 201
호엿는고로 ......... 134, 169 and
  II. Chap. X. Sec. 9. ......... —
호엿는딕 ............. 134, 169, 199
호엿는지 .............. 134, 169, 197
호엿는지라 Book form marking
  a partial break ............... —
호엿네 ........................ 134, 138
호엿노 ................... 134, 141 (5)
호엿노라 .......... 134, 140 and 118
호엿노라고 ........... 134, 140, 228ﬀ
호엿소오니, honorific form of
  호엿스니, q.v. ............... —
호엿소온즉, honorific form of
  호엿슨즉, q. v. ............... —
호엿습고, honorific form of
  호엿고, q. v. ............... —
호엿습니다 ................... 139 (7)

호엿습느잇가 ................... 142 (8)
호엿습는듸 ...................... 139 (8)
호엿습메다 ...................... 135, 140
호엿습메니 ...................... 135, 182
호엿지오 .................... 134, 139 (4)
호엿서도 .................................. 134,

  II. Chap. VII. § II.
    Sec. 7, 2 (c).

호엿섯습니다 ............ 134, 139 (6)
호엿섯소 ................... 134, 139 (3)
호엿섯다 ................... 134, 139 (1)
호엿섯지오 ................ 134, 139 (4)
호엿슴니다, for 호엿습느이다
                                   139 (6)
호엿슴닛가, for 호엿습느잇가
                                   142 (8)
호엿슴메가, contr. for the
  following.
호엿습메니가.................. 135, 143
호엿슬듯호다 ............... 167, 225
호엿스며 ..................... 134, 194
호엿스면 ................134, 183, 185
호엿스나 ..................... 134, 189
호엿스니 ..................... 134, 186
호엿스닛가 ................... 134, 187
호엿스되 ..................... 134, 190
호엿슨들 ..................... 134, 190
호엿슨즉 ..................... 134, 187
호엿스리오 and 호엿스리라
                                 134, 140
호엿슬걸  ⎫
호엿슬거시 ⎬ ..........................
호엿슬것  ⎪
호엿슬거슬 ⎭
호엿슬거시니................. 223, 186
호엿슬거시오 ........... 223, 138 (3)
호엿슬거시니라............. 223, 140
호엿슬거시로듸.............223, 190
호엿슬고 .....................167, 197

## INDEX OF VERBAL FORMS. 467

| | |
|---|---|
| 호엿슬적에 ............... 167, 227 | 호오면 ............... 137, 185 |
| 호엿슬지라도 ............... 167, 198 | 호온 ............... 137, 163 |
| 호엿스티 ............... 134, 190 | 호오나 ............... 137, 189 |
| 호엿쇼 ............... 139 (3) | 호오니 ............... 137, 186 |
| 호엿다 ............... 139, (1) | 호온잇가 ............... 137, 187 |
| 호엿다가 ............... 134, 202 | 호온가 ............... 137, 197 |
| 호엿다고 ............... 134, 228 | 호온티 ............... 137, 199 |
| 호엿다마는 ............... 134, 191 | 호온즉 ............... 137, 187 |
| 호엿다더니, for 호엿다호더니 | 호온지 ............... 137, 197 |
| 호엿에 ............... 134, 138 (2) | 호옵겟습느이다 ...... 137, 134, 141 |
| 호엿답에다, for 호엿다홉에다, | 호옵고 ............... 137, 200 |
| or 호엿다말홉에다 ......... 228 | 호옵니다 ............... 138 (6) |
| 호엿더이다 ............... 135, 140 | 호옵느이다 ............... 138 (6) |
| 호엿더면 ............... 135, 185 | 호옵느잇가 ............... 141 (8) |
| 호엿던ㅣ ............... 135 | 호옵시오 ............... 145 |
| "half talk" for 호엿더냐 | 호옵시고 ............... 137, 200 |
| 호엿더냐 ............... 135, 141 (1) | 호옵신 ............... 137, 163 |
| 호엿더니 ............... 135, 186 | 호옵시닛가 ............... 137, 141 (9) |
| 호엿더닛가} ............... 135, 141 (8) | 호옵시다 ............... 141 (4) |
| 호엿던잇가} | 호옵쇼셔 ............... 137, 145 |
| 호엿더뇨 ............... 135, 141 (2) | 호옵더이다 ............... 140 |
| 호엿던가 ............... 135, 197 | 호옵메다, Contr. for above. |
| 호엿던고 ............... 135, 197 | 호옵더니 ............... 137, 134, 186 |
| 호엿던들 or, 돌 ............... 135, 190 | 호옵던잇가 ............... 143 (4) |
| 호엿더라 ............... 135, 140 | 호옵지오 ............... 137, 138 (4) |
| 호엿도다 ............... 134, 201 | 호오러니와 ............... 137, 176, 190 |
| 호엿지 ............... 142 (4) | 호오리잇가 ............... 137, 143 |
| 호엿지오 ............... 139 (4) | 호오리라 ............... 137, 140 |
| 호엿지마는 ............... 139, 191 | 호오리이다 ............... 137, 140 |
| 호여지이다, or 호여지어다 ... 145 | 호오릿가, Contr. for 호오리잇가 |
| 호여지다 ............... 211ff | 호오티 ............... 137, 190 |
| 호여주다 ............... 211ff | 호셔 ............... 197 |
| 호오 ............... 138.3 | 호게 ............... 159 |
| 히 요, or 호요, Verbal Participle | 호게오 ... 150ff F. V. P. with 이오 |
| with 이오 | 호게호려호다 ......... 159 3rd, 204ff |
| 호와 ............... | 호게호다 ............... 159 3rd |
| 호와이다, Appen. B. I. ......... | 호겟습니다 ............... 134, 138 (7) |
| 호외다, Appen. B. I. ............. | 호게되다 ............... 219 |
| 호오매 ............... 137, 187 | 호겟것마는 ............... 134, 191 |
| 호오여 ............... 137, 194 | 호겟거든 ............... 134, 185 |

# INDEX OF VELBAL FORMS.

하겟기 .................... 172
하겟기에 ................ 172, 174
하겟기가 ................... 172ff
하겟기를 ................... 172ff
하겟기로 ................... 172ff
하겟길늬 ..................... 188
하겟고 ................. 134, 200
하겟고나 ................ 134, 201
하겟나 .................. 134, 189
하겟나보다 ............... 134, 214
하겟노이다 ............. 134, 138 (7)
하겟노잇가 ............ 134, 141 (8)
하겟노냐 ............... 134, 141 (1)
하겟노니 ............... 134, 141 (1)
하겟노니라 .............. 134, 140
하겟는잇가, for 하겟노잇가
하겟는뇨 ............... 134, 141 (2)
하겟는가 ............... 134, 197
하겟는고 ............... 134, 197
하겟는고로 ............... 134, 169

**II. Chap. X. Sec. 9.**

하겟는듸 ............... 134, 199
하겟는지 ............... 134, 197
하겟는지라, Book form of future.
하겟네 ................. 134, 138
하겟니 ................ 134, 141 (1)
하겟스닛가 ............. 134, 187
하겟노 ................ 134, 141 (5)
하겟노라 ......... 134, 140 and 118
하겟습고, Honorific for 하겟고 q. v.
하겟슴니다 ............ 134, 138 (6)
하겟슴노잇가 ........... 134, 141 (8)
하겟슴데다, 하겟슴데이다 ......
  ................... 134, 140
하겟슴지오 .............. 138 (5)
하겟스며 ............... 134, 194
하겟스면 ............... 134, 185
하겟스나 ............... 134, 189
하겟스니 ............... 134, 186

하겟스닛가 ............. 134, 187
하겟슨들 ............... 134, 190
하겟슴데닛가 ........... 134, 143 (4)
하겟스디 ............... 134, 190
하겟쇼 ............... 134, 138 (3) or 141 (6)
하겟다 ............... 134, 138 (1)
하겟다가 ............... 134, 202
하겟다고 ............... 134, 228ff
하겟다마는 .............. 134, 191
하겟다더니 ............ 134, 191, 186
하겟더라 ............... 135, 140
하겟데 ................. 135, 140
하겟답데다, for 하겟다하옵데다.
하겟더이다 .............. 135, 140
하겟더면 ............... 135, 185
하겟더냐 ............... 135, 143 (1)
하겟더니 ............... 135, 186
하겟더닛가 ............. 135, 143 (3)
하겟던잇가, for above.
하겟더뇨 ............... 135, 143 (2)
하겟던가 ............... 135, 197
하겟던고 ............... 135, 197
하겟더라 ............... 135, 140
하겟도다 ............ 134, 138 (9)
하겟지 ............... 134, 141 (4)
하겟지오 ............. 134, 138 (5)
하겟지마는 ...... 134, 138 (5) 191
하거나 ..................... 192
하거나말거나 .............. 192
하거늘 ..................... 193
하거니 ..................... 192
하거니와 .................. 190
하거니말거니 .............. 192
하건마는, for 하것마는 ......... 191
하건티 ..................... 187
하거든 ..................... 185
하것마는 ................... 191
하기 ..................... 171ff
하기에 ..................... 174

## INDEX OF VERBAL FORMS. 469

ᄒᆞ기가 ............... 171ƒ
ᄒᆞ기는 ............... 173
ᄒᆞ기를 ............... 173
ᄒᆞ기로 ............... 173
ᄒᆞ길ᄂᆡ ............... 188
ᄒᆞ고 ............... 200
ᄒᆞ고셔
  II. Chap. VII. ? II. Sec. 26, 1.
ᄒᆞ고십흐다 for ᄒᆞ고십소 ...... 217
ᄒᆞ고도
  II. Chap. X. Sec. 5, 1.
ᄒᆞ고는
  II. Chap. X. Sec. 8, 2.
ᄒᆞ고쟈ᄒᆞ다 ............... 205
ᄒᆞ고져ᄒᆞ다 ............... 205
ᄒᆞ고지고 ............... 236, 241 (f)
ᄒᆞ고말고 ............... 232, 241 b.
ᄒᆞ구나, for ᄒᆞ고나
ᄒᆞ ............... 171
ᄒᆞ마 ............... 118
ᄒᆞ매 ............... 187
ᄒᆞ마고 ............... 228 and 118
ᄒᆞ머 ............... 194
ᄒᆞ면 ............... 185
ᄒᆞ면셔 ............... 203
홈은, Appositive of 홈. Introduces the reason.
홈이 ............... 171, 53
홈이어나 ............... 171, 192
홈이오 ...... 홈 with verb 이오.
  It can be carried through all forms.
홈인며
홈일시니라
홈ᄂᆡ다 ............... 138 (6)
홈빈다 ............... 138 (8)
홈ᄂᆞ잇가 ............... 141 (8)
홈네, A provincialism for ᄒᆞ네
호 ............... 163
ᄒᆞ나 ............... 189

ᄒᆞ나보다 ............... 214
ᄒᆞ냐 ............... 141 (1) for ᄒᆞᄂᆞ냐
ᄒᆞᄂᆞ이다 ............... 138 (6)
ᄒᆞᄂᆞ잇가, for ᄒᆞᄂᆞ니잇가 ... 141 (8)
ᄒᆞᄂᆞ ............... 162
ᄒᆞᄂᆞ냐 ............... 141 (1)
ᄒᆞᄂᆞ니 ............... 141 (1)
ᄒᆞᄂᆞ이, Pres. Rel. Part with 이 "person who."
ᄒᆞᄂᆞ니잇가 ............... 141 (8)
ᄒᆞᄂᆞ이잇가, for ᄒᆞᄂᆞ니잇가. q. v.
ᄒᆞᄂᆞ이가, ᄒᆞᄂᆞ이 (q. v.) with nom. ending.
ᄒᆞᄂᆞ이는, ᄒᆞᄂᆞ이 (q. v.) with appos. ending.
ᄒᆞᄂᆞ니라 ............... 140
ᄒᆞᄂᆞ잇가, for ᄒᆞᄂᆞ니잇가 q. v.
ᄒᆞᄂᆞ뇨 ............... 141 (2)
ᄒᆞᄂᆞ가 ............... 197
ᄒᆞᄂᆞ가보다 ............... 214
ᄒᆞᄂᆞ고 ............... 197
ᄒᆞᄂᆞ고면 ............... 195
ᄒᆞᄂᆞ고면 ............... 195
ᄒᆞᄂᆞ고나 ............... 201
ᄒᆞᄂᆞ고로 ............... 162

  II. Chap. X. Sec. 9.

ᄒᆞᄂᆞ바 ............... 162, 73
ᄒᆞᄂᆞ쎄 ............... 162, 260
ᄒᆞᄂᆞ디 ............... 199
ᄒᆞᄂᆞ듯ᄒᆞ다 ............... 225
ᄒᆞᄂᆞ동마ᄂᆞ동 ............... 234, 241d.
ᄒᆞᄂᆞ도다 ............... 138 (9)
ᄒᆞᄂᆞ헤ᄒᆞ다 ............... 221
ᄒᆞᄂᆞ쟈 ............... 162, 73
ᄒᆞᄂᆞ지 ............... 197
ᄒᆞᄂᆞ지마ᄂᆞ지 ............... 231, 241, a.
ᄒᆞᄂᆞ지라, Book form marking a partial break.
ᄒᆞᄂᆞ줄 ............... 162, 221

# INDEX OF VERBAL FORMS.

호눈줄을 .................. 221
  II. Chap. I. § III. Sec. 6 a.
호눈줄노 .................. 221
  II. Chap. I. § III. Sec. 12.
호누보 .................. 211, 214
호누베 Conversational form among equals from 호누보다.
호누보다 .................. 214
호네 .................. 138 (2)
호이 .................. 163, 97
호니 .................. 186, or 143 (1)
호이가 .................. 163, and 97
호니와 .................. 182, 187
호니싸니 .................. 182, 187
호니깐드로 .................. 182, 187
호니마니 .................. 232
호니라 .................. 140
호닛가 .................. 182, 187
호노 .................. 142 (5)
호노니 .................. 118, 186
호노라 .................. 118, 140
호노라호고 .................. 228
호노라고 Contr. for above.
호뇨,=호누뇨 .................. 141 (2)
호가 .................. 197
호가베, Conversational form from
호가보다 .................. 214
호거시어늘 .................. 220ff, 193
호거시오 .................. 221, 223
호거시니 .................. 223, 186
호것 .................. 163ff
  P.R. Part with 것.
호고 .................. 197
호고로 .................. 193ff
  II. Chap. X. Sec. 9.
호바 .................. 165ff, 73
호다 .................. 138 (1)
호셰 .................. 163, 226
호다호들 .................. 229, 190

호다호다 .................. 229, 138 (1)
호다고 .................. 229
호다마는 .................. 138 (1), 191
호다네 .................. 229, 138 (2)
호답니다 .................. 229, 138 (6)
호답데다 .................. 229, 140
호다더라 .................. 229, 140
호단다 .................. 229
호다더니 .................. 229, 186
호티 .................. 229, 199
호드시 .................. 229, 167
호둣 .................. 163, 225
호들 .................. 163, 190
호둣호다 .................. 225, 139 (1)
호동만뎡 .................. 234, (d)
호쟈 .................. 163
  with 쟈 (者).
호죽 .................. 187
호죽손 .................. 187
호지 .................. 197
호지만지 .................. 231
호지라 book form of past.
호줄 .................. 221
호줄을 .................. 221
호줄노 .................. 221
  II. Ch. I. § III. Sec. 6, 2 (a) and Sec. 12. I; Ch. VII. § III. Sec. 3 (note).
흡니다 for 호옵누이다 .................. 138 (7)
흡누잇가 for 호옵누잇가 .................. 141 (9)
흡네 .................. 138 (2)
흡네다 .................. 138 (6)
흡세 .................. 144 (2)
흡셰다 .................. 144 (5)
흡시오 .................. 145
흡시다 .................. 144 (4)
흡쇼=호옵쇼 .................. 135, 145
  "half talk" much used among women.
흡데다=호옵더이다 .................. 140

## INDEX OF VERBAL FOLMS. 471

홉멘다, for 흐옵더이다 ......... 140
흡더이다 ............................ 140
흡더닛가, 흡뎃가 ...... 143 (3), (4)
흡던잇가, same as above.
훌 ...................................... 166
흐라 contr. for 흐여라 ......... 145
흐래라 ............... 229 to inferiors
흐라오 ............................... 229
흐라흐여게시다 ................... 229
  Verb, Part. form with 게시다 q. v.
흐라흐여라 ..................229, 145
흐라흐라, contr. for above.
흐라흐려흐다 ............... 229, 204
흐라흐다 ............ 229 (indefinite)
흐라다가 ..................... 229, 202
흐라겟다 .............................. 229
흐라고 ................................ 229
흐라고흐다 ........ 229. (indefinite).
흐락말낙흐다  235=흐낙말낙
  흐다.
흐라면 ........................... 229, 185
흐란다, for 흐라흐다 ............ 229
흐랍시더니, for 흐라흡시더니
  229, 186 and chap. honorifics.
흐랍더니, contraction for 흐라
  흐옵더니
흐랍던잇가, for 흐라흡더니잇가
  143 (4)
흐라더니 .............................. 229
  with 흐더니 q. v.
흐랴 ................................... 176
흐랴오 ............. 204 for 흐랴흐오
흐랴흐다 ........................... 204*ff*
흐랴겟다 .............................. 204
흐랴고흐다 ....................... 204*ff*
흐랴면 ........................... 204, 185
흐랍니다, for 흐랴흐니다
  204, 138 (7)
흐랴나 ......... 204, 141 (3) or 189

흐랴는 ....................... 204, 162
흐란다, for 흐랴흐다 ............. 204
흘양으로 ............................. 225
흘양이면 ............................. 225
흐랴더니 .................... 204, 186
흐랏다, for 흐랴흐엿다 ......... 204
흐리라, for 흐라고흐여라 ..... 229
흘어가다, for 흐러가다 ........ 170
  supine with 가다.
흐려 ................................. 176*ff*
흐려흐여라 .................. 204, 145
흐려흐들 ..................... 204, 190
흐려흐다 .............................. 204
흐려고흐다 .......................... 204
흐렴 ................................... 240
흐려면 ........................ 204, 185
흐려무나 ............................. 240
흐려니와 ..................... 204, 190
흐련마는, for 흐려흐것마는 ...
  204, 191
흐련다, for 흐려흐다 ........... 204
흐련다마는, for 흐려흐다마는..
  204, 228, 191
흐럿마는,=흐련마는, q. v. ...... —
흐럿다,=흐랏다, q. v. .......... —
흐려지마는 .................. 204, 191
  =흐려흐지마는.
흐리 ................................... 140
흘이 ................................... 166
  F. Rel. Part. with 이
  "person who."
흐리이다 ............................. 140
흐리잇가 ............................. 143
흐리잇고 ..................... 135, 143
  book language.
흐리오, F. tense in 리 with 오
  138 (3)
흐리니 ......................... 134, 186
흐리라 ................................ 140
흐리로다 ................. 131, 138 (9)

## INDEX OF VERBAL FORMS.

호리다, for 호리이다 ............ 140
호린가, for 호리잇가 ............ 143
호료, for 호리오 q. v. ............ —
호 ............................................ 166
홀가, 홀짜 ........................ 166, 197
홀가말가 ........................ 197, 231
홀가보다 ................................ 214
홀가시부다 ... 217 to inferiors.
홀걸, for 홀거슬 .................. 223
홀거시 .................................. 223
홀거시어늘 .................... 223, 193
홀거시나 ........................ 223, 189
홀거시니 ........................ 2-3, 186
홀거시니라 .................... 223, 140
홀거시라 ........................ 223, 140
"니" is omitted from above.
홀거실다 ................................ 223
홀고 ........................................ 197
홀만호다 ................................ 222
홀나 ........................................ 237
홀나다가, for 호랴호다가 ...... 204
홀나고, for 호랴고 ................ 204
홀낙말낙호다 ............ 235, 241 (c)
호논지 .................................. 197
홀너니 ........................ 239, 241 (i)
홀너라, ending 라 on above.
홀년지 .................................. 197
홀바 ................................ 166, 73
홀번호다 ................................ 224
홀법 ........................................ 222
홀샌일다 ................................ 221
홀샌더러 .................. 221 with 더러
홀시 ........................................ 226
홀수록더욱 ............................ 227
홀셰라 .................................... 166
  with 세 and 이오 express fear
  similar to 홀나.
홀색, for 홀시 q. v. ................ —
홀삼부르다 ............................ 166
  with 삼 (相) and 부르다 =

He appears as though he will.
홀셩부르다, for above.
홀수 ........................................ 221
홀수업다 ................................ 221
홀수잇다 ................................ 221
홀때 ........................................ 226
홀듯 ................................ 220ff, 225
홀듯호게 ........................ 225, 159
홀듯호다 ........................ 220, 225
홀듯시부다, for 십다 ............ 217
홀동말동 ........................ 234, 241d
홀터 ................................ 221, 223
홀터이오니 .......... 223, 138 (note)
홀터이면 ........................ 223, 185
홀터이니 ........................ 223, 186
홀지로다, Fut. Rel. Part. with
  갈지 & 이오 ............ 138 (9)
홀줄 ........................................ 221
홀줄을 .................................... 221
홀줄노 .................................... 221
  II Chap. I. § III Sec. 6, 2,
  (a) and Sec. 12. 1.
  Chap. VII § III Sec. 3
  (note).
호사, hon. from 호시오 for
  호여 .................................. 153
호소이다, Appen. B. I. ........ —
호숩니다, for 호소읍누이다. 138 (7)
호셧누이다 ............ 134, 138 (6)
호셔 ...................................... 153

II. Chap. VII. § II. Sec. 26.
호셰 ...................................... 144
호셧나 ........ 134, 142 (3) or
  189 fr. 호시오.
호셧누잇가 ........ 134, 142 (8)
  fr. 호시오.
호셧눈고 ...... 134, 197 fr. 호시오
호셧네ㅡ...134, 189 (2) „ „

… INDEX OF VERBAL FORMS. 473

ㅎ셧습지오...134, 139 (5) or 142
  (7) fr. ㅎ시오.
ㅎ셧쇼 ...... 134, 139 (3) or 142
  (6) fr. ㅎ시오.
ㅎ셧지 ...... 134, 142 (4) fr. ㅎ시오
ㅎ셧지오 ...... 134, 139 (4), or
  142 (7) fr. ㅎ시오.
ㅎ시오 .................. 145, or 273
ㅎ신, Fr. Hon. ㅎ시다 ......... 167
ㅎ십셰다, Contr. for ㅎ시옵셰다
                                144 (5)
ㅎ시도소이다, Appen. B. I. ... —
ㅎ쇼,=ㅎ소 ... .................. 145
ㅎ쇼셔 ........................... 145
ㅎ다 .................. 140 book form.
ㅎ다가 ........................... 202
ㅎ다고 ........................... 228
ㅎ답데다,=ㅎ다홉데다 ........
                                228, 140
ㅎ다더라 ................... 228, 140
ㅎ단, for ㅎ던 q. v. ............. —
ㅎ더 ............................. 199
ㅎ듯시 ..................... 225
ㅎ듯............................. 225
ㅎ데 ............................. 140
ㅎ더이다 ........................ 140
ㅎ더고나, for ㅎ다고냐 ......... 240
ㅎ더면 ...................... 140, 185
ㅎ던 { Rel. part ............... 168
     "half talk" for ㅎ더냐 q. v,
ㅎ더냐 ........................ 143 (1)
ㅎ더니 ........................... 186
ㅎ더니라 ........................ 136
ㅎ더니마는 ................. 186, 191
ㅎ더닛가, Contr. for ㅎ더니잇가
                                143 (3)
ㅎ던잇가, same as above.
ㅎ더뇨 ........................ 143 (2)
ㅎ던가 ........................... 197
ㅎ던가보다 ............ 194, 139 (1)

ㅎ던고 ........................... 197
ㅎ던지 ........................... 197
   II. Chap. VII. §I, Sec. 3, 4.
ㅎ던지마던지 ............ 197, 231
ㅎ더라 ..................... 135, 140
ㅎ더시다........................ 135
  with hon. 시 and term ... 139 (1)
ㅎ든, for ㅎ던 q. v. ............. —
ㅎ들, 돌 ........................ 190
ㅎ듯 ............................. 225
ㅎ도 ............................. 196
ㅎ되 ............................. 190
ㅎ도록, for ㅎ드록 ............. 227
ㅎ도소이다, Appen. B. I. ...... —
ㅎ도다 ........................ 138 (9)
ㅎ자 ............................. 144
ㅎ자고 ........................... 205
ㅎ자고ㅎ다 ..................... 205
ㅎ잔타=ㅎ지아니ㅎ다 ......... 206ff
ㅎ지 ................... 141 (4) or 177
ㅎ지아니ㅎ다 ................. 206ff
ㅎ지이다=ㅎ여지이다 ......... 145
ㅎ지오 ....................... 141 (7)
ㅎ지마는 ................. 141 (4), 191
ㅎ지마오 ........................ 208
ㅎ지를 ...... 177, 100, Acus past
  added to Neg. Base ......... —
여 .................................. —
이 .............................. 96ff 160
이야, A verbal form of 아 ...... 103
  fr. 이오 used in expressing
  alarm.
이어늘 .......................... 193
이어든 .......................... 185
이여, Appen. B. II. ............ —
이오 ............ 160 with verb ㅎ오.
이완더, for 이건대 ............. 187
이읍시다 ........................ —
이거든ㆍ............... for ㅎ거든 185
이기에 ................... 174 (note)

# INDEX OF VERBAL FORMS.

| | |
|---|---|
| 이고 | 200 |
| 이며 | 194 |
| 이면 | 185 |
| 이나 | 189 |
| 이냐 | 141 (1) |
| 이니 | 186 |
| 이니라 | 140 |
| 이닛가, for 이ᄂ니잇가, fr. 괴오. | 141 (8) |
| 이닛까, for 이ᄂ니잇가 | |
| 이뇨 | 141 (2) |
| 인가 | 197 |
| 인가보=인가보오 | 214 |
| 인가베, Conversational form | 138 (2) |
| 인가보오 | 214, 138 (3) |
| 인가보다 | 214, 138 (1) |
| 인고 | 197 |
| 인고로 | 162 |

### II. Chap. X. Sec. 9.

| | |
|---|---|
| 인데 | 199 |
| 인들 | 190 |
| 인즉 | 187 |
| 인지 | 197 |
| 인줄 | 221 |
| 입뎬다, for 이옵더니이다 | 140, 138 (7) |
| 입뎻가, for 이옵더잇가 | 143 (4) |
| 이라 | 140 |
| 이라도 | 198 도 with 이라. |
| 이란다 | 228, 138 (1) |
| 이랴 | 176 |
| 이러니, The Progressive sign 더 is sometimes with 이오 changed to 러. This then is 186 or 239 | |
| 이러라, See above and 더라 | 140 |
| 이리라 | 134, 140 |
| 이로고, Usage has allowed the introduction of a connective 로 between the stem and termination or particals with the verb 일다. This then equals 이오 or 일고 | 200 |
| 이로고나 (See 이로고) | 201 |
| 이로세, (See 이로고)=일세 | 138 (2) |
| 이로소이다, (See 이로고 and Appendix B. I) | — |
| 이로라, (See 이로고) | 140 |
| 이로다, (See 이로고) Appen. B. II. | 138 (1) |
| 이로되, (See 로고) | 190 |
| 일너 | 188 |
| 길 changed into 일 from verb 이오. | |
| 일너니 | 239, 241 (1) |
| 일넌지 | 197 |
| 일세 | 138 (1) |
| 일다 | 138 (1) |
| 일더냐 | 135, 143 (1) |
| 일더니라 | 135, 140 |
| 일더라 | 135, 140 |
| 일던가 | 135, 143 (note) |
| 일뜻ᄒ다 | 220, 225 |
| 일지라도 | 198 |
| 일줄 | 221 |
| 이시니 | 272, 186 from 이오. |
| 이시니라 | 272, 140 |
| 이시닛가, Contra. for 이시ᄂ니잇가 | 272 141 (8) |
| 이시라 | 272, 140 |
| 이실다, hon. form of 일다 272. | |

| | |
|---|---|
| 이더 ……………………… 190 | 이던지 ……………………… 19, 7 |
| 이더면 ……………… 135, 185 | **II. Chap. VII. § I. Sec. 3, 4.** |
| 이더냐 …………… 135, 143 (1) | 이더라 ……………… 135, 140 |
| 이더닛가 ………… 135, 143 (3) | 이되 ……………………… 190 |
| 이더뇨 …………… 135, 143 (2) | 이지오 ………………… 141 (7) |
| 이던가 ……………………… 197 | 이지마는 ………… 141 (4), 191. |

大正三年十二月三十日印刷
大正四年一月十二日發行

不許複製

發行所　朝鮮耶穌教書會
　　　　朝鮮京城鍾路

印刷所　福音印刷合資會社
　　　　横濱市山下町百〇四番地

印刷者　村岡平吉
　　　　横濱市太田町五丁目八十七番地

著作兼發行者　神學博士　米國人　元　エチ、ヂー、アンダーウツド　尤
　　　　朝鮮京城南大門外御成町三十四番地

定價金三圓五十錢

www.ingramcontent.com/pod-product-compliance
Lightning Source LLC
Chambersburg PA
CBHW021417300426
44114CB00010B/528